PRAISE FOR JON ENTINE'S *TABOO*

"Provocative and informed. . . A well-intentioned effort for all to come clean on the possibility that black people might just be superior physically, and that there is no negative connection between their physical superiority and their IQs."

> —John C. Walter, director of the Blacks in Sports Project at the University of Washington, *The Seattle Times*

"Entine boldly and brilliantly documents numerous physiological differences contributing to black athletic superiority."

> —*Psychology Today*

"Notable and jarring. It brings intelligence to a little-understood subject."

> —*Business Week*

"A highly readable blend of science and sports history."

> —*The New York Times Book Review*

"A powerful history of African-Americans in sports. At long last, someone has the guts to tell it like it is."

> —*St. Petersburg Times*

"Compelling, bold, comprehensive, informative, enlightening."

> —Gary Sailes, Associate Professor of Kinesiology, Indiana University and editor of the *Journal of the African American Male*

"*Taboo* clearly dispenses with the notion that athleticism in Africans or African-Americans is entirely due only to biology or only to culture. Entine understands that as scientists continue to study the complex interactions between genes and the environment, population-based genetic differences will continue to surface. *Taboo* is an excellent survey of a controversial subject."

> —Human Biology Association President Michael Crawford, University of Kansas professor of Biological Anthropology and Genetics, and former editor of Human Biology

"Carefully researched and intellectually honest."

—Jay T. Kearney, Former Senior Sports Scientist, United States Olympic
Committee

"Entine has compiled abundant evidence to support this politically incorrect belief, and it is more than convincing."

—*The Black World Today*

"I believe that we need to look at the causes of differences in athletic performance between races as legitimately as we do when we study differences in diseases between the various races. Jon Entine shows a lot of courage in publishing *Taboo*. Only by confronting these enormous issues head-on, and not by circumventing them in the guise of political correctness, do we stand a chance to evaluate the discriminating agendas and devise appropriate interventions."

—Claude Bouchard, geneticist and director of the Pennington Biomedical
Research Center at Louisiana State University

Taboo helps us understand and even celebrate that while we're mostly the same, we are also wonderfully different."

—Amby Burfoot, *Runner's World* editor

"The real value of the book is its willingness to address racist thought in the context of the black athlete and seek an honest dialogue on the topic."

—Brian Gilmore, Africana.com.

"This is an important book for biological anthropologists."

—American Journal of Physical Anthropology

"You might expect that claiming to show a genetic basis for the dominance of certain sports by people of African descent would raise a firestorm. But in fact Entine's book gets warm reviews."

—*Slate.com*

TABOO

WHY

BLACK ATHLETES

DOMINATE

SPORTS

AND WHY

WE'RE AFRAID

TO TALK ABOUT IT

JON ENTINE

PublicAffairs
NEW YORK

Photo Credits: Cartoon courtesy of the *Sunday Nation*, Nairobi, Kenya. Photo of Kenyan runners © Vinny Dusovic/Photo Run. Photo of Kipchoge Keino, courtesy of the author. Photo of the Oberlin College baseball team courtesy of the Oberlin College Archives. Photo of Jack Johnson © Brown Brothers. Photo of Jesse Owens courtesy of the *Chicago Daily Defender*. Photo of the Eastern League basketball champions courtesy of Naismith Memorial Basketball Hall of Fame. Photo of Joe Louis courtesy of the *New York Daily News*. Photo of Stella Walsh courtesy of the Track and Field Library/Butler University. Photo of Wilma Rudolph © Deutsche Presse Agentur/Archive Photos. Photo of the Texas Western basketball team courtesy of The University of Texas at El Paso. Photo of Tommie Smith and John Carlos © AP/Wide World Photos. Photo of Cathy Freeman © Brian Myers/Photo Run. Photo of John Godina © Victah Sailer/Photo Run. Photo of Kinoshiki by Chris Cole, © AllSport Photo Gallery. Photo of the Tarahumara Indians © Natalie B. Fobes Photography. Photo of Herschel Walker on a bobsled © Nancie Battaglia. Photos of Herschel Walker running and playing football courtesy of the University of Georgia. Photo of Frankie Fredericks © Mark Verbaan/Rex Features. Photo of Roger Bannister © Mike Hewitt/AllSport Photo Gallery. Photo of Sebastian Coe © Victah Sailer/Photo Run. Photo of Hicham El Guerroj © AP/Wide World Photos.

Book design by Jenny Dossin.

Library of Congress Cataloging-in-Publication Data

Entine, Jon.

    Taboo: why black athletes dominate sports and why we're afraid to talk about it / Jon Entine.

        p.   cm.

    ISBN 1-58648-026-X

    1. Athletes, Black.   2. Blacks—Race identity.   I. Title.

    GV706.32.E57   2000

    796'.089'96073—dc21   99-41889

                                                                       CIP

CONTENTS

Preface: Reflections on Sports and the Genetic Revolution   vii
Foreword by Earl Smith   xv

PART I
THE TABOO

1. Breaking the Taboo on Race and Sports   3
2. The Education of Sir Roger   11

PART II
THE EVIDENCE

3. By the Numbers   17
4. The Most Level Playing Field   29
5. Nature's Experiment: The "Kenyan Miracle"   43

PART III
HISTORY OF RACE SCIENCE AND SPORTS

6. "More Brains or More . . ."   71
7. Evolution (of Great Athletes)   81
8. Race Without Color: The History of Human Differences   96
9. The Origins of Race Science   117

PART IV

THE SEGREGATION AND INTEGRATION OF SPORTS

10. The Superiority of White Athletes	137
11. Jack Johnson in the Ring Against Jim Crow	151
12. American Eugenics	161
13. Jesse Owens and the German Race	172
14. A Knockout Blow to Race Science	188
15. The "Scheming, Flashy Trickiness" of Jews	198

PART V

NATURE OR NURTURE?

16. The Integration of Sports	207
17. The Sixties	218
18. Sports and IQ	232
19. Winning the Genetic Lottery	246
20. The Environmentalist Case Against Innate Black Superiority in Sports	272

PART VI

WHAT ABOUT WOMEN?

21. The Superiority of White Female Athletes	295
22. East Germany's Sports Machine	305
23. The Renaissance of the Black Female Athlete	317

PART VII

FINAL THOUGHTS

24. A Genteel Way to Say "Nigger"?	331
Acknowledgments	343
Notes	346
Index	375

REFLECTIONS ON SPORTS AND THE GENETIC REVOLUTION

Although *Taboo* draws its empirical evidence from the sports world—there is a vast trove of statistics from almost every population group in the world—its scope is far broader than athletics and race. My intention was to answer questions and debunk myths about human biodiversity in the context of the unfolding genetic revolution. As *Scientific American* wrote in its review, "Few issues are as provocative and as poorly understood as biological differences among the races."

For the most part, the science community has welcomed an honest discussion of issues frequently addressed only in the most circumspect or politicized ways. "Entine has put together a well-researched . . . and lucidly written case," the same review noted. "[His] proposed biocultural theory offers an attractive explanation, suggesting that cultural conditions can amplify small but meaningful differences in performance related to heredity."

The most deeply felt criticism came from those who believed that the book reflects a historical "white obsession" about racial differences. Ken Shropshire, a thoughtful Wharton business school professor, asked rhetorically "Why care? Why care if there are some minor anatomical or genetic differences between blacks and whites? . . . Will acknowledging some measure of black superiority in a handful of athletic maneuvers help us achieve social understanding? I don't think so."

Although professor Shropshire's sentiments are understandable, I believe he underestimates the importance of the dramatic revolution in genetics that is now unfolding. The challenge is not whether we should address such issues—we have no choice short of shutting down genetic research—but whether we can discuss human biodiversity in ways that enhance human dignity.

Over the past months, I've reflected on that concern, turning over in my mind a conversation I had with Arthur Ashe, Jr. shortly before he succumbed to AIDs. I had asked Arthur what was his greatest challenge, fully expecting him to cite his battle with the disease that would ultimately claim his life. But his life-and-death struggle was not what he voiced. "It's being black," he stated in his matter of fact voice that spoke of an utter absence of disingenuousness. "It's waking up in the morning and realizing that no matter what I've achieved, I will still be thought of first as a black man." It was a startling statement to me, for I had always assumed that Ashe was of such stature that he transcended race and the daily indignities, large and small, which blacks face.

Shortly thereafter, I got the tiniest inkling of what millions of African Americans experience daily when I traveled to the Nandi Hills in western Kenya. I visited the open market in Eldoret, where the early morning crowd bargains over the day's selection of fresh chicken and vegetables. I was one of the few white men for miles around and acutely aware of my skin color. People stared, though no one was hostile.

Later that afternoon, I turned to my host Ibrahim Hussein, one of the world's all time great marathoners. "Do you think of yourself as a 'black man' or just as a man," I asked. I was immediately embarrassed for fear that he would be offended, but I pressed on. "I mean, are you aware of your blackness."

Ibrahim looked at me as if I had just landed from Mars. "No, of course not," he said, breaking into a gentle Kenyan smile that immediately put me at ease. "I am just a man. Do you see yourself as white in your country? Certainly not. But in America, I became aware of my color. There are not many whites in this part of Kenya. Here *you* are a white. It is *I* who is just a man." For one of the few times in my life, I shared with American blacks the omnipresent awareness of being judged, analyzed, dissected, and abstracted by the dominant culture.

There exists a blurry line between a healthy fascination about human differences and a white obsession. It's that concern that led dozens of journalists and media outlets to refuse to even discuss *Taboo*—as a matter of conscience, some asserted. It was popularly perceived as a skunk in heat. For instance, shortly before *Taboo* appeared in bookstores, *The New York Times Magazine* dropped plans to publish an adaptation because the very idea of discussing human differences—not the book itself, was too hot to handle. "Our reluctant decision to drop it is no reflection of my regard for your work, which remains high," wrote Kyle Crichton, who had championed the article. "In brief, the whole subject worries my editor . . . ." I encountered such reactions repeatedly, most pointedly from those who had not read the book.

Even raising the issue of racial differences is considered racist in some circles, an odd stance considering the lip service given to cultural diversity. "It is perhaps the existence of these lingering attitudes—still prevalent throughout much of this country—which explains some of the backlash against *Taboo*'s central thesis," wrote Michael Crawford, University of Kansas biological anthropologist, president of the Human Biology Association, and former editor of the journal *Human Biology*. "While the sections concerning Entine's hypothesis will surely attract the greatest attention, they actually form a relatively small portion of the book," he added. "The majority of Entine's tome is concerned with outlining the origins and history of the 'taboo' itself—the reasons why Americans are reluctant to talk about human differences in general, and athletic differences in particular—and it is here that Entine is at his best."

In general, black scholars and journalists were the most enthusiastic about the cultural history of the race concept. "I am an editorial columnist," wrote Bill Maxwell of the *St. Petersburg Times* in a personal note to me. "I reviewed your book because I enjoyed reading it. It cut through all of the bullshit. I am black." What are we to make of the phenomenon in which some whites, so quick to crow about their own racial sensitivity, inject racial divisiveness into a debate in which many African Americans see refreshing candor?

It's apparent that many blacks have become irritated to the point of anger by the patronizing censorship and condescension of some journalists and academicians. "You will be accused of spouting old fashion racism for even raising the issue of African American superiority in athletics," I had been warned by Earl Smith, an African American scholar and head of the sociology department at Wake Forest University who took a considerable personal risk by writing the Foreword to *Taboo*. "All this beating around the bush has to stop. This is a good book. I am quite excited with the arguments that are raised."

"Taboo is both provocative and informed," added John Walter, professor of American Ethnic studies and director of the Blacks in Sports Project at the University of Washington, in the *Seattle Times*. "Entine has provided a well-intentioned effort for all to come clean on the possibility that black people might just be superior physically (for the record, *Taboo* asserts not superiority but anatomical differences between populations, a crucial distinction), and that there is no negative connection between that physical superiority and their IQs."

Although only briefly addressed in the book, the potential link between athletic differences and the genetics of intelligence provoked a surfeit of not-so-thoughtful reactions, mostly from right wing zealots who saw an opportunity to promote a racist agenda. But there was also a reflexive criticism from ideologues on the left who believe that any mention of human difference is the first step down a slippery slope. "There has never been a single study linking a genetic trait, racial or otherwise, with athletic performance," claimed Berkeley sociologist Harry Edwards. "The existing genetic data testify that known DNA variations do not respect the boundaries of human groups," echoed University of North Carolina/Charlotte anthropologist Jonathan Marks.

Both are wrong, literally dead wrong. Medical researchers have already isolated the genetic basis for multiple sclerosis that targets whites and colo-rectal cancer that disproportionately affects blacks, to name just two of dozens of population specific diseases. As *Taboo* documents, there are innumerable anatomical traits, from basic body shape to muscle composition to metabolic efficiency to skeletal structure that are genetically based, more pronounced in some populations, and critical to athletic performance.

It may be breaking news to Edwards and Marks but it's conventional science that humans have evolved in response to differing environmental conditions in different regions of the world. The

explosive issue is not the science of human differences but the historical tendency to misuse the ever-evolving data to promote insidious ends. Simplistic generalizations have linked vague concepts
such as intelligence, violence, and sexual aggressiveness to populations grouped by skin color. "Race" confounds even the most careful
thinkers. *Taboo* acknowledges the inherently fuzzy nature of the concept. Trait variations that are the result of waves and cross currents
of migrations belie folkloric racial categories based largely on skin
color. That's why *Taboo* draws from the work of top geneticists, such
as Stanford University's Luigi Luca Cavalli-Sforza, who recognize
patterned biological differences between populations.

Are these differences enough to account for the growing phenomenon in which different population groups tend to excel in specific
sports? To answer this conundrum, scientists employ Ockham's Ra-
zor, also called the rule of parsimony: *non sunt multiplicanda entia
praeter necessitatem*; i.e., entities are not to be multiplied beyond necessity. Simply stated, when there are two competing theories that
make exactly the same predictions, the one that is simpler is favored.

In this case, the biocultural explanation espoused in *Taboo*—biological factors specific to populations can exaggerate the impact of
small but critical anatomical differences—is opposed by a belief in
the primacy of culture. "Black dominance in sports is a combination of opportunity and access," asserted Percy Hintzen, chair of
the African American Studies Department at University of California-Berkeley. "[To claim that genetics plays a role] doesn't make
sense."

What does the evidence tell us? What are we to make of the fact
that an athlete of African ancestry holds every major running record,
from the 100 meters to the marathon?

Running is truly the most international of sports. Athletes face
with the lowest social and economic barriers. Let's look at Kenya, a
tiny country in East Africa that has carved out a reputation as one of
the world's athletic hotspots. Little boys dream that one day, they
might soak up the cheers of the adoring fans that regularly crowd
the stands at the National Stadium in Nairobi to celebrate the country's national sport. The best players are national icons. The selection

process to spot stars begins very young. Coaches backed by federal outlays comb the countryside. The most promising of the lot are sent to special schools and provided extra coaching. It's not an exaggeration to call Kenya's national sport a kind of national religion, the passion of the masses.

According to conventional and socially acceptable wisdom, this is a familiar story—the sure cultural explanation for the remarkable success of Kenyan distance runners. Only one problem: The national sport, the hero worship, the adoring fans, the social channeling, the confluence of "opportunity and access" that Berkeley professor Hintzen talks about as if it were a revealed truth—that all speaks to Kenya's enduring love affair with soccer, not running.

Despite the enormous success of Kenyan runners in the past fifteen years, running remains a relative afterthought in this soccer-crazed nation. Unfortunately, Kenyans are among the world's worst soccer players. Even with the expenditure of hundreds of thousands of dollars of sparse sports resources, Kenya is regularly trounced by Nigeria as well as far poorer countries in West Africa such as Ghana, Ivory Coast, and Cameroon. In fact, there is no such thing as an East African soccer powerhouse. Key skills necessary for soccer success including sprint-like speed are in short supply. East Africans are ectomorphs: relatively short and lean in the upper body, with huge natural lung capacity and a preponderance of endurance-sustaining slow twitch muscle fibers. That's a perfect biomechanical package for distance running, but not so great for soccer or sprinting.

In contrast, in Sydney, for the fifth Olympics in a row, all of the runners sprinting for gold in the 100 meters could trace their primary ancestry to West Africa. And consider this: while the qualifying time for the men's 100 meters was 10.6 seconds, pokey by modern standards, one of the world's historical running meccas, Finland, could not produce a qualifier. This came as no surprise to Olympic analysts, as no Finn has ever topped 10.27 in the 100 meters. Neither has a runner from Denmark (10.23), New Zealand (10.27) or Taiwan (10.27). In fact, while Maurice Greene has cracked 10 seconds more than thirty times, that barrier has proved impenetrable for runners of Caucasian, Hispanic or Asian descent. East Africans, who dominate world distance running, fare no better. The best Kenyan time ever in the 100 meters—10.28 seconds—ranks somewhere near 5,000 on the all-time list.

Genes may not determine who are the world's best runners, but they do circumscribe possibility. "The basis for the success of black runners is in the genes," asserted Bengt Saltin, physiologist and director of the Copenhagen Muscle Research Institute (and author of the September 2000 *Scientific American* cover story, "Muscles and Genes," on why athletes are born and not made). "There is no question about that."

The Sydney Olympics underscored that reality. There were no prominent Chinese sprinters, or male East Asian runners of any note, except at the longest distances, and no jumpers. East Asians do flourish in the martial arts, diving, and gymnastics. Is this totally a product of cultural factors? Perhaps, but doubtful. "Chinese splits," a rare gymnastics maneuver demanding extraordinary flexibility, has roots in this unique anthropometric capacity of East Asians. Even Asian domination of Ping-Pong is likely to have a genetic component; test after test has shown that Asians have significantly faster hand-to-eye coordination of any population group. Why? Scientists can only speculate about the genetic basis for this phenotype, but the facts, documented on the field and confirmed in the laboratory, are certainly intriguing.

A few critics remain defiantly resistant to the confluence of empirical (in this case, on-the-field) evidence, anatomical data, and population genetics. Kenan Malik, a science journalist, argued that that anyone who even acknowledges human differences, even multiculturalists, are fellow travelers. "By emphasizing differences rather than equality, anti-racists are resorting to the same philosophies as gave rise to racial thinking itself," he wrote. Such views appear well motivated, but the call for censorship is a cynical prescription.

As Barbara Ehrenreich and Janet McIntosh wrote in the liberal weekly *The Nation* in 1997, this unrelenting attack on genetics by a coterie of social thinkers is an attempt to subvert science to politics. "What began as a healthy skepticism about misuses of biology," they wrote, [has become] a new form of dogma. Like the religious fundamentalists, the new academic creationists defend their stance as if all of human dignity—and all hope for the future—were at stake.

[But] in portraying human beings as pure products of cultural context, the secular creationist standpoint not only commits biological errors but defies common sense."

Demonizing genetics in the name of social justice is a dangerous (and ultimately futile) gambit. Today, no credible scientist disputes that evolution has helped shape Kenyan distance runners, white weight lifters with enormous upper body strength, and the explosive runners and jumpers of West African ancestry. "Entine understands that as scientists continue to study the complex interactions between genes and the environment, population-based genetic differences will continue to surface," wrote professor Michael Crawford. "We can speculate in private, or openly probe, debate, and seek answers. *Taboo* is not only an excellent survey of a controversial subject, it is also an impassioned argument in favor of this more democratic approach."

Respecting human differences enhances the possibility that we can constructively, but critically, confront the breathtaking changes that genetic research is spurring. "Entine writes carefully on a very touchy topic, and made me a bit more optimistic that some decent people have the courage to broach important questions of genetics and race," wrote George Mason University professor Walter E. Williams in *American Enterprise*. "If decent people don't discuss human biodiversity, we concede the turf to black and white racists."

That is the guiding spirit of *Taboo*.

JON ENTINE
Agoura Hills, California
November 2000

ADDRESSING TOUGH QUESTIONS: AFRICAN AMERICAN ATHLETES, SPORT, AND GENETICS

In the United States, a country obsessed with sports, race and athletics are inextricably linked. But it is a subject that is often difficult to discuss because of our long and deeply antagonistic racial history. All of us—professional scientists, weekend sports enthusiasts, athletes, coaches, and even "soccer moms" may wonder why Jon Entine, a journalist, has jumped into these stormy waters? Collectively we may also ask: "Why this particular topic at this point in time?" Is there some way to take on such tough questions, especially by someone who is white, and not be labeled a racist? I definitely think so.

Jon breaks with the stereotypes of nineteenth-century racial discourse that represented African Americans as a race of physical bodies (athletes) without minds or spirits. He has skillfully rekindled the burning questions of the innate physical abilities of African American athletes that have been the focus of speculation, research, and scholarship for more than 100 years.

Most importantly, though, *Taboo: Why Black Athletes Dominate Sports and Why We're Afraid to Talk About It* opens the possibility for concrete dialogue. It will cause people to think. It allows for professional disagreements. I have convened a panel of experts for a professional society meeting to discuss it and have had numerous opportunities to engage Jon in many a varied discussion about the book. Overall, the book has prompted me to reconsider the types of questions I now ask myself, especially those that were once deeply recessed in my mind. What accounts for athletic superiority, real or imaginary? Why, for example, is every finalist in the elite Olympic 100-meters dash (or 400 meters for that matter) of African origin?

Over two decades ago, in 1978, the eminent Harvard University sociologist William J. Wilson was lambasted by his peers—both African American and White—for writing a book entitled *The Declining Significance of Race: Blacks and Changing American Institutions.* Wilson's thesis that social class had become more important in determining the life-chances of African Americans than were issues related to race (e.g., mobility through different class strata) was a bold, new, and extremely unpopular perspective. This was especially true coming from an African American scholar on the heels of the tumultuous 1960s and the Vietnam War era.

By today's standards, Wilson's argument was mild, but the initial response to the book was mostly negative. What struck me most were the tenor of the public denouncements, a high pitched rancor, and the source of the loudest denouncements, a group of African American sociologists. "The Association of Black Sociologists is outraged over the misrepresentation of the black experience," read the widely circulated critique. "We are also disturbed over the policy implications that may derive from this work and that, given the nature of American society, are likely to set in motion equally objectionable trends in funding, research and training." The die was cast. Yet, looking back, William J. Wilson was not far off the mark. His analysis, considered controversial at the time, proved to have been right.

And so it may be with *Taboo.* I will argue that Jon's book will take its place in historical scholarship, but as with the Wilson book, it may have to wait years before full assessments are realized.

The distance between journalistic inquiry and scholarly research has received much attention. It is a sort of "Two Cultures" debate, rooted in the notion that a journalist cannot and should not tackle difficult subjects. Why? They don't have the time to do the necessary research for good, solid analysis. This is not true in this case. Jon has not rushed his subject, and he has certainly done the research.

This book argues that different populations, dominate certain athletic events because they have innate skills that are critical in certain athletic events. African American athletes dominate in North American sports because they are able to run faster, jump higher, and perform some incredible feats that athletes from other racial or ethnic groups cannot. Is this the primary reason that Michael Jordan became the best basketball player in the world? Or, is Jordan the best because he has an insatiable work ethic? Jon's book forces us to rethink such questions. Hopefully, it will contribute to finally putting to rest the torturous stereotype of the "dumb black jock." For sure, this distorted view of African American athletes does not apply to Michael Jordan!

People are attracted to simple cause/effect relationships. Yet it does not work that way in life or sports. Since this is the case, the public should ask for more from journalists, researchers, and scholars. Hopefully, *Taboo* does not mark the end of the dialogue, but acts as a stimulus to new research. In particular, I would like to see addressed the origins—the etiology—of African American athletic domination. At what point did a despised, segregated people come to "dominate" many North American Individual and team sports? My suspicion is that if African American athletic domination exists at all, it began with the destruction of the high walls of segregation in sports.

In rummaging through old magazines, I came across a *Sports Illustrated* that pictured the start of an Olympic 100-meter dash. It showed only the athletes' feet, wearing Nike, Adidas, and Puma running shoes. In viewing such a picture I often wonder: "Why are all the feet black?" Anyone seriously interested in knowing about the "double-edged sword" of athletic achievement for African American athletes need look no further than Jon's book. If nothing else, *Taboo: Why Black Athletes Dominate Sports and Why We're Afraid to Talk About It* will make it possible to more openly discuss this issue.

EARL SMITH, PH.D.
Dr. Ernest Rubin Distinguished Professor
of American Ethnic Studies, and Professor and Chairman,
Department of Sociology, Wake Forest University

To the Rose in our life, who reminds us,
each and every day, in so many wonderful ways,
that love, patience, and tolerance
are nature's gifts to all of us.

TABOO

THE TABOO

CHAPTER 1

BREAKING THE TABOO

ON RACE AND SPORTS

"I know that the American system is very sensitive to statements of black and white. But you cannot defy science. You cannot just say that day is night and night is day. These are facts. And I think it's to the advantage of the black athletes to be proud that God was on their side."[1]

Gideon Ariel,
Biomechanist, former Israeli Olympic athlete

"What really is being said in a kind of underhanded way is that blacks are closer to beasts and animals in terms of their genetic and physical and anatomical make up than they are to the rest of humanity. And that's where the indignity comes in."[2]

Harry Edwards,
Professor of Sociology, University of California at Berkeley

Imagine an alien visitor chancing upon a basketball arena on a wintry night. It sees a curious sight: most of the faces of the extended tree trunks scampering around the court are black; the crowd, on the other hand, is almost all white. This alien would see much the same racial division at football games, boxing matches, and at track meets and running races around the world. Even in sports in which blacks are not a majority—baseball, soccer, rugby, cricket, even bobsledding in some countries—blacks are represented in greater number than their share of the population.

Why is this so? Are blacks modern *übermenschen*, Friedrich Nietz-sche's supermen in baggy shorts and Air Jordans? Are race and ge-netics significant components of the stunning and undeniable dominance of black athletes? Or is this notion nothing but white voodoo designed to banish blacks to the modern plantation—the track, the basketball court, and the football field—while whites con-trol the boardrooms?

To the degree that it is a purely scientific debate, the evidence of black superiority in many sports is persuasive and decisively con-firmed on the playing field. Elite athletes who trace most or all of their ancestry to Africa are by and large better than the competition. The performance gap is widest when little expensive equipment or facilities are required, such as running, the only true intentional sport, and in widely played team sports such as basketball and foot-ball. Blacks not only outnumber their nonwhite competitors but, more often than not, are the superstars.

This disparity, which we can expect to increase as socio-economic barriers continue to erode, results from a unique confluence of cul-tural and genetic forces. The favored and socially acceptable expla-nation for this phenomenon—a dearth of opportunities elsewhere, does not suffice to explain the dimensions of this monopoly. The de-cisive variable is in our genes—the inherent differences between populations shaped over many thousands of years of evolution. Physical and physiological differences, infinitesimal as they may ap-pear to some, are crucial in competitions in which a fraction of a second separates the gold medalist from the also-ran.

When willing to speak openly, black and white athletes freely ac-knowledge what we intuitively suspect. "Blacks—physically in many cases—are made better," says Carl Lewis, one of the best sprinters of all time, shrugging as if to say, "Does anyone really question that?"[3] This is the same Carl Lewis who, by his own estimation, worked out eight hours—per week, that is, not per day—in the run up to win-ning four gold medals at the 1984 Olympics. But such anecdotes alone cannot resolve this controversy. Lewis's belief that he is a breed apart can be seen as either an expression of black pride or a simplistic stereotype so powerful that even successful blacks have come to recite a racist party line.

Even raising the subject of black athletic superiority brings angry rebukes from some quarters. William Rhoden, a distinguished African American columnist with the *New York Times*, derides it as "foolishness," a white "obsession," and an "unabashed racial feeding frenzy."[4] Lurking in the background, suggests Rhoden, are racial stereotypes of black mental and moral inferiority. In this garbled translation, black success in sports is not a compliment, but a proxy for racism—a "genteel way to say nigger," in the cut-to-the-chase words of fellow *Times* columnist Bob Herbert.[5]

Herbert and Rhoden make an important point. The world's historical romance with slavery and the persistent misuses of racial science have served permanent notice of what can happen when an intellectual interest in human differences hardens into an obsession based on class, ethnicity, or race. White fascination with black physicality has been part of a dark undercurrent since the first stirrings of colonialism. In the minds of many, the notion of physical differences is tethered to racist stereotypes of an "animalistic" black nature and the implication that blacks are somehow intellectually inferior.

And we should not forget that though black *athletes* may dominate sports, blacks in general do not: the ownership and high-level management of every major sports franchise and the various leagues are still in white hands to the virtual exclusion of African Americans.[6] Whiteness has come to symbolize political power, wealth, economic advancement, rationality, and civilized culture, whereas blackness is equated with the natural, sensuality, hyper-sexuality, musicality, laziness, intellectual deficiency, cultural pathology—and athleticism.[7] With some variation, these stereotypes hold true throughout much of the world. These deeply ingrained stereotypes help explain why the image of a raging Mike Tyson spitting out the torn piece of ear of his opponent stirred such personal reactions among both blacks and whites.

"People feel if you say blacks are better athletically, you're saying they're dumber," noted Frank Deford, the respected author and sports reporter. "But when Jack Nicklaus sinks a 30-foot putt, nobody thinks his IQ goes down."[8] Even saying blacks and whites are merely *different* can echo of racism, as the Golden Bear learned. In

1994, Nicklaus was asked by a Canadian sports writer why there are so few blacks playing at the highest levels of golf. "They have different muscles that react in different ways," he said. It was an innocent enough statement, whether true or not, yet it provoked an immediate storm and inevitable back-pedaling. "God created all of us equally," said a chastened Nicklaus in response to charges that he was racist. "We are then influenced by our environment. That is all I have said."[9] Thereafter, he refused to talk of the subject again.

Given all the controversy involved in addressing such a potentially divisive issue, it is worth asking why it even matters whether blacks are better athletes. It's a fair question and there isn't a short and simple answer. *Taboo* does its best to understand both the question and the skeptics. As a necessary consequence, the book is self-referential: it grapples with the issue of whether it should have been written at all, considering America's troubling racial history.

In 1989, Tom Brokaw and I sliced off a sliver of this controversy in the NBC News documentary *Black Athletes: Fact and Fiction*. "It was probably as complicated and controversial a story as I've ever gotten involved in, certainly up there with Watergate," Brokaw remembers. "There were times right before and after it aired that I worried if the storm would ever die down. Those were delicate moments."[10]

Here we were, two prototypical "white men who couldn't jump," tackling a racial controversy that was certain to touch raw nerves. "Friends said 'Don't do it,'" recalls Brokaw. "But I thought that it was important enough to address. Then as the broadcast got near, people came around very quietly and would say to me 'You're doing the right thing.' On the other hand, they didn't want to be associated with it."

Widely praised—the *Denver Post*, for example, applauded NBC "for its bold venture, for the willingness to tackle a sensitive subject . . . and for taking risks in the name of truth-seeking"[11]—the documentary divided journalists, frequently along racial lines. A white columnist at *Newsday* called it "a step forward in the dialogue on race and sports,"[12] while a black colleague at the same daily wrote that "NBC had scientists answer questions that none but a bigot would conjure up."[13] "[Brokaw] utterly ignore[d] the facts in favor of the speculation of several scientists," charged Ralph Wiley in *Emerge* magazine. "His program played like a badly cast farce."[14]

Some of the reaction was intensely personal. "Why are we constantly fighting this superiority battle, instead of asking why and how anyone in the human race develops the ability to excel?" wrote Sybil Smith, a former All-America swimmer at Boston University and then a swim coach at Harvard, in *Sports Illustrated.* She said she was driven to tears by the unpleasant memories the show stirred of her days as a young athlete. Smith had starred in a sport in which blacks have been notably unsuccessful and the subject of a controversy about whether they are physiologically incapable of competing at the elite level. Yet teammates used to explain away her swimming accomplishments by glibly saying, "You're so lucky that you don't have to work that hard."[15]

After the program aired, a number of Brokaw's black friends, the late Secretary of Commerce Ron Brown in particular, called with kind words. "Even Brown was going through a tough time with it, though," says Brokaw. "But I knew him well enough, and we worked through it. But I had another friend who shall go nameless, who is a distinguished black American, had been an athlete, and excelled at the highest levels in other fields. He never ever raised the subject with me. He just quietly withdrew our friendship for about two years."

Black Athletes may have stirred controversy, but it also stimulated a dialogue about the underlying issue: the destructive categorization of people based simply on their ethnicity or the color of their skin. Human differences have never been easy to discuss. And over the past decade, racial suspicions appear to have grown wider, even in the world of sports, which has long operated under the illusion that it is an oasis of tolerance. In 1968, as a black power boycott of the Mexico City Olympics gathered steam, sociologist Harry Edwards, then at San Jose State University, noted, "The prevailing wisdom was that sports were the best thing that ever happened to black people in this country. The question was not how do we correct the problems in sports; the question was how do we make the rest of society like sports."[16] Today, despite decades of progress and the remarkable accomplishments of black athletes, sports remain a haven for some of our most virulent stereotypes.

Taboo is out to do some damage to these prejudices. It was written in the optimistic belief that open debate beats backroom scuttlebutt. Although discussing racial differences is likely to provoke strong reactions, on balance and in proper context, strong emotions are healthy. Issues of race left unexamined can do a lot of damage— just look at the polarized reactions to the O.J. Simpson verdicts, the Rodney King trials, and the 1994 mega-seller book, *The Bell Curve*. It may not be easy to address some of the questions *Taboo* poses, but considering the path racial understanding has taken over the past quarter century, it is a risk worth taking.

There is another reason why this is the right time to look at this issue. At its core this book is about what it means to be human. Today, science is catching up to curiosity. We are unlocking the mystery of genes, the sequence of DNA on a chromosome that forms the molecular basis for heredity. Geneticists are rushing to complete a map of the three billion base pairs of the human genetic code, in effect reconstructing the path of human development. We may not yet be able to definitively deconstruct the relationship of nature to nurture, but we are refining our questions. The coming revolution of our understanding of human nature and behavior will be as profound as the discovery by Copernicus that the earth circles the sun.

For the first time in history science promises a glimpse of how the world's different populations—popularly called races—have evolved. Think of genes as the frame of a house: they determine the shape and set limits, but much of the important stuff gets added over time. Complex phenomena such as intelligence, sociability, and creativity are difficult to dissect without resorting to huge generalizations. Success will always remain a mysterious brew. But we are certainly closer than ever to unraveling the enigmatic forces, biological and social, that shape great athletes, gifted musicians, or top scholars. Within the performance range in which most of us fall, the environment may be critical. But when we talk about people such as Einstein and Mozart—or Mark McGwire, Jim Brown, and Péle—genes count a lot.

Yet the explanatory power of biology has its limits. The "why" of human differences—black/white, male/female, Italian/Irish, between Slavic ethnic groups or one African tribe and another—is likely to remain only crudely measurable. Race—based on ancestry and marked by skin color, ethnicity, and geography—is a fuzzy concept. This fuzziness is compounded by the historical reality that theories about race have been frequently superficial and almost always reflective of a social agenda, whether stated or unrecognized. In the not-too-distant past, conjecture and cultural prejudices costumed as science provided much malignant fuel for the fires of slavery, segregation, and the quiet but insidious racism that continues to haunt relations between blacks and whites. Though frequently exploited in the service of racism, science can now help demolish stereotypes.

In *Taboo*, the importance of the individual remains paramount. Winning athletic competitions does not make one superior in any moral sense. It does signify that you have hit on your lucky number playing the roulette wheel of genetics, cultural serendipity, and individual drive.

Simply stated, *Taboo* is written for those intrigued by one of the more remarkable phenomena of our times—the monumental success of the black athlete in defiance of considerable odds. It plumbs the stories of street-smart playground hoopsters, from Jewish and Black basketball stars of the thirties and forties—to the later-day acrobatics of Connie Hawkins, Julius Erving, and Allen Iverson. The model for the world's greatest athlete is no longer Babe Ruth waddling around the bases nor gimpy-kneed Joe Namath, but a sculptured black athlete: loping long distance runners from the highlands of Kenya; Muhammad Ali with his washboard stomach, lightning moves, and even quicker tongue; speedsters Maury Wills, Lou Brock, and Rickey Henderson; soccer superstar Ronaldo; Randy Moss, who makes catching a football in traffic look like a frolic in the park with a Frisbee; or "Tiger" Woods.

Although the book focuses primarily on male athletes, it devotes an entire section to the history of women in sports. Female athleticism has its own set of celebratory images: Chamique Holdsclaw

twisting through the paint on the way to the basket; the metronomic success of sprinter Marion Jones; and the growing exploits of
tennis superstar siblings Venus and Serena Williams. And *Taboo*
does not shy away from addressing a dark side of athletics, the use
of performance-enhancing drugs. The sports world, women's sports
in particular, still struggles with the legacy of the East European
sports machines.

But *Taboo* is as much about the history of humankind as it is
about hoop dreams and Olympic glory. While not embracing the de-
terministic role of genes, *Taboo* challenges the orthodoxy that all
meaningful differences between populations are cultural, an issue so
sensitive that many people have come to believe that self-censorship
is a mark of tolerance given the racial suspicions that run through
society like an underground river. Human biodiversity may be a danger zone, but pretending that there are no slippery questions does
not prevent them from being asked, if only under one's breath.
Stereotypes are like a mythical herd of elephants in the living room:
everyone hopes that if we refuse to acknowledge their existence,
maybe, just maybe, they will go away. Of course we know they won't.
And they certainly can't be driven away by ignoring what is so obvious, even to a child.

This book uses sport as metaphor, the access point, if you will, to
examine why blacks and whites have such a difficult time acknowledging our differences—the first and most important step in bridg-
ing them. Athletic competition, which offers a definitiveness that
eludes most other aspects of life, is a perfect laboratory for a serious
exploration of such a subject. The challenge is in whether we can
conduct the debate so that human diversity might be cause for celebration of our individuality rather than fanning distrust. After all, in
the end, for all our differences, we are far, far more similar. That's
Taboo's only real message.

CHAPTER 2

THE EDUCATION OF SIR ROGER

A s a scientist rather than a sociologist," the speaker began, "I am prepared to risk political incorrectness by drawing attention to the seemingly obvious but understressed fact that black sprinters and black athletes in general all seem to have certain natural anatomical advantages." The distinguished neurologist had been asked to address the 1995 meeting of the British Association for the Advancement of Science. Because of his personal history—he was a former world-class miler—few were better qualified to assess the issue of breaking barriers in sports than this patrician gentlemen. Nonetheless, the retired Oxford dean, Sir Roger Bannister, would come to regret using the "N" word—natural.

Forty-one years before, in 1954, Bannister had accomplished what many had claimed was beyond the limit of human capability: on a crisp May afternoon, the young medical student had cracked the four-minute-mile barrier. He was an unlikely trailblazer in the eyes of most track aficionados of his era. American Wes Santee and Australian John Landy were considered the top contenders to break four minutes. But Bannister, who had finished fourth in the 1,500 meters at the 1952 Olympics, had quietly launched a crash training program and targeted a relatively obscure meet for his effort.

Bannister had recruited teammates Chris Chataway and Chris Brasher to act as "rabbits." Brasher took off quickly, as planned, setting a fast pace for the first half mile. Chataway took over on the third lap, pulling Bannister to a shade over three minutes at the three-quarter mark. Then, with the crowd of less than one thousand urging him on, Bannister tore down the stretch, hitting the tape in 3:59:4 before collapsing.

For years it was assumed that Bannister's science background had given him a special edge, but he believed that idea was presumptuous. "A medical training aims at increasing the power of careful observation and logical deduction,"[1] he would say, adding that running takes grit and God's will.

Now almost a half century later, as we chat in the living room of his modest Victorian townhouse across the street from Pembroke College of Oxford, his perspective on human performance leavened by years of medical research and experience, Bannister was in hot water for offering his views on the secret of athletic success. But who was outraged? His colleagues were unruffled by his remarks, which were in accord with current genetic and anthropological thinking. Yet his frank address provoked critical headlines around the world.

"I don't think it matters what the biological conclusions are. It forges a distinction between black and white athletes which is unhealthy, unhelpful, and untrue," said Garth Crooks, an African British former professional soccer star and head of the players' union.[2] "It is potentially racist to look at the biological factors," added Theresa Marteau of the Psychology and Genetics Research Unit at Guy's Hospital in London. "I don't need to know whether what Bannister said is correct. And I don't think there needs to be research."[3]

The reaction in the United States was more muted, but no more supportive. "The essence of what Bannister said is not inherently racist," noted *Sports Illustrated*. "It would not, for instance, be prejudicial to note that blacks tend to have different hair and lip structure than Asians, or that Asians on average, are smaller than Caucasians."[4]

So why, muses Bannister out loud, is it racist to suggest that there are biomechanical or physiological differences between populations? He crosses the room to a wall of books where he locates a copy of *The First Four Minutes*, his account of his barrier-breaking run. The narrow spine of the book, with its suggestive title, is the only visible evidence in the entire room that he was once a world-class athlete. He turns the pages almost aimlessly. "I never assumed to be an expert in the physiology of sport. I am a scientist. I observe phenomena. I love to talk about breaking barriers. That was the premise of my talk. It's the kind of inquiry that science should pursue." He taps his left temple with his fingers. He closes the book but does not raise his eyes. "Let's remember, anatomy is not the most important factor. I wasn't the best miler of my time." Then as if filing away that part of his life, he slides the volume neatly back into its accustomed position in the wall library.

Looking tired and worn, very different from the sleek runner who engraved his name in the annals of sports history, Bannister returns to his tattered, plush red chair. Although he insists he has nothing to apologize for, he had refused to allow the session to be recorded. "You just don't know how reporters will report things. It's just safer this way."

He looks up at the ceiling and presses his fingertips together, searching for words. Our discussion is nearing its end. "The brain," he emphasizes in an epilogue designed to rebut the worst interpretations of his speech. "It's the brain, not the heart or lungs, that is the critical organ, it's the brain. But one would have to be blind not to see a pattern here. I hope we are not at a time and place where we are afraid to talk about remarkable events. I hope not."[5]

THE EVIDENCE

CHAPTER 3

BY THE NUMBERS

ore than twenty years after his retirement as a competitive runner, Brooks Johnson looks as fit as the day he last laced up his spikes. Lean and handsome, with a touch of gray at the temples, he looks more like a professor than a college running coach. On this day, the former Olympic and Stanford coach takes his athletes—almost all of them are white—through a demanding drill mixing fast bursts with relaxed jogging. Coach Johnson shouts encouragement as one runner after another throws his exhausted body over the finish line.

"I've been an Olympic coach twice," he muses as he reviews the lackluster times of his charges. "I've had Olympic champions, world-record holders. The big challenge left for me is to put these silly notions to rest. To rub their noses in it. I want to find the white Carl Lewis. That's my mission."[1]

How could it be, Johnson is asked, that elite white sprinters are virtually extinct? "It's racism, pure and simple." He pauses. "But against whites." Johnson speaks with conviction but smiles impishly. It is not clear whether he believes his own words. "Whites are brainwashed to think that because I'm black, I'm going to be faster than you. That means that from the time you were a little kid, you were scared every time you saw me at the starting line, and that gives me an unbeatable edge."

Johnson is repeating a popular, if tired, refrain from the late 1960s, as the racial transformation brought about by desegregation rippled through America. Blacks began to dominate the most popular American sports, erasing once-and-for-all the Anglo-Saxon myth of white physical superiority. According to sociologists, in reaction, whites began to believe that they could not compete in certain sports. "The 'white race' thus becomes the chief victim of its own myth," wrote Harry Edwards in 1973.[2]

By his own admission, Coach Johnson has become obsessed with disabusing people of what he believes is the silly notion that blacks are naturally superior athletes. He sighs, acknowledging for a moment the quixotic nature of his quest to find a white 100-meter champion. "I'm going to find him. In fact for every Carl Lewis, there are nine white Carl Lewises out there. I'm going to find one of them."

"Dear Brooks," wrote Scott Ostler, then a sports columnist with *The Los Angeles Times* when he heard of Johnson's comment, "Pack a lunch."[3]

BIOLOGY CIRCUMSCRIBES POSSIBILITY

Simply stated, the opposing and incompatible claims that black athletic success can be explained by environmentalism or evolution are equally simplistic. Sports success is a bio-social phenomenon. There is extensive and persuasive research that elite black athletes have a *phenotypic* advantage—a distinctive skeletal system and musculature, metabolic structures, and other characteristics forged over tens of thousands of years of evolution. While people of African descent have spent most of their evolutionary history near to where they originated, the rest of the world's populations have had to modify their African adaptations after migrating to far different regions and climates.

Preliminary research suggests that different *phenotypes* are at least partially encoded in the genes—conferring *genotypic* differences, which may result in an advantage in some sports. But all such differences are mediated through experience, from our prenatal health to the educational opportunities while growing up. In other words, our environment and culture can enhance or diminish whatever tiny variations linked to evolution that may exist. Considering the wide variation within each geographic, racial, and ethnic population, such differences may appear minuscule, but at the elite level, they are the stuff of champions.

These inbred differences influence who does how well and in what sports. Asians, who constitute about 57 percent of the world's population, are virtually invisible in the most democratic of world sports, running, soccer, and basketball. Blacks of sub-Saharan African ancestry comprise approximately 12 percent of the world's 6 billion population, yet their hold on many sports, particularly running, is staggering. In the United States, 13 percent of the population is black. In the mid-1960s the racial breakdown in the National Basketball Association (NBA) was 80 percent white, 20 percent black; today it's almost exactly reversed—the NBA is more than 85 percent black. Women's pro basketball is 75 percent African American. The National Football League (NFL) is 70 percent black. In college, 65 percent of men's basketball players and 50 percent of football players are African Americans.[4]

Becoming a professional athlete is still a long-shot for aspiring teenagers, but it's a lot longer for whites. A black male would have about 1 chance in 4,000 of playing in the NBA, as compared to about a 1 in 90,000 shot for a white. And even as African Americans are abandoning baseball in droves for basketball and football, more than one-third of Major League Baseball and a higher percentage of the top stars are blacks from North and Latin America.

Even these eye-popping numbers grossly understate the trends. Check the NBA statistics: not one white player has finished among the top scorers or rebounders in recent years. White running backs, cornerbacks, or wide receivers in the NFL? Count them on one hand. Roll the calendar back decades, to the 1950s, to find the last time a white led baseball in steals. A white male toeing the line at an Olympic 100-meter final? Not in decades.* Don't expect to see a white man set a world record in a road race—any race, at any distance from 100-meters to the marathon. It may happen. In some future decade. But don't hold your breath.

*Four whites, including the gold and bronze medalists, did compete in the 100-meter final at the 1980 Moscow Olympics, which were boycotted by many nations, including the United States.

There is a new racial barrier in sports. Positions that require speed and jumping ability are almost exclusively black. In street parlance this phenomenon is blamed on a malady, virulently infectious but apparently limited to Caucasians—white man's disease. "The NBA is perhaps the only arena of American life," opined sports writers Bob Ryan and Terry Pluto in their book *48 Minutes*, "where to be white is to be immediately judged inferior. [It is] not necessary to have a Ph.D. in kinesiology to realize that the average black player can jump higher and run faster than the average white player."[5]

Standing 5 feet, 7 inches in high-tops, former NBA guard Spud Webb used to dunk the ball in warm-ups. "Just to keep everybody honest," he would say.[6] Even Mugsy Bogues, at 5 feet, 3 inches, can dunk. White players, many of whom line the bench, wonder what kind of future they have. "White people can't jump as high," sighs Scott Brooks, a white guard who bounced around the league in an undistinguished NBA career. Another itinerant guard, Jon Barry, son of Hall-of-Famer Rick Barry, believes he is the last of a "dying breed."[7] Only the demand for mutant giants of any background is likely to forestall a near total washout of nonblacks in coming years.

This is a worldwide phenomenon. Black athletes are now stars in many western countries, from Europe to Asia. For example, tiny Senegal, population 8 million in a country the size of South Dakota, had seventeen citizens playing college basketball in the United States as of 1998. It has also sent dozens of athletes to play in professional basketball leagues in Greece, France, and Israel.[8] In a nation with just one indoor basketball court, it is a triumph of natural talent and tremendous desire over almost insurmountable odds.

That familiar trend is readily apparent in the world's most popular team sport, soccer. Nigeria won the Olympic gold medal in 1996 and qualified two years later for the World Cup along with Cameroon, Tunisia, and South Africa. With the global hopscotching of top players, Africans have become fixtures in Europe's top clubs, even with sharp restrictions on signing foreign players. The Netherlands national team, which made it to the semifinals in the '98 World Cup, includes stars from Suriname, and is about one-third black. France, winner of the 1998 World Cup, has a large contingent of players of African descent, including Ghana-born Marcel Desailly, one of the heroes of the World Cup.[9] Even in England, which was slow to allow foreigners and has a black population of less than 2 percent, 1 in 5 professional soccer players in the premier division is black.[10]

As the world playing field continues to level, natural abilities are more likely to come to the fore. East Asians are disciplined and very competitive, yet because of their small stature and natural flexibility—a result of evolutionary forces—they make better ice skaters, and gymnasts than basketball players or sprinters. Is it more than just cultural serendipity that Brazilians are time and again the best soccer players, the Chinese among the best divers, black Dominicans among the best baseball players, and African Americans the top basketball and football players? Clearly, "racial" patterns in sports do not lend themselves to a facile black and white explanation.

WHAT ABOUT BASEBALL?

The relative dearth of black Americans in baseball—about one in six major leaguers—is frequently cited as proof that blacks do not dominate sports. When a "racial report card" published a few years ago by Northeastern University's Center for The Study of Sport in Society noted that the percentage of American black baseball players had fallen slightly, an outraged editorial entitled "A White Man's Place to Be" appeared in the *New York Times*. Warning of an imminent white takeover of the base paths, it expressed "renewed anxiety about the whiteness of players." It noted the sky-high black participation rates in other sports, then quoted a scout as predicting that "African Americans would soon disappear from the game."[11]

In fact African Americans make up approximately 15 percent of top professionals, higher than their 13 percent of the general population. Americans so reflexively expect black domination that anything less than an NBA or NFL-sized black majority is taken as a sign of renewed discrimination—against blacks. To invoke racism for a slight drop in the percentage of American blacks (the raw numbers have actually increased with expansion) shows how deeply the belief in black athletic superiority is ingrained in Americans, black and white.

The racial report card's numbers distort the racial trends. There are actually far more black players in baseball than ever before. Only 60 percent of Major League Baseball players are American-born whites, and the number is decreasing every year. Over the past twenty years, Hispanics, many of whom are black, have jumped from 8 to 24 percent. Today, 40 percent of professional baseball players are of primarily West African ancestry.

By the numbers, black Hispanic ballplayers are the most likely to make it to the big leagues, followed by players of mixed black and white heritage, then whites, with Mexicans (who, according to physical anthropologists, typically have shorter legs and are less muscular in the lower body than Caribbean blacks as a result of their Native Indian heritage) having the toughest time.[12] The largely black Dominican Republic, which currently has more than ninety players in the major leagues, is a baseball hothouse.

Although the overall numbers of blacks in baseball do not approach those in football or basketball, the stars are disproportionately black. A "dream team" recently put together by USA Today sports writers included only one white among the position players.[13] This phenomenon is not a recent development. In the fifty years since Jackie Robinson became the first black to be named Most Valuable Player (MVP), a black player has been chosen National League MVP thirty-three times. Since 1963, when Elston Howard of the New York Yankees became the first nonwhite named MVP in the American League, black players have won the honor nineteen times. A clear majority of MVP's are black. Whites are far more likely to be the marginal players filling out a roster.

Baseball historian Bill James, author of dozens of books on the statistical twists of his favorite sport, believes this trend is not a fluke. In an intriguing study conducted in 1987, he compared the careers of hundreds of rookies to figure out what qualities best predict who would develop into stars.[14] He noted many intangible factors, such as whether a player stays fit or is just plain lucky. The best predictors of long-term career success included the age of the rookie, his defensive position as a determinant in future hitting success (e.g., catchers fare worse than outfielders), speed, and the quality of the player's team. But all of these factors paled when compared to the color of the player's skin.

"Nobody likes to write about race," James noted apologetically. "I thought I would do a [statistical] run of black players against white players, fully expecting that it would show nothing in particular or nothing beyond the outside range of chance, and I would file it away and never mention that I had looked at the issue at all."

James first compared fifty-four white rookies against the same number of black first-year players who had comparable statistics. "The results were astonishing," he wrote. The black players:

- went on to have better major-league careers in 44 of the 54 cases
- played 48 percent more games
- had 66 percent more major-league hits
- hit 93 percent more triples
- hit 66 percent more home runs
- scored 69 percent more runs
- stole 400 percent more bases

James compared Reggie Jackson, who began his career as a right-fielder with the Oakland Athletics in 1969, to Bob Allison, who broke in with a splash ten years before with the Washington Senators. A star running back in college, Allison was fast as lightning and strong to boot. The young centerfielder hit a solid .261, smacked a rookie-high 30 homers, knocked in 85 runs, scored almost as many, swiped 13 bases, and led the American League in triples. He also sparkled in centerfield.

Allison's rookie year was remarkably comparable to Jackson's (see Table 1). Like Allison, Jackson was a star football player. Both were

TABLE 3.1

ROOKIE-YEAR STATISTICS FOR BOB ALLISON AND REGGIE JACKSON

	G	AB	R	H	2B	3B	HR	RBI	SB	AVG
Allison	150	570	83	149	18	9	30	85	13	.261
Jackson	154	553	82	138	13	6	29	74	14	.250

speedsters. But while Jackson got better and better, Allison went into a long decline after a few fine seasons with the Minnesota Twins. By 1965, he had lost his speed and was splitting time between left field and first. A few years later, he was out of the game altogether. Meanwhile, Jackson played on five World Series teams, earning the moniker "Mr. October" before retiring into the Hall of Fame.

Flabbergasted at what he had found, James ran a second study using forty-nine black/white comparisons. Again, blacks proved more durable, retained their speed longer, and were consistently better hitters. For example, he compared Ernie Banks, a power hitting shortstop for the Chicago Cubs, and Bernie Allen, who broke in with Minnesota. They both reached the majors when they were twenty-three years old, were the same height and weight, and were considered equally fast. Over time, Allen bombed and Banks landed in the Hall of Fame.

Or contrast the careers of Gus Bell, who played mostly for Pittsburgh and Cincinnati, and Hank Aaron of the Braves. In their early years, Bell was faster and comparable to Aaron as a slugger. But a few years along in their careers, Aaron was stealing 30-plus bases a year and gunning for Babe Ruth's all time homer record; Bell deteriorated into a part-timer with "wooden legs."

In an attempt to correct for possible bias, James compared players with comparable speed statistics such as the number of doubles, triples, and stolen bases. He ran a study that focused only on players who had little speed. He analyzed for "position bias" and made sure that players in the same eras were being compared. Yet every time he crunched the numbers, the results broke down along racial lines. When comparing home runs, runs scored, RBIs, or stolen bases, black players held the advantage a startling 80 percent of the time. "And I could identify absolutely no bias to help explain why this should happen," said James in disbelief.

James also compared white Hispanic rookies, whom he assumed faced an uphill battle similar to that for blacks, with comparable groups of white and black players. The blacks dominated the white Latinos by even more than they did the white North Americans, besting them in 19 of the 26 comparisons. Blacks played 62 percent more games, hit 192 percent more home runs, drove in 125 percent more runs, and stole 30 percent more bases.

So why have blacks become the stars in baseball far out of proportion to their relative numbers? James eventually concluded that there were only two possible explanations: "Blacks are better athletes because they are born better athletes, which is to say that it is genetic, or that they are born equal and become better athletes."

COOL RUNNERS

That whites dominate golf, rugby, or the America's Cup yacht race is hardly big news, considering the fact that English-speaking whites invented the sports. More remarkably, black athletes are coming to prominence even in sports in which, by culture, economics, or geography, they are unlikely participants. For example, bobsledding.

As a young boy growing up in Memphis, Garrett Hines certainly never fantasized about running the chutes. He dreamed about being a professional basketball player, dunking hoops with Dr. J, or sliding past Magic Johnson for an easy layup. He was fast—like a gazelle, he was told. Instead of pursuing basketball, however, he ended up running high school track and playing football, eventually becoming a two-sport star at the Southern Illinois University. In 1992, after graduation, one of his college buddies decided to try out for the U.S. bobsled team. What the heck, Hines thought. So they piled into the car for the twenty-two-hour drive to Lake Placid to pursue their crazy whim.

When he and his friend pulled into town after a day-long drive, there was more snow than Hines had ever seen in his life. "I was so scared I almost quit right there," he recalled thinking after his first training run.[15] He went on to shock even himself by making the team as a pusher—the second person in the two-man and one of the two runners in the four-man bobsled whose job it is to launch the sled careening down the mountain.

Hines's journey from urban basketball junkie to star college athlete to Olympic bobsledder is not as improbable as it may appear.

The most critical factor in bobsledding is the start. If it's explosive, it can give a two- or four-man team an edge that can sometimes overcome a lesser-quality sled or a bumpy ride. With quickness so critical, it makes sense that the most explosive contemporary athletes—blacks who trace their ancestry to West Africa—would be among the best bobsled pushers. As unlikely as it sounds, that notion is becoming true.

Six years after that harrowing practice run, in 1998, Hines mused over the twists of fate that had lifted him from the streets of Memphis to a mountaintop in Nagano, Japan. As he settled his nerves and prepared to hurtle down an ice-slick bobsled run at speeds topping 80 miles an hour, he glanced across at his Olympic teammate and fellow pushman Randy Jones, a former football and track star from Duke University, who now owns his own computer upgrading and repair company. Jones was the side-push and brakeman on the 1994 U.S. team and winner of three gold medals during 1996 and 1997 World Cup competitions. The two were attempting to become the first African American men to win a medal at the Winter Olympics. "I never imagined this," said Hines. "Not in a million years."

There is already a tradition of black bobsledders and lugers. In 1988, the U.S. bobsled team sought out two track Olympians: Edwin Moses, who was in the midst of a 16-year, 122-race streak as world-record holder in the 400-meter hurdles, and sprinter Willie Gault. Gault was selected but didn't compete. The British team included several athletes of Caribbean heritage. The Calgary Winter Olympics also marked the quixotic debut of the "Cool Runners" from Jamaica. Egged on by the country's tourist board, which saw the adventure as a way to boost Jamaica's sagging image, the islanders competed in two- and four-man events using hand-me-down sleds. With the world prepared for a chuckle, the four-man team rocketed out of the gate with one of the fastest starting times in the event, before crashing spectacularly. Still, they finished a respectable twenty-second among thirty-one teams.

The Jamaicans became an instant legend, with the crash forming the climactic scene in a Walt Disney movie, *Cool Runnings*, which was loosely based on the experiences of the bobsledders. They celebrated with an international victory-less tour, including a guest appearance with the Los Angeles Lakers complete with tributes from Magic Johnson and Kareem Abdul Jabbar. Almost overnight, bobsled federations in several countries were clamoring to find the fastest runners to draft into the sport.

Within a few years, the United States, Britain, France, and Canada had drawn upon a deep well of black sprinters to stock their teams. In 1992 Brian Shimer recruited professional football player and former University of Georgia track star Herschel Walker to be his pusher in a two-man US team. Although they barely had time to practice together—Walker chose to finish the 1991 season with the Minnesota Vikings rather than hit the World Cup circuit—the media touted the duo as a pre-Olympic favorite. But their rustiness showed in Lillehammer, where they blew the start and finished a disappointing seventh. But the upstart Jamaicans finished fourteenth, ahead of both US teams, which had state-of-the-art high-tech sleds

By 1998 black bobsledders were commonplace. The Jamaicans were even given an outside shot at a medal. They were joined by long-shot wanna-bes from Trinidad and Tobago, the Virgin Islands, and Puerto Rico. The top pushers on Team Canada traced their ancestry to Africa via the Caribbean. Sheridon Baptiste, a football, basketball, and track star at Queen's University in Kingston, Ontario, was one of the top brakemen in the world and the fastest man on the Canadian squad. His African-Canadian teammates included Ricardo Greenridge, a former 200-meter champion, and Ian Danney. The United States had high hopes that it could capture its first bobsled medal in decades. The previous November, at the World Cup in Winterberg, Germany, Shimer's four-man had crushed the course start record in both heats, a testament to the blazing speed of its two runners, Jones and Hines.

On the final day of competition at Nagano, Germany established an insurmountable lead in the four-man. The two Canadian teams faltered while Jamaica slid to twenty-first. With Switzerland clinging to second, it came down to the final slide. The start was phenomenal, as usual, with the US team blazing through the first 50 meters in

4.90 seconds, the fastest of the heat. But even the African American pushmen were not enough to overcome a sloppy run, as the US bob-sledders missed a medal by .02 seconds. The unheralded French and British teams tied for the bronze medal. Two black pushers, Court-ney Orville Rumbolt and Paul Jason Attwood, both star sprinters, powered Britain.

What are we to make of this? For years, faster times in bobsled-ding were driven by technique and the development of ever-sleeker sleds. With the technology gap between countries now almost nonexistent, the human factor has again become paramount. Faster starts mean faster times. It's no surprise that bobsledding is turning to the fastest men alive: blacks who trace their ancestry to West Africa.

CHAPTER 4

THE MOST LEVEL PLAYING FIELD

I t was a long bus ride home for Alfonce Muindi. While most of his Kenyan countrymates celebrated loudly, he stared glumly out the window. The annual 10 miler in Flint, Michigan, attracts more than five thousand runners. Muindi, one of a dozen Kenyans entered in the 1996 race, was considered one of the favorites. The hilly Michigan course was tailored to his style. Race-day conditions, with temperatures in the 60s, were not unlike a cool morning in the Kenyan highlands where he had grown up.

Muindi took off fast and was among the leaders in the early going. The pace was blistering. He held with the pack until the midpoint, but faded near the end. Muindi was inconsolable. Although he had handily finished ahead of all the non-Kenyans, including elite runners from North America, Europe, Asia, and Latin America, in the only competition that mattered–the race among his countrymen–he had failed miserably. Kenyans swept the top twelve places; in the race of the elite, Muindi had finished dead last.[1]

Kenyan domination of distance running, and the virtual takeover of elite-level track by athletes of African descent, is powerful anecdotal evidence of innate physical differences between populations. If there is a level playing field in athletics, it is the earth–literally. "A scientist interested in exploring physical and performance differences couldn't invent a better sport than running," wrote Amby Burfoot, editor of *Runner's World* and former winner of the Boston marathon..

It's a true world-wide sport, practiced and enjoyed in almost every country around the globe. Also, it doesn't require any special equipment, coaching, or facilities. [Ethiopia's] Abebe Bikila proved this dramatically in the 1960 Olympic Games when–shoeless, little coached, and inexperienced–he won the marathon. Given the universality of running, it's reasonable to expect that the best runners should come from a wide-range of countries and

TABLE 4.1
WORLD RUNNING RECORDS

Distance	Athlete	Time	Date	Ancestral Origin
100-meters	Maurice Greene (USA)	9.79	6/16/99	West Africa
4x100m relay	Marsh, Burrell, Mitchess, Lewis (USA)	37.40	8/8/92	West Africa
110m hurdles	Colin Jackson (GRB)	12.91	8/20/93	West Africa
200m	Michael Johnson (USA)	19.32	8/1/96	West Africa
400m	Michael Johnson (USA)	43.18	8/26/99	West Africa
4x400m relay	Young, Pettigrew, Washington, Johnson (USA)	2:54.20	7/22/98	West Africa
400m hurdles	Kevin Young (USA)	46.78	8/6/92	West Africa
800m	Wilson Kipketer (KEN)	1:41.11	8/24/97	East Africa
1000m	Noah Ngeny (KEN)	2:11.96	9/5/99	East Africa
1500m	Hicham El Guerrouj (MOR)	3:26.00	7/15/98	North Africa
Mile	Hicham El Guerrouj (MOR)	3:43.13	7/7/99	North Africa
3,000m Steeplechase	Bernard Bermasai (KEN)	7:55.72	8/24/97	East Africa
5,000m	Halle Gebrselassie (ETH)	12:39.36	6/13/98	East Africa
10,000m	Halle Gebrselassie (ETH)	26:22.75	6/3/98	East Africa
Marathon	Khalid Khannouchi (MOR)	2:05:42	10.24/99	North Africa

racial groups. This isn't, however, what happens. Nearly all the sprints are won by runners of West African descent. Nearly all the distance races are won, remarkably, by runners from just one small corner of one small African country.[2]

For all practical reality, men's world championship events might as well post a sign declaring, "Whites Need Not Apply." Indeed, with the breaking of Sebastian Coe's 18-year-old 1,000-meter world record in 1999 by Kenyan Noah Ngeny, every men's world record at every commonly-run track distance belongs to a runner of African descent (see Table 4.1).[3]

While Africa is the mother-lode of the running world, talent is not evenly distributed across the continent but is concentrated in three areas: a swath of western African coastal states, notably Senegal, Nigeria, and Cameroon, extending south to Namibia; the northern African countries of Algeria and Morocco; and a long stretch of eastern African states from Ethiopia, Tanzania, and Kenya to mountainous South Africa (see Figure 4.1).

Each sport, or running distance, demands a slightly different mix of biomechanical, anaerobic, and aerobic abilities. Not surprisingly, athletes from each region tend to excel in specific athletic events as a result of both cultural and genetic factors: West Africa is the ancestral home of the world's top sprinters and jumpers; North Africa turns out top middle distance runners; and East Africa is the world distance running capital. Amazingly, whereas only one in every eight of the people in the world are black, more than 70 percent of the top times are held by runners of African origin. (see Figure 4.2).

A look at the ancestry (or home country) of the runners holding the top 100 times in eight distances, from the 100 meters to the marathon, makes it clear that African domination is deep as well as broad.[4]

- Blacks who trace their ancestry to West Africa, including African Americans, hold 494 of the top 500 100-meter times and 98 percent of top sprinting times;
- Whites are virtually absent from the top ranks of sprinting;

though whites have traditionally done well in the longer endurance races, particularly the marathon, their ranks have
thinned in recent years as Africans entered the sport;

- Athletes from one country, Kenya, make up 40 percent of top

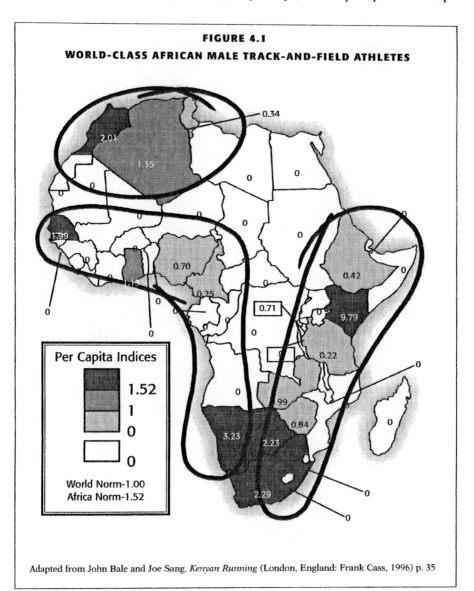

FIGURE 4.1

WORLD-CLASS AFRICAN MALE TRACK-AND-FIELD ATHLETES

Per Capita Indices

1.52
1
0
0

World Norm-1.00
Africa Norm-1.52

Adapted from John Bale and Joe Sang, *Kenyan Running* (London, England: Frank Cass, 1996) p. 35

33

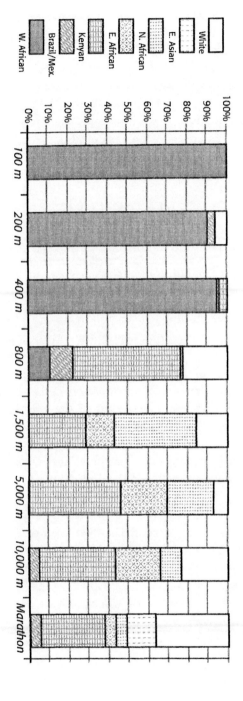

FIGURE 4.2

TOP 100 TIMES BY COUNTRY OR ANCESTRY

times in middle and long distance races; including top performances by other East Africans (most from Ethiopia), that domination swells to more than 50 percent.
- North Africans excel at the middle distances;
- Mexicans, mostly Native Indians, are strong at the longer
races, 10,000 meters and the marathon;
- East Asians–Chinese, Koreans, and Japanese–are competitive
at the event requiring the most endurance, the marathon.

SPRINTS

Remember the last time a non-black set the men's world record in
the 100-meter sprint? One has to go back to 1960, when German
Armin Hary won the Olympic gold medal in 10.2 seconds. The best
time by a white 100-meter runner is 10 seconds, which ranks below
two hundred on the all-time list. There are also no elite sprinters of
note from Asia, which has 57 percent of the world's population, even
with the Confucian and Tao traditions of discipline and an authori-
tarian sports system in the most populous country, China.

Today, the 100-meter distance is monopolized by blacks of West
African ancestry. They are quicker out of the starting blocks and
demonstrate blazing speed. Former "world's fastest human" Donovan Bailey clocked a mind-bending 27 miles per hour at the midpoint of his record-breaking sprint at the Atlanta Olympics.[5] Dozens
of blacks but no Asians or whites have cracked the 10-second barrier
(see Table 4.2).

All of the forty finalists in the last five Olympic men's 100-meter
races are of West African descent. The likelihood of that happening
based on population numbers alone–blacks with ancestral roots in
that region represent 8 percent of the world's population–is
0.000000000000000000000000000000000000000001 percent.[6]

There have been a small handful of non-West African 200- and
400-meter runners over the years. In 1979 Italy's Pietro Mennea
shattered the 200-meter record, running 19.72 seconds, still the best

TABLE 4.2

BREAKING 10 SECONDS AT 100 METERS

	Sub–10s	Personal Best
Maurice Green, (USA)	31	9.79
Frankie Fredricks, NAM	26	9.86
Alto Boldon (TRI & TOB)	22	9.86
Donovan Bailey (CAN)	15	9.84
Carl Lewis (USA)	15	9.86
Dennis Mitchell (USA)	13	9.91
Linford Christie (USA)	9	9.92
Jon Drummond (USA)	9	9.92

time by a non-African. Although he ran in Mexico City's 7,300 foot altitude and was aided by a tailwind of 90 percent of the allowable limit, Mennea's moment-in-the-sun is invoked as "proof" that whites can run as fast as blacks of West African ancestry. Mennea's record held for seventeen years before being pulverized in 1996 by Michael Johnson in a stunning 19.32 seconds, an improvement of more than 2 percent, an unheard of breakthrough in sprinting.[7] Intriguingly, many southern Europeans (including Mennea[8]) who are disproportionately stand-outs in running, trace a significant percentage of their genes to Africa as a result of interbreeding.[9]

MIDDLE DISTANCES

Whereas runners of West African ancestry monopolize sprinting from 100 meters to 400 meters, with rare exception, they do not even compete in elite middle distance races. Malvin Whitfield of the United States won gold medals in the 800 meters in the 1948 and

1952 Olympics in times that by today's standards, set by North and East Africans, are pokey. The current list of athletes holding the all-time top 800-meter times includes only two men who might claim West African ancestry: Johnny Gray of the United States and Joaquim Carvalho Cruz of Brazil (although Cruz's racial ancestry, like that of many Brazilians, includes Amerindian/Asian genes).

In contrast, East Africans and North Africans (who have substantial white ancestry, whether Arab or Berber is not certain), who are hapless in the sprints, dominate endurance races. Even tiny Burundi, has become a power of sorts, winning a gold in the 5,000-meters and coming in fourth in the 10,000 meters at the Atlanta Olympics, a better showing in distance running than the United States. Not surprisingly, all seven members of the Burundi team were slender Tutsis, of the same Nilotic-Saharan background as athletes from the world's top running super-powers, Ethiopia and Kenya.

As the economic barriers that long limited participation by Africans have eroded, the rest of the world runners, even in some widely-contested races such as the 10,000 meters, drift further and further back in the pack (see Table 4.3).

Kenya is far and away the world power at 800 meters and the 3,000 meter steeplechase. Excepting two extraordinary North Africans, Noureddine Morceli of Algeria and Morocco's Hicham El Guerrouj, Kenyans set the pace at the other middle distances, the 10,000 meters and the marathon, holding more than half of the top times. Kenyan men have won the World Cross-Country Championships every year since 1986 and are often so dominant that they would have beaten the rest of the world combined.

The depth of the country's talent is so dazzling that Daniel Komen, considered by many to be the world's premier middle-distance runner in 1996, could not make his country's Olympic team. At the World Juniors in 1994, the Rift Valley native took the 5,000- and 10,000-meter titles. But in the Kenyan Olympic Trials two years later, Komen could not finish among the top three in any race. As a result, he ended up watching the Games on television from his summer training base in the London suburb of Teddington, just a few miles from the fields of Harrow, where Roger Ban-

TABLE 4.3
TOP TEN NON-AFRICAN TOP TIMES IN THE 10,000 METERS

1	27:08.17	BARRIOS Arturo	MEX	89.08.18	WORLD RANK	23
2	27:12.47	PINTO António	POR	99.07.07		34
3	27:13.81	MAMEDE Fernando	POR	84.07.02		37
4	27:14.44	RONCERO Fabian	ESP	98.04.04		40
5	27:15.76	PINTO António	POR	98.04.04		45
6	27:16.50	ANTIBO Salvatore	ITA	89.06.29		46
7	27:17.48	LOPES Carlos	POR	84.07.02		50
8	27:18.14	BROWN Jon	GBR	98.08.28		57
9	27:18.22	BARRIOS Arturo	MEX	90.17.08		59
10	27:18.45	BARRIOS Arturo	MEX	89.03.07		69

nister had prepared for his assault on the four-minute mile-barrier four decades before, and where Sebastian Coe still lopes through the hills to stay in shape.

Shortly after the Olympics concluded, as if in revenge for not being selected, Komen embarked on one of the great months in running history. In mid-August in Zurich, he crushed then 5,000-meter world-record holder Halle Gebrselassie of Ethiopia. Nine days later in Brussels he took on Morocco's Noureddine Morceli at 3,000 meters and left him sniffing vapors. The next week at Rieti in Italy, he broke the 3,000-meter record, running 7:20:67. Komen moved on to Milan, where he won the 5,000-meter Grand Prix finals. In less than a month, a Kenyan Olympic team also-ran had destroyed three world records at a variety of distances, earning more than $400,000.

The following year, 1997, Komen added the 5,000-meter record, along with two indoor world marks. Still not in his prime, he has run a scintillating 7:58.61 over two miles, the first athlete to cover that distance in less than eight minutes. While the world rightly considers Bannister's sub-four minute mile a momentous accomplishment, Komen ran his first mile in 3:59.2–then turned in a second mile of 3:59.4.

What's most striking about Komen and many other top East African runners is their remarkable range in middle- and long-distance events. Gebrselassie began the 1999 outdoor track season with 15 world records in his career at distances from 2,000- to 10,000-meters. Kenya's Moses Kiptanui, the first athlete to run the 3,000-meter steeplechase in under eight minutes, and countryman Wilson Kipketer, are both capable of record-setting performances over a variety of distances.

Unlikely new stars blossom every season. Ondoro Osoro, who had never previously run a marathon, even in practice, and is primarily a 5,000-meter runner, did nothing less than run the third-fastest marathon in history in Chicago in 1998. "It truly blows me away," says Keith Brantly, a 1996 U.S. Olympian and one of America's top marathoners, of the combination of speed and endurance in East African runners. "It's really nice to be naïve sometimes and run like it's a distance run and sprint at the end."[10]

Is this success just a temporary phenomenon? Not likely. The pipeline is full of young Kenyans, who have captured almost every men's new world junior record in road racing in recent years. Among the females, only a few Chinese women have cracked Kenyan hegemony over the world junior circuit. And the staggering reality is that while Kenyans continue to improve in the middle distances, runners from the rest of the world have stagnated.

THE MARATHON

Until the mid–1980s, no country dominated marathoning. Africa was an international also-ran. "We were told when we were younger that the marathon was not good for your health, that you might not be able to have children," says Kenya's Moses Tanui, who won his second Boston Marathon with a near-world record run in 1998.[11] That changed with the emergence of the Kenyans, spurred in part by the breakthrough success of Ibrahim Hussein in marathons in Honolulu, Boston, and New York in the late eighties. With Hussein's very visible victories, and as money and prestige washed over the event, such cultural constraints were soon swept away.

Now Kenya is the hands-down best at both middle- and long-distance running. At Boston, considered the world's premier marathon, Kenyan men have not lost since 1990. Even the slow Kenyans leave the rest of the pack behind. Each year, the top fifty fastest Kenyan marathoners can expect to break 2:13, a time out of reach of most whites, and Asians, and blacks of West African ancestry.

KENYA UNDER THE MICROSCOPE

Let's turn a high-powered microscope on this tiny powerhouse. Kenya is a diverse country with many ethnic tribes and only a loose and somewhat recent concept of a nation. All told, Kenya has collected forty-five Olympic medals since the 1964 Olympics. That includes fifteen gold in men's races, a haul exceeded by only the sprint-rich United States, with a population ten times larger. At Seoul in 1988 Kenyan men won the 800, 1,500, and 5,000 meters, along with the 3,000 meter steeplechase. Based on population percentages alone, the likelihood that this Texas-sized country could turn in such a remarkable medal performance is *one in 1.6 billion.*[12]

Increase the power on our microscope to focus on the highlands along the western rim of the Great Rift Valley adjacent to Lake Victoria. Three-fourths of Kenyan world-class athletes trace their ancestry to this region, a level of dominance that has remained remarkably consistent over the decades. How remarkable is this juggernaut? Kalenjin runners have won more than seventy percent of Kenya's Olympic medals in world running and all but one of Kenyan-held world records.[13] Over the past decade, athletes from this tiny dot on the world map have won more than 40 percent of all the biggest international distance-running honors available and nearly three times as many Olympic and World Championship distance medals as athletes from *any other nation in the world.*[14]

Yet even these remarkable figures understate what's going on in

Kalenjin country. Ratchet the magnification up another notch. One small district, the Nandi, with only 1.8 percent of Kenya's population, has produced about half of the world-class Kalenjin athletes and 20 percent of all the winners of major international distance-running events.[15]

By almost any measure, this tiny region in west-central Kenya represents the greatest concentration of raw athletic talent in the history of sports. "As far as Kalenjin running is concerned," observes John Manners, a former Peace Corps teacher in Kenya and author of two books on Kenyan running, "I think it's unlikely that anyone who spends any time in Kalenjin country and watches what untrained kids can do (especially when compared with other Kenyans of ostensibly similar backgrounds) will come away thinking that anything but genetic factors are paramount in their success. The evidence is impressionistic and anecdotal, but the *prima facie* case is pretty persuasive," he says, though he insists that he remains skeptical of biological theories of athletic success.[16]

Kenyan dominance of international endurance running is so complete that there was a movement afoot by some race directors to limit their number at future races.[17] "They are not only slaughtering the Americans," said Brantly after finishing behind eight Kenyans in the 1998 Cherry Blossom 10-mile race in Washington, "they are slaughtering everybody."[18]

It's gotten to the point where most of the world's best non-Kenyan men have all but given up contesting the middle distances in elite races.[19] "When you are trying to earn your living on the road, it is getting silly," remarked a top British runner. "There are 10 or 15 Kenyans everywhere."[20] Fabián Rancero, the brilliant Spaniard who has run one of the best marathon times ever, is skeptical that anyone can match up against the top Kenyans. "The only athlete capable of going close to 2:05 at this moment is probably [Kenyan] Paul Tergat," he said in 1998. "No white man is capable of running that sort of time."[21]

The best of the non-African runners are dubbed "white Kenyans" in the same slightly patronizing way that Hank Aaron was once called the "black Babe Ruth." Many white runners such as Germany's Dieter Baumann, the surprise gold-medal winner at 5,000-meters in the 1992 Barcelona Olympics, are stunned to find themselves slipping further and further back in the pack. "We Europeans

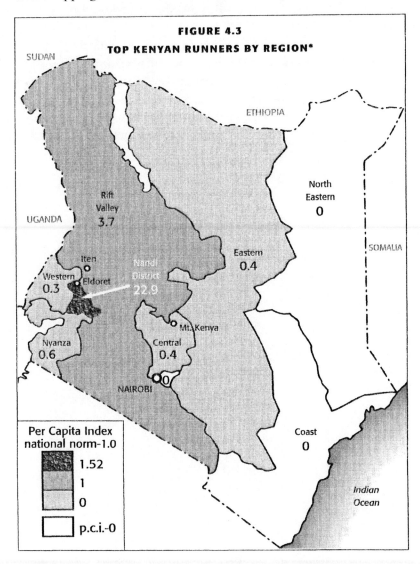

Adapted from John Bale and Joe Sang, *Kenyan Running* (London, England: Frank Cass, 1996) p. 141

are just as good as them and no less suited for distance running," he bellyaches. "I don't see myself on the defensive because the Africans are simply normal opponents." Bauman was suspended in 1999 for two years after twice testing positive for the steriod Nandrolone.

Normal, yes. Beatable? That's another story.

"The record-holders used to be athletes from industrialized nations who had access to technology and financial incentives," says Frank Shorter, in search of an explanation. "As more Kenyans and Ethiopians could achieve the same access to agents, money and a lucrative running career, the balance of power changed. The Africans finally got a level playing field. Then, the game was over."[22]

CHAPTER 5

NATURE'S EXPERIMENT:

THE "KENYAN MIRACLE"

he slumbering giants of Mount Kilimanjaro and Mount Kenya tower over the mountainous region that slices through Ethiopia, Kenya, Tanzania, and Uganda. It is part of a larger geological formation, an enormous depression that stretches from the mouth of the Zambezi River northward through East Africa into the Jordan Valley. During the Pliocene epoch some five million years ago, the earth's crust buckled and boiled, spewing forth lava, creating the Great Rift Valley, a 4,000-mile-long gash, 20 to 60 miles across the heart of East Africa.

With no outlet to the sea, the floor of the valley filled with narrow, shallow lakes and steaming hot springs. It is one of the few ecosystems in the world that has remained unchanged for centuries. Here on the shores of Lake Turkana and Olduvai Gorge in Tanzania, Richard Leakey discovered the 1.9-million-year-old Koobi Fora fossils and stone tools, among the most important discoveries establishing the history of early modern man. It is here in East Africa that archaic humans crossed a threshold into tool-making. It is believed that marked a transition to meat eating, helping to spur a dramatic growth of the brain and the eventual evolution of modern humanity.

Lake Victoria, the source of the Nile, anchors the southwestern corner of Kenya. The various tribes who have long called the Rift Valley home enjoy a near-perfect year-round climate, a result of the altitude and ample rains. It is the mother-lode of world-class endurance runners. "If you take a look at the Olympic medals that have been won in long distance running by Africans," observes former Kenyan coach John Velzian, "they nearly all come from this region. It's a very, very small area, but there is an endless supply of world-class runners."[1]

Nairobi, Kenya's capital, is East Africa's largest city and the gateway to the world's greatest sports empire. It is noisy, plagued by honking drivers, endless traffic jams, and deteriorating public services. Political corruption and a tattered economy are considered a way of life. From here, tourists head east to gorgeous tropical beaches along the Indian Ocean or south to the wild open grasslands with a spectacular array of wildlife. But the past decade has seen a different kind of tourism: lean young men and women from all points on the globe heading northwest from Nairobi into the high moorlands, carrying duffel bags emblazoned with brand symbols of Nike, Reebok, and Asics. They come in search of the Holy Grail of road racing, the secret of Kenya's running miracle.

The road from Nairobi cuts across miles of brush populated by herds of galloping zebra and hartebeest. Bright pink lily pads covering Lake Nakuru flutter into the sky, revealing themselves as thousands of flamingos. The road snakes into the mountains through pine forests before crossing the equator and dropping gently into the hill country. During the rainy season, from April to July, the doughy mess that passes for roads can make traveling and running an extra challenge. Jacaranda trees with bright purple blossoms give way to maize fields and then at higher elevations to dusty plains spotted with cacti.

The drive ends at a village framed by dilapidated billboards for Coca-Cola and Tusker, a Kenyan beer. "Drive Carefully," reads a sign. "Bloodless Road Looks Good." There is a sultry and incongruous feel to this town. Farmers herd cows, sheep, and goats down a rutted main road. Produce spills from baskets balanced on the heads of local women. Bleached white stucco-covered shops stand side by side with colonial-era buildings. With its dusty streets, the town looks like an all-black version of the American Old West. Along the lower main road, entrepreneurs hawk haircuts and flea-market clothes from makeshift, open-air shacks. Most people here are poor, but not in character. Their faces, deep ebony, break into warm white smiles at the sight of strangers. This is Eldoret.

Almost every afternoon, the central byway is sprinkled with Mercedes and recent-vintage sporty trucks that belie the town's modest prosperity. Its owners can be found sipping tea in the local café. World-record holder Moses Kiptanui is a frequent visitor. Gold medalists Peter Rono and Joseph Kitur, sharing a joke at a corner table, are joined by rising stars Paul Ruto and David Kibet. Moses Tanui, who has won two Boston Marathons and owns a home nearby, sits off to one side reading a running magazine. While the group chatters away, Mary Chemweno and her husband, Kipsubai Koskei, both veteran international competitors who live on a farm just outside town, drop by. It is a remarkable gathering of top athletes, made more so by the fact that it happens almost daily.

"If one were to circumscribe a radius of 60 miles around the town of Eldoret, you would get about 90 percent of the top Kenyan athletes," observes Fred Hardy, a retired college track coach who began recruiting from the region more than thirty years ago. "Something special has happened here in the Nandi Hills."[2]

Many of Kenya's top runners call Eldoret home. It is also the home of the famed Kipchoge Keino, the father of Kenyan running and the favorite son, who has an office down the street. The phenomenal success of local sons and daughters in international road racing has brought a blush of prosperity to the ranchland that lines the road between Eldoret and Kapsabet, the largest towns in the area. The occasional rattle of a passing matatu, a windowless minibus hauling stragglers home for supper, is the only sound in the heavy late-afternoon air. As the sun begins to set, the rolling hills are bathed in an orange glow. Dozens of young boys and girls can be found running in the mountain breezes that come as the African sun begins to cool.

Fifteen minutes outside Eldoret, a side road veers sharply left. After a few hundred yards it deteriorates into a series of ruts. Every quarter mile or so stands a tiny concrete home with a tin roof and an outside kitchen. The early-evening light gives way to a moonless black. There is an almost total absence of illumination because the cost of bringing in electricity is so prohibitive. A flicker of light finally becomes visible in the distance. It is coming from the living room of a modest house where a half-dozen young men crowd around the only light source for miles around. The television is on; it's like a campfire keeping the people warm. Ibrahim Hussein, Kenya's first great marathoner, is laughing uproariously. They are watching the movie, *The Gods Must Be Crazy*.

Hussein is a gracious benefactor. With his considerable running earnings, he founded the Ibrahim Hussein Track Club, which provides living expenses and trains top area runners. He has also built two homes and purchased a hotel in Eldoret. Hussein owns one of the few VCRs in the area, which he kept running by generator until power lines were finally installed. Next to his small house sits a huge construction bulldozer and the frame of what promises to be a Kenyan-style mansion, a gift to his parents. They have finally relented and are allowing him to build a kitchen in the house instead of off to the side in a separate hut.

Like his hero Kip Keino, Hussein loved running as a boy. "It happens that I lived about two miles from my primary school," he says, remembering his days as the school bell ringer. "It's not like the American system where schools are very near. I would run in the morning and then run back for lunch and run back again in the afternoon. If you are late, they would punish you."[3] Even today the road between Kapsabet and Eldoret is filled each morning with schoolchildren in uniform running in bare feet. "It's a way of life here. It's a type of indirect training. It gave me a competitive edge."

Despite his relatively late appearance on the international racing circuit—Hussein did not win a major marathon till he was well into his twenties—he became a fearless competitor, winning 40 percent of the marathons he entered. He captivated New York in 1987 but is proud of one win above all others: Boston, 1988. Hussein pops a tape into the VCR and grins. He has played and replayed this tape of his victory hundreds of times. "It was the smartest race I ever ran. When you're running a marathon, there is a stage where you hit the running high, where you feel like you're pumped up, you have the energy. The race starts here, about 21 miles for me. It worked according to my plan."

He ran steadily, lurking in a pack well behind the leaders. It was only after the infamous Newton hills that have claimed so many Boston hopefuls that he challenged the favorite and leader, Juma Ikangaa of Tanzania. "We were dueling. And there was a point at which I was behind Juma and I was smiling. I was saying to myself, 'I'm winning this one.'" In the final 50 yards, Hussein shot past Ikangaa. "I changed into the fifth gear, and I passed him. Up to the time I hit the tape, my brain was working. It was a great feeling. So long as I'll live," he says, "I will always remember Boston."

The victory helped make Hussein wealthy beyond his dreams, but it was a win for Kenya too, for he was the first African to win the Boston Marathon. Kenyans have not lost at Boston since an Italian won in 1990. "There's a word in Swahili, *kuvumulia*, which means to endure," Hussein says. "You have to be mentally and physically prepared. It's our tradition."

THE KALENJIN SPIRIT

All kinds of suppositions have been advanced to explain the Kenyan miracle, from tradition to diet to genetics to geography. The mountain towns peak at 5,000–8,000 feet, an altitude many physiologists contend is a "magic zone" for endurance athletes. At this elevation athletes can naturally build aerobic capacity to maximum efficiency; over a certain elevation, the body strains to utilize oxygen, and altitude becomes a hindrance. But numerous countries, from Mexico to Ecuador to central Europe, have similar elevations. There must be other factors unique to the Great Rift Valley.

Almost every attempt to decipher the East African mystique includes an elegiac description of the warrior spirit of the Kalenjin. The suggestion by some that this is romantic blather, and that the Kalenjin are actually no more than a linguistic conceit, does not hold up under scrutiny. That theory, suggested John Manners, has been propounded by scholars who have relied on the writings of Kenyan historian Henry Mwanzi, a Luhya, whose work has been effectively discredited as the product of tribal animus bred either of traditional resentments or of modern ones about the Moi administration.

Few who now proudly use the Kalenjin name realize that it has both a cultural and evolutionary pedigree. The term Kalenjin and the consciousness of a collective ethnic identity as a tribe is a relatively new construction. It was devised only in the 1940s by schoolboys who had come to an elite high school near Nairobi from various parts of the same territory and found they shared their Kalenjin language and customs with teenagers from other groups.[4]

Kenya is a melting pot. All evidence—linguistic, archaeological, and folkloric—suggests that the three million people who today call themselves Kalenjin originated as a small group of pastoral nomads and sheepherders in the Nilotic core area of what is now southern Sudan, eventually migrating south to the Mount Elgon region. It is almost universally acknowledged that the current population arrived within the past 2,000 years or so. Pastoralist Cushites arrived from southern Ethiopia, displacing and absorbing a very sparse population presumed to have been Khoisan.[5]

Along the way, small populations of perhaps hundreds of people who appear to have been indigenous forest dwellers, commonly known as Okiek or Dorobo, were partially engulfed by the migrating Kalenjin and adopted their own variants of the language. The likely course of events is that the incoming populations split and that language differences among their descendants who now speak Bantu, Nilotic, and Cushitic, resulted from geographical separation and incidental contact with other groups.[6]

Centuries later, sometime in the second millennium, it is believed they dispersed to their present homeland along the rim of the Rift Valley northwest of Lake Turkana, with some spreading into and across the valley when their movement was not obstructed by the Masai. Nilotic people pressed in from the north, intermarrying with the Cushites and bringing their own customs, particularly the ritual of circumcision.

The principal groups that today constitute the Kalenjin "tribe" all appear to have been segments of the core population from the Mount Elgon area.[7] By the 1600s, as the Bantu expanded eastward from central West Africa, the Kalenjin retreated to their highland strongholds, breaking into numerous smaller groups, mostly cattle

rustlers and warriors, who defended against outsiders but sometimes quarreled among themselves. Raiding parties would celebrate
victories with a ceremonial drink of milk mixed with cow's blood.
One of the largest of the native groups came to be known as the
Chemwal, the Kalenjin word meaning "raid cattle," or those who
steal. It is the forerunner of the Nandi, who have been a distinct
tribe for almost three centuries.[8]

Although Kenya came under the sway of the British Empire, the
Nandi tradition of fierce independence remained intact. Indeed, at
the turn of the century British colonialists armed with the most sophisticated weaponry needed five campaigns over a decade of
fighting before they secured control of the Kalenjin district, where
almost half of the population of the Rift Valley province is concentrated. By this time Kenya had become a missionary center, beginning a long tradition of Anglo-Saxon cultural influences.
Colonialists set up the King's African Rifle Regiment, establishing a
crude infrastructure to nurture athletics to tame the independent
tribes in western Kenya, who it seemed would rather go on cattle
raids.

"[The British] jailed the raiders and put them to work leveling and
marking out running tracks," wrote Manners. "Because the Kalenjin,
and especially the Nandi, were such frequent offenders, they got a
disproportionate number of tracks in their districts and the biggest
push to participate."[9] In the Anglo-Saxon tradition of melding sports
with the military, the British soon organized track meets throughout
the highlands, a tradition that would be continued after Kenyan independence.

Although the conquerors respected the ferocity of the Kalenjin,
they were startled by some of the tribal traditions. Young Kenyans,
particularly the boys, were put through a gauntlet of physical trials
and weeks of seclusion and instruction culminating in the initiation
into adulthood, circumcision. British diplomat Sir A. Claud Hollis
described the ritual in 1906 shortly after the British colonial victory:
"The boy's face is carefully watched by the surrounding crowd of
warriors and old men to see whether he blinks or makes a sign of
pain," he wrote. "Should he in any way betray his feelings, he is

dubbed a coward and receives the name of *kipite*. This is considered a great disgrace."[10]

Circumcision and clitoral extirpation, although the latter practice is officially discouraged, are still defining moments in the lives of many young Kalenjin, much like confirmation or Bar Mitzvah. "Circumcision Rituals in Full Swing; December is always a busy month," ran the headline in the largest-circulation paper, *The Daily Nation*.[11] The youth is expected to accept such rituals with the steel nerves of a champion cattle raider. No potions to deaden the pain are allowed before or after.

"Circumcision parallels what the military does to a draftee," explained Mike Boit, Kenya's minister of sport and a former silver medalist. "The elders shave his head, give him a new name, and subject him to rigorous discipline, all to remove his individuality and replace it with a new identity of toughness and obedience." Many Kenyan athletes believe that the circumcision ritual has acted as a form of unnatural selection, selecting for only the most disciplined. Of course, many East Africans undergo this rite, yet only the Kalenjin turn out world-class runners in such disproportionate numbers.

"HALF MAN, HALF HARTEBEEST"

According to popular myth, these centuries-old tribal practices and the inspiration of local heroes such as Kip Keino have converged to create a formidable tradition of running success. Keino's importance to running can't be overstated. He is a living symbol of Kenya and a magnet for worshipful Olympians, past and present. Except perhaps for Nelson Mandela, he is the most revered man in Africa. Indeed, his name echoes throughout Kenya: many towns have a Kipchoge Keino Stadium or other public building.

When not traveling the world, Keino can be found chatting amiably outside the sporting goods and book shop he owns on a rutted side street in Eldoret or at the family farm nearby. "Young Kenyans, they imitate me," he says, shaking his head in wonder. There is no hubris in his voice, for he is a profoundly modest man. "In schools, whoever wins a race, they say 'I am Kip Keino.'"[12] A warm smile breaks across his face, revealing wide gaps in his teeth.

Although Kenya produced a number of Olympic-class runners during the 1950s and early 1960s, Keino was the first from his country to become widely known. Keino's trophies and medals are stacked in a corner of his living room at the farm. On the wall is a fading world map dotted with hundreds of red and yellow pins marking his races. Keino now pays it no notice.

Competing in an era when amateurs made no money, Keino earned only $20,000 in his career.[13] But it was enough to purchase this farm and people it with dozens of playful girls and boys. Hundreds of children have been taken in by the Keinos and sent off, healthy and confident, to face the world. As he shares some tea with his guests and his wife Phyllis, he determinedly steers the discussion to the orphanage that has become his life.

Keino grew up poor, one of seven children. He traces his love of running to his father, who ran on the plantation where he worked. He says he never fantasized about becoming a competitive runner. "School played a very important role for me," he says. He leads his visitors on a tour through rows of tea plants that skirt the stone houses where the children bunk. "I used to run from the farm to school and back. We didn't have a water tap in the house, so you run to the river, take your shower, run home, change, go to school. I didn't even put in a lot of formal training. Everything is running. I had a lot of stamina."

At age thirteen, Keino ran his first race, placing fourth and winning a bar of soap. By the time he was fourteen, he was keeping records of his times, recording each mile and each race in a book. His goal was to break six minutes in the mile, which he soon began to do with monotonous regularity. He fantasized that he was Maiyoro or Chepkwony, nationally known Kenyan runners. Like many Kalenjin, he was schooled in the tradition of asceticism. While most boys were off playing soccer, Keino and other Kalenjins could be found running alone or in small groups.

Keino later joined the military, becoming a policeman, which offered the promise of a better life and an opportunity to keep running. Because of the colonial role of the British, African sport was concentrated in the military, which supervised soccer and cricket matches along with annual track events. It was then that Keino encountered older soldier-athletes who regaled him with their trips to Europe for races, with the tab and extra spending money provided by the government. "When you are winning and doing well, the Forces put no demands on you as long as you represent them in the major competitions," explained Simeon Rono, who was later a star runner on a government team.[14]

In 1959, only nineteen years old, Keino demonstrated promise with fine showings at some police inter-squad meets. The stability of military life nurtured his development. He finished fifth in the 5,000 meters at the 1964 Tokyo Olympics. He burst upon the international scene in 1965 by setting world records in the 3,000 and 5,000 meters, and running an impressive mile time of 3:54 at a race in London.[15]

By 1968, Keino was named the leader of a spirited group of fifteen Kenyan men and three women sent off to Mexico City. It was only Kenya's fourth Olympics, but expectations were high. In the 10,000 meters, one of the first races, Keino set a grueling early pace. But shortly before the finish, he doubled up in pain, staggering onto the infield. His teammate Naftali Temu sliced through the pack to take the lead. Keino dragged himself to his feet and resumed jogging just as the stretchers arrived, eventually finishing far behind Temu, who captured Kenya's first-ever gold medal.[16]

Unbeknownst to many, Keino suffered from gallstones and an infection. He could eat no solid foods. Yet over the next eight days he would compete in two more events, repeatedly ignoring warnings from doctors that he was literally risking his life. He performed bravely in the 5,000 meters, winning his heat before being edged out by two-tenths of a second in a memorable duel with Tunisian track star Mohamed Gammoudi. Still the terrible pain persisted. To insiders on the team, the likelihood of Keino being able to race again in these Olympics seemed a long shot. But, hoping for a miracle recovery, the team kept mum.[17]

The premier track event, the 1,500-meter race, then called the "metric mile," pitted Keino against the favorite, Jim Ryun from

Kansas University. The two had met the year before. Keino had run his fastest time ever, only to be destroyed by Ryun, who smashed the world record, by more than 30 yards. Although Ryun had not lost at this distance in three years, Keino had trained relentlessly, and the high altitude added a wild card.

The duel had been hyped as the lanky farm boy versus the "half man, half hartebeest" who could "beat a leopard to a zebra carcass."[18] The urge to associate black athletes with primitiveness infected even the best intentioned of commentators. "Kipchoge Keino came off the slopes of Mt. Kenya about a decade ago with no more idea of how to run formfully than a rhinoceros," wrote Jim Murray, the respected sports columnist of the *Los Angeles Times*. "You reconstruct how they must have found him. They came into a clearing one day and here was this pride of lions with their tongues hanging out and a rich lather of sweat on their flanks—and the tracks show they had been on the spoor of this man who is calmly staying safely ahead of the lions relay team while munching on a sandwich."[19]

On race day, Keino finally acceded to his doctors' orders and stayed in the athletes' village, resigned to not running his sixth race in eight days. But as the start time approached, he grew restless. "How could I go home failing?" he remembers thinking. Keino pulled himself out of bed and hopped into a cab. Yet another challenge loomed—a mile from Aztec Stadium, the infamous Mexico City traffic closed around him.

"This is the most important race of my life," he thought. "In the Nandi tribe, the warriors used to walk miles and miles to find water and food. That is our spirit, the spirit of the Nandi and the Kalenjin. You always feel that you should achieve something, come home with glory. That is my heritage." He jumped out of the stalled cab and jogged to the stadium. Courage. Determination. Endurance. *Kuvumulia*.

Puffing and drained, Keino arrived moments before the gun. Fellow Kenyan Ben Jipcho set a blistering early pace, with Keino close behind. Ryun came out slowly so as not to burn himself out in the thin air of Mexico City. While the two Kenyans shadowed each other,

Ryun fell almost 30 meters off the pace. Few in the crowd or press box were worried at this point, for Ryun had a fearsome kick. And as *Track & Field News* would report, "[Keino] was expected to fall flat on his face at any moment."[20] Almost everyone, it seems, underestimated him and the toll that the 7,300-foot Mexico City altitude would take on most of the field.

On the final lap, the Kansas farm boy reached for his familiar kick but came up woefully short. Dazed, Ryun could not stay with Keino. Few remember that Ryun ran a terrific race of his own, 3:37.9 in smoggy Mexico City—one of the best 1,500-meter marks in Olympic history. Yet it looked pitifully inadequate when matched against the Kenyan's remarkable 3:34.9, his career best and an Olympic record. On this day of personal glory, Keino was awarded a gold medal and a daughter; minutes before the race, his wife had given birth. "In a week, Keino went from being a talented runner to national hero," says Mike Boit. "Keino's emergence came at an opportune time," agrees Velzian. "It coincided with independence. Here you had a young, newly emerging nation, struggling for its own identity. Suddenly, along comes a great athlete. And he has become Kenya's best ambassador."

THE KEINO CONNECTION

Keino became a monumental role model for aspiring runners and a key figure in the international recruiting wars which started in the late '60s. Keino was approached by Fred Hardy, then the head track coach at the University of Richmond. Ever alert to help his extended family, Keino convinced Hardy to recruit Limo Kolum, who had developed a reputation as a good student and runner. Kolum went on to become an All-American, firmly establishing the Keino-Hardy recruiting pipeline.

Now in his eighties, Hardy was one of the first U.S. coaches to tap into the Nandi gold mine. Within a few years, University of Texas at El Paso coach Ted Banks developed a pipeline of his own to the Kikuyu tribe. In large measure because of their efforts, Kenya has sent track recruits to the likes of Virginia, UTEP, North Carolina, Washington State,

Iowa State, Richmond, and Lubbock State. "Why do I come to this area so exclusively?" Hardy asks rhetorically. "That bank robber, Willie Sutton, was asked why he robbed banks. He says, 'That's where the money is.' Well, this is where the runners are."

On this day and with Keino at his side, Hardy sets out from Eldoret to visit a local family, the Kurgats. Hardy is trying to land Josiah, who recently completed high school and is working for the Kenya Power and Lighting Company while he sorts through scholarship offers. The main road turns off into a dirt path. Goats and cattle look up lazily, then return to their grazing as the pair pulls up. The small family farm sits next to a Seventh-Day Adventist church, where Josiah's father is an elder. The main house is constructed of mud with a corrugated metal roof. Alongside are three traditional-style mud-and-thatch huts. As Keino and Hardy approach, the three younger children emerge from one of the huts, the family kitchen, followed by mom and dad.

"*Habari.*" Hardy offers greetings in Swahili, then switches to English with Keino acting as translator. "Good to see you," Hardy says. The warm cadence makes it clear that they are old friends. "Hello, Momma. Good to see you all." Hardy formally greets the senior Kurgat, then shakes every hand in sight.

"How is Ben?" asks the elder Kurgat, hoping for word from his oldest boy, an earlier Hardy recruit.

"He's running fine, and he is among the best at the university in his studies," replies Hardy. He then delivers a gift box from Ben. Inside is a leather jacket, an impossible dream for a subsistence farmer. The family is thrilled. After a respectful wait, Hardy presses on. "I want to have a word with you and momma about Josiah. You know, I'm hoping that he can come to the University of North Carolina." He turns to Keino. "Kip, can you tell them?" Keino's appearance is the equivalent of Michael Jordan making a personal pitch for a high school basketball star to attend his alma mater. It is difficult to say "no."

"Now, you've given me one son," says Hardy. "I want to be sure that I have permission to take the second son. I think he would be successful and happy at the University of North Carolina. Do I have Momma's and your permission for him to go?"

.Keino and the elder Kurgat traded words in the local dialect. "It's a long way," he says to Hardy, who appears to hold his breath. Just then they are joined by Grandmom Kurgat, who had been dozing nearby. She has just turned 110. She gives Hardy a big hug. "The family trusts in you," Keino translates, adding with a smile, "we in Kalenjin respect someone who is an elder."

Hardy laughs, at once relieved and delighted. "Elder?" he jokes. "I am very young."

"To us Kalenjin, an elderly person is given respect," quips Keino with a grin. The Kurgats smile broadly as they embrace this small white man with a face turning beet red in the mid-day sun. The talk turns to planning a *harambee*, a community gathering for raising funds for a cause, in this case the airfare to the United States for Josiah.

"We try to treat them as our own," says Hardy solemnly.

When the details are worked out, Hardy, visibly elated, joins hands with the family to share in a Kalenjin prayer. "Thank you. Thank you for the gift of your son."

DIAMONDS IN THE ROUGH

The apparently bottomless fount of talent feeds the belief that raw diamonds require no polish, and some coaches believe there is more than a grain of truth to that idea. Even today few young Kenyans receive much formal training. Coach Hardy is struck by the proliferation of nameless, untrained young athletes who run local races in Kenya in times that would qualify them for international competitions. "Most of the runners are self-trained and get a coach only later," he says. "Some show up at events in bare feet, win a race, and disappear again. They are a dime a dozen. No one even knows who they are."

Most Kenyans cannot afford high school, in effect extinguishing their dream of college and a running career. Primary school is free, but high school can cost $350, about equal to per capita annual income and a prohibitive sum in rural Kenya. The most talented, the more affluent, and the luckiest compete for spots at a few local religious schools such as St. Patrick's in Iten.

Despite international renown, St. Patrick's, "the mecca of Kenyan running" still has but one clay-red, weed-overgrown dirt track. The weight room, if one could call it that, is a shady area outside one of the bunking quarters stocked with weights made of cement connected by rusty pipes. The complex is reminiscent of a down-in-the-heels summer camp in the Poconos.

Yet St. Patrick's is a phenomenon because of its remarkable human resources: an endless supply of local talent and Coach Colm O'Connell, a short, pudgy man with a bright red face. A member of the Patricians, the Irish teaching brotherhood, he is an unlikely athletic guru. When he first arrived in Kenya from Ireland in 1976, track was far from his mind. But within days of his arrival he attended a meet and was hooked. For the first two years, he simply observed. "My great advantage," he says wryly, "was that when I came, I knew no athletics. I had no formal training as a coach. I learned about the athletes first, then the sport."[21]

O'Connell went on to become the school's headmaster while developing an impressive stable of elite runners. "Within a 50-mile radius of here, there is no better ground in the world for athletic talent," he says, pointing out the plaques of world champion runners, now in the dozens, that line the wall of the school cafeteria.[22] Most of his graduates have gone on to college. Wilson Kipketer, the 800-meter world-record holder, who came to study at St. Patrick's in 1986, caught O'Connell's attention because of his studiousness, not his running prowess. "Wilson didn't seem like anything extraordinary [as an athlete]," O'Connell says, "but I'm often attracted to athletes by a faithful commitment they make to what sport will help them become. Wilson was a profound learner. At 5:30 each morning, never 5:35, it was 'What can you teach me today?'"[23]

Peter Rono, the first of O'Connell's prodigies to win an Olympic gold medal, still worships him. "Brother Colm is the best coach I've ever had. He encouraged us every step of the way. He became like a father to me."[24] On display in the school cafeteria are the pictures of dozens of athletes O'Connell has helped reach the Olympics.

O'Connell was a father to a generation of young women, too. On this typically bright and sunny day, a dozen girls, led by Rose Cheruiyot, who is destined to go on to become a world-record holder, lope around the track. Only a few wear running shoes. The rest, by choice or necessity, run barefoot. Brother Colm turns to his guests. "Listen, you can hear the sound of their feet coming together." The diminutive coach, stopwatch in hand and wearing baggy khaki pants and safari cap, gently commands his runners. "Try to get in harmony with everyone else."

The runners are protégées of Colm or attend St. Patrick's sister academy, Singore Girls Secondary School, where O'Connell also is coach. Kenya's premier school for young female athletes has no workout facilities, not even a track. Although Kenyan women are now beginning to demonstrate the kind of dominance long shown by the men, poverty and tradition remain formidable barriers. Most families are reluctant to spend precious funds to send a young girl to high school when they can support the family by marrying her off. "Parents acquire cows as dowry as the bride price for a daughter," says Mike Boit. "It makes a wife more of an economic object than a partner in a joint venture."[25]

Rose Chepyator, who held Kenyan records in the 800 and 1,500 meters, yielded to the inevitable when she retired while still in her prime to marry and have children. But three years later she came out of retirement to run again, provoking outrage in some quarters. "Running is for children, not for married women with children," she was excoriated in a Kenyan newspaper in 1977. "She should have retired the day she got her wedding ring. And she should now devote her time to looking after her children, not running."[26]

Competition is still regarded as unladylike. Girls who have excelled at the junior level are prevailed upon to give up sports to attend to finding a husband. "Most people in Kenya think women are supposed to say home and care for the kids," agrees marathoner Sammy Nyangincha.[27] According to tribal tradition, women are not to be distracted by their own ambition or pleasure. "There is no way that girls can command respect here if they are not circumcised and ready for marriage," remarks one farmer. After undergoing the ritu-

als of adulthood, which include female circumcision, they traditionally take a husband, get pregnant, and quit school.

As a result of these cultural taboos, which are slowly weakening,
Kenyan women have become a force in international road racing
only recently. There is now a core of rising stars, particularly Tegla
Loroupe, two-time New York Marathon winner, and Pauline Konga,
who became the first Kenyan woman to win an Olympic medal
when she finished second in the 5,000 meters at Atlanta.

"It's becoming more Westernized," says Pasqualine Wangui, a former national-record holder in the marathon who has since earned a
medical degree in London. "Women, especially in cities like Nairobi,
don't have to get married. Some can get divorced. Women can set up
businesses. As runners, we are more accepted."[28]

TRAINING THE KENYAN WAY

For both his male and female charges, Coach O'Connell eschews
the kind of mega-training that is so common among distance runners in Europe and North America. That doesn't mean that he goes
easy on his athletes. He just believes that a little goes a long way. He
steers them clear of weight lifting and prescribes only minimal exercise. "Running is enough. It's a necessity not to overtrain. If you get
hurt, there's nothing you can do about it but rest. There are no doctors or therapists up here."

O'Connell expects his runners to do a daily speed workout, usually at mid-morning. In the late afternoon, he has them run a hard 6-
to 10-mile run. Nobody keeps track of mileage. Rarely do his runners cover more than 50 miles a week. He says he has adapted his
techniques to what his athletes respond to best—high intensity, low
mileage.

John Velzian recalls that when he began his coaching career in
Kenya in the late 1950s, he too was forced to abandon his absolute
reliance on 100-mile weeks. "I came here with ideas about quantity
of running because that's what the world was talking about in those
days," he says. "But I very rapidly gave that idea up. There's altitude

here. *Everything* we do is high-quality training. So when a Kenyan talks about having run 20 miles, he's talking about the sort of quality that very few others ever get."

Wilson Kipketer, for example, is renowned for the most prodigious workout in running: twenty repeats of 200 meters in 26 seconds with a one-minute rest in between; a five-minute rest, then another twenty 200s, again with only a minute between each repeat. The total time running is only 17 minutes, during which Kipketer covers about 5 miles.[29] That works out to a death-by-running 3:28 per mile average. No surprise that he ran undefeated for more than two years before being temporarily felled by malaria.

Not every Kenyan endorses this low-mileage strategy, however. Some of the best runners opt to attend the annual cross-country training camp, which is almost always held at St. Mark's College along the slopes of snow-capped Mount Kenya, a mile and a half above sea level. It used to be run by then national track coach Mike Kosgei, a wanna-be international sprinter who had lucked into a track scholarship at Washington State during the heyday of US recruiting. Kosgei believed in high intensity *and* high mileage.

The living quarters at the training center are sparse. There is no running water in the cinder-block dorms—just some communal wash-stands and toilets in between the various dorms and a few taps shared during the school year by all 1,700 students. "This is the secret, this is what makes us strong," laughs Ondoro Osoro, a future marathon champion, as he lugs a bucket of water back to the dorm.[30]

The meals are filling but hardly extraordinary: no cow's milk and blood but plenty of beans, cabbage, vegetables, stew, and the ubiquitous *ugali*, the staple of the Kenyan diet, a gritty porridge made from ground maize. (Most Kenyans subsist on maize, sorghum, and millet, crops that are easy to raise in the verdant valleys and temperate climate.)[31]

The running day begins at dawn with an easy 40-minute jog. Children emerge from straw huts along the way to gawk at their heroes or run along for a few hundred yards. By mid-morning it is steaming. The athletes travel by dilapidated bus, kicking up dust from the red dirt road as it rattles along, to the base of a long hill for workout number two. Once there, they run 6 miles of *fartlek*, a form of running that alternates speed work and easy running with no rest periods.

After lunch comes the killer workout, a 10-mile run. "It's high speed, near racing speed," demands Coach Kosgei. The young men clock 5:20 training miles, a respectable race time. There are no easy long runs, the staple of European and American endurance athletes. As much as one-third of the weekly grind is at competition pace. Sunday is a day of rest: a steady 15-mile run along undulating hills. The weekly total amounts to more than 150 miles.

Visiting foreign athletes to the camp have likened the experience to prison or being a caged animal. It's certainly far from the romantic picture of "natural" athletes rolling out of bed and into the Olympics. Tom Ratcliffe, a top American long distance runner, has trained there briefly on several occasions. He returned home from his first visit after only a week—Kenyans usually attend for three weeks—exhausted but singing the praises of the astonishing work ethic. "I had figured that Kenya's success in distance running was driven by life-style, altitude and genetic pre-disposition," wrote Ratcliffe. "I discovered an equally compelling explanation: an exhausting regimen that inflicts pain with resounding fury."[32]

Although many top runners, convinced that lower mileage yields better results, refuse to attend, Coach Kosgei has some impressive converts to his high-mileage regimen. John Kagwe, who won the 1997 New York Marathon in near-record time, logs up to 150 miles a week. "My body likes climbing," says Kagwe, who runs the hills in Valley Forge National Park near his summer training base outside Philadelphia. Back in New York in 1998, Kagwe surged past countryman Joseph Chebet on an uphill at mile 23, winning by more than a minute.[33] Chebet has to be wondering whether he is doing enough mileage in training; earlier that year, at Boston, he finished second by three seconds to a surging Moses Tanui, who is known to do 180-mile weeks.

ANY KALENJIN CAN RUN

Such stories have fueled the myth that there is a secret Kenyan training formula. But with athletes putting in weeks ranging from running less than twenty miles to well over a hundred miles, it's impossible to point to training as the key ingredient. The most important factor appears to be the fitness level of the athlete, whether a product of conditioning, a consequence of superior genetics, or both. Kenyans are renowned for their resiliency. For example in 1997, John Ngugi, who helped establish the tradition of intense workouts, eased up considerably going into the national cross-country competition, finishing only seventy-sixth. Yet he was still selected to represent Kenya in the world championships because he had won the year before. He won easily. The following year, he won again.[34]

John Manners likes to tell the story of Paul Rotich, the son of a prosperous Kalenjin farmer who sent him to the United States in 1988 to get a quality education. He certainly wasn't a pampered athlete on scholarship. He was 5 feet, 8 inches tall and weighed 180 pounds—in other words, he was fat. His father gave him $10,000, enough to pay for two years at South Plains Junior College in Texas. But Paul got himself into a bind. He lived the high life the first year, and by spring he had blown all but $2,000. Facing the prospect of having to return home to his angry father, Paul decided that he would try to do the impossible—transform himself and win a track scholarship. Manners picks up the story:

> He began training—running at night because he was embarrassed to be seen lumbering around the track. In the autumn, he managed to make the cross-country team, and by the end of the season he finished in the top 50 in the national junior college championships. But that was just the beginning. He landed a track scholarship—to nearby Lubbock Christian University—and over the next two years he earned All-America honors 10 times in cross country and various track events. When he went back to Kenya and told his cousin what he had done, the cousin replied, 'So, it is true. If you can run, any Kalenjin can run.'[35]

Or consider Paul Ereng, a lanky teenager from the Turkana tribe who came to St. Patrick's in 1986 for a tryout as a 400-meter runner. Coach O'Connell soon realized that he had had no formal training and was not particularly dedicated. "I told [him] 'Go away. You wouldn't even make our relay team.'"

After the rejection—O'Connell still kicks himself for not spotting his potential—Ereng was recruited to the University of Virginia by Hardy, who appreciated his raw talent. Hardy remembers sitting with Ereng in a coffee shop in Eldoret as they made final plans for his move to Charlottesville. "I said to him, 'You know, you're a good 400-meter runner. But when you come to America, I'd like you to run the 800 meters.'" Ereng had fancied himself a speedster, but the coach knew that he did not have the legs to compete against the best sprinters of West African ancestry. "He looked at me as though I were crazy," Hardy recalls, but the young runner agreed to made the transition.

For months, Ereng trained on his own, usually at his favorite spot atop the 8,000-foot dormant Menengai volcano, but never running more than 20 miles a week. "Most people say I float when I run. Just make it easy and float graceful. Running is just fun to me. I don't put much effort. It comes naturally."[36] In the early morning, as the mist dissolved into an indescribable vista of verdant plantations, Ereng glided along in a stride that is technically near perfect.

"He looks like a loping antelope," glows Velzian. "You see somebody who moves so smoothly that he doesn't look as if he's straining at all. He's calm. He's relaxed. He looks as if it's a complete joy to be running, even at the end of a tough race."

The transition to middle-distance running did not come easily at first. "I ran my first 800 meters and I felt terrible. It was slow. I felt so tired. And I thought it was a mistake. But Coach Hardy told me not to give up. 'Give it a shot,' he said, 'we can make the Olympic team.'"

Ereng's learning curve was a straight line to the sky. In less than two years the St. Patrick also-ran became the upset 800-meter gold medalist at Seoul. After he crossed the finish line in a late surge past the favorite, Morocco's Said Aouita, the victorious Ereng joyfully grabbed a Kenyan flag from a spectator and took a lap around the Olympic oval.

"You know, he had only run about sixteen 800s in his life," says Hardy. "It was a remarkable achievement. He knew that carrying that Kenyan flag represented something besides himself."

"RUNNING IS IN OUR BLOOD"

So what are the keys to Kenyan success? Certainly there are powerful cultural and environmental factors at work. "They come from great, extended families," says O'Connell. "You hear them speaking of 'my father and my other father and my other father,' because they are brought up to think uncles are fathers. Cousins are brothers or sisters. The mentality is community. They run for their people, and when they come back, they aren't put on a pedestal. They're absorbed back into the family. That's a great release of pressure for them. They don't have a great fear of losing because the loss is distributed over the group."[37]

Still, all of the unique cultural factors—altitude, diet, tribal traditions, role-model worship, dedicated training—don't add up to the enormity of what is occurring in Kenya. It's pretty lame to suggest that simply a fierce hunger by Kenyans to escape the clutches of poverty can explain the country's spectacular running success. After all, athletes from across Asia and around the world are arguably as poor and dedicated, and still the gap between Kenyans and all other distance runners increases from year to year. And Kalenjins were running into history a long time before the sport yielded any material rewards. The theory that Kenyans "train themselves" as children is no more persuasive. Wilson Kipketer, for one, never ran miles to school each morning as a young boy. "I lived right next door," he says with a wide grin. "I walked, nice and slow."[38]

It's tempting to invoke the mystical. "There must be something very special about the Kalenjin that make them the great middle- and long-distance runners," says Velzian. "It's a fascinating question. We don't know the answer. I certainly can't put forward one single answer. And we haven't even scratched the surface of Kenya's potential." Velzian pauses, knowing he is about to venture onto dangerous territory. "I've always believed in the supremacy of the black athlete."

Everyone who has coached, visited, or run in Kenya has an opinion. Stories about Kenya's remarkable running conquests are almost always infused with a romantic paean to natural black athleticism. "People used to say that the African just stepped out of some little mud hut on a hillside and broke a world record," Hardy says with a smile. He tells of a local physiologist who believed that the Nandi people have disproportionately long femurs. Hardy was skeptical, especially since the femur is one of the most difficult bones to measure in the living. In an attempt to find out whether that was the "smoking gun" behind the Kenyan success story, he measured the femurs of sixty-five Nandis and an equal number of North Americans. He found no differences. "I concluded that the guy didn't know what he was talking about."[39]

Still, Hardy has his own pet theories. "There is a phenomenon here. It's inescapable. It's obvious." He believes it is part psychological, part physical. "It doesn't affect the Kenyans if they win or lose," he observes. "They just love to run. And it's not ambition. It's their life. They live to run." So psychology is important. But, like O'Connell, Hardy is convinced that the social and cultural components are only part of the equation. He also believes that Kenyans may be more efficient at metabolizing oxygen, a theory to which scientists give some credence. "It may be in their genes," he concludes.

If one had a more efficacious transfer of oxygen with the bloodstream, within the cardiovascular and respiratory systems, an athlete might be able to run a little further, a little faster. I think it's tribally associated. It's in the physical nature of the people. That's the best I can tell you. During a marathon, sometimes you reach a point where you can't go any further. That's because when we breathe, we're exchanging gases in the lungs. The oxygen is taken to the musculature which is doing the work and the carbon dioxide is returned to exhale. So we breathe heavier and heavier, we get more and more fatigued, our respirations go deeper and deeper, and finally we reach a point where we can't go any further. Kenyans just aren't as vulnerable to this exhaustion.[40]

Velzian believes that his runners seem both more focused and more relaxed. "Perhaps they are more mature than runners from other countries, for many do not begin running, formal training, until they are maybe fifteen or sixteen. Maybe they are better able to make a decision about whether they even want to be in athletics." He contrasts their relaxed attitude with the mindset of athletes from Britain, Europe, and the United States, who he believes are consumed by ambition.

"The key is their spirit," says Brother Colm. "I don't coach them, they coach themselves. They run with a certain inevitability. It helps them if they make up their mind and say, 'I am a runner.' The athletes take running as being natural. They often use that term here."

The "N" word again; everyone uses it in Kenya, although whites are sensitive that such remarks may be taken the wrong way. "If you can imagine the hours, the months, the years of work that go into producing a champion, any athlete is going to be slighted if you suddenly suggest to him that he's the great athlete he is because of natural ability," says Velzian. "But within themselves, they know that they are special people. It's incredible."

Africans are less reserved. "To be world class," says Hussein, "you have to be a natural athlete. It's not that I won't work as hard as the person who does not have as much natural ability. I like people to think I'm a natural athlete. It helps me beat them mentally." In Africa, he adds, the word natural is said with pride, not tainted by echoes of racism. "I don't take it as an insult. I take it as a compliment."

"We are natural athletes," agrees Keino. "Most of our runners are naturally born athletes. We have only to work on improvement, the technical part of it. We feel that running is in our blood."[41]

The on-the-track evidence certainly lends credence to this belief. And few scientists who have actually examined the data on body types dispute that on average East African runners have a singular body type and physiology, perfect for distance running. Yet Kenyans, like all East Africans, are relatively poor sprinters. The best Kenyan time ever in the 100 meters—10.28 seconds—ranks somewhere near 5,000 on the all-time list.

So why is this subject of race, body type, and sports considered so inflammatory? Context is critical. The history of blacks in sports is inspiring but often heartbreaking. It is inextricably tied to the history of race science, which has often been used for despicable ends. Only by looking at both can we lay the foundation for understanding what is going on in the world of sports.

HISTORY OF RACE SCIENCE

AND SPORTS

CHAPTER 6

"MORE BRAINS OR MORE . . . "

S tating the obvious can be dangerous. Jimmy "the Greek" Snyder was a fixture as a prognosticator on CBS's NFL pregame show, though he was known for being more entertaining than accurate. In January 1988, Snyder was in Washington to scout the National Football Conference champion Redskins, led by Doug Williams, one of pro football's few black starting quarterbacks. The former Las Vegas bookie was working the tables at his favorite haunt, Duke Zeibert's restaurant, when a television crew in search of colorful comments approached. A tipsy Snyder off-handedly mused that slave owners had bred blacks to produce the best physical specimens, which he believed had contributed to black success in sports.

His comments, made on Martin Luther King Day, ripped open a wound in a pool of sharks. Carl T. Rowan, writing in the *Washington Post*, compared Snyder to Nazi propaganda minister Joseph Goebbels. The *Boston Globe* ran a cartoon featuring a hooded Klansman consoling Snyder with the words, "I certainly didn't find you offensive."[1] *Sports Illustrated* editorialized that "Snyder's ramblings betrayed an ignorance of both American history and sport."[2] John Jacob, president of the Urban League called the remarks "dumb . . . ludicrous . . . and silly."[3] Willis Edwards, president of the Beverly Hills-Hollywood chapter of the NAACP, said Snyder "could set race relations back 100 years or more, particularly in the area of sports."[4] Edwards publicly called for Snyder's scalp. A few days later, CBS Sports handed it to him.

What did Snyder say that cost him his job, his reputation, and ultimately his health? Consider the following:

- "On the plantation, a strong black man was mated with a strong black woman. [Blacks] were simply bred for physical qualities."[5]
- "The Negro was brought to this country as a physical specimen, a physical thing, to work the land. He was right away involved in physical labor. And he was involved in sports by the white slave owner. One owner might say to another, 'My nigger can outrun your nigger,' or 'My nigger can beat up yours.' This started a pattern of physical excellence. . . . Competition gave him an out, and it has continued that way through the years."[6]
- "Think of what the African slaves were forced to endure in this country merely to survive. Black athletes are their descendants."[7]

It's always a challenge to see beyond our own knee-jerk reactions. While Snyder did shoot his mouth off, he actually uttered none of these remarks. The first was spoken by Calvin Hill, the Yale graduate and Dallas Cowboys all-star, whose son Grant is tearing up the NBA. Another African American, Lee Evans, made the second observation when he was the world-record holder at 400 meters and a militant supporter of the Black Power protest at the 1968 Olympics. The final comment originated with African American Bernie Casey, a star receiver during the 1960s with the San Francisco '49ers and Los Angeles Rams. Needless to say, no one ever suggested that what *they* had said was racist.

So what exactly did Snyder say? "The black is a better athlete because he's been bred to be that way. . . . During slave trading, the slave owner would breed his big woman so that he would have a big black kid, see. That's where it all started." Snyder opined that blacks could "jump higher and run faster" because of their "high thighs and big size."

It never dawned on him that he was out of line. Such talk is all too familiar in the multicolored world of the locker room, where hyperbole about women and race is as ubiquitous as breathing. That was Snyder's world.

And these issues have long been discussed among athletes and academics, particularly in the black community. No less a critic of the notion of black athletic superiority than William Montague Cobb, one of the most distinguished black anthropologists of this century, subscribed to the "breeder" theory. "No other group of Americans in such large numbers has had to pass such rigorous tests of survival as has the Negro," Cobb wrote in 1939. "From this standpoint he is the most highly selected stock in America. . . . [The Negro] is physically strong, showing great endurance at strenuous labor under severe climactic and nutritional hardships, and producing a disproportionately large number of champions in representative fields of athletics."[8]

Were Snyder's words crude? Absolutely. Deserving of condemnation or worse? That clearly depends on who utters such sentiments. Overlooked in the jihad was the context of his comments. In another part of the interview, Snyder observed that whites were finding it increasingly difficult to compete on the field against blacks. "The black talent is beautiful, it's great, it's out there," he noted. "There are ten players on a basketball court. If you find two whites, you're lucky. Either 4 out of 5 or 9 out of 10 are black."

Snyder then offered his explanation for this phenomenon. "That's because they practice and they play and they practice and play. They're not lazy like the white athlete."[9] As a result, he claimed, white ex-players were trying to hoard the coaching positions, the only jobs left. Few read those words before Snyder was fired.

SCIENCE ON TRIAL

Despite intriguing scientific evidence and overwhelming on-the-field results, some academicians and journalists go through contortions to have us believe that tens of thousands of years of fighting for survival in radically differing climates in vastly different terrain has left no genetic footprint on Europeans, Africans, Asians, and other population groups. This postmodernist ethic holds that human differences are for the most part "not in our genes," the title of a well-known polemic against linking behavior to population genetics.[10] Even though group differences within species abound naturally in the animal kingdom and selective breeding may explain fleet-footed thoroughbreds and rats that can solve the most complicated of mazes, these critics contend that evolution cannot account for any meaningful variations between human populations.

Postmodernist reasoning places science itself on trial. With all knowledge filtered through a cultural prism, relativity threatens to reign. In the extreme, race, ethnicity, religion, or even gender are reduced to mere linguistic or social constructs. Although people accept the role of genetics in individual differences—not many of us would expect to survive a one-on-one game of hoops with Allen Iverson—any evidence that innate differences exist between races or the sexes is considered inflammatory and inadmissible by the prevailing intellectual zeitgeist.

It is no surprise that the negative associations attached to the stereotype of black athletic success can sometimes overwhelm reason. In the United States, where the binding religion is a belief in equality, discussions of race take on metaphysical significance. For many, the concept of "equal in opportunity" has come to mean "identical in capacity": everyone is born with equal potential, with what amounts to a *tabula rasa* or empty slate on which life experiences write our biography. There are no differences, or at least none that can be traced to such ephemeral concepts as race, ethnicity, or nationality. A country nurtured on the myth that all people are created equal is understandably uncomfortable talking about innate differences, particularly when it comes to race.

So when blacks are referred to as physically superior or natural athletes, hackles are raised. What's the *real* and *underlying* agenda? If blacks are better at sports, are they better "sexual athletes"? Are they more brutish? Is black physical superiority inextricably connected to intellectual inferiority, like a seesaw—"more brains or more penis"?*[11]

---

*This phrase was used by Geraldo Rivera on his talk show in 1989 to caricature the controversial research of one of his guests, J. Philippe Rushton, a developmental psychologist at the University of Western Ontario, Canada. Rushton believes that intelligence has an evolutionary basis and is distributed along a racial hierarchy with Asians the most gifted, whites in the middle, and blacks on the bottom.

The prejudice that blacks rest at the bottom of an intellectual totem pole has merged over time with another stereotype, that of the "dumb jock," a somewhat recent and very North American belief. For much of modern history, physical and mental activity were inextricably linked but with a positive bias. The Greeks believed that physical fitness was essential to achieve a proper balance of mind and body, a tradition advocated during the Renaissance by Jean Jacques Rousseau in *Emile*, published in 1762. An early pioneer in physical education, Johann Christoph Friedrich Gutsmuths helped institutionalize the same positive view of physical education in Germany. English writers added a moral component to the mix in the eighteenth and nineteenth centuries, forming the core of what came to be known as "muscular Christianity," with sports competition as its ultimate expression. It was in the best Anglo-Saxon tradition to be an athlete.[12] Athletic success remains a mark of privilege in many cultures today, such as the Commonwealth countries of Nigeria and Kenya, as well as in Russia, Latin America, and much of Asia. Athletes are looked upon as civic leaders and endowed with a mystique of intelligence and accomplishment. Moreover, a great deal of evidence suggests that in fact there is a positive relationship between physical and mental fitness.

But the stereotype of the dumb jock, often tinged with racism, is far more pervasive, at least in the United States. In the 1960s, after the sports establishment finally opened its doors to young blacks, their immediate success triggered a reflexive backlash grounded in the lingering racist belief that blacks were not "smart enough" to handle the demands of "thinking" positions in sports, most notably quarterbacking in football. Whether consciously or as the result of deep-seated prejudices, it was believed that blacks could not cope in situations that placed a premium on strategy.

"Nobody had ever believed that a black man could handle the planning and pacing that it took to run any distance over the 800 meters," remembers John Velzian, a white Kenyan who directed the country's national track team for more than thirty years. That kind of presumptive prejudice hung heavily in the smoggy Mexico City air in the summer of 1968, when Jim Ryun faced off against Kip Keino, in the Olympic finals of the 1,500-meters. Of course, Keino annihilated the field.

Such racial assumptions continue to haunt the sports world, and not only in the United States. Not too long ago it was the common wisdom in England that blacks would never become great soccer players because they lacked the "mental capacities."[13] From Wales to South Africa, rugby is played almost exclusively by whites—except in New Zealand where an influx of Maori and Pacific Islanders has led to the kind of backroom whispers long familiar to black North Americans. According to some, they don't have "the discipline for physical conditioning. They lack the right kind of mental attitude. They just turn up and play."[14]

In Australia, the outsized success of athletes with aboriginal genes in running, tennis, boxing, rugby, and Australian-rules football— Cathy Freeman, Tony Mundine, Lionel Rose, the Ella and Kracker brothers, Dale Shearer, and Evonne Goolagong Cawley—has led to under-the-breath comments about their supposed mental limitations. There is a widespread belief that their success can be explained away by their genetic advantage.[15]

BEYOND "RACIAL INTELLIGENCE"

Rightly or wrongly, "racial intelligence" has become a subtext for all discussions about athleticism. "The obsession with the natural superiority of the black male athlete is an attempt to demean all of us," charges sportswriter Ralph Wiley. Beneath expressions of admiration, he avers, public fascination serves a less noble fixation. "The search for genetic explanations would deny black athletes the right to dream, to aspire, to strive. It suggests that black men cannot set goals, which implies the struggle to survive, to triumph. That is the crux of the question. Our answer should be obvious."[16]

"[Blacks] didn't [become stars] because they were smart," adds former Olympic running coach Brooks Johnson sarcastically. "They're just naturally good . . . they're just naturally fast." His eyes, usually inviting and friendly, focus into narrow brown darts. "That's the racist attitude that blacks are naturally lazy, so anything they get they don't get from hard work, they get because God just gave 'em the right gene."[17]

Johnson is disturbed that even many blacks are seduced by what he believes is the pabulum of the belief in black physical superiority. "You have to understand that the whole secret of racism and sexism and all these other 'isms' is that the people who are oppressed end up spouting the party line of the oppressor. The whole idea is to convince black people that they're superior in some areas—sports—and therefore by definition must be inferior in other areas. It's interesting that the white people always have the best talent in the areas that pay the best money."

Most politically-liberal white sociologists are equally adamant. "Isn't it strange," writes Richard Lapchick, founder of Northeastern University's Center for the Study of Sport in Society, "that no one feels very compelled to look for physical reasons for white dominance in sports?"[18] University of Texas sociologist John Hoberman, who has written a number of cogent books on race and sports, dismisses genetic theories as "Euro-American white racialist thinking . . . quasi-scientific . . . irresponsible . . . sensational . . . scientifically invalid" and "tabloid science."[19] Feminist sports sociologist Laurel Davis, an assistant professor of sociology at Springfield College in Massachusetts, contends that "reports that purport to show black genetic advantages in sports [are] built upon racist assumptions" and reinforce "white power structures."[20]

Neither blacks nor whites have totally clean hands in this matter of racializing intelligence. Consider black racial romanticism and Afrocentrism, which have turned athletic accomplishment into a symbol of black superiority. At the furthest extreme, so-called melanin scholars, including Leonard Jeffries at City College in New York, Wade Nobles at San Francisco State University, Asa Hilliard at Georgia State University, and retired professor Yosef A. A. ben-Jochannan, promote the notion that the pigment responsible for skin color acts as an energy sponge, endowing dark-skinned peoples with everything from superior intelligence to musical ability to superior speed. According to these scholars, black is a marker of all things advanced. Africa is home to the "Sun People" and Europe the "Ice People."[21] Extreme Afrocentrists go so far as to claim that the ripest fruits of Western civilization, from philosophy to science, art and literature, originated in Africa, not Greece and Rome. Hundreds of years of Anglo-Saxon arrogance may make these ruminations understandable but no less bizarre and historically unsupportable.

The quest to understand intelligence has probably inspired more bad science than any other intellectual quest of modern times. "All of this has a connection with a very disagreeable history," acknowledged George Will, political analyst, long-suffering Chicago Cubs fan, and author of two best-selling books on baseball. "The decent, democratic American impulse is to say we have a lot of pluralism in this country but none in the chromosomes."[22]

Politics threatens to overwhelm the science. It is striking that so many hardened critics of the study of human biodiversity are themselves so willing to play the race card. "The danger that interracial comparisons will be inhibited by considerations of political correctness," writes Nature in an article questioning the propriety of pursuing the issue of racial differences in sports, "is less serious than that interracial studies will be wrongly used."[23]

Is it necessary to walk the edge of censorship to protect us against ourselves? Overreaction can be as dangerous as recklessness. The fear of even sounding racist has conspired to stifle debate and suppress legitimate scientific inquiry. Anyone who attempts to breach this taboo to study or even discuss what might be behind the growing performance gap between black and white athletes must be prepared to run a gauntlet of public scorn, survival not guaranteed.

"When you say you want to look at [differences between black and white athletes], you get labeled a redneck," notes Ken McFadden, a retired professor of anatomy from the University of Alabama. "But it's nothing to do with racial discrimination. Studying athletes will tell us what bodies are capable of, and I don't think people should get upset just because you are comparing different racial groups."[24]

Considering the hotter-than-hot nature of the debate, it is not surprising that many of the most balanced views originate with those outside the racially charged borders of the United States. "There is an environment in the US which prevents individuals from even talking about this topic," says Claude Bouchard, an exercise physiologist and geneticist formerly from Laval University in Canada, but now director of the Pennington Biomedical Research Center in Baton Rouge. "I did not feel this pressure at all in Canada. We talked openly about this issue and treated it as a scientific matter. I believe that we need to look at the causes of differences in performance between races as legitimately as we do when we study or discuss differences between the various races."

Internationally respected for his pioneering studies of twins and the genetics of obesity, Bouchard has documented that endurance, muscular strength, amount of lean tissue in the body, and distribution of body fat are largely determined by heredity and not distributed uniformly across populations. As a result of his research, he has come to believe that science shouldn't recoil from exploring how nature impacts human development. "I have always worked with the hypothesis that ignorance fosters prejudice. [Critical inquiry] is the greatest safeguard against prejudice."[25]

Measured by fractions of a second, or wins and losses, sport comes as close as we can get to an objective, racially neutral scoring system. "I've been asked many times how an academic can waste time studying the differences between black and white people," comments Kathy Myburgh, an exercise physiologist who has turned up measurable differences between black and white long-distance runners. "I said, 'Well, if you're a scientist and you're studying obesity, who do you compare obese people with? You compare them with thin people. But if you are a physiologist and you want to compare your best runners with those not quite as good, you compare the black ones with the white ones, because the blacks clearly are performing better.'"[26]

The controversy has put some of the most thoughtful black intellectuals on the spot. "The phenomenon of African Americans performing better than whites in certain areas does exist, and it is worth studying," says David Hunter, head of the department of health and physical education at Hampton University in Virginia. Although he remains convinced that much of the over representation in sports by blacks can be explained by sociological factors, mounting genetic and physiological evidence has seeded his curiosity. "If we say, 'This might cause problems, let's not study it,' we simply perpetuate whatever thoughts we've had."[27]

Arthur Ashe, Jr., the first black man to win the U.S. Open, Australian Open, and Wimbledon singles tennis titles, wrestled with this conundrum for much of the last decade of his life while writing his groundbreaking *A Hard Road to Glory*, which catalogues the history of black accomplishment in sports. He accumulated thousands of anecdotes of how cultural and environmental forces had shaped black success in sports. Still, Ashe couldn't put the genetic issue to rest. When asked about what he had come to believe after years of research, whether blacks had a physical advantage, Ashe responded deliberately: "The results are outstanding, nothing short of stellar. Sociology can't explain it. I want to hear from the scientists. Until I see some numbers [to the contrary], I have to believe that we blacks have something that gives us an edge."

"Damn it," he sighed, frustrated at the political incorrectness of his own beliefs. "My heart says 'no,' but my head says 'yes.'"[28] So which is right—Ashe's head or his heart?

CHAPTER 7

EVOLUTION (OF GREAT ATHLETES)

ver since farmers in the Neander Valley near Düsseldorf in Germany discovered a human-like skullcap in 1856, the story of human evolution has been gradually assembled, a bone and stone at a time. But it remains a maddening puzzle with most of the pieces irretrievably lost. Scientists have reached a consensus on one key point, however: Internet-savvy modern humans are not the product of a simple evolution from an ape-like primate. The familiar image of an evolutionary tree has been replaced by a dense bush with many dead branches. Rather than a steady march to modernity, competing hominid species are believed to have engaged in an evolutionary elimination tournament with modern *Homo sapiens* the winner by knockout.

As recently as the 1960s, it was believed that to account for the differences between humans and our ape cousins—chimpanzees, gorillas, and orangutans—humans and apes must have evolved separately for as long as 28 million years. That belief was overturned in dramatic fashion in 1966, when anthropologists Vincent Sarich and Allan Wilson of the University of California, Berkeley, analyzing blood proteins, concluded that divergence was more likely about 6 million years ago. (Recent DNA studies have shown that chimpanzees and gorillas are much more closely related to humans than they are to orangutans.)[1] Around this time, for reasons unknown, an ape-like creature who plied the forests of Africa began to walk on two legs, although its gait was very different from modern humans and it still spent a good deal of time in trees. It probably stood about

4 feet tall. Because it was better able to walk, it diversified its diet, feeding brain growth, which was further accelerated by the invention of primitive tools and weapons. These creatures evolved into—or were supplanted by, depending on one's interpretation of the sketchy fossil record—a succession of hominids with body shapes and brain capacity more and more like modern humans.

It's at this point where the consensus of how evolution unfolded begins to fray. Orthodox "out-of-Africa" theorists hold that the first modern humans did not appear until some 200,000 or so years ago, the offspring of an actual woman dubbed "Eve." The emotional appeal of this story is undeniable for it echoes biblical beliefs and reaffirms that humans are all one family with a single universal Mother. "Human unity is no idle political slogan," proclaimed Stephen Jay Gould, the noted Harvard anthropologist and biologist, who dismisses racial classifications as divisive. "All modern humans form an entity united by physical bonds of descent from a recent African root. I advocate this . . . view with such delight for it sits so well with my own."[2] (See Figure 7.1.)

Despite the emotional attractiveness of the Eve theory, there has never been a convincing explanation for what triggered the emergence of these art-loving, tool-creating *Homo sapiens* or what led to the disappearance of less sophisticated hominid species.[3] Those unsolved mysteries have kept alive a competing theory, "multiregionalism." Generally, multiregionalists agree that all of modern humanity originated from a single ancestor, but millions rather than hundreds of thousands of years ago. By this theory, some members of the community of early humans then broke off and migrated to other regions. Subject to differing selective pressures, these somewhat insulated populations, although in contact along their fuzzy edges, evolved differently and have maintained regional continuity to the present day.

University of Michigan anthropologists Milford Wolpoff and Rachel Caspari question the out-of-Africa theory as both improbable and not supported by the paleontological evidence. "The issue is about whether people have multiple ancestors from many places or one ancestor from one place," writes Wolpoff.[4] They contend that modern *H. sapiens* evolved as colonies of more primitive *Homo erectus*, some of which left Africa around two million years ago but interbred in a global network of genetic relationships.

It is not likely that the differences between these two interpretations of the fossil and genetic record will be resolved any time soon. The question at hand, however, is whether either of these theories enhances or precludes the thesis of this book—that populations have evolved functional biomechanical and physiological differences. The answer is no, although some strict out-of-Africa advocates have claimed that there has not been enough time since the birth of mitochondrial Eve's first love-child to have evolved populations with any meaningful differences. They are wrong.

THE EVOLUTION OF EVOLUTION

Race marks the intersection of science, history, popular culture, and most of all, religion. Before the late nineteenth century explosion in fossil discoveries, speculation and mythology infused the debate over human origins. The dominant ideology was Christian creationism, which set the time clock for life's origin (and all species of plants and animals) at about six thousand years ago. All living beings were thought to be ordered by the Almighty Creator according to moral worth along a vertical great chain of being, with European whites at the pinnacle.

Beyond these key points of agreement, creationists were bitterly divided about how modern man had come to be. So-called monogenists contended that all modern humans were descendents of Adam and Eve. The races descended from the sons of Noah who settled throughout the world: Shem (near Korea), Japeth (near Norway), and Ham (in Africa near Ghana).[5] The cursing of Ham for looking on his father Noah's drunken nakedness, was cited by some fundamentalists as justification for enslaving blacks. Early polygenists claimed that God created these three races at once. Fundamentalists considered such beliefs heretical, for that suggested multiple Edens in conflict with the Bible.

The debate raged for centuries, mostly in the absence of hard evidence. That changed abruptly in 1890 when the Dutch physician Eugène Dubois stumbled across a curious set of bones while excavating caves on the island of Java. Taken by Darwin's theory of natural selection, Dubois had joined the army as an excuse to travel to the Dutch East Indies, now Indonesia. Populated by orangutans, which are a close cousin of modern man, Java offered Dubois hope that he might discover the "missing link" between the great apes and early humans. He was ecstatic when, from the banks of the Solo River, he dug up human-like thighbones and a skullcap with a sharp, sloping forehead that resembled an ape's. But was it animal or human?

Dubois believed that the fossils, which he named *Pithecanthropus erectus*, and later called *Homo erectus*, represented a transitional hominid. Java Man touched off an intellectual earthquake that rumbled through the religious and anthropological world. For Dubois, the discovery meant instant fame and a university appointment, but he was bitterly attacked. Religious traditionalists considered his views blasphemous, and jealous colleagues contended that the fossils were nothing more than a variety of ape, or at best a distinct but prehuman species. The denunciations were so vociferous that even Dubois came to doubt his original conclusion. According to legend, he went to his death suspecting that his ape-man was probably a giant gibbon.[6]

Nonetheless, the discovery of the first archaic human fossils fired an explosion of interest in evolution and was followed by other finds. The significance of Java Man was contentiously debated. It's place in evolutionary history was not resolved until after World War II. Sir Julian Huxley, who had proposed as far back as 1935 that race was not a scientifically valid concept but rather a "subjective impression,"[7] along with geneticist Theodosius Dobzhansky and the ornithologist Ernst Mayr, attempted to clarify the nature of the evolutionary process. Working with numerous other scientists, they proposed what came to be called the "modern synthesis" (in effect the synthesis of Darwin and Mendel). It placed the theory of DNA-based reproduction and evolution, the fundamental core of Darwinism and now beyond dispute among scientists, at its center.[8]

Dobzhansky and Mayr advanced the notion that "evolutionary

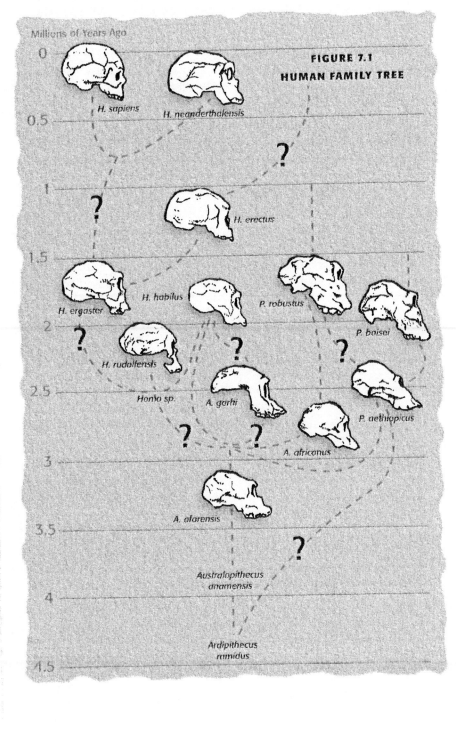

Millions of Years Ago

FIGURE 7.1
HUMAN FAMILY TREE

H. sapiens

H. neanderthalensis

H. erectus

H. ergaster

H. habilus

P. robustus

P. boisei

H. rudolfensis

Homo sp.

A. garhi

P. aethiopicus

A. africanus

A. afarensis

Australopithecus
anamensis

Ardipithecus
ramidus

change consisted simply of the gradual modification within lineages of organisms over long spans of time under the guiding hand of natural selection." As for human evolution, Dobzhansky proclaimed that Java Man, and Peking Man which was found in China years later, were from creatures so similar that they made up a single, although highly variable, human-like species. Mayr believed that *H. erectus*, which included Neanderthals, was a unique human species that died out in competition with larger-brained *H. sapiens*, modern man.[9]

This scenario appeared to be confirmed in 1974 when anthropologist Donald Johanson, then at Case Western Reserve University, unearthed in Ethiopia a 3 feet, 6 inch tall skeleton he dubbed Lucy (he named the fossils after the Beatles' "Lucy in the Sky with Diamonds," which he was listening to in his tent while examining the find). Since dated at 3.3 million years, this early human appeared to be an even more distant evolutionary link. In other words, said anthropologist Ian Tattersall of the American Museum of Natural History in New York, human evolution appeared to be "the story of a long, single-minded struggle from primitiveness to perfection."[10]

But that picture now appears far too tidy. Several species of early man apparently appeared and died out from the time prehumans began to walk and more modern hominids began to craft stone implements rather than just use rock and stick tools, about 2.5 million years ago. These were the first truly modern humans, hairless and with an upright manner of walking. It was not long, within 500,000 years or so, before some of these early humans migrated out of Africa. Carl Swisher of the Berkeley Geochronological Center reasoned that the African and Asian *H. erectus* might even have evolved into two separate species.[11]

This scenario has reignited the long smoldering debate between multiregionalists and the more numerous out-of-Africa advocates. Orthodoxy holds that Africa is twice the birthplace of humankind. These original "ape men," *Homo habilis* and the more modern *H. erectus*, ultimately lost the evolutionary battle and died out. They were replaced during a second evolutionary push by a larger-brained human, who first appeared a few hundred thousand years ago, mothered by a literal Eve. Small bands of these more modern hu-

FIGURE 7.2: PROBABLE ROUTES AND DATES OF HUMAN MIGRATIONS

(shaded areas correspond to modern population density)

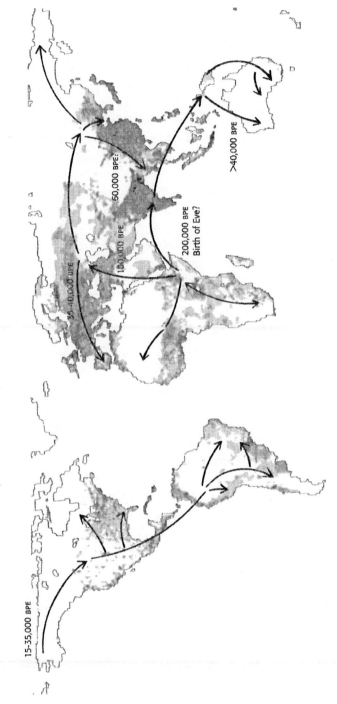

Adapted from LL and PR Cavalli-Sforza, *The Great Human Diasporas* (Reading, Massachusetts: Addison-Wesley, 1995) p. 122

mans split off from the main population group and traveled through the Middle East to settlements in Europe. About 40,000 years ago, after emerging from an ice age, they began populating wildly, eventually splitting off branches that reached into Asia, Australia, and the Pacific. Modern humans eventually made their way to the Americas only within the last 15,000 to 35,000 years.[12] (See Figure 7.2.)

Multiregionalists disagree, and based on the fossil evidence, there is certainly ample wiggle room for ambiguity. If the Eve theory was correct, asserted Wolpoff and Alan G. Thorne, an anthropologist at the Australian National University, the vast collection of human-like fossils represents lineages that left no descendents and all went extinct, which they have concluded is unlikely. Their review of the fossil record suggests that Neanderthals never disappeared, but lived on in various European populations.[13] "Humans have been a single widespread polytypic species, with multiple, constantly evolving, interlinked populations, continually dividing and merging," wrote Wolpoff and Caspari.[14] Multiregionalists claim an unbroken genetic continuity from various Asian and African strains of *Homo erectus* into geographically corresponding contemporary modern human groups.

"Today, human genes flow between Johannesburg and Beijing and between Paris and Melbourne," says Thorne. "Apart from interruptions from ice ages, they have probably been doing this through the entire span of *Homo sapiens'* evolution."[15] Neighboring populations bred with each other often enough to exchange genes and create a common humankind, but not enough to erase some regional racial differences such as a susceptibility to certain diseases.

THE DNA REVOLUTION

There was considerable disagreement in the early 1980s when Gunter Brauer of the University of Hamburg proposed that modern humanity was rooted in Africa. It was widely hoped that revolutionary DNA research would resolve, once and for all, this mystery of evolution. Anticipation surged when results began trickling out of Allan Wilson's Berkeley laboratory. In preparing her doctoral dissertation in the early 1980s, one of Wilson's students, Rebecca Cann, made the ingenious decision to focus on mitochondrial DNA (mtDNA) found in the cells of all animals. Mitochondria convert stored food into energy with the assistance of oxygen.

Cann's analysis turned on the realization that rapidly evolving mtDNA do not derive from the combining of chromosomes but reproduce asexually. In other words, all children from the same mother will have identical mtDNA even if the father is different, in much the way that a family name is passed along even though the mothers' surnames differ in succeeding generations. As a result of this cloning of the mitochondria, each chance mutation is preserved in the next. And while nuclear DNA changes rapidly every generation as the result of interbreeding, mtDNA changes only by mutation, which takes place relatively slowly—on average, about 1 or 2 percent every 100,000 years. And because there is so much less mtDNA than nuclear DNA, it is much easier for geneticists to rely on it to draw archaeological maps of evolution.

Cann, Wilson, and Mark Stoneking (now a molecular anthropologist at Penn State University), drew mtDNA samples from women from all around the world. Based on a belief (now seen as too simplistic) that mutations occur regularly, like a chronometer or the ticking of a molecular clock, they built a genetic family tree by following the mtDNA trail. By their calculations, those with the most mutations, who turned out to be from Africa, would be of the oldest lineage. Cann declared Africa the actual birthplace of Eve, or the "lucky mother" as she put it, and set the date of her debut at approximately 200,000 years ago.

These findings, published in 1987, suggested that groups of early modern humans had indeed left Africa and populated the rest of the world, ultimately outlasting the smaller-brained Neanderthals.[16] These hunter-gatherers, who had endured for millennia only to dwindle to extinction in a relatively short time, were quickly supplanted by their more sophisticated hominid rival. Cann and her colleagues did not find any Neanderthal mtDNA in modern humans, raising doubts that this archaic lineage was even the same species as *H. sapiens*. They also found that differences in mitochondria were remarkably uniform from population to population: two randomly chosen Europeans were only slightly more genetically similar than a European to a Chinese or an African. In other words, in terms of mitochondrial DNA, populations were genetically different, but not dramatically so, and therefore racial lines were invariably blurry. This added up to a crushing blow to the multiregionalists, who had based their theory mostly on the spotty paleontological evidence.

When Cann's pioneering work was made public, Eve became the toast of the town and even made a heralded appearance on the cover of *Newsweek*.[17] And why not? A belief in a primal mother bolstered by cutting edge technology was certainly politically correct, for it reinforced the belief in a brotherhood of mankind. By the late 1980s, supported by this early romance with DNA research, the tentative belief that all modern humans share a common ancestry had hardened into a new scientific orthodoxy.[18] With it came the politically satisfying conviction that meaningful genetic differences, if not impossible, were unlikely given the relatively short time since man crossed a Rubicon into modernity.

ARE MODERN "RACES" DIFFERENT LINEAGES?

The most contentious issue dividing out-of-Africa and regional continuity theorists has been the when and where of the mysterious emergence of modern humans. Are humans a relatively recent and distinct species, the only surviving branch of the evolutionary bush of humankind? Or is it possible that major population groups evolved from separate lineages of *H. erectus*? Strict out-of-Africa theorists have maintained that modern humans appeared suddenly, 100,000–200,000 years ago. That contention is under renewed fire by some geneticists and anthropologists.

In 1991, geologist Ernesto Abbate of the University of Florence discovered a skull with two teeth and fragments of a pelvis while excavating in Eritrea, not far from the Red Sea coast of Africa. The skull is long and oval, pointed at the back, with massive browridges characteristic of the small-brained *Homo erectus*. But it also has parietal bones, which form the curved sides and wider top of the skull typical of *Homo sapiens*, and has since been dated at one million years old. "The age of this skull indicates that morphology like that of *Homo sapiens* had begun to differentiate in Africa one million years ago," contended Abate.[19]

Recent genetic studies that question the reliability of mitochondrial dating techniques underscore the fragility of the Eve theory. It's now clear that mitochondria do not mutate like a biological clock with metronomic precision. Instead, genes mutate at different rates in different lineages and at different times. Sections of a sequence of nucleotides may undergo rapid changes, even within one or a few generations. And now that scientists see mitochondrial analysis as a relatively blunt (if revolutionary) tool, they are wary of assuming that mtDNA sequences can pinpoint ancient divergences.[20]

Evolutionary theory is now edging away from the neo-Darwinist dogma that all evolutionary change occurs gradually. A quarter century ago, American Museum of Natural History Curator Niles Eldredge and Stephen Jay Gould advanced what they called the concept of "punctuated equilibrium" to explain why the fossil records appear to show that plants and animals undergo little change for long periods of time and then experience sudden, dramatic mutations. They argued that new species do not evolve slowly but rather erupt, the result of a chain reaction set off by a tiny fraction of our genetic makeup known as the homeotic, or regulatory, genes.

This theory, though controversial and still widely debated, helps explain the limited number of bridge, or intermediary, species in the fossil record (as Creationists never fail to point out). Either as a mutation or in response to an environmental shock, these regulators could trigger a chain reaction with cascading consequences, creating new species in just a few generations. The model for evolutionary change, once a rolling ball, is now pictured as a multisided block that needs to be pushed to its next stable state.[21]

More changes to neo-Darwinism are afoot. Even those who accept the Eve theory are revising the date of the migration out of

Africa. In March 1999, population geneticist Jody Hey and anthropologist Eugene Harris of Rutgers University estimated the split at
200,000 years ago, not 40,000–100,000, or so years, as had been believed. That would predate the earliest modern human fossils, which
raises the likelihood that the transformation to modern humans occurred in a subdivided population, with one group giving rise to
modern Africans and the other to all modern non-Africans.[22] They
have estimated that to remain distinct, the two ancestral populations
must presumably have lived in different places, developing unique
modern traits that were then spread around the world by migrating
bands of the ancestors of modern humankind.

"It's important evidence," acknowledged University of Utah anthropologist and geneticist Henry Harpending. "A lot of us thought
[the question of human origins] was answered." And although Harpending doesn't subscribe to multiregionalism, he asserted that "if we
follow the implications of this, then the out-of-Africa hypothesis is
wrong."[23]

Harpending and John Relethford, a biological anthropologist
from the State University of New York at Oneonta, had reached
somewhat similar conclusions in their joint research.[24] "Our results
show human populations are derived from separate ancestral populations that were relatively isolated from each other before 50,000
years ago," they concluded.[25] Their findings are all the more surprising because they come from somewhat opposite scientific camps:
Harpending advocates the out-of-Africa paradigm while Relethford
embraces regional continuity. Furthermore, their studies suggest
that the genetic variation found in Africa—about 10–15 percent
more than in people from anywhere else in the world—could result
from the fact that there were more people in Africa than everywhere
else combined during most of the period of human evolution. In
other words, greater African genetic variability may be the result of
fast population growth, not because Africa is the home of the original Eve.[26]

THE CONVERGENCE OF THEORIES
OF HUMAN EVOLUTION

A spate of recent archaeological and genetic studies have narrowed even more what once seemed like irreconcilable theories of evolution. In one of the more intriguing finds, in November 1998, an archaeologist working an ancient burial site in Portugal's Lapedo Valley, 90 miles north of Lisbon, stuck his hand down a rabbit burrow and pulled out a well-preserved bone of a human forearm. João Zilhão, director of the Institute of Archaeology at the University of Lisbon, who quickly traveled to the site to take a look for himself, was stunned. After days of frantic digging, they turned up an unusually complete skeleton of a child, intact but for the skull. The boy, believed to be about four years old, had the prominent chin, teeth, and other facial characteristics of a fully modern human, but the stocky body and short legs of a Neanderthal. How could that be?

Radiocarbon analysis dated the skeleton to 24,500 years ago, about 4,000 years after the last Neanderthals were thought to have disappeared from the Iberian Peninsula.[27] The archaeologists dubbed the boy a love-child. "It's as certain as any new scientific hypothesis can be," said Zilhão.[28]

"[Hybridization] seems to be the best possible explanation," agreed Erik Trinkaus, a Washington University in St. Louis palaeoanthropologist who went to Portugal to help with the analysis.[29] After examining the boy's limbs, he called it a "dead ringer" for Neanderthal skeletons. "This is the first definite evidence of admixture between Neanderthals and European early modern humans," he commented. "They intermixed, interbred and produced offspring.[30] In fact Trinkaus has long offered a kind of watered-down out-of-Africa theory, contending that the Neanderthal line "disappeared" only because it interbred with the more modern *Homo sapiens*.[31]

However many of his peers are not nearly as certain. They note that it is problematic to make too much out of the remains of one child, particularly one without a skull. "It's just a chunky modern kid," claims Ian Tattersall dismissively. "There's nothing special about it."[32]

These is not a mere academic squabble. Conventional thinking has held that modern humanity is a single species descended from Cro-Magnons, believed to be the first hominids to have what might loosely be called culture. Even that belief is under question. Recent excavations have uncovered Neanderthal tool making and cave art picturing humans that has been dated to 38,000 years ago. "I've always argued that the transition is a mosaic, not a 20th century-style invasion," declares Lawrence Straus, an anthropologist at the University of New Mexico.[33]

Is it possible that different populations or "races" may contain more or less Neanderthal genes depending upon what part of the world in which they evolved? The out-of-Africa model can tolerate a little extra-species fooling around, but not much. One oft-cited mtDNA study concluded that Cro-Magnons and Neanderthals were unlikely to have cavorted in the same gene pool with modern humans.[34] But it also dealt a blow to the orthodox out-of-Africa theory by suggesting that a common African ancestor for all of modern man existed, but in the more distant past, about 600,000 years ago, three to four times earlier than traditionally estimated. Milford Wolpoff blurred the picture even more with his assertion that natural selection may have gradually erased any signs of Neanderthal admixture, rendering most studies less than definitive.[35]

There are other inconsistencies. Since the brain sizes of Neanderthals appear to be at least equal to our own, if not slightly larger, and since there is not one anatomical detail from their brain casing to suggest any different neurological functioning from our own, it is difficult to believe, without indulging in speculation, that their behavior was that much different than our own. And if Neanderthals independently made the same leap into modernity along with Cro-Magnons, it is at least possible, if not likely, that they took an extended swim in the modern gene pool.[36]

The net effect of the flurry of recent studies is the convergence of what were once believed to be two incompatible models of evolution. "The supposed behavioral gap between them and us has narrowed," says Chris Stringer of the Natural History Museum in London, one of the originators of the out-of-Africa model. "This, together with an apparently long period of coexistence in Europe, makes a simple scenario of massive cognitive or technological superiority of [Cro-Magnons] much less plausible. In the end there was only one real history . . . and ultimately the different approaches should converge on this."[37]

So no matter the details of the story of evolution, the claim that there are no functional differences between populations or ethnic groups appears increasingly passé. There has been more than ample time for differences to have evolved whether or not the world's populations are proven to share a recent or more distant ancestry. But do these population differences amount to meaningful "racial" distinctions? That's one of the most politicized questions in all of science.

CHAPTER 8

RACE WITHOUT COLOR:

THE HISTORY OF HUMAN DIFFERENCES

The simple fact," wrote Harry Edwards in 1972, italicizing his conclusion for emphasis, *"is that the scientific concept of race has no proven biological or genetic validity*. What emerges from any objective analysis of supposed physical differences between so-called races is the undeniable fact that there exist more differences between individual members of any one racial group than between any two groups as a whole."[1]

The concept of race is problematic at best, a political hot potato, part social construct and part science, built like a huge Dagwood sandwich. For the most part, social theorists have united behind the belief that "race" is so layered with centuries of racist stereotypes that it is not only a meaningless concept but a dangerous one.

"Race is a social invention," declared Audrey Smedley, an anthropologist at Virginia Commonwealth University in Richmond and chief author of the 1998 American Anthropological Association statement on race. "We've been conditioned to the idea that physical differences are much more important than they actually are. I would never say that race doesn't exist. It very much exists, and it exists because people invented it."[2]

Yet forensic scientists can distinguish with considerable accuracy a person's ancestry, whether it be Asian, European, or African. "Given one person each from Sweden, Nigeria, and Japan," wrote Jared Diamond, a professor of physiology at the UCLA School of Medicine, "none of us would have any trouble deciding at a glance which person was from which country. . . . The most visibly variable features in clothed people are of course skin color, the color and form of the eyes and hair, body shape, and (in men) the amount of facial hair. If the people to be identified were undressed, we might also notice differences in amount of body hair, the size and shape and color of a woman's breasts and nipples, the form of her labia and buttocks, and the size and angle of a man's penis. All those variable features contribute to what we know as human racial variation."[3]

That said, most scientists hoist a warning flag when people casually assume that such skin and facial characteristics signify an unshakable biological reality. Skin pigmentation and eye color are but two of thousands of genetic variations. Looks can be skin deep. In Africa skin color ranges from almost white (the Tuareg of the Sa-

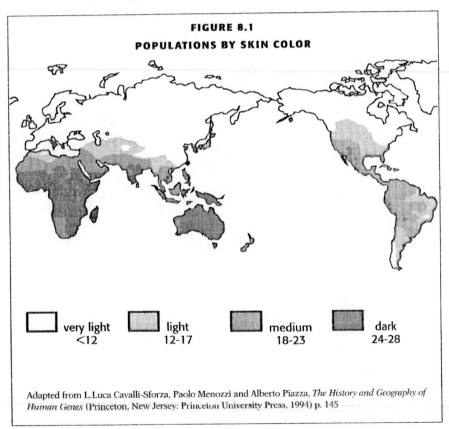

FIGURE 8.1

POPULATIONS BY SKIN COLOR

very light <12   light 12-17   medium 18-23   dark 24-28

Adapted from L.Luca Cavalli-Sforza, Paolo Menozzi and Alberto Piazza, *The History and Geography of Human Genes* (Princeton, New Jersey: Princeton University Press, 1994) p. 145

hara) to light skinned (the Bushmen of the Kalahari) to ebony black. Amazonian Indians and Southeast Asians have relatively pale skin but live at the same latitude as dark-skinned Africans. Australian aborigines are similar in color to Bushmen, but the two groups have traveled a different evolutionary path. In contrast, some of the inhabitants of northern India have relatively dark skin but are genetically close to Europeans. Clearly, skin color and facial features can be confusing markers of "race."

This issue is of particular import in the United States, which turns out some of the world's best—and most genetically scrambled—athletes. Golf star Tiger Woods is a prototypical American mutt. His father, Earl, is half African American, one-quarter American Indian, and one-quarter Chinese. His mother, Kutilda, is half Thai, one-quarter Chinese, and one-quarter white. With a wry touch, Woods calls himself a "Cablinasian." But to the African American community and most of the media, he is seen as a young black man who has succeeded against considerable odds in a mostly white sport.

Woods's very American story underscores the fluid nature of scientific categories of race in contrast to the rigid popular concept. Many commentators have advanced the argument that the African American gene pool has been so watered down as to render the concept of a "black race" meaningless. Critics often invoke the analogy of pouring black syrup into white milk to form a light chocolate drink. "I have looked at every piece of information [about black/white differences] that has come down the pike for the last 25 years," writes Harry Edwards.

> When you say 'this is a black group' you're already in trouble. One drop of black blood makes you black. We have a much more basic and fundamental problem here and that has to do with the whole concept of race itself. We know for example that the African American population arose from an admixture of European, American, Aboriginal, and African stock. The issue emerges: how black does one have to be to make any sense of these things they are testing and talking about?[4]

Although North American blacks do contain a significant percentage of non-African genes, it is far less than popular estimates that
range as high as 30 percent. DNA analysis of some ten populations
of African descent from across the United States and in Jamaica
found that blacks had a European genetic ancestry ranging from 6.8
to 22.5 percent. There was no significant sign of Amerindian genes.[5]

Over time, if racial mixing becomes widespread, it will wash away
many genetic differences. But that time is quite far off and reflects a
simplistic understanding of how genetics works. Genes are not diluted
but passed on whole; they are not individually selected but are organized in sets and "gene group selected." Not all human characteristics
vary linearly with the degree of admixture, but may be mediated by
genes, sometimes many genes, each of small effect. Geneticists are far
from figuring out how the mechanisms of evolution work and which
traits are likely to be passed on. They do know that two hundred years
of racial interbreeding, less than 0.1 percent of the evolutionary history of the world, would not be enough time to dilute all of
the genes that are distinct to each population—including, for example,
the genes that influence athletic performance such as more efficient energy production or quick-firing muscle fibers.

Therefore, to resolve the question about whether it makes sense
to even talk of human races, we need to go back farther in time, to
the origins of the concept of race itself.

THE RACIAL PYRAMID

Humans are inveterate classifiers. The first attempt to systematize
the different "races" appears in the historical record in the thirteenth
century BPE (before present era). Paintings on the ancient tomb of the
Egyptian King Seti I depict four races: Libyan, Nubian, Asiatic, and
Egyptian.[6] By 450 BPE, Herodotus, the father of Greek history who is
considered by some to be the first anthropologist, described three population groups other than the Greeks—the Pygmies of West Africa, the
black-skinned Ethiopians, and a blue-eyed, red-haired tribe in Russia.[7]

In the first century PE, the Roman naturalist Pliny the Elder described Africans as "burnt by the heat of the heavenly body near them, and are born with a scorched appearance, with curly beard and hair." Those from northern climes had "white frosty skins, with yellow hair that stands straight."⁸ It was thought that these different peoples had different amounts of the four "humours"—blood, yellow bile, black bile, and phlegm—and that temperament as well as disease supposedly arose from an excess of one of the humors. The historical links between "race," medicine, psychology, and behavior, were permanently forged.

For the most part differences between peoples were characterized as matters of degree and geography, not of value. The urge to rank populations is a relatively recent historical phenomenon, originating with the explosion of the European population and the age of foreign exploration and colonialism symbolized by the voyage of Christopher Columbus in 1492. It is no coincidence, contends University of Michigan anthropologist C. Loring Brace, that those who "lived at the end of the Europeans' trade routes" in Africa and China came to be considered inferior to whites.⁹ Naturalists and journalists attempted to sort order out of a kaleidoscope of humans, from dark-skinned savages who roamed the "Heart of Darkness" to "civilized" white Europeans. By the eighteenth century race began to eclipse other forms of social differentiation, including religion, ethnicity, and class.¹⁰

Swedish naturalist Carolus Linnaeus is credited with first systematically categorizing the races in his *Systema Naturae*, first published in 1734. In what he believed to be a scientifically neutral system based on character and anatomy, Linnaeus created four geographical subdivisions: white Europeans, red Americans, yellow Asians, and black Africans, with no species, not even humankind, ranked higher than any other,¹¹ although his characterizations did reflect prevailing stereotypes: the indigenous Indians of America were considered "red, ill-tempered [with] hair black, straight, thick; nostrils wide, obstinate . . . contented . . . ruled by habit"; Europeans were "serious, strong, hair blond, eyes blue, very smart . . . inventive . . . ruled by law"; Asians were "melancholy, greedy . . . hair black . . . eyes dark . . . severe, haughty . . . ruled by opinion"; Africans were "impassive, relaxed ... hair kinked ... nose flat ... lips thick ... crafty, slow, foolish ... ruled by caprice."[12] Linnaeus also suggested a fifth racial category that he called *Homo sapiens monstrous*, which consisted of "remote, deformed or imaginary people" such as the Flatheads of Canada and the coneheads of China.[13]

Although some scientists, such as University of North Carolina–Charlotte evolutionary biologist Jonathan Marks, have ridiculed Linnaeus for introducing "disparaging value judgments about other peoples ... [and legitimizing] the proposition that the human species could actually *be* divided into a smaller number of basic biological groups,"[14] that's certainly not a majority opinion. Stephen Jay Gould noted that Linnaeus fiercely contested the popular belief that white Europeans represented the highest form of God's creation. "With regard to the human race," he quoted Linnaeus, "one might be induced to think that Negroes have a rather peculiar origin but for my part I refuse to believe this."[15]

That same spirit of human equality infused the writings of Linnaeus's prize pupil, the German anatomist Johann Friedrich Blumenbach, considered the founder of physical anthropology. Blumenbach referred to Africans as his "black brethren" and campaigned for the abolition of slavery. "No doubt can any longer remain," he wrote in his doctoral thesis, *De Generis Humani Varietate Nativa* (On the Natural Variety of Mankind), "but that we are with great probability right in referring all ... varieties of man ... to one and the same species."

The most conspicuous of traits, skin pigmentation, dominated the views of late eighteenth century scientists, as it does our popular consciousness today. Blumenbach was also influenced by French naturalist George Louis Leclerc de Buffon, who embraced monogenism, the belief that humans were of a single species. "After multiplying and spreading over the whole surface of the earth, [humans] have undergone various changes by the influence of climate, food, mode of living, epidemic diseases, and the mixture of dissimilar individuals," he wrote.[16] Although Buffon was an avowed abolitionist, he nonetheless reflected the common wisdom that white was the original color of humanity. "The most temperate climate produces the most handsome and beautiful men. It is from this climate that the ideas of the genuine color of mankind, and of the various degrees of beauty, ought to be derived."[17]

Building on the writings of Linnaeus and Buffon, Blumenbach devised his taxonomy based not on claims of mental ability or moral differences but on what might be called poetical or aesthetic considerations. Caucusia, which borders Iran and Azerbaijan, was believed to contain an astonishing number of elderly people, evidence enough for Blumenbach that something special was going on. He concluded that those who lived along the southern slope of the Ural Mountains were the original and "the most beautiful race" of men. "I have allotted the first place to the Caucasian," he wrote. "[Their skin] is white in color which we may fairly assume to have been the primitive color of mankind, since . . . it is very easy for that to degenerate into brown, but very much more difficult for dark to become white."[18]

Blumenbach hypothesized that the various races, all degraded versions of white, were not distinct but "run into one another" as a result of adaptations to different habitats so that "you cannot mark out the limits between them."[19] In concert with the times, he designed a ranking that placed European whites closest to perfection at the peak of nature's pyramid. "This diverges . . . on the one side, namely into the Ethiopian, and on the other into the Mongolian. The remaining two occupy the intermediate positions between that primeval one and these two extreme varieties, that is, the [Native] American between the Caucasian and Mongolian; the Malay between the same Caucasian and Ethiopian."[20]

Although Blumenbach appeared to equate race and skin color, he anticipated more contemporary concepts of race when he referred to Jews. Marked by a historical determination to maintain their religion and culture no matter where they lived, Jews seemed to fit his definition of race yet stand outside the "rules of nature" that determined skin color and other "racial" characteristics. "The nature of the Jews," he wrote, "who under every climate remain the same as far as the fundamental configuration of face goes, [is] remarkable for a racial character almost universal, which can be distinguished at the first glance even by those skilled in physiognomy, although it is difficult to limit and express by words."[21]

Even after the dawning of the Enlightenment, and despite revolutionary changes well underway in France and the New World, it was generally believed that the races could be ranked, morally and intellectually. Considering themselves liberals, anthropologists referred to Africans as "noble savages" who were cursed (or blessed) with childlike innocence. The savages might be superior to Europeans in strength, but the black man paid for his physique with a moral "insensibility" and a weakness of will. Could it be, asked the French zoologist François Péron, that "moral perfection must be in inverse ratio to physical perfection?"[22] By this measure, intelligence and physicality were forever inversely linked in popular consciousness.

Linnaeus, Blumenbach, and Buffon, liberal egalitarians all, reflected the emerging Eurocentrism of the times. By the end of the century, the historical fix was in. "The shift from a geographic to a hierarchical ordering of human diversity," said Gould, "must stand as one of the most fateful transitions in the history of Western science—for what, short of railroads and nuclear bombs, has had more practical impact, in this case almost entirely negative, upon our collective lives?"[23]

99.8 PERCENT PURE

History has provided more than enough evidence that race is not a scientifically neutral concept. Does that necessarily mean that differences are purely social categories? Even some hard scientists question whether it makes sense to classify humans.

"Black isn't really a category that a biologist can recognize," Gould has said, disparaging the interest in racial differences as an "obsession" that exaggerates our sense of separateness." He maintains that individual differences have a biological basis but group differences are not provable.[24] In other words, races cannot exist because of significant within-group ("race") phenotypic and genotypic variation. "The differences between the races are small, just tiny compared to the variation within races."[25]

Racial categories themselves are suspect. "There are many different, equally valid procedures for defining races [other than skin color]," wrote UCLA's Jared Diamond in an oft-quoted article in *Discover* in 1994.[26] He served up a bouillabaisse of alternate theoretical categories that cuts across traditional racial lines. "Depending on whether we classified ourselves by anti-malarial genes, lactase, fingerprints, or skin color, we could place Swedes in the same race as [respectively] either Xhosas, Fulani, the Ainu of Japan, or Italians."[27]

Diamond offered a more colorful version of an argument advanced in 1972 by Richard Lewontin, a Harvard University geneticist. Lewontin had become convinced that virtually all meaningful differences between races are either random or culturally determined. Based on his review of the then available data, he concluded that only a tiny fraction of the differences between individuals could be considered "racial." In other words, Lewontin maintained that the differences that separate "races" are little more than what distinguishes two random fans at a World Cup match—statistically nothing, genetically speaking. The article, published in the prestigious journal *Evolutionary Biology*, amounted to a frontal attack on the popular concept of race.[28]

For sure genetic differences between any two individuals are extremely small in percentage terms.[29] Coming from a geneticist, rather than a sociologist or anthropologist, Lewontin's article had enormous influence, although not everyone was convinced. Lewontin's finding that on average humans share 99.8 percent of genetic material and that any two individuals are apt to share considerably more than 90 percent of this shared genetic library is on target. Interpreting that data is another issue, however. Lewontin's analysis suffers both scientifically and politically.

Although the politics of a scientist is not necessarily an issue in evaluating their work, in Lewontin's case it is crucial. According to his own account, his sensibilities were catalyzed by the civil rights movement of the 1960s. He made it very clear that his science was in part a mission to reaffirm our common humanity. To geneticists and biologists with less of an avowed agenda, Lewontin appeared to leaven his conclusion with his personal ideology.[30]

From a scientific perspective, Lewontin and those that have relied on his work have reached beyond the data to some tenuous conclusions.

In fact the percentage of differences is a far less important issue than which genes are different. Even minute differences in DNA can have profound effects on how an animal or human looks and acts, while huge apparent variations between species may be almost insignificant in functional terms. Consider the cichlid fish, which can be found in Africa's Lake Nyas. The cichlid, which has differentiated from one species to hundreds over a mere 11,500 years, "differ among themselves as much as do tigers and cows," Jared Diamond has noted. "Some graze on algae, others catch other fish, and still others variously crush snails, feed on plankton, catch insects, nibble the scales off other fish, or specialize in grabbing fish embryos from brooding mother fish." The kicker: these variations are the result of infinitesimal genetic differences—about 0.4 percent of their DNA studied.[31]

In humans too, it is not the percentage of genes that is most critical, but whether and how the genes impact our physiology or behavior. Diamond mused that if an alien were to arrive on our planet and analyze our DNA, humans would appear, from a genetic perspective, as a third race of chimpanzees. Although it is believed they took a different evolutionary path from humans only six million years ago, chimps share fully 98.4 percent of our DNA. Just 50 out of 100,000 genes that humans and chimps are thought to possess—or a minuscule 0.3 percent—may account for all of the cognitive differences between man and ape. For that matter, dogs share about 95 percent of our genome; even the tiny roundworm, barely visible to the naked eye, share about 74 percent of its genes with humans.[32]

Most mammalian genes, as much as 70 percent, are "junk" that have accumulated over the course of evolution with absolutely no remaining function; whether they are similar or different is meaningless. But a minute percentage of regulatory genes can and do have a huge impact on all aspects of our humanity. In other words, small genetic differences do not automatically translate into trivial bodily or behavioral variations. The critical factor is not which genes are passed along but how they are patterned and what traits they influence.

Lewontin did collate genetic variability from known genetic markers and find that most of it lay within and not between human populations. Numerous scientists since have generalized those findings to the entire human genome, yet no such study has been done. Now it is believed that such an inference is dicey at best. The trouble with genetic markers is that they display "junk" variability that sends a signal that variability within populations exceeds variability between populations. However, the "junk" DNA that has not been weeded out by natural selection accounts for a larger proportion of within-population variability. Genetic makers may therefore be sending an exaggerated and maybe false signal. In contrast, the harder-to-study regulatory genes (that circumscribe our physical and athletic abilities) signal that between-group variability is far larger than has been believed.[33] In other words, human populations are functionally far different than Lewontin and others who have relied on his work realize.

LUMPERS VERSUS SPLITTERS

It is certainly true that "race" and other popular concepts such as homosexuality and intelligence have many links to folk psychology and biology, and are only loosely grounded in underlying causal structures. However, on examination, arguments by Diamond and Lewontin are more clever than persuasive. They based their critique on the assumption that the fuzziness of any biosocial concept, such as race, intelligence, or homosexuality, is a vague social construction *by definition*. Race is certainly an inexact indicator of human population differences—as are all categories of human biodiversity—but it is demonstrably more effective than fingerprint whorls or tongue-rolling abilities. It's one thing to say that race is a folk concept; it's far more problematic to make the claim that populations have not clustered and evidenced some cosmetic *and* functional differences.

There has been little historical consensus about the number and size of human populations groups or races. Charles Darwin cited estimates ranging from two to sixty-three.[34] The pioneering research by biologists Masatoshi Nei and Arun K. Roychoudhury in the 1960s and 1970s provided a genetic basis for the classic folk groupings of Caucasoids, Negroids, and Mongoloids (along with the much smaller population of Australian Aborigines or Australoids).[35] These groupings are the product of geographic cul-de-sacs, where populations remained relatively insular and clear phenotypic differences emerged.[36] Although these racial categories are based on gene frequencies and ancestry, they loosely correlate with broad social categories defined by pigmentation, hair form, blood component reactions such as clotting, disease susceptibility, and the like.

Most geneticists dispute the sociological orthodoxy that holds that racial categories represent merely an infinite spectrum of overlapping and inseparable populations. "The classification of human ethnic or racial groups remains a viable, important feature in understanding the nature and mechanism of human evolution," writes Ranajit Chakraborty, a population geneticist at the University of Texas Health Science Center at Houston.[37] Chakraborty distinguishes between the popular concept of race, which includes cultural dimensions, including self-definition, and the term now used by geneticists and evolutionary biologists to mean a common biological inheritance.[38]

However, the precise number and grouping of races will always be somewhat arbitrary—race is in part a social construct. Typology, the typing of humans into categories, is akin to wrestling an octopus into a shoe box: no matter how hard you fight with it, you still have something dangling out somewhere. Modern typologists still cannot agree whether it is more meaningful to lump races into large fuzzy groups or to split them into smaller units of dozens or even hundreds of populations.[39]

The genetic evidence does appear to point to three migratory waves out of Africa, one to Oceania, one to Asia and subsequently to America, and a third one predominantly to Europe.[40] That conforms with our popular notion of around four major populations or races. Chinese scientists, using microsatellite analysis (repeats of short segments of DNA), recently produced a racial map that consisted of Africans, Caucasians, Aborigines, Amerindians, South Asians, and North Asians.[41]

Such mega-groupings are more or less meaningful depending on what traits are analyzed. Many geneticists involved in the Human Genome Project are avowed "splitters," estimating that there are dozens or even hundreds of bio-geographic population groups but no "races." In effect, they play semanticist by substituting the terms "ethnic groups," "demes" or "population clusters" for race. Technically, clusters are composed of a succession of migratory waves or genetic overlays as smaller populations migrated and mated.

Splitters can come up with any number of "races" defined by shared genetic and environmental cues. One of the most renowned is Stanford University geneticist L. Luca Cavalli-Sforza. His thousand-page classic of population analysis, *The History and Geography of Human Gene*,[42] coauthored with Paolo Menozzi, and Alberto Piazza, identified 491 world populations. Although Cavalli-Sforza and his colleagues go out of their way to note that "the concept of race has failed to obtain any consensus,"[43] their research belied such a facile assertion. They breakdown the world populations into 42 smaller groups and further divided them into 9 clusters: Africans (sub-Saharan), Caucasians (European), Caucasians (extra-European), Northern Mongoloids (excluding Arctic populations), Northeast Asian Arctic populations, Southern Mongoloids (mainland and insular Southeast Asia), New Guineans plus Australians, Inhabitants of Minor Pacific islands, and Native Americans.[44]

The Stanford team further identified four populations—the word "race" is never used—that look remarkably similar to what are conventionally known as races. "The most important conclusion . . . is that the greatest difference within the human species is between Africans and non-Africans," they wrote, adding later, "the cluster formed by Caucasians, northern Mongoloids, and Amerinds is reasonably compact in all analysis."[45]

The issue of racial differences is usually framed in black and white, but human biodiversity appears in a kaleidoscope of populations across a wide range of characteristics. Skin color is one, sometimes helpful, but not always accurate, marker of a population cluster. Consider the Lemba, a Bantu-speaking people in

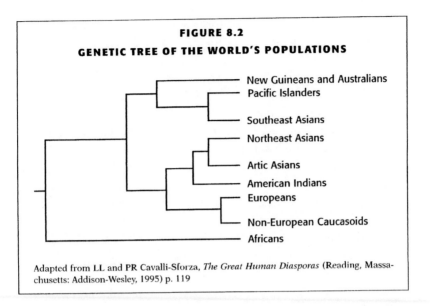

FIGURE 8.2

GENETIC TREE OF THE WORLD'S POPULATIONS

New Guineans and Australians
Pacific Islanders

Southeast Asians

Northeast Asians

Artic Asians

American Indians
Europeans

Non-European Caucasoids
Africans

Adapted from LL and PR Cavalli-Sforza, *The Great Human Diasporas* (Reading, Massachusetts: Addison-Wesley, 1995) p. 119

southern Africa numbering about 50,000. Although they consider themselves Christians, some of their traditions suggest links to Judaism. The Lemba have clan names like Sadiqui and Hamisi that are clearly Semitic and have an enigmatic identity that traces their origins to an ancient Jewish community in what is now Yemen. Although scholars had long dismissed their claims as having been adopted from tales spun by missionaries, research now confirms that the black-skinned Lemba are genetic cousins of white Sephardic Jews. A team of geneticists has determined that many Lemba men carry in their male chromosome a set of DNA sequences that is distinctive of the Jewish priests believed to be the descendants of Aaron, one of the twelve original Jewish tribes.[46] Clearly, skin color is an inexact marker of a population.

Although the mobility of world populations ever so slowly flattens human biodiversity as genes are exchanged from one population to the next, functional differences nonetheless remain. Science may never be able to identify how many races exist, or what are their definitional boundaries, but we well know that the ancestors of a

Nigerian, a Scandinavian, and a Chinese have traveled significantly different evolutionary paths.

THE "FUZZY LOGIC" OF RACE

While the concept of race may seem ambiguous in a technical, biological sense, acknowledging that there are racial categories (even if we disagree on the makeup and boundaries of those categories) simply reflects their very real significance in social and medical contexts. That there may be no universal agreement on the name, number, or precise qualities that define each race does not undermine the reality of human differences.

To escape this trap, retired Berkeley anthropologist Vincent Sarich has suggested that it might be useful to think of races as akin to what mathematicians call "fuzzy sets," almost like an extended family. "Races are populations, or groups of populations, within a species, that are separated geographically from other such populations or groups of populations, and distinguishable from them on the basis of heritable features—and races exist to the extent that you can look at individuals (and/or their genes) and place them into the area of origin of themselves or their recent ancestors," he wrote.[47] In other words, races reflect a continuous biological reality, they are not a discontinuous classificatory system. The boundaries are always blurry (although there *were* geographical filters such as deserts, mountains, or oceans that helped shape distinctions).

Natural selection, punctuated equilibrium, and even catastrophic events are invoked to explain how "racial differences" arose. For example, University of Illinois archaeologist Stanley Ambrose has offered the hypothesis that the earth was plunged into a horrific volcanic winter after a titanic volcanic blow-off of Mount Toba in Sumatra some 71,000 years ago.[48] The eruption, the largest in 400 million years, spewed 4,000 times as much ash as Mount St. Helens, darkening the skies over one third of the world and dropping temperatures by more than 20 degrees. The catastrophe touched off a six-year global winter, which was magnified by the coldest thousand years of the last ice age, which ended some 14,000 years ago. It is believed to have resulted in the death of most of the Northern Hemisphere's plants, bringing widespread famine and death to hominid populations. If geneticists are correct, some early humans may have been wiped out entirely, leaving no more than 15,000 to 40,000 survivors around the world.

What might have been the effect on evolution? "Humans were suddenly thrown into the freezer," said Ambrose. Only a few thousand people in Africa and a few pockets of populations that had migrated to Europe and Asia could have survived. That would have caused an abrupt "bottleneck," or decrease, in the ancestral populations. After the climate warmed, the survivors resumed multiplying in what can only be described as a population explosion, bringing about the rapid genetic divergence, or "differentiation" of the population pockets.[49]

This new hypothesis may resolve the paradox of the recent African origin model: Why do we look so different if all humankind recently migrated out of Africa? "When our African recent ancestors passed through the prism of Toba's volcanic winter, a rainbow of differences appeared," Ambrose has said.[50] The genetic evidence is in line with such a scenario. Anna DiRienzo, a postdoctoral fellow working out of Wilson's lab at Berkeley in the early 1990s, had found evidence in the mtDNA data of a major population spurt as recently as 30,000 years ago.[51]

The relative shortness of time since the population explosion after the conclusion of the last ice age may even have contributed to human racial differences. "The shorter the period of time required to produce a given amount of morphological difference, the more selectively important the differences become," Sarich has written.[52] Since the gene flow as a result of intermingling on the fringes of population pockets was only a trickle, relatively distinct core races would likely have been preserved even where interbreeding was common.

Human differences can be ascribed to any number of genetic, cultural, and environmental forces, including economic ravages, natural disasters, genocidal pogroms, mutations, chromosomal rearrangement, natural selection, geographical isolation, random genetic drift, mating patterns, and gene admixture.[53] Taboos such as not marrying outside one's faith or ethnic group exaggerate genetic differences, reinforcing the loop between nature and nurture.

The most genetically heterogeneous regions are the way stations of great population migrations, such as the Middle East, which was the gateway to both Asia and Europe. Nature, in the form of oceans, deserts, mountains, and glacial sheets, has also historically formed a natural barrier to gene flow. The Atlantic Ocean has ensured that the genetic homogeneity of the tiny North Sea island of Iceland was not easily muddied by outsiders. It has only 270,000 residents, almost all of whom share the genetic codes of the small number of original Viking explorers who settled there more than 1,100 years ago. Scientists estimate that going back about ten generations, every Icelander is more or less related[54]

"A homogeneous population with great genealogical and medical records is the scarcest resource in human genetics today," said Jeffrey Gulcher of Decode Genetics, which is analyzing the blood samples of 10,000 Icelandic volunteers. Decode is also compiling the genealogical histories of 580,000 of the 750,000 or so Icelanders who have ever lived, including everyone alive today.[55]

Geneticists readily speak of core populations in cases where clusters remained relatively isolated for an extended time, with little outside genetic admixture. So, for example, the very large cluster "Asian" provides limited genetic and medical information, "Japanese" gives a lot more, and the core population group "Hokkaido Ainu" gives even more.

Populations that stand side by side, or even intermix, may have traveled by quite different genetic paths. Consider the seemingly endless tension in northern Ireland, which is often described as a religious conflict between Catholics and Protestants. It would be better thought of as a racial struggle between the native Irish and the transplanted Ulster Protestant Scots, brought in by the English to solidify their hold on the Emerald Isle. Indeed, some English people have long thought of the Irish as a "savage sub-race," distinct from the civilized English masters. In fact, the English and Irish have quite different cultural and genetic histories. Ireland was first populated by Gaels who arrived from Spain in the first millennium. They became amalgamated with the Picts who came from northern Scotland and with a race of aboriginals called the Firbolgs. These groups are the genetic ancestors of today's Irish Catholics.

Most northern Irish Protestants, on the other hand, who came over from Scotland only in the seventeenth century, traveled a different historical path. When the English arrived in Britain in the fifth century, Scotland was inhabited by a mix of peoples, mostly Celts but including Picts from the north. The English who made it to the north were overwhelmed by Scandinavian invaders in the ninth to eleventh centuries. It is likely that the genetic makeup of what became the lowland Scots and later Ulster Protestants consists mainly of Scandinavians and Picts, with small admixtures of Gaelic, English, and some aboriginal types. Thus, except for some common Pict heritage, the Catholics and Protestants of northern Ireland have about as few genes in common as any other two European groups.[56]

The salient point is that human populations are continually subdividing, expanding, declining, and disappearing along genetic and cultural tracks. Although there is considerable disagreement, significant if fuzzy anthropometric and physiological differences began to emerge as distant as 100,000 years ago as waves of migrations swept out of Africa to different regions. It's possible that the sub-Saharan black population may only have begun to differentiate from a more generalized or perhaps pygmoid-like African population with the development of primitive agriculture in West Africa as recently as 10,000 to 14,000 years ago.

THE PEACOCK OF CONTINENTS

The sharpest genetic delineation anywhere on earth is that between sub-Saharan Africans and the rest of the world. Today's Sahara Desert, with its mammoth stretches of parched earth and blinding white sand, looks far different than the forested and fertile land that prevailed after the end of the last ice age. Greater rainfall then nourished vegetation which spread wild wheat and barley across wide savannas dotted with streams, ponds, and lakes. These fertile lands attracted grazing animals and, in turn, hunter-gatherers, some of whom abandoned their nomadic ways to settle into small villages.

By 4500 BPE, indiscriminate grazing and a persistent dry spell had turned the once fertile region into an arid wasteland. Once a sponge that drew people to its verdant plains, the dry, infertile soil now squeezed them out—mostly southward but in some cases out of Africa altogether. The desert became a relatively impermeable genetic barrier. For the most part, the sub-Saharan tribes that settled in central and western Africa survived by hunting in the vast tropical rainforests.

While primitive hunters roamed the forests, North Africa attracted blacks from the south and whites from the north. There was considerable mixing and mating with populations that flourished in the Iberian peninsula. Northwest Africa also drew Neolithic farmers from the Middle East, pastoral tribes from East Africa, Ethiopia, and the Nile Valley, and pastoral blacks.[57] This mix has persisted over time. DNA analysis finds a heavy concentration of Europe and Near East genes and "mitochondrial motifs" that make it all but certain that the Northwest African population has been relatively intact for thousands of years.

East Africa attracted a variety of tribes, but it was not so much a melting pot as a collection of co-existing populations because the groups remained economically distinct: Khoisan hunter-gatherers; tribes from the West Rift Valley, with their dry-country grain crops, sheep, and cattle; South Nilotes at high altitude, with their cattle; and South Cushites in the eastern grasslands. The Bantus, relative late-comers, were able to gain a foothold in East Africa because they farmed in wet forest areas rather than in the drier climes favored by other tribes who grew primarily grains.

By 4000 BPE, there are signs that the resettled East Africans, isolated by the mountains along the Great Rift Valley, had begun domesticating rice and yams. Over time the Bantus added dry agricultural grain crops and domesticated cattle. They developed the use of iron tools, turning them into one of the most self-sufficient and prosperous tribes. Within a few centuries of reaching the east coast of Tanzania, Bantu food producers advanced southwards for several thousand miles to reach southern Africa.[58]

Over the centuries, this region was in contact with the Greek and Roman empires, Middle Eastern dynasties, and by the year 600 BPE, Arab traders who plied the eastern and southern coasts and undoubtedly left their genetic imprint. So whereas the West African population remained relatively isolated, East Africa was a genetic stew. The visible mix of Caucasian and European racial features in East Africans, and in some tribes in far southern Africa that it is believed migrated from East Africa, suggests considerable inbreeding among racial groups. This has been confirmed by recent gene studies that show Ethiopians with a mixture of about 60 percent African and 40 percent Caucasian genes.[59]

Given such variation, Africa is considered the peacock of nations. Its many tribal communities, from tiny Pygmies to pencil-thin Bantu tribesman, from muscled Nigerians to the small, slender denizens of the East African hill country, were variously isolated by geographical, religious, and cultural barriers. Khoisan populations that once occupied most of sub-Saharan Africa are now confined to a few pockets in Namibia and South Africa. Some tribes may have disappeared entirely, like the Tasmanians did in Australia. Numerous other races have expanded, shrunk, or even vanished, many leaving no trace in the historical record.

In his work for the Human Genome Project, Yale University geneticist Kenneth Kidd is mapping African diversity. In 1996, he led a team to Zaire and the Central African Republic to examine two Pygmy tribes and take DNA samples. Blood-protein studies suggest that DNA differences between Africans only one valley apart may be greater in some cases than between two population groups that based on superficial characteristics (such as skin color) appear far different.[60]

Because Africans were likely first out of the genetic blocks and have been reproducing the longest, it stands to reason that black Africans have more genetic variability than any other population in any other geographic region. "It's logical that if running fast has a genetic component, in any African population you'd expect to find more fast runners, more slowpokes, and fewer ordinary runners in between than in the rest of the world," said Kidd.

Kidd's point is crucial. The popular belief that genetically meaningful differences between populations have not had time to evolve is outdated. Even Eve theorists now acknowledge the existence of relatively distinct population clusters. So whether one accepts the out-of-Africa theory or multiregionalism, science supports the notion that populations can be different from one another. Does that lend credence to the possibility that at the elite level, we are likely to find more athletes of African origin? "It's a probability, even," says Kidd. "I don't question for a moment that star black athletes have a genotype that enables them to be great runners and jumpers."[61]

"There has recently been a push to proclaim that race differences are recent frosting on the human cake," agrees Utah's Henry Harpending. "It is all ideology dressed up as scholarship." Harpending even offers his personal theory of racial differentiation, which though different than most anthropological views that populations split relatively recently, would account for racial differences such as we see in athletics. "The ancestral populations must have been subdivided into partially isolated races [that] are older than our species' ecological success," Harpending has claimed.[62] In other words, different races may not be modifications of *Homo sapiens*, they may originate before the emergence of *Homo sapiens*. Race may have preceded modern humankind, not the other way around.

CHAPTER 9

THE ORIGINS OF RACE SCIENCE

By 1831, the fever of exploration had touched young Charles Darwin, a former divinity student turned scientist and adventurer. As expedition naturalist on the HMS *Beagle*, Darwin embarked on an ambitious five-year sail to the Australasian and South American coasts, painstakingly collecting samples of flowers at every stop. During his travels he became an avid reader of the social theories of English political economist Thomas Malthus. He wrote later that he was struck by the similarities between what he observed in nature and Malthus's belief in the inevitable conflicts between fast-growing human populations.

When Darwin returned to England, he regaled the ornithologist John Gould with stories of the flora and fauna on the Galápagos Islands, the isolated and pristine archipelago off the coast of Ecuador. During that stop, Darwin had thought little of the warbler finches he had seen, thinking they were varieties of a single species that had reached the islands long before. Gould startled him with a different theory: there were many distinct species of finches on the islands. Although they looked similar, their beaks were shaped and colored differently, each meeting a special need, such as eating seeds on the ground, picking ticks off iguanas, or chiseling insects out of bark cracks. Gould's surprising news touched off a chain reaction in Darwin's thinking that ultimately led to his daring conclusion that the earth's animals and plants might not in fact be fixed and unchangeable.[1]

As these revelations sank in, Darwin came to reject the French naturalist Chevalier de Lamarck's theory that living beings passed on advantageous adaptations to future generations.* He devised a far more radical hypothesis. Darwin believed that through chance mutations (which he called natural variation), finches were born with different-shaped beaks, which helped them consume food in trees, on cacti, or on the ground. It was these congenital mutations, not adaptations, as Lamarck had suggested, that the survivors passed along to their offspring. As this process was repeated again and again, some thirteen finch species had evolved on the Galápagos Islands and one more on a nearby island.

From the very first Darwin scoffed at the radical environmentalism that one hundred years later, would twist his explanation for human and animal differences. "The external characteristic differences between the races of man cannot be accounted for in a satisfactory manner by the direct action of the conditions of life," he wrote, rejecting the Lamarckian belief in the impact of the environment to produce heritable change.[2]

For a blueprint of how natural selection might work, Darwin drew parallels between natural selection and the conscious selection by British horsemen who, since the thirteenth century, had bred prize stallions and mares for qualities of speed, endurance, hardiness, and gait to turn out the top-performing racehorses.[3] He borrowed the phrase "survival of the fittest" from Herbert Spencer, a self-taught philosopher who in turn, in later years, would combine Darwin's theories with his own similar beliefs and apply them to every aspect of everyday life.

Darwin's theory is elegantly simple and proved testable and predictive. Greatly influenced by Malthus's proposition that populations "naturally" compete for a limited supply of food, Darwin supposed that plants and animals whose chance variations gave them an edge in the struggle for life would be more likely to survive and repro-

*A botanist by training, Lamarck awkwardly grafted long-standing religious dogma about creationism onto the nascent science of nature. He reaffirmed the mystery of creation by suggesting that new life forms are the result of "spontaneous generation." But he also believed that contemporary life forms did not resemble their long-ago ancestors. Anatomical variations, he suggested, resulted from adaptations to changes in the environment. In the spirit of the Enlightenment, which had taken France by storm, Lamarck believed that the various species represented an ever-evolving progression to a higher state of perfection.

duce. If these mutations were inherited, then the characteristics of the survivors would change over time. Dramatic changes, from small-celled creature to complex one, and from ape to human, would occur successively over eons.

Although increasingly confident of his findings, Darwin was agitated by the potential impact of the revolutionary ideas that swirled in his head. He was well aware that his epic thesis would be as heterodox as Galileo's discovery that the sun, not the earth, was the center of our universe. It would challenge two Christian values: Darwin divorced the concept of evolution from that of progress—he contended that humans were not necessarily improving morally or intellectually—and he made the case that humankind was not superior to all other beings but was just one living product of evolution among many.[4] Darwin's challenge to the cherished belief that humans and only humans were made in the "image of the likeness of God," but shared an ancestry with monkeys, drove Bible-thumpers ape.

Fearing rejection and even ridicule from a wall of political correctness constructed by the church, he held off formalizing his findings for more than twenty years, finally publishing *On the Origin of Species by Means of Natural Selection* in 1859. The distinguished biologist Thomas Huxley and other British naturalists were immediately taken by the elegance and simplicity of Darwin's explanation. Many mainstream Christians were not nearly so impressed. A storm erupted, immediate and violent, splitting intellectual Britain in two. Stirred up by establishment outcries, the press caricatured Darwin variously as a snake-oil salesman, heretic, or fool. They vulgarized his cautiously constructed hypothesis that groups of animals shared a common ancestry, miswriting that Darwin claimed that humans were "descended" from apes.

It is startling how quickly Darwin's heretical thesis slew the establishment evangelical ghost. Less than a year after the publication of *Origin*, Huxley, Darwin's most passionate advocate, and the bishop of Oxford, Samuel Wilberforce, met in a dramatic face-off sponsored by the British Association for the Advancement of Science. The stage was Oxford's University Museum. Over a thousand students, clerics, scientists, and curious journalists gathered for what promised to be a fiery debate. Wilberforce lit into Darwin's theories—effectively if without much scientific substance, according to most accounts—before shooting himself in the foot.

"I should like to ask Professor Huxley, who is sitting by me, and is about to tear me to pieces when I have sat down," he intoned with self-importance, "as to his belief in being descended from an ape: Is it on his grandfather's or his grandmother's side that the ape ancestry comes in."[5]

Unintimidated by the bilious wisecrack, Huxley slapped his hand on his knee and exclaimed, "The Lord hath delivered him into my hands!" Huxley offered a wide-ranging rebuttal of the bishop's invocation of a higher order, then ran through the gaping hole that Wilberforce had so generously left open:

> ... A man has no reason to be ashamed of having an ape for his grandfather. If there were an ancestor of whom I would feel shame in recalling, it would be a man, a man of restless and versatile intellect, who, not content with an equivocal success in his own sphere of activity, plunges into scientific questions with which he has not real acquaintance, only to obscure them by an aimless rhetoric, and distract the attention of his hearers from the real point at issue by eloquent digressions, and skilled appeals to religious prejudice.[6]

As Huxley finished, one lady in the audience collapsed from the tension. After a momentary silence the dazed crowd reportedly broke into laughter and applause. Huxley's speech, and the obvious glee with which it was received, signaled the beginning of the end of the clerical jihad against natural selection. Within less than a decade the fight for acceptance of evolutionary theory in scientific circles was effectively over.[7]

As with most battlefield victories, Huxley's tour de force carried with it unintended consequences. Though *Origin* may have revolutionized humankind's self-image, it also unleashed a theory so powerful that it would dramatically advance and forever haunt science.

RACE, BRAIN SIZE, AND INTELLIGENCE

Darwin's evolutionary thesis introduced into the human sciences intellectual rigor, coherence, consistency, and predictive dimensions, epistemic qualities that were not present in the more speculative ruminations of his naturalist predecessors. Ironically, the effort to bring a similar rigor to the premodern sciences of medicine and biology and to ground anthropology in objective science, spawned the highly speculative pseudo-sciences of craniology and phrenology. These bastard creations would ultimately come to infect evolutionary theory and erode public confidence in its scientific underpinnings.

By the mid-eighteenth century, Dutch anatomist and artist Petrus Camper was attempting to steer human sciences on a more mathematically based and theoretically objective course with his work on the shape and size of the human skull. Camper regarded prognathism—facial features such as a protruding jaw or heavy brow—as signs of primitiveness and retarded intellectual development. The flatter the face, he believed, the more advanced the being. He devised what he called a facial index to determine beauty and perhaps intelligence that extended from white Europeans, who he believed (incorrectly it turns out) had the flattest faces, down to the Negro, the monkey, the dog, and finally the woodcock, whose face protruded the most.[8]

Camper's quest to define a universal beauty based on the Greek ideal reflected the artist's passion for aesthetics. But as the nineteenth century beckoned, talk of progress and a fascination with evolution took hold in Europe, replacing Enlightenment ideals such as egalitarianism and humanity. With the emergence of anthropology as a discipline, the focus shifted away from our common humanity to human differences. This new obsession was fueled by tales brought back from Africa, South America, and the Pacific by European explorers. "Race" took on meaning not as a measure of aesthetic differences but as a way to rank human worth as well as a collective expression of fears and myths about dark-skinned people, with blacks banished to the lowest rung on the ladder of civilization.

In the grip of the Enlightenment, French naturalist Georges Cuvier, a founder of paleontology and comparative anatomy, had been convinced that racial differences were environmental. This also reflected his creationist belief that all humans were descended from Adam but had developed into three different races after a catastrophe some 5,000 years before. But by 1817, he had come to believe that human differences were inherited and permanent—racial in origin. Cuvier classified blacks as "the most degraded of human races, whose form approaches that of the beast and whose intelligence is nowhere great enough to arrive at regular government."⁹ Reflecting the dominant Eurocentric ideology, he blamed the "stupidity" of Negroes on their "lack of civilization," which he believed was the province of whites. To document his claims, Cuvier assembled a collection of skulls of "savages" procured by European adventurers.¹⁰

A flourishing commerce in human skulls helped fuel interest in the pseudo-science of phrenology. Franz Joseph Gall, a German physician, became one its earliest proponents, enthusiastically taking up the challenge of systematizing the burgeoning research on human anatomy. In *The Anatomy and Physiology of the Nervous System in General, and of the Brain in Particular*, published in 1808, Gall claimed that he could accurately determine the character, morality, and intellect of a person by measuring the bumps and curves of the skull. He noted twenty-seven organs within the brain, each responsible for a particular mental function such as "domesticity" or "sublimity." It was believed that the better these organs worked, the larger shape they assumed.¹¹

Gall inspired contemporary Swedish botanist Anders Retzius, who devised a "cephalic index" that he calculated by the ratio of the width to length of the skull.¹² Out of such musings emerged the science of biometrics, the mathematical study of evolution. Leading craniometrists churned out statistical tracts that purportedly proved that skull shapes delineated distinct races: Nordic, Alpine, and Mediterranean. Not surprising, wild exaggerations appeared in the press. Alpines were described as short-headed, which made them "detail-loving" and "plodding." Mediterraneans were best suited to "lighter branches of engineering, electric and motor-car work." Nordics, of course, represented the proper balance of the mental and the physical and could be expected to handle both complex and physically demanding tasks.[13]

The predictive promise of craniometry infused all of science. "In general," wrote Paul Broca, a professor of clinical surgery and founder of the Anthropological Society of Paris, who adopted the technique of measuring craniums and weighing brains, "the brain is larger in mature adults than in the elderly, in men than in women, in eminent men than in men of mediocre talent, in superior races than in inferior races."[14] Proposing a direct relationship between fertility and race, Broca stated that racial hybrids were likely to be mentally, morally, and physically inferior.[15]

Most physical anthropologists of this generation, both in Europe and the United States, eagerly marched down this blind alley of craniology. Anecdotal evidence was marshaled to bolster anti-black beliefs. For example, the British anthropologist Charles Hamilton Smith, who saw military service with British troops in the West Indies, noticed how even the smallest British army caps issued to black troops proved too big. Caps for the noncommissioned officers, who were in part of white descent, fit nicely, however. Smith went on to speculate that the human brain developed linearly according to race, "successively assum[ing] the form of the Negroes, the Malays, the Americans, and the Mongolians before it attains the Caucasian," who was most developed at birth.[16]

Samuel George Morton, a Philadelphia physician, helped transform the United States into an epicenter for craniological research. A leader in the so-called American school of anthropology, Morton amassed a personal museum of more than six hundred skulls, the largest collection of its kind in the world. He established a ranking of intelligence based on cranial size, with Asians and whites on top followed by Native Americans, Malays, Ancient Caucasians, and Africans. Differences in brain size, he implied, explained differences in the capacity for civilization.[17] His measurement techniques might seem absurd by today's standards—he determined endocranial volume by filling skulls with mustard seed and later BB shot—yet his work was so well established that Charles Darwin would later cite it as evidence in favor of his theory of human origins in *The Descent of Man and Selection in Relation to Sex* in 1871.[18]

Morton's work was pivotal in the evolution of an American brand of race science, although he himself was a Quaker and an outspoken abolitionist. The belief in black inferiority was deeply ingrained in the United States. The Declaration of Independence may have proclaimed, "We hold these truths to be self-evident, that all men are created equal," but that truth never applied to most blacks—even Thomas Jefferson stocked his Virginia plantation with slaves. "I advance it . . . as a suspicion only," Jefferson wrote, "that blacks, whether originally a distinct race, or maybe by time and circumstance, are inferior to the whites in the endowment of both body and mind."[19]

Intentionally or not, Morton's research legitimized the rabid convictions of outright racists. He reported that Africans had smallish crania and lower brain weight. As a result, the Negro was assigned a lowly position in the human order. Of course whites had the largest skulls. (It would be years before the first Neanderthal skeletons would be uncovered, which would throw a hefty wrench into such thinking; these archaic humans had larger, though more inefficient, brains than the more modern humans that are thought to have replaced them, undermining the belief that cranium size determines intelligence).

Morton's findings were noted in Europe, where they were used to buttress the general case for white supremacy. Professor of anatomy Karl Vogt, who became known as "monkey Vogt" when he began actively promoting Darwinian theory, was certain that the capacity for culture and the size of the cranium were directly linked. Since it was accepted that Negro intellectual development stopped at puberty, Vogt proposed that slaves "must be treated like neglected and badly brought up children."[20]

By the 1880s, John Beddoe, president of the Royal Anthropological Institute in London, was circulating what he called an Index of Nigressence. Beddoe argued that based on skull shape, the Irish were close to Cro-Magnons and thus were connected to the "Africinoid" races, which he considered a distinct, and the most primitive, human species.[21] Even Thomas Huxley, Darwin's pit bull, looked favorably on the predictive powers of skull shape. "It is simply incredible," he wrote, "that . . . our prognathous relative . . . will be able to compete successfully with his bigger-brained and smaller-jawed rival, in a contest that is to be carried out by thoughts and not by bites."[22] Although he was referring to the Negro, facial projection was also identified in the Irish.

The public became fascinated by the stream of studies on cranial dimensions spewing out of academia, crudely assuming they might explain the deterioration in civic discipline that appeared to rage around them. Maybe, they wondered, social problems were predetermined. In Europe and particularly in England, people lined up at analytical parlors where a cephalic index and cranial measurements became the basis for the new pseudo-science of phrenology. It was wildly popular, rivaling even astrology in some circles.

Although many people who embraced craniometry and scientists who studied it considered themselves open-minded, their views were grounded in assumptions that were not very different than those with more rigid views. "The dark races are the lowest on the scale," Joseph-Arthur, Count de Gobineau, a French diplomat, in his *Essay on the Inequality of Races*, had written in the 1850s. Gobineau fed the darkest stream of racist ideology: "The negro's narrow and receding forehead seems to mark him as inferior in reasoning capacity." He also noted "the negro's . . . moral cowardice" evidenced by their stoicism in facing pain as well as their inferior muscle power.[23]

According to Gobineau's racial hierarchy, Africans were permanently and ineradicably mental, moral, and physical weaklings. He eagerly promoted Morton's speculations linking brain size and cultural development and fervently advanced his own belief that the blond Aryan, or Teuton, represented the most evolved expression of the naturally strong and superior white race. His theories would not only infect German racialist thinking and eventually the views of Adolf Hitler, but rare scientists for generations to come.

SOCIAL DARWINISM AND EARLY EUGENICS

Social theories do not emerge in a social vacuum. Late nineteenth century Europe was a social and political hothouse. Although the economy boomed, the crude evolution of capitalism widened the gap between the destitute, the working poor, and a growing plutocracy. Newly established trade routes led to a dramatic increase in the importation of grain, which sent prices crashing. Hungry and desperate, farmers abandoned their land and poured into cities to work in the expanding mill and coal industries, uprooting traditional patterns of life and creating squalid tenements in grubby industrial centers. An epidemic of cholera ensued. To compound the chaos, the aftershocks of international credit crises roiled many cities, sending hordes of the newly unemployed to join the hungry in the streets. Europe began to balkanize along ethnic and economic fault lines. The tensions peaked with the bloody revolutions of 1848.

The changes were felt most directly in England where the industrial revolution was furthest along. The influx of poor laborers to build the mammoth railroad system fed suspicions about foreigners. The dailies were filled with florid stories about "moral decadence" and jingoistic attacks on the Irish, the Welsh, southern Europeans, and rival countries in general. The deepening economic cleavages called forth all sorts of conjecture about race, many targeting blacks. Many theorists turned to the exciting theory of the "survival of the fittest," splicing it to everything from politics to biology.

Darwin's thesis that evolution was shaped by natural, society-wide competition was not his unique idea. It was first articulated in 1851 in the writings of Herbert Spencer, then an editor at the *Economist*.[24] Whereas Darwin would come to see nature as evolving along a natural path dictated by a need to survive, Spencer saw it as progressing to a better end, based on the desire to thrive. By his accounting, material success was a sure sign of superior genes. The squalor and social strife that marked the plight of the poor was not something to be feared as an aberration, but was only part of nature's way of selecting the hardiest to breed an even better race of humans. Blacks came under particularly harsh judgment. "Conditioned as he is," wrote Spencer, "the savage lacks abstract ideas."[25]

With his juicing of natural selection, Spencer caught the fancy of Darwin's cousin, Sir Francis Galton, perhaps the most important historical figure in shaping the modern view of race. Brilliant and privileged, Galton had struggled as a young intellectual, eventually seeking analysis at the London Phrenological Institute. The chief phrenologist measured his skull at twenty-two inches around and pronounced him "sanguine" with a powerful mind fit for "roughing it" in "colonising."[26] Filled with renewed self-confidence, Galton took off for Africa, where he indulged his fascination with the "inferior race," bringing back details of the Damara people in what is now Namibia.[27]

Although feted on his return, he soon sank into what he described as an existential despair at the Dickensian chaos of European cities. Reading Darwin's work and Spencer's synthesis was like a conversion experience, inspiring him with hope that he could guide the ship of progress back to stable moorings. Galton loosely applied Darwin's theory of natural selection to the mind in an attempt to ground psychology in science rather than speculation. He tried to devise an intelligence test based on the idea that mental capacity correlated with sensitivity in sight, hearing, and touch. His tests, crude by today's standards, became the inspiration for the French psychologist Alfred Binet who would develop the first intelligence tests years later.[28]

Galton outlined the main tenets of his new-found ideology in *Hereditary Genius*, published in 1869, a seminal work in the sociology of race and intelligence. He contended that Europe's hegemony over much of the world reflected natural selection in the same way that nature determined that lions ruled the jungle. He claimed that man's intelligence and abilities were a product of the same evolutionary forces that shape the natural world and that whites were naturally and considerably more intelligent than blacks, who were often referred to as a "child race."[29]

By some measures, the broad echoes of Social Darwinism would soon eclipse in impact the original theory on which the notion was based. Political movements from the extreme left—Marxist communism—and the extreme right—ultranationalism—would invoke Darwin's ideas to justify their world views that class and racial conflicts were inevitable.

The movement unleashed by Galton was so powerful and appeared so progressive that Darwin himself was seduced. He may
have preached that no species was superior to any other—they were
all just different—but he felt no contradiction in his book, *The Descent of Man*, in describing the tribesmen of Tierra del Fuego in Ar-
gentina as "wild animals . . . their mouths, frothed with excitement
. . . possessing great size, strength, and ferocity" but lacking the
"higher mental qualities" of Western cultures."[30] Thus, with Darwin's
unwitting blessing, evolution became securely moored to the folk
prejudices of the times—nonwhites were both mentally and physically inferior.

Social Darwinism also spawned the progressive embrace of eugenics as a way to improve the lot of the downtrodden through interbreeding with superior white European stock. The future of the
world came down to the quality of breeding. By 1883, in *Enquiries
into Human Faculty*, Galton applied his hereditary theories to the
entire race of humankind and in the process coined the term "eugenics." Galton and his followers suggested that social progress
could be attained only by purging "undesirable genes"—which
meant for the most part restricting the mentally ill, the poor, immigrants, and nonwhites from propagating.[31] It was to be for the overall good of the race—the human race. Left unchecked, the lower
stratum would propagate recklessly and drag society down with it.

Anthropometric laboratories proliferated, competing to develop
statistical tools to isolate the most intelligent and highly developed
humans so as to "save the world" through selective procreation.[32]
Eugenicists from all parts of Europe embarked on a massive project,
subjecting some 25 million people to anthropometric measurements.
The stated goal was to determine ideal skull types and identify a perfect Nordic skull. The effect was to publicly identify and brand those
considered permanent and unsalvageable members of the under-
class.

Such thinking was sanctified by the turn-of-the-century estimable
Encyclopædia Britannica, which defined "Negro" in part by cranial
size: according to this racial hierarchy, the average European had 45
ounces, the Negro 35, and the highest gorilla 20.[33]

In 1906, American physical anthropologist Robert Bennett Bean, after measuring 152 brains of Negroes and whites, would find significant differences between the two races in total brain size and relative size of their frontal lobes. Although the data on overall brain size appear historically accurate, Bean's claims about the significance of his findings are more personal than scientific:

> The Caucasian is subjective, the Negro objective. The Caucasian—more particularly the Anglo-Saxon . . . is dominant and domineering and possessed primarily with determination, will power, self-control, self-government, and all the attributes of the subjective self with a high development of the ethical and aesthetic faculties. The Negro is primarily affectionate, immensely emotional, then sensual and under stimulation, passionate. There is love of ostentation, of outward show, of approbation; there is love of music, and capacity for melodious articulation; there is undeveloped artistic power and taste—Negroes make good artisans, handicraftsman—and there is instability of character incident to lack of self-control, especially in connection with the sexual relation.[34]

For decades the skull had offered what appeared to be irrefutable proof of a social hierarchy, with black "barbarians" at the bottom. It wasn't until after World War II that it became clear that the heritability of skull shape and size was sensitive to short-term environmental effects.[35]

Although Social Darwinism, phrenology, and eugenics have been portrayed by contemporary historians as quirky theories used to bolster the status quo, they were all seen at the time as the most progressive impulses of a socially conscious meritocracy. Those who embraced and popularized these views considered themselves humanitarians whose idealistic goal was to better society. But these theories became so exaggerated and vulgarized that they eventually came to be used as an excuse for everything from inequality of wealth, to the gutting welfare programs for children and women, to the limitation of immigration—many of the gross inequalities of industrial society. It was this fateful fusion of science with political and social ends that would come to haunt the twentieth century. To the old-guard and the new plutocrats, the spoils obviously accrued to those who deserved it most.

THE RISE OF ULTRANATIONALISM

While Social Darwinists in England and America struggled to apply these new insights, however flawed, to better understand human nature, political theorists took the Darwinian paradigm to another level. Leading socialists of the late nineteenth century, such as Galton's biographer and protégé, Karl Pearson, a Quaker, equated the struggle for survival with the growing tension between countries. Race and nation came to be synonymous. Pearson reaffirmed the contention that intelligence and character were as heritable as hair color or height. Under his guidance the emphasis in eugenics gradually shifted from defining the ultimate society into breeding to construct it.[36]

Radical conservatives viewed natural selection as a justification for ultranationalism. Carlos Losson, considered an American apostle of Social Darwinism, promoted the Hegelian-like belief that all history was a struggle that produced a constant redistribution of the racial elements in nations according to various "laws of social selection." A Harvard graduate who lectured in economics before becoming a real estate broker, Losson believed there was strong evidence of a pure race—the Aryan *Homo Europaeus*, numbering some 49 million Europeans.[37]

While romanticism settled into stolid England, the florid *Sturm und Drang* of the work of Johann von Goethe and Johann von Schiller set the intellectual tone in Prussia. At first, the German eugenics movement appeared remarkably similar to those in other countries. But its conception of race was colored by the peculiarly Germanic belief in spiritual and historic destiny. For more than a century, German intellectuals actively promoted *volksgeist*, which they claimed was shaped by the spirit of the age, the *zeitgeist*. That metaphysical legacy can be traced to Johann Gottfried von Herder, a philosopher and mentor of Goethe, whose *naturaphilosophie* would influence generations of German intellectuals. Herder believed that each race had its own distinct consciousness. It was a mystical blend of nationalism and racial chauvinism, with Germany touted as the embodiment of God's master plan.

Darwin's most enthusiastic proponent in Germany was Ernst Haeckel, a botanist who was also taken by Goethe's romantic musings about German destiny. Unlike Darwin, he believed fervently in the concept of progress determined by natural law, postulating what came to be called "organic evolution." Haeckel was also smitten by the ideas of Galton and Spencer, believing that as a natural result of progress through natural selection, European superiority would result in the extermination of inferior races.[38] Greater Germany, he concluded, possessed a soul that predisposed it to lead the march into the future.

Haeckel's mysticism represented an impossible reconciliation of hostile religious and racial theories of human origins. Before Darwin, polygenists had believed that different races of humans have distinct and separate origins and were created more or less in their present form. Darwin demolished that idea, but polygenism refused to die. Its adherents rejiggered their theory, accepting common descent from Darwin but rejecting natural selection as the only mechanism for change. They reasoned that if evolution was controlled by some internal mechanism, or god-like soul, then races could have evolved in parallel. It wouldn't have been necessary for humans to have competed, with only the fittest surviving and breeding.

As a result of such twisted reasoning, within a decade after the publication of *Origin of Species,* Darwin's theories had been bastardized to the point that one could be either a monogenist, believing in common descent from an ape-like human, or a polygenist, believing that there were a number of separate, early modern human populations, and still call oneself a true believer.[39]

Haeckel's ruminations elevated him to the chic status of a cult figure in a Prussian society stewing in the nationalist fervor stirred by Otto von Bismarck, the first political leader to tap into German mysticism. Bismarck had come to power with the support of the middle-class after the collapse of the revolution of 1848. A conservative populist, he finessed the liberal majority, engineered his election as chancellor of Prussia in 1862, and immediately played the dormant German *volk* card. Bismarck embarked on a "blood and iron" strategy of unification and launched three wars in nine years, culminating in a heady victory over France and the establishment of the German Reich in 1871.

To solidify his control, Bismarck sprinkled his militaristic nationalism with numerous reforms, including a comprehensive social security system and new labor laws for children and women. The first organized anti-Semitism in Germany began to emerge at this time. The Christian Social Party and other public figures orchestrated a campaign to ban the admission of East European Jews into Germany and exclude German Jews from public life. This combination of nationalism, socialism, and racism would eventually provide a blueprint for the Nazis.[40]

Energized by an ultranationalist zeal that swept through Germany, Haeckel gained even more prominence. He turned his attention to politics, for he believed that only Germans possessed the *volk* spirit to renew European dominance. In *The Riddle of the Universe*, published in 1899, which sold hundreds of thousands of copies, he outlined his new goal of remolding Germany into a unified people by revamping the educational system. He explicitly rejected the "sickly" Christian belief in the equality of humankind, writing that because "lower races" such as Negroes are "physiologically nearer to the mammals, apes and dogs, than to civilized Europeans, we must, therefore, assign a totally different value to their lives."[41] Haeckel's jingoism made him a hero to many in the German political establishment.

His intellectual rival was his former mentor, Rudolf Virchow, a German pathologist, who led the opposition to Bismarck's militaristic nationalism. While Haeckel was a freethinking racist, Virchow was a rigid Christian humanist who believed that the fad of evolutionism was feeding a nationalistic frenzy. It is hardly surprising that Haeckel's romantic mysticism about a "state-soul" sent Virchow into a tizzy. Ironically, given his desire to contain soft-headed thinking, his response was equally unscientific. Despite his professed desire to separate church and science, Virchow could not come to accept that humans shared ancestry with any animal, let alone apes.[42]

Virchow vowed to stop the spread of evolutionary theory at all costs. He targeted its most ardent German proponent, Haeckel, whose nationalistic drumbeating grew more bizarre by the month. In an attempt to destroy the myth of the tall, blond, blue-eyed Aryan ideal, Virchow marshaled establishment science to initiate a massive anthropological survey of some 7 million German school children. Published in 1886, it definitively established that no Aryan ideal existed, but it had almost no effect in denting the myth of Nordic supremacy. In fact it had the opposite effect, for it unwittingly endorsed the mania for measuring skull size and racially determined aptitudes, tools that were being used throughout Europe to bolster the popular belief that Aryans *were* a superior species or subrace.

Houston Stewart Chamberlain, an Englishman who popularized this notion of Aryan supremacy, asserted the historical superiority of the German race, stretching back thousands of years, in his scathing two-volume work, *The Foundations of the Nineteenth Century*, published in 1899. Inspired by the racist ideology of Gobineau, he assembled a rogues' gallery of aristocratic scientists to justify his condemnation of Negroes and Jews as degenerate. He also drew on the writings of Swiss psychiatrist August Forel, who had studied "intellectually inferior" races in the United States and the West Indies. "The brain of the Negro is weaker than that of the white," Chamberlain wrote, quoting Forel. "Even for their own good the blacks must be treated as they are, an absolutely subordinate, inferior, lower type of man, incapable themselves of culture. That must once and for all be clearly and openly stated."[43] As science it was ridiculous, but as propaganda it was powerful.

By the turn of the century, Germany was fully in the grip of folk racism. In 1905, German professor Alfred Ploetz launched the German Gesellschaft für Rassenhygiene (Society of Racial Hygiene) to focus on the societal problem of the "mentally unfit." Ploetz, a leading socialist of the time, was convinced that the "Jewish problem"—

Jews were Germany's largest minority, although they constituted only 1 percent of the population—could be solved if Jews would only allow themselves to be absorbed into German society and not insist on retaining their "separateness." Ploetz and his followers did not consider themselves anti-Jewish and in fact trained Jewish physicians with hopes of encouraging the spread of assimilationist thinking.[44]

Despite superficial pronouncements of liberalism, there was no mistaking the peculiarly German romantic notion of *rassenhygiene*. Medicine, nationalism, and the new pseudo-scientific leanings of anthropology were hopelessly entangled. By this time, Darwin's theory of natural selection had been twisted far beyond recognition. Race was no longer based on empirical science and no longer designated a population group that shared physical traits. Instead it had become a way to stigmatize "anyone but us"—Jews, Gypsies, Serbs, Africans, whomever. Science was being transformed into a handmaiden to the state, with race purity as its driving ethic.

What had begun two hundred years before as a benign system of classification had by now devolved into an increasingly rigid hierarchy of social worth and intelligence. To compound the problem, the bright stream of evolution had turned into a raging river polluted by the eccentric ideas of the well meaning and the frightening pronouncements of the simply racist. It was only a small step from claims of racial superiority to calls for the purging of those who didn't fit the Aryan model. But that would come later.

IV

THE SEGREGATION AND INTEGRATION

OF SPORTS

CHAPTER 10

THE SUPERIORITY

OF WHITE ATHLETES

I t was a steamy June day in 1890 with 25,000 fans rocking the rickety stands at the Coney Island Track. A band of horn players hired to stir the crowd was drowned into silence. According to one account, "newspapers sent their page one byliners abetted by staff artists to depict the event in line drawings."[1] Everyone was on the edge of his seat as the country's two best jockeys, "the Great White Hope" and "the Colored Archer," guided their steeds onto the track for the race of the century.

Isaac Murphy, who had been given his nickname in honor of a famed British jockey, had little to prove. He had begun riding professionally at fourteen and was a star three years later. In 1879, while wearing the red-and-white colors of the Reynolds Stable, he rode Falsetto to victories in the Phoenix Hotel Stakes and the Clark Handicap in Louisville and a second-place finish in the Kentucky Derby. On a stirring July 4, in Detroit, he jockeyed four of the five races and won them all, a rare clean sweep. Energized, Murphy moved on to Saratoga, where he rode Falsetto to victories in both the Travers and Kenner Stakes. It was a great showing, even if it was dismissed by some as only "nigger work."[2]

There weren't many white faces in horse racing in the years after the Civil War, when the sport started to gain in popularity. Because whites considered the work degrading, black "boys" who had trained plantation thoroughbreds took over as jockeys-of-choice after emancipation. In the first Kentucky Derby in 1875, ex-slaves rode fourteen of the fifteen horses. Negro jockeys won eleven of the first twenty and fifteen of the first twenty-eight Derbys.[3]

Murphy was the sport's biggest star and arguably the first great, nationally recognized African American athlete. He was the first jockey ever to win three Kentucky Derbys, four American Derbys, and five Latonia Derbys. All told, he racked up an amazing 44 percent winning percentage in more than 1,400 mounts, which earned him the honor of being the first jockey voted into the National Racing Hall of Fame in Saratoga Springs when it opened in 1955. At the height of his career, he was pocketing $20,000 a year, quadruple the earnings of the other best jockeys and almost ten times the average salary of a white person. For a time, he owned homes in prosperous white neighborhoods in Lexington, Kentucky and Chicago.[4]

Murphy was not the only black jockey. But as the sport began drawing both publicity and money, whites angled for a bigger piece of the pie. The changing of the color guard in horse racing gave the Coney Island match race between Murphy and his white challenger, "Snapper" Garrison, all the more poignancy.

According to news accounts, Murphy, riding Salvator, and Garrison, on Tenny, ran a wild race, exchanging the lead back and forth. Murphy was famed for close races—in 1889, a *New York Tribune* reporter had written that he had a "penchant for gallery finishes, the temptation to . . . lounge along in the rear of the field till he strikes the homestretch and comes in range of the clear vision of the admirers in the grand stand . . . then letting his mount move up and get his nose in front of the leader."[5] But in the end, Murphy held off Garrison and won by a head.

After Murphy won the Kentucky Derby the following year, his career and life went into a tailspin. Known as a hard drinker and battling the plague of racism that quickly swept blacks out of horse racing, Murphy found it increasingly difficult to get mounts. By 1893, he was reduced to doing walk-ons as a stage actor, luring crowds with his fading reputation. Three years later, still fighting for mounts, he was dead.

According to Arthur Ashe, Jr., for a brief few decades after the Civil War, Negro athletes like Murphy were "the most well known and among the richest of black Americans."[6] But like so many of this era, Murphy's success was poisoned by the racism that greeted Reconstruction. White jockeys banded together to form the Jockey Club to license riders and lobbied the blue-bloods who owned the horse farms to keep the sport white. As before the war, blacks were relegated to feeding and grooming the horses. Shortly after the turn of the century, there were no black jockeys riding premier steeds. Horse racing, like most American sports, was again an all-white enterprise.

THE ANGLO-SAXON SCHOLAR-ATHLETE

Murphy was an anomaly among blacks who became sports stars in the later half of the nineteenth century. Rather than being former slaves or poorly educated, the top black athletes were frequently from the middle class and well educated, often graduates of mostly white universities. Except for boxing and to some extent baseball, poor blacks, and poor whites for that matter, had virtually no chance to join the elite sports clubs. For well-to-do whites, sports came to symbolize education, intelligence, and wealth in a society increasingly marked by class distinctions.

The first stirrings in America of this elite sensibility occurred at Harvard, where students were observed playing games with "bats, balls, and foot-balls."[7] The earliest baseball games were modeled on rounders, a British game that uses a ball and a bat. The sport was most popular with new professionals, America's first yuppies. The rosters of the Rochester town-ballers of the 1820s; the Philadelphia Olympics of the '30s; and the Knickerbockers, New York's first team which played in Manhattan before moving across the Hudson river to Hoboken, New Jersey, in the '40s, were filled with doctors, lawyers, and other white-collar workers.[8]

The tradition of the black scholar-athlete grew out of this Anglo-Saxon athletic aesthetic. In British bastions in Africa, America, and the Caribbean, the colonialists encouraged black participation in sports, for it helped the British maintain control and ingratiate themselves with a potentially unruly population. A cricket reference book in Trinidad noted that "black men add considerably to the strength of a side, while their inclusion makes the game more popular locally and tends to instill a great and universal enthusiasm among all classes of the population. The black men are especially fine fieldsmen," it read; "they throw very well and seldom miss a catch."[9]

For the large percentage of American blacks, who were concentrated in southern plantations, sports were limited to contests among slaves. Slave owners staged boxing, track events, or other spectacles that were more akin to cock fights. According to legend, a slave named Thomas Molineaux, born in 1784, allegedly won his freedom by defeating an opponent in a match.[10] "Our sports and dances was big sport for the white folks," recalled Will Adams, a former Texas slave, in one of many narratives of former slaves from interviews conducted by the Works Progress Administration (WPA) during the Depression.[11] "Old master would have my father and Uncle Jacob and us boys run foot races," added Charles Hinton of Arkansas. "I could outrun a wild animal, barefooted and bare headed."[12] As Henry Coleman of South Carolina remembered in his makeshift dialect, "De white fokes used to bet amongst dem selves as much as $20 dat I could outrun dat horse."[13] Boxing was also popular and was one of the few sports in which English blacks were occasionally permitted to compete against whites.

Until the end of slavery, however, playing organized sports was less a dream than a fantasy for most American blacks. Sundays, Easter, and Christmas were among their few days of respite. "The majority [of slaves] spent the holidays in sports, ball-playing, wrestling, boxing, foot racing," wrote Frederick Douglass.[14] Children generally were not required to work until they were fourteen, leaving some time to develop a zest for sports, such as they were in the 1800s. "Most slave children thought of themselves as skillful 'athletes'; their white counterparts were generally felt to be less competent physically, unable to dance, run, jump, or throw."[15]

Needless to say, sports were not the highest priority immediately after the Civil War. Most organized athletic competitions were overseen by the new gentlemen's clubs that had sprung up in the major cities of the United States to encourage the British tradition of amateur competition. Competitive athletics did not capture a wider audience and draw more diverse participants until after the first-ever track meet between Oxford and Cambridge Universities in England in 1864. The contest generated unexpected excitement throughout the English-speaking world.

The British Empire Games, a forerunner of the modern Olympics, followed in 1866. The hoopla that greeted these events sparked the opening of dozens of sports clubs in Britain and the former colonies. Most were private associations, a mixture of male-only social clubs and athletics. They sponsored teams in cricket, track, boxing, and water sports. Team sports, such as soccer and rugby, and baseball in the United States, which were popular in the factory towns spawned by the industrial revolution, were looked down upon as fads of the lower classes.

As with most social clubs of the times, the sports clubs were open to everyone—everyone, that is, who was white, male, Anglo-Saxon, wealthy, and well connected. "A superior athlete," read one account, "unless he be black, a recent immigrant, or too crude in social demeanor, could expect little difficulty in finding a club that would grant him membership."[16] The barriers that restricted participation by Italians, Irish, and Jews applied doubly, and openly, to blacks. The New York Athletic Club and other Eastern metropolitan sport associations explicitly barred "Negroes." Though hostile to black membership, many of these same clubs were not above sponsoring lucrative events featuring star black athletes, particularly boxers. Without such sponsorship, most blacks, and most whites for that matter, could not afford the equipment and time necessary for the few organized sports that existed at the time.

EARLY INTEGRATION OF SPORTS

Overjoyed at first by the prospect of freedom, former slaves found the going rough. With little education, most Southern blacks had few of the survival skills necessary to make their way in a hostile world. Education, particularly in rural areas, was close to nonexistent, and health problems were rampant. Despite such horrendous conditions and in defiance of incalculable odds, some of the best athletes between 1870 and the new century were blacks, who were frequently better educated than their white counterparts. They had to be, for their entrée into sports was largely through the university system, at that time the whitest of white American institutions.

Those few who managed to defy the odds and achieve modest success do not fit the stereotypical profile of today's sports stars, black or white. Only those blacks who had already dug their way out of poverty could consider getting involved in athletics. "In those days of no athletic scholarships, and sports as a sidelight, only the well-to-do could afford to go to college," wrote Bryant Gumbel, who was the founding editor of *Black Sports* magazine before moving into broadcasting. "Above all, the Black man was in college to study, not to perform on the athletic field. Those Blacks who were in college came from backgrounds and environments similar to their white counterparts. And still later, after athletics had come under the auspices of college faculties, the primal objective of academics was still in force."[17]

Track was the most popular participation sport among young blacks, for it required almost no special equipment or formal training. The few who entered formal races did extraordinarily well. In the mid-1890s, Napoleon Bonaparte Marshall, a graduate of Phillips Andover Preparatory School and a student at Harvard, ran 51.2 in the 440-yard dash, just a shade off the world-record. Marshall paved the way for a series of scholar-athletes. George Poage from the University of Wisconsin was the first black to earn an Olympic medal, taking home bronzes in the 100- and 200-meter hurdles at the 1904 St. Louis Games. University of Pennsylvania veterinary student John "Doc" Taylor, a two-time world-record holder in the 400, became the first black to win an Olympic gold medal, in the relays, in 1908. Ted Cable, the first black field star, twice won the Intercollegiate hammer throw in 1912 and 1913 and was a champion broad jumper as well.[18]

Even with such successes, blacks were not perceived as being naturally fast or great jumpers. That perception soon changed with the exploits of Howard Porter Drew, the first sprinter widely regarded as the "world's fastest human." Drew was a champion high school sprinter from Lexington, Virginia, when he tied the world 100-meter mark of 10.8 seconds at the 1912 Olympic trials. "Never in my life have I seen any sprinter with such wonderful leg action," commented U.S. coach Mike Murphy. "Trainers and experts say that he has the quickest start of any man ever seen upon the track."[19]

Renowned for seldom training, Drew pulled up lame at the Olympics; some believed that he injured himself precisely because he was forced to train in Stockholm at the pace of the rest of the U.S. team, which for him amounted to over-training.[20] Yet he had recovered enough by November to lower the 100-meter record to 10.2 seconds—at an indoor meet. Drew later added Amateur Athletic Union titles in the 100- and 220-yard dashes and the world record for the 220. The highwater mark of his career came in 1913 when he sped the through the 100-yard dash, then the most coveted of speed records, in 9.6 seconds. From there, he went on to the University of Southern California, and later to Drake University, where his running floundered after the cancellation of the 1916 Olympics because of the war.

Football, perhaps because it started as a college sport, was never exclusively white. The origins of the game can be traced to the early 1800s, when Harvard and other Ivy League schools, along with Rutgers, Amherst, Bowdoin, and West Point, would play each other in annual games, usually held on the eve of the beginning of classes.[21] The first black to be selected as an All-American, William Henry Lewis, a son of former slaves freed before the Civil War, starred at "center rush" for Amherst in 1889. The next year he was elected captain. After graduating to Harvard Law School in 1892, he helped defeat Dartmouth 46–0 in his first game. He later became an assistant district attorney in Boston.[22]

A steady trickle of blacks was recruited to Northern and Midwestern colleges, from Cornell to Northwestern to Nebraska. However, some schools, such as Princeton, remained all white, and few colleges featured more than two black players. By the turn of the century, the racial schisms in the post-Reconstruction United States had grown even larger, and the opportunities at premier colleges for blacks actually decreased. Most young athletes ended up at one of the black colleges, such as Talladega, Howard, Alabama State, and Fisk, which came together as the Colored Intercollegiate Athletic Association in 1912.[23] Some players would "graduate" from the all-black schools and matriculate at white colleges in the North.

Frederick "Fritz" Pollard and Paul Robeson, scholar-athletes, were two of the first blacks to be named All-Americans. Entering Brown University in 1915 as a twenty-one-year-old freshman, Pollard quarterbacked his team to a Rose Bowl and was selected the top running back in college football the next season. "You're a nigger, but you're the best goddamn football player I ever saw," said a Yale player after one of Pollard's sterling performances.

Robeson was considered the finest wide receiver of his era. The son of a part-Indian mother and runaway slave father, Robeson worked hard enough in high school to earn a scholarship to Rutgers University. He won twelve letters in four sports and was a star quarter-miler. In his spare time, he won three public speaking prizes and was selected commencement speaker, Phi Beta Kappa, and class valedictorian before graduating in 1919. Robeson moved on to law school at Columbia University, financing his studies by playing semipro football on the weekends. Racial prejudice prevented him from fully developing his law practice, so he moved on to another love, the theatre, becoming a distinguished actor. He learned to speak more than twenty languages, which he incorporated in a singing repertoire that ranged from classical music to Negro spirituals.[24]

Like so many black entertainment and sports stars before and since, Robeson saw his career derail when he became too free-speaking for the white establishment to tolerate. In 1940, he voiced his opposition to enlisting in the armed forces. The next year he filed a racial discrimination suit against a San Francisco restaurant that refused to seat him. Believing that racism in the United States was intolerable, he packed his son off to the Soviet Union to study. Shortly thereafter, he sang at a benefit concert to raise aid for the Soviet soldiers killed in the Allied front fighting the Germans.

Robeson, who dedicated his life to dispelling the racist belief that blacks were mindless machines, paid a terrible price for his out-

spokenness. He was branded a communist and his passport was re-
voked, his reputation forever sullied.[25] Although his accomplishments on and off the field far eclipsed those of most athletes of this
era, black or white, Robeson is best remembered as a renaissance
man who balanced body, mind, and soul—an achievement that was
not an aberration among many African American athletes of the first
half-century.

THE AFRICAN AMERICAN LOVE AFFAIR
WITH BASEBALL

In his account of slave life, the historian John Blassingame
quoted an illiterate white laborer describing a Civil War-era game
that served as a precursor to baseball. "We played what we called
'Town Ball,'" said Henry Baker. "We had bases en we run frum one
base tuh de udder 'cause ef de runner wuz hit wid de ball he wuz
out. We allus made de ball out a cotton en rags. We played wid de
niggers on de plantation."[26] It was probably a plantation version of
rounders.

By the end of the Civil War, baseball in more or less the form we
have today, had emerged as America's most popular team sport. Although a few of the earliest leagues attempted to keep out immigrants and blacks, the game became a magnet for working class
whites and the more well-to-do blacks. The National Association of
Baseball Players, formed in 1858, included both blacks and whites.
But that tolerance faded after the war. Pressure from Irish and German clubs led the NABBP to deny membership to the black Pythian
Club of Philadelphia, which applied for membership in 1867. When
owners began taking control away from players and the National
League was formalized, the league officially refused admission to
"any club which may be composed of one or more colored players."[27]
For almost a decade, the National League was lily white.

Nonetheless, the sport was hugely popular among blacks. Most of
the players who made up the twenty or so professional and semipro
leagues that operated in these formative years were from the black

upper class. Black clubs flourished in the inner cities of the South and Northeast. Before one big game in 1867 between the Philadelphia Excelsiors and the hometown Brooklyn Uniques and Monitors, a Brooklyn *Daily Union* reporter wrote, "These organizations are composed of very respectable colored people, well-to-do in the world. . . . We trust, for the good of the fraternity, that none of the 'white trash' who disgrace white clubs by following and brawling of them will be allowed to mar the pleasure of those social colored gatherings."[28]

Perhaps as many as seventy of the most extraordinary Negro athletes worked their way onto previously all-white teams. The best of the lot, Bud Fowler (nee John W. Jackson), played for semipro teams in New Castle, Pennsylvania, and Stillwater, Minnesota. "He is one of the best general players in the country," reported *Sporting Life* in 1885, "and if he had a white face, he would be playing with the best of them." One Denver journalist deadpanned, "Fowler has two strong points: He is an excellent runner and proof against sunburn. He don't tan worth a cent."[29]

The color barrier in the owner-run National League crumbled briefly when the Cincinnati Red Stockings and other dissidents bolted from the league in 1884 after owners instituted a "reserve clause" limiting the players' bargaining power. The "Redlegs" joined the renegade American Association, which included the semipro Toledo Mud Hens, which had a Negro star, bare-handed catcher Moses "Fleet" Walker. The son of a physician and a graduate of Oberlin College, Walker had left law school at the University of Michigan to pursue his dream of playing baseball.

It was a tough year for baseball's first Negro professional and the only black in the league. Walker played respectably but was frequently under attack by one racist lunatic after another. He feared for his safety after many games and actually skipped one contest in Richmond after management received a letter from "75 determined men" threatening to "mob Walker" and cause "much bloodshed."[30]

Walker's trying experience reflected the difficult time in an America that furiously resisted post–Civil War integration. Reconstruction ground to a halt in the aftermath of the disputed election in 1876 when Democrat Samuel J. Tilden appeared to score a close win over Republican Rutherford B. Hayes. Hayes was eventually awarded the election by decision of an electoral commission set up by Congress. As part of the backroom dealing, Tilden agreed not to contest the finding in return for which the Republicans agreed to remove Northern troops from the South, effectively ending the enforcement of any Reconstruction civil rights laws. With public support for integration fading, the Supreme Court, in 1883, declared the federal Civil Rights Act of 1875 unconstitutional. The following year, Abraham Lincoln's Republican party lost the White House for the first time since the war, putting the last nail in Reconstruction and legalizing the South's unofficial program of apartheid.

The rancor spilled over into baseball. Fowler, Walker, and other blacks who thought they had found a home of sorts, suddenly found themselves on the firing line. "How far will this mania for engaging colored players go?" read a typical article in *Sporting Life*. Not far, it turned out. By 1887, a seething revolt by white fans and players began picking up steam. Fans in Toronto reportedly chanted, "Kill the nigger" when teams with black stars visited. That August, the Chicago White Stockings star and manager Adrian "Cap" Anson led a group of white players who threatened to quit unless the league banned Negroes, including Walker, who had long since proven themselves. Although the four teams with black players voted against the measure, the six all-white teams passed a rule forbidding future contracts with the "colored element."[31] It was the only formal vote ever taken to ban black players from baseball.

It took less than a month for another flare-up. In September, eight members of the St. Louis Browns refused to take the field against an all-black squad. "We . . . do not agree to play against negroes tomorrow," read a letter sent to the team owner. "We will cheerfully play against white people at anytime, and think by refusing to play we are only doing what is right, taking everything into consideration." The all-white Detroit Tigers were substituted at the last minute.[32]

By the end of the 1887 season, although a few black players still played for white teams, the door on integrated baseball was closing fast. During the off season, teams from Buffalo and Syracuse tried to overturn the ban, but to no avail. Moses Walker's brother, Weldy, who had starred at the University of Michigan, wrote a plaintive letter to the league after he was dropped from the Akron team. "The law is a disgrace to the present age," he wrote. "There should be some broader cause, such as lack of ability, behavior and intelligence, for barring a player, rather than his color." Not all quarters were unsympathetic. Labeling the "objection to colored men . . . ridiculous," the *Newark Call* noted, "If anywhere in the world the social barriers are broken down it is on the ball field."[33]

The embarrassing and very public controversy did prompt the barons of baseball to rescind their ban on blacks, but it was an empty maneuver, all for show. Over the next two years the half-dozen remaining black players were pushed out of the major leagues and relegated to "colored" semipro teams. A de facto gentlemen's agreement gradually fell into place that effectively prohibited blacks from the Major Leagues for almost sixty years.

WHITENING SPORTS

The racism faced by black players infected almost every aspect of post-Reconstruction America. Even multiethnic New Orleans, which had made great strides toward total integration of blacks, resegregated its schools. In 1890, the city passed the Separate Car Act, which required blacks to sit in a special "colored" car in all public transportation. On June 7, 1892, a thirty-year-old shoemaker named Homer Plessy, who had one black great-grandparent but was otherwise of Aryan stock, was jailed for sitting in the "white" car on the East Louisiana Railroad. Plessy was found guilty, and after several appeals the case ended before the Supreme Court.

Plessy v. Ferguson rebuilt the walls of separation that had tumbled after the Civil War. In an infamous 8-to-1 ruling, the Supreme Court established the doctrine of "separate but equal" at the highest judicial level. The Fourteenth Amendment abolishing slavery, declared the justices, "could not have been intended to abolish distinctions based upon color, or to enforce social, as distinguished from politi-

cal equality, or a commingling of the two races upon terms unsatis-
factory to either."

Within days "whites only" signs sprouted everywhere. "Jim
Crow"—the name was lifted from a minstrel act—provided an excuse for keeping blacks in the back of the bus, away from white rest
room facilities, and out of the best schools. That meant no more experiments in integration in baseball, horse racing, football, or other
sports.

As new sports came into fashion, opportunistic black athletes
who defied the odds and got a chance to demonstrate their skills
were soon discarded by the white establishment. The great Indi-
anapolis bicyclist Marshall "Major" Taylor, the first black to enter the
world cycling championship, swept both the 1- and 2-mile events in
1899. He also won the American title and was a standout in the grueling six-day races. The situation didn't sit well with the whites-only
League of American Wheel Men, which had banned bicyclists of the
"inferior race" in 1896.[34]

Baited into bicycling when he was thirteen by pranksters at a cycling competition, Taylor had fought an endlessly uphill battle even
to participate. It is reported that after he broke a white racer's track
record when he was only fifteen, it was not so politely suggested that
he never return. A model of modesty, self-reliance, and clean living,
Taylor "battled under bitter odds against the dreadful monster prejudice"[35] in the United States, where he came to dominate the short
and middle distance events. Regularly assaulted by his competitors,
on and off the track, Taylor ended up throwing in the towel and
heading to Australia, which had a rigid color line of its own but accepted the American racer warmly.[36]

The reversal of fortune for blacks in race-walking was particularly
startling, for blacks were integral to the sport's early popularity.
Pedestrianism, as it was called, had become all the rage after the
Civil War. Papers had been filled by the exploits of athletes on what
was called the "sawdust circuit." In 1879, the Englishwoman
Madame Anderson walked 2,700 quarter miles, collecting headlines
across America and several thousand dollars. Edward Weston, who
held numerous world records, was both rich and famous. But the

emerging star was Fred Hirchborn, an African American from Boston dubbed the "Black Dan" after his financial backer, former star race-walker Daniel O'Leary.[37]

After doing well in a number of local matches, Hirchborn entered the prestigious six-day O'Leary Belt race in 1879. According to press accounts, the race at New York's Madison Square Garden attracted tens of thousands of spectators, many of whom crowded the arena for the start of the race by the "dark horse." He was given special presentations by the Young Men's Colored Club of Boston and two Colored Republican Clubs of New York. Yet no competitors would shake his hand at the starting line. The race turned into a gauntlet as Hirchborn suffered racial taunts and threats of violence. On the third day a stranger offered him some soda water and he fell ill, apparently from mild poisoning. Dehydrated and near quitting, he struggled on to cover 482 miles, finishing fourth and beating the famed Weston.

Hirchborn considered it a disappointing performance, but it was inspiring to other blacks. Two other African Americans, William Pegram and Ed Williams, joined the tour and quickly moved into the forefront of the sport. That December, all three shattered the 500-mile barrier in the Rose Belt race in New York. Hirchborn won the race, traveling 540 miles, only 1 mile short of the world record. When he took a victory lap, carrying U.S. flags in both hands, the Garden fans reportedly cheered at a "deafening level." The next April, Hirchborn won the O'Leary Belt, setting a new six-day world record of 565 miles and collecting an amazing $17,000 in gate receipts. Pegram finished second and Williams seventh.

But Hirchborn's exploits were short-lived. Within a decade, the color barrier would be erected in race-walking as well. The sport was turned over to lesser competitors and eventually died out. It was one more thwarted attempt at integration. By the 1890s, experiments in tolerance in sports were being swept aside by the tide of nationalism and racism rolling across the Atlantic to receptive shores in the United States.

CHAPTER 11

JACK JOHNSON IN THE RING

AGAINST JIM CROW

If there was ever a black man who embodied the noxious stereotypes held by white racists, Jack Johnson was that man. John Arthur Johnson dominated the sport of boxing for much of the first two decades of this century. In 1908, after having been denied a shot at the title for years, he became the first black to fight for and win the heavyweight championship. An imposing physical presence—he stood 6 feet, 2 inches tall and had a classically sculpted body—Johnson dressed the way he wanted, talked up a storm, and paraded his flashy and very public affairs with white women. He was a hero in much of the black community, which viewed his defiance with tolerance and even pride. This was a man who didn't stoop to shine any white man's shoes.

It was no surprise that white America took a less sanguine view of this "uppity nigger." Ebony and proud, Johnson was an affront to the establishment, which had long linked athletics to privilege and saw in this young black man a raw and threatening dignity. He challenged the lie that a black man would turn tail in a fight against a seasoned white boxer. Johnson feared no one, faced all comers, and had to resort to taunting the best white boxers to embarrass them into fighting him. When they did fight, he showed no mercy. After invariably beating his white opponent to a pulp, he would stand over him smirking.

But white racism had the last laugh. In response to his gargantuan talent, Johnson's athletic achievements were devalued as a character flaw, a by-product of his primitive African heritage. He

compounded his heresy by refusing to act the docile role demanded
of blacks trying to make it in a white world. Johnson's defiance
earned him the enmity of the white establishment and a reputation
as a "bad seed." His less than submissive attitude would cost him his
heavyweight title, and eventually his liberty.

THE INFIRMITY STEREOTYPE

Black stars such as Johnson had to face down the sacred doctrine
of racist intellectuals that blacks were too fragile of will and spirit,
and not physically hardy enough, to compete in sports. Blacks could
not seem to shake the paradoxical stereotype, which had prevailed
for more than a century, that they were strong but physically fragile.
Success presented a double-edged sword. Winning a boxing match
or scoring a touchdown only reinvigorated the belief that blacks
were near animals and brutes; their "natural" abilities and "animal-
like" physiology got the credit, not their dedication and skills. Losing
confirmed racist notions that blacks were intrinsically inferior.

The stereotypes were deeply rooted in an America that had actively embraced or at least tolerated slavery for hundreds of years.
By the nineteenth century, prominent Southern physician Samuel
Cartwright would provoke little controversy when he contended that
Negroes exhibited a "weakness of . . . will" and were lazy to boot. He
argued that blacks had an inferior nervous system that "rendered the
people of Africa unable to take care of themselves . . . [and is] the
true cause of their indolence and apathy."[1] Slaves were supposedly
prone to a disease he called "drapetomania"—the insane desire to
run away. Although he was considered an extremist even in the
South, such views were not uncommon and seeped into the public
consciousness.

This racialized perspective prevailed even in the North, where slavery was outlawed. "The Negro had little elasticity of temperament . . .
and lacked nervous endurance and moral courage," claimed W. J. Burt,
a well-known physician of the time.[2] According to Stanford Hunt, a sur-
geon for the Negro Volunteers during the war, Union officers were con-

vinced that the Negro soldier could not handle the rigor of combat: "Had he the necessary physical courage? Would he not, when his savage blood was up in the fever-heat of battle, entail disgrace upon our cause by acts of outrage?" Black men were portrayed as "brutish, ignorant, idle and treacherous" while women were described as "loose, wanton, immoral, and matriarchs."[3]

Although these outspoken views were certainly not universal, it can't be overstated how deeply white superiority was ingrained in the American racial imagination. Even Abraham Lincoln in his famous debate in 1858 with Stephen Douglas would state, "There is a physical difference between the white and black races which I believe will forever forbid the two races living together on terms of social and political equality."[4] Lincoln struck a moderate position for the times—between abolitionists and the virulent racism epoused by many of his fellow Republicans.

There were muted voices of reason. One respected Boston physician, John Streeter, stated unequivocally that "colored" men "compare favorably in intelligence and aptitude for military service with white recruits. In muscular development and freedom from physical disqualifications, they are superior to the average white men I have examined."[5] But in the racialized heat of the Civil War era, those who disagreed with the popular cant were mostly quiet.

Although frequently caricatured as weak in character and deficient in endurance, blacks were also prized as purely physical specimens. That was the stereotype of John Henry, the "steel drivin' man," the mythical nineteenth-century railroad worker who stood over 7 feet tall, was as "strong as thirty men," and went head to gear against the new steam-powered drill. In *A Treasury of American Folklore*, B.A. Botkin referred to him as a "role model" because he "stands for something which the pick-and-shovel Negro idolizes—brute strength."[6] Botkin believed his observation was well intended. Although John Henry won his contest with the steam drill, he died from the effort, becoming a symbol of the man-against-the-heartless-machine age but also of congenital black frailty.

This myth complemented the stereotype of Negro indolence. The inborn apathy of blacks, it was said, could be overcome only by discipline and training. Implicit was the prejudice that brains and brawn are inversely proportional—the "law of compensation," as it came to be known. By the turn of the century, this common prejudice had deepened. The almost complete absence of medical care for black people after Reconstruction had contributed to the spread of many health problems, not least of which was the killer-disease syphilis. It was now widely assumed that blacks were congenitally inferior to whites, both physically and intellectually. The fragile health of the Negro population was even offered up as proof of a fundamental physical frailty that would lead to the extinction of the race.

In fact, everyday life for most blacks was so onerous and educational opportunities so limited that this prejudice was grounded in reality. The situation became so dire that community leaders actually begged young men to pay more attention to their physical health. "Athletic sports must in the future play a larger part in the normal and mission schools of the South," W.E.B. Du Bois, a leading black intellectual, wrote, "and we must rapidly come to the place where the man all brain and no muscle is looked upon as almost as big a fool as the man all muscle and no brain."[7]

SEPARATE AND UNEQUAL

Both as a man and as a boxer, Jack Johnson challenged such smug assumptions. As a young boy, he never looked for handouts. By the sixth grade, he had quit school to work on a milk wagon for $1.25 per week. Taken by fantasies of the big city, Johnson left Galveston, Texas, for New York and Boston, only to return home after breaking his leg while working at a racetrack. When he was only sixteen years old, he skipped home again for Dallas. He made horse buggies and was befriended by an ex-boxer, who introduced him to the sport. For the first time in his life, Johnson had a passion and purpose. He became a regular at the local gym. Entranced by the possibility of making real money—he pocketed $25 after getting whipped in one four round match—he quit his job and joined a boxing troupe.

Johnson's skills were raw in 1895 when he first began traveling the Negro circuit. Only seventeen years old, he would regularly face off against fighters far more experienced than he. But no one intimidated him. Like many black fighters, he was forced to appear in vaudeville exhibitions, playing the docile Negro, flashing a wide smile while fiddling and tap dancing for white patrons. When even those opportunities dried up, he returned home to Texas, where he started serious training and turned his sights on the Negro title. By 1903, he was the black champion of the world, which unfortunately still left most doors jammed shut.

Although Negro boxers were shut out of most world championship fights, they regularly fought white opponents in lesser bouts. But the world heavyweight championship, which had come to symbolize the Anglo-Saxon ideal of white racial superiority, was white only. In 1904, Jim Jeffries, the undefeated white champion, declared self-righteously, "I will not fight a colored man." Apparently not wanting to appear intimidated by a Negro, however, Jeffries bragged, "I think I can lick him as I have the rest."[8] It was a safe boast because Jeffries was not about to risk losing to this "savage," which was how the press referred to Johnson. For his part, the black champion regularly taunted Jeffries, but to no avail. Two years later Jeffries retired, complaining that there was no competition. Johnson seethed.

Determined to get a shot at the title, Johnson signed with a white manager and fought the best challengers, black and white. It was no use. Few boxers would consider entering the ring against him. Black fighters were not eager to become his latest victim, and whites begged off, out of either fear or prejudice.

Almost five years slipped by. Johnson remained incorrigible, too hot to handle, refusing to tone down his defiant, very public profile, often traveling openly with two or three white prostitutes. According to legend, during sparring sessions he would jape white insecurities about black sexuality by wrapping his penis under his shorts to make it look bigger.

In 1908, his manager finally broke the logjam by offering Tommy Burns, a white Canadian who had succeeded to the world heavyweight crown, $30,000 to fight Johnson. It was a small fortune at that time. The boxers agreed to a title fight in Australia. The match was publicized as a battle between civilized man and the jungle. If his relatives had not been "rescued" from Africa by slaver traders, wrote one writer before the match, "Johnson might still be up a tree."

Burns, considered the overwhelming favorite, had agreed to the fight on condition that his manager be allowed to referee. That stipulation didn't help Burns much. Johnson floored the lumbering Canadian almost as soon as the fight started and continued to batter him almost at will. "There was all the hatred of 20,000 whites for all the negroes in the world," commented one postfight retrospective that portrayed Burns as a martyr to the cause of white supremacy. "The white beauty faced the black unlovingness, forcing the fight, bearing the punishment as if it were none. Weight and reach [of Johnson] were telling against intrepidity, intelligence and lightness [of Burns]."⁹ The police finally stepped in to stop the match in the fourteenth round.

By this time, the Aussies had come to appreciate Johnson. Blacks were overjoyed when word of the result reached the United States, but it was not greeted with much celebration by whites. Johnson's victory prompted an emotional appeal by Jack London, author of *Call of the Wild*, for the return of the "Great White Hope": "The fight!—There was no fight! . . . It had all the seeming of a playful Ethiopian at loggerheads with a small white man—of a grown man cuffing a naughty child. . . . But one thing now remains. Jim Jeffries must emerge from his alfalfa farm and remove the golden smile from Jack Johnson's face. Jeff, it's up to you."¹⁰

Johnson returned home and defended his title five times in one year against the best white challengers. That ensured his unpopularity. Turn-of-the-century America would not easily suffer a black heavyweight champion. Johnson was like an earlier-day Dennis Rodman, and his in-your-face persona and insistence on setting the white establishment on its ear evoked mixed feelings, even among blacks. He took on an Irish girlfriend, and when members of a hometown welcoming committee in Galveston demanded that he not bring her to a planned celebration, Johnson told them to "go to hell." His independence and his profession—boxing was considered to be degrading—irked the small middle-class Negro establishment, particularly black intellectuals, who feared his success would only confirm hated prejudices. "[White America] would accept from a Negro physical and athletic superiority," wrote William Pickens, a professor at Talladega College, "but . . . stand aloof when one approaches with moral or intellectual superiority."[11]

But others held with him. In the National Association of Colored People's official magazine, *Crisis,* Du Bois labeled boxing immoral but wrote that Johnson's greatest failing was his "unforgivable blackness"—he was the antithesis of an Uncle Tom.[12] "Although pugilism is that end of civilization that is adjacent to barbarism," seconded the *Chicago Defender,* "it was a good deal better for Johnson to win than for Johnson to have lost and all Negroes to have been killed in spirit by the preachments of inferiority."[13]

SNATCHING DEFEAT FROM THE JAWS OF VICTORY

With Johnson's victory over Burns, the drama had been cast. Jim Jeffries was cajoled out of retirement in 1910 to play the role of the "Great White Hope." He declared that he was "not going to disappoint . . . that portion of the white race that has been looking to me to defend its athletic superiority." To underscore the symbolic significance of the fight, the boxers agreed to meet on July 4 in Reno, Nevada. Because of the racial subtext, the Johnson-Jeffries match turned into the most anticipated sporting event in US history. Black churches held prayer vigils. Thirty thousand people crammed into Times Square to follow the action on the electronic news ticker.

Jeffries's return was anticlimactic, to say the least. He was alternately pummeled and jeered at by Johnson, in much the way that Muhammad Ali would toy with lesser fighters, black or white, when he was at the height of his powers. The ex-champ staggered around the ring spitting blood before the referee mercifully stepped in. Johnson made $70,000 for the win, which riled whites to no end.

After the fiasco no one dared suggest that blacks were cowards or that whites were naturally superior athletes. But the old order played a trump card. Physical prowess, once the proud domain of whites, might be ceded to a black man, but it would henceforth be considered of diminished value. Two days after Johnson pulverized Jeffries, the *Los Angeles Daily Times* published an editorial, "A Word to the Black Man," which summed up white sentiment towards the average black-on-the-street: "The white man's mental supremacy is fully established and for the present cannot be taken from him," it read.

> His superiority does not rest on any huge bulk of muscle, but on brain development that has weighed worlds and charmed the most subtle secrets from the heart of nature. Do not point your nose too high. Do not swell your chest too much. Do not boast too loudly. . . . Let not your ambition be inordinate or take a wrong direction. . . . Remember, you have done nothing at all. You are the same member of society you were last week. . . . You are on no higher a plane, deserve no new consideration, and you will get none.[14]

In case that expression of white supremacy was too subtle, whites took to the streets. On the night of Johnson's triumph, angry whites targeted celebrating blacks in New Orleans, Houston, and Philadelphia. One black was almost lynched in Baltimore, where seventy people were arrested. In Macon, Georgia, a mob of drunken whites went on a rampage. All told, thirteen blacks around the country were reported killed. The race riots that accompanied Johnson's victories prompted the federal government in 1912 to ban the interstate shipment of fight films, which were then popular movie-theater entertainment. Johnson became a marked man.

Johnson may have destroyed Jim Jeffries, but he fared less well against the federal government. That same year he was charged with crossing a state line to have sex with a young white woman. The verdict was a foregone conclusion. Deliberations by the all-white jury lasted less than two hours. Johnson was convicted and sentenced to a year in jail. Released on bail but banned from fighting in the

United States, Johnson married the white prostitute with whom he had been consorting and slipped off to Canada. He went on to barnstorm in Europe but was always short of money. In effect, the Internal Revenue Service succeeded in a way that no boxer could; it effectively destroyed his career—and with it his dignity and eventually his life.

Still heavyweight champion, Johnson finally agreed to fight Jess Willard in Havana in 1915 for $30,000. Thirty-two thousand people were on hand. The bout remains controversial to this day. According to most observers, the thirty-seven-year-old Johnson won the first twenty-four rounds, then fell to a sucker punch in the twenty-sixth.

Johnson, of course, was devastated. Bitter, he claimed that he had tanked as part of a deal with the promoters, whom he claimed had promised to help ease his way back to the United States. The story might very well have been true. During the last round Johnson supposedly looked over Willard's shoulder and signaled to his wife to leave with Jack Curley, Willard's partner and the man who put up the purse for the fight.[15]

After his victory, Willard announced that he would never give Johnson a rematch again or fight any black boxer. Willard's comments, made to a Negro paper, the *Chicago Defender*, may now be read as prescient by some.

> Jack Johnson did more to hurt his people than Booker Washington did to help them. I am not saying this in a mean way. I'm not excusing white men for feeling that way. I think it shows ignorance. But lots of white men did feel that way. Who doesn't remember all the sickening "white hope" business. And just as ignorant white men thought their race disgraced, so did a lot of ignorant colored men think that their race had been proved the better by Johnson's victory. That's why I'm going to draw the color line. I say this because I don't want anybody to think that I'm doing it from any mean, petty little prejudice.[16]

Willard was more or less bowing to public opinion, even among some middle-class blacks who were increasingly embarrassed by

Johnson. The former heavyweight champion was eventually allowed to return to the United States, but on condition that he go to jail. He spent eight months at Leavenworth and was made the prison's physical director before being released. But he was a broken man. Johnson even agreed to speak at a Ku Klux Klan rally in 1924.[17] He spent the following years in slow decline, fighting bulls in Barcelona, performing stunts in circuses, playing a comic version of Othello, and at sixty-eight, boxing all comers to scratch out an existence.[18]

Many boxing experts consider Jack Johnson the greatest fighter of all time. According to Arthur Ashe, he was the "most significant black athlete in history."[19] His reign, though celebrated by those who reveled in his defiance of segregated America, was anathema to many whites. At the championship level, boxing once again became a whites-only sport. As with every other sport in the United States, the path to opportunity was effectively blocked. The only real winner was Jim Crow.

CHAPTER 12

AMERICAN EUGENICS

The eugenics movement took a sensational turn in 1900 with the rediscovery of the half-century-old research of an Austrian monk—findings that would lay the foundation for our modern understanding of heredity. Working in his monastery in the 1850s and 1860s, Gregor Mendel became fascinated with raising peas in his experimental garden. He bred some thirty thousand plants, examining seed size, flower color, and plant size to determine how these attributes were passed along. He mated tall plants with short ones and found that all the offspring were tall. Yet when these hybrid tall plants were mated, one-quarter of the new plants were short.

Mendel concluded that genetic traits are the result of pairs of genes, one from each parent, each with a genetic message, in this case "tallness" or "shortness." It didn't matter which parent contributed which genetic message. Dominant traits such as tallness in peas would show up at a consistent ratio of 3 to 1. It was a revolutionary discovery but was greeted with yawns when this reclusive monk published his research in an obscure journal in 1865. The science intelligentsia was just too busy resisting the revolution over evolution unleashed by Darwin to take much notice.[1]

The rediscovery of Mendel's research in 1900—a number of botanists appear to independently have stumbled across his original paper—touched off a research boom that seemed to confirm Mendel's basic model of genetic inheritance. In the process, his work provoked a bitter battle between old-line social Darwinists and a new generation of geneticists. This new breed, inspired by the promise of eugenics, was committed to the project of replacing supposition with biometric data and unlocking, once and for all, the mystery of human inheritance.

Based on Mendel's discovery that a single gene determined height and a number of other traits, Harvard-educated zoologist Charles Davenport assumed, incorrectly it turned out, that there existed a single gene for human intelligence. "The idea of a 'melting pot,'" observed Davenport, "belongs to the pre-Mendelian age. Now we recognize that characters are inherited as units and do not readily break up."[2]

Emboldened by his new, if mistaken, perspective, Davenport established the Eugenics Record Office with financial backing from Andrew Carnegie. The organization's stated goal was to preserve the "national protoplasm" that Davenport was certain was found in Americans of Anglo-Saxon heritage. He collected massive data on everything from eye color to the number of people with hemophilia, albinism, athletic ability, and pauperism, all traits, that were inherited in a simple Mendelian model.

In a manner reminiscent of nineteenth-century craniometry, Davenport attempted to link physical features and personality traits. Based on any number of characteristics, he concluded that Poles were "independent and self-reliant, though clannish." Italians tended to "crimes of personal violence." Bohemians were given to "thieving," though not to "personal violence" like the Italians. "Hebrews" were thought to fall somewhere between slovenly Serbs and Greeks and the fastidious Swedes and Germans.[3]

Another leading American physician and physical anthropologist, Robert Bennett Bean, studied brain shape and facial features. He relied on an extensive collection of European anthropological studies on the brain and skull but frequently moved beyond his otherwise cautious scientific approach to speculate on the meaning of the differences he so carefully calibrated. Bean went so far as to speculate that the Jew's penchant for indignation had led to the evolution of pronounced noses.[4] He also devised his own racial rankings by analyzing the size of parts of the corpus callosum, the brain structure that contains fibers connecting the right and left hemispheres. Based on this analysis of the frontal lobes, he concluded that Negroes were less intelligent but more emotional than whites. He noted their "peculiar bumptiousness," and a general "instability of character . . . especially in connection with the sexual relation."[5]

Though the pronouncements of this new school of American eugenics are offensive by today's standards, the scientists who formulated them were, by and large, respected and respectable. Their work was very much mainstream, and their speculation, which they considered reasoned, sounded reasonable to an establishment convinced that it was threatened by an invasion of sorry immigrants from Europe. The scientific establishment even offered a progressive solution to the social chaos caused by flow of immigrants moving into Europe and from Europe to the United States: "positive eugenics," which would encourage society's elite to have more children, and "negative eugenics," which discouraged breeding and promoted sterilization among the lesser classes. If only "human matings could be placed upon the same high plane as that of horse breeding," Davenport mused. "The general program of the eugenicist is to improve the race by inducing young people to make a more reasonable selection of marriage mates; to fall in love intelligently. It also includes the control by the state of the propagation of the mentally incompetent."[6]

Although Davenport claimed that he opposed eliminating the "unfit," his reckless speculation about societal defectives served as a casual endorsement of social "cleansing." Eugenicists grouped those whom they judged "defective" under the umbrella term of feeblemindedness, a trait that was considered recessive. Social outcasts were considered to have a bad gene as well as "bad blood" that "no amount of education or good environment can change."[7]

INTELLIGENCE TESTING

The early infatuation with eugenics inspired the development of the first intelligence tests. An initial follower of craniometry, Alfred

Binet eventually came to believe it was little more than quackery. In 1904, at the request of the French government, he developed a range of tests designed to detect children who were underperforming in school and might need special help. "Our purpose is to be able to measure the intellectual capacities of a child who is brought to us in order to know whether he is normal or retarded," he wrote. "We do not attempt to establish or prepare a prognosis, and we leave unanswered the question of whether this retardation is curable, or even improvable."[8] Although Binet fashioned the concept of "mental age," he made it clear that he was not suggesting there was a hierarchy of intelligence or that intelligence was inborn.

Binet's ground breaking but cautiously written studies fell into the hands of American psychologist Henry Goddard, director of research at the Vineland Training School for the Feeble-Minded. Mendel's work had prompted Goddard to look for a genetic explanation for the mental illnesses he treated at his New Jersey institution. Echoing Davenport's oversimplified notion of intelligence, Goddard postulated that feeblemindedness could be explained by a single recessive gene and that intelligence was a single heritable trait, which came to be called "general intelligence" or *g*. In other words, the complex behaviors that make up the nebulous human quality we call "intelligence" could be expressed by a single number. He also argued that high intelligence not only aided in reasoning but underlay all moral behavior. Low intelligence was a serious societal problem that had to be attacked.

Although it was perhaps not his intention, Goddard opened the door for a ranking of individuals from genius to moron, and by implication for the intellectual ranking of races and ethnic groups. He later continued his work at Ellis Island, where he sampled arriving immigrants for signs of feeblemindedness. And by hitching morality to intelligence by attributing deviant and criminal behavior to inherited mental deficiencies, his well-publicized studies fed the xenophobia of the times.[9]

Goddard introduced intelligence testing to the United States, but Stanford University psychologist Lewis Terman turned it into a mass-market commodity. Terman extended Binet's scale to measure the teenaged years. In 1916, he revised it again to measure adult intelligence and rechristened it the Stanford-Binet. Terman had a strong prejudice that class and intelligence were linked and that prestige and income were direct measures of one's biological capacity.

> A low level of intelligence is very common among Spanish-Indian and Mexican families of the Southwest and also among Negroes. Their dullness seems to be racial, or at least inherent in the family stocks from which they come. . . . The writer predicts that . . . there will be discovered enormously significant racial differences in general intelligence, differences which cannot be wiped out by any scheme of mental culture. . . . From a eugenic point of view they constitute a grave problem because of their unusually prolific breeding.[10]

Intolerance was in the air, and it infected even those who viewed their work as a force for good. Under the supervision of Harvard psychologist Robert M. Yerkes, intelligence testing was soon adopted by the military, which set out to grade every army recruit. The testing would yield a eugenicists' map of American mental capacity that would have enormous influence in the coming decades. Based on this data, the average mental age of white adults was pegged at 13.08, a shade above moronic. Intelligence was correlated with skin color and geographic location. Nordics were the most intelligent. Russians had a mental age of 11.34, Italians 11.01, and Poles 10.74. Negroes tested at 10.41. Although the tests were supposed to measure "innate intelligence," they were filled with questions about baseball ("Who is Christy Mathewson?") and consumer products ("What is Crisco?"). Fully 89 percent of American blacks (and 37 percent of whites) under age 13 were projected to be morons.[11]

Although some of the assumptions of intelligence quotient (IQ) testers have proven fallacious, these early-century theorists are far from unindicted coconspirators of racism and genocide as they have been portrayed in some quarters. They were keenly aware of how the environment and culture might affect their data. However, their studies did become fodder for popular demagogic tracts by Lothrop

Stoddard, who attracted a cult following by warning against "mongrelization," while including in his writings almost all of the fashionable inflammatory generalizations, quarter-truths, and folk prejudices of the times.[12]

Stoddard's vitriol was matched only by the torrent of pseudo-science in *The Passing of a Great Race*, a 1916 polemic by Madison Grant, a close friend of Davenport. "The cross between a white man and an Indian is an Indian," Grant wrote. "The cross between a white man and a Hindu is a Hindu; and the cross between any of the three European races and a Jew is a Jew."[13]

This was not just empty rhetoric. In 1918, Davenport and Grant cofounded the Galton Society, dedicated to the study of "racial anthropology." Only Americans who were considered anthropologically "sound" were permitted to join. The society's members included some of the top scientists of the day, such as John Merriman, a leading biologist who became the society's president, and Henry Fairfield Osborn, a Columbia University paleontologist and president of the American Museum of Natural History's Board of Trustees.[14]

Osborn, who had written a glowing introduction to Grant's diatribe, would later expound on his own racialized view of intelligence. "The Negroid stock is even more ancient than the Caucasian and the Mongolians, as may be proved in an examination not only of the brain, of the hair, of the bodily characteristics ... but of the instincts, the intelligence," he wrote. "The standard of intelligence of the average adult Negro is similar to that of the eleven-year-old-youth of the species *Homo Sapiens*.[15]

Certainly not everyone was seduced by this "Nordic nonsense," which is what some called it, but a flood of racist tracts chalked up monumental sales in the United States. The country was gripped by xenophobia that was stirred up by the flood of immigrants and the war in Europe. Establishment America was consumed by the question of what to do with "defective" social outcasts and immigrants. "These new immigrants were no longer exclusively members of the Nordic race as were the earlier ones," Grant wrote. "Our jails, insane asylums and alms houses are filled with this human flotsam and the whole tone of American life, social, moral and political has been lowered and vulgarized by them."[16]

Shortly thereafter, Grant joined Davenport as appointees to the National Research Council, which was set up to design immigration-restriction legislation. Eugenics was key. "Sterilization," wrote Grant, "is a practical, merciful, and inevitable solution of the whole problem, and can be applied to an ever widening circle of social discards, beginning always with the criminal, the diseased, and the insane, and extending gradually to types which may be called weaklings rather than defectives, and perhaps ultimately to worthless race types."[17]

In 1924, Congress passed increased restrictions on immigration, which imposed quotas restricting immigration from what some believed to be biologically inferior areas in favor of immigrants from northern Europe.[18] "The United States Department of Agriculture already has stringent laws to prevent the importation of dangerous weeds, parasites and organisms of various kinds," wrote one prominent geneticist. "Is the inspection and supervision of human blood less important?"[19] Involuntary-sterilization legislation was ultimately enacted during the 1920s and 1930s in the United States, Canada, Denmark, and Norway, among many countries. As late as 1942, thirty states retained a ban on marriages between "whites and Negroes," purportedly to keep the white race from degrading.[20]

Until impending war softened the hardest edge of intolerance, some thirty-two states passed laws requiring sterilization of "degenerates," criminals, syphilitic Negroes, those judged mentally incompetent, and other social outcasts, as well as those convicted of drug or alcohol crimes. However, few states carried out purges; although Henry Goddard estimated that the United States was threatened by a "feebleminded menace" of as many as 400,000 people, fewer than 9,000 had been eugenically sterilized by 1928.[21]

PROGRESSIVE EUGENICS

Despite the heated rhetoric at the extremes, eugenics struck a hopeful chord with the Protestant establishment that had guided the United States and Europe through the nineteenth century and was now distressed by what it believed was a deep decay in moral values. By the mid-1920s more than 350 colleges reported teaching courses in eugenics, and eugenics institutes sprang up in almost every major city.

At the height of the movement's popularity, the American Eugenics Society was invited to erect an exhibit at the Sesquicentennial Exposition in Philadelphia in 1926. The display included a scoreboard, like today's national-debt clock, that flashed multicolored lights every forty-eight seconds to signal that a "mentally deficient" person was born in the United States. Only every seven and a half minutes did the country welcome "a high grade person . . . who will have the ability to do creative work and be fit for leadership." A nearby placard added, "How long are we Americans to be so careful for the pedigree of our pigs and chickens and cattle—and then leave the ancestry of our children to chance or to 'blind sentiment.'"[22]

Few were unaffected by this strong tide of hereditary thinking. Its message of the overall betterment of humanity crossed racial and ethnic barriers. As a result, unlike similar movements in Germany and like in Britain, American eugenics was never exclusively a movement of conservatives. Eugenics supporters included, with varying degrees of fervor, such political opposites as Davenport on the right, progressives Gifford Pinchot, H. G. Wells, Beatrice Webb, Charles Eliot, and Emma Goldman. Women, clamoring for moral purity, were particularly taken by the new science. Most mainline eugenicists were hardly feminists, however, because there was a general belief that higher education of women might divert attention from their preordained role as God's breeders. But eugenics did inspire supporters of the sex-education movement, such as Englishman Havelock Ellis, who believed teenagers should be instructed on sexual hygiene to ensure the propagation of the healthiest offspring.[23] Even the founder of Planned Parenthood, Margaret Sanger, was an eager although qualified supporter of eugenics before she became disillusioned with its increasingly elitist and racist focus.[24]

With extremism threatening to tar the promise of positive eugenics, a group of reformist eugenicists emerged. Conservative Ronald A. Fisher in England, moderate liberal Julian Huxley, utopian communist J.B.S. Haldane, and Hermann J. Muller, a Marxist who

would go on to win a Nobel Prize for his work in genetics, joined together to promote a generally progressive agenda, including the abolition of slums, fair wages, and a range of welfare programs from
improved housing to guaranteed education and health care. "Eugenics, in asserting the uniqueness of the individual, supplements the
American ideal of respect for the individual," wrote the distinguished American anthropologist Frederick Osborn, another reformist. "Eugenics in a democracy seeks not to breed men to a
single type, but to raise the average level of human variations."[25]

Although they were at odds politically, the scientists were united
by their belief that biology mattered and that humans were not born
with an empty slate of intellectual and emotional possibility (as
some environmentalists would later contend). And they were committed to doing the meticulous, peer-reviewed research needed to
bolster their convictions. "We can't do much practical eugenics,"
Huxley stated, "until we have more or less equalized the environmental opportunities of all classes and types, and this must be by
leveling *up*."[26] But despite their best efforts to save eugenics from being dismissed as a mutant sibling of Nazi ideology, the reformists
found themselves unable to hold back the extremist tide. Muller
would write sorrowfully that eugenics had become "hopelessly per-
verted" by "advocates of race and class prejudice, defenders of vested
interests of church and state, Fascists, Hitlerites and reactionaries
generally."[27]

THE VIRUS OF WORLD RACISM

The United States was but a microcosm for the racist-tinged ultra-
nationalism that prevailed in much of the world leading up to World
War II. The post–World War I boom in industrial production and living
standards had given way to a prolonged slump in trade and heavy industry. Germany, previously the engine of Europe, grappled with runaway inflation, political instability, and heavy reparations to pay off its
war debts. It wasn't until the late 1920s that Europe began to stand on
its wobbly collective feet.

Then in 1929, prosperity came to a crashing end with the stock market debacle and a financial panic. World unemployment doubled within a year. The postwar hope of international reconciliation shattered into competing factions driven by nationalist and ethnic chauvinism. The scapegoats were the ethnic minorities, particularly Negroes and Jews, who were easily identifiable by their skin color or anatomical stereotypes. Like blacks, Jews were believed to have disproportionately sized skulls; prominent jaws; and distinctively shaped noses, lips, and earlobes. These stereotypes conferred an illusory biological legitimacy on discrimination.

Escalating public hysteria hit black Americans particularly hard. Blacks were regularly terrorized on the basis of white paranoia that they planned to Africanize America through indiscriminate breeding. Breeding became a catchword that scientists wielded when nigger was considered too blunt. Samuel J. Holmes, a University of California at Berkeley biologist, suggested that the stock of Negroes might improve appreciably if society encouraged the "bleaching" of the race through miscegenation.[28] But the standard view was that blacks were unsalvageable and that the mixing of the races would prove disastrous.

New data were sometimes massaged to fit the predetermined predilection. When one study found that blacks who lived in Northern cities did better, on average, on army IQ tests than certain white groups in the rural South, the accepted explanation was "selective migration." Psychologist Otto Klineberg challenged this hypothesis in his groundbreaking study "Negro Intelligence and Selective Migration." He proposed instead that the superior test performance of Northern blacks was the result of a more supportive cultural environment.[29] For the most part, neither the extremist naturists or nurturists seriously pondered whether both genetics and culture could play a role in test scores.

Race science became so much the rage and so mainstream among middle- and upper-class Americans that its perceived potential to improve humanity made it popular even among ethnic groups that were themselves targets, including blacks and Jews. In a Mother's Day sermon delivered during the 1920s, Kansas City Rabbi

Harry H. Mayer went so far as to declare, "May we do nothing to permit our blood to be adulterated by infusion of blood of inferior grade."[30]

Eugenics also held out the possibility of managing birth rates in the black community. Kelly Miller, one of the leading black writers of this period, was deeply concerned about the low fertility rate of the black intellectual elite.[31] Inspired by the vision of positive eugenics, W.E.B. Du Bois, the founder of the NAACP, even mused how the "talented tenth" of the Negro population should be the focus of efforts to ensure the mainstreaming of the black community. He came out strongly in favor birth control, which was seen as a powerful tool for reducing infant mortality and poverty. "The mass of significant Negroes, particularly in the South, still breed carelessly and disastrously," wrote Du Bois, "with the result that the increase among ignorant Negroes, even more than among whites, is [in] that portion of the population least intelligent and fit, and least able to rear children properly."[32]

Swept up by the optimism of the "Roaring Twenties," it seemed that most black and white intellectuals considered themselves eugenicists.

CHAPTER 13

JESSE OWENS

AND THE GERMAN RACE

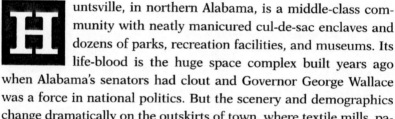untsville, in northern Alabama, is a middle-class community with neatly manicured cul-de-sac enclaves and dozens of parks, recreation facilities, and museums. Its life-blood is the huge space complex built years ago when Alabama's senators had clout and Governor George Wallace was a force in national politics. But the scenery and demographics change dramatically on the outskirts of town, where textile mills, paper plants, and chemical factories give way to cotton fields that stretch as far as the eye can see. Broken-down barns dot the countryside, and, if the light is just right, with a squint of the eye, a ramshackle sharecropper's house might appear in the distance.

In the tiny town of Oakville, thirty miles southwest of Huntsville, there are two road markings likely to catch the eye of a tourist. Along County Road 203 is an impressive sign commemorating Oakville's most distinguished former resident: "Jesse Owens Memorial Park," it reads. Down the road a piece, on the other side of 203, is a hand-scrawled sign slapped on a bridge overlooking a gully. Its sign, misspelled in block letters, is not so uplifting: "Nigerville 3 miles." More than sixty years after Jesse Owens returned to the United States from Berlin as America's most famous athlete, the racial strains that roiled the south are not healed.

It took more than a dozen years and a determined effort in the face of a largely indifferent white community to honor Owens with the park. First authorized in 1983 by the born-again integrationist Governor Wallace, the project languished for lack of funds. A few local residents did manage to clear some weed-infested fields, build a basketball court, erect a flagpole, and put up two granite markers. "On this site in 1914 was born Jesse Owens, all-time track great," read one marker, although Owens was actually born across the way in 1915. "He inspired a world enslaved in tyranny and brought hope to his fellow man," read the other marker.[1]

The project finally got back on track when the Atlanta Olympic Committee decided to route the torch relay through town. A few local residents complained—one woman who was asked to donate some siding from her broken-down barn to build a replica of the sharecropper's house in which Owens was born, flat-out refused. "I won't give nothin' to a nigger project," she said.[2] But the times had changed and most of the county, more than 80 percent white, supported the memorial. Finally, in 1996, eighty-two years after he was born, Oakville dedicated the park, complete with sports facilities, a museum, and a towering statue of Owens, to its favorite son.

Few whites, or blacks for that matter, can appreciate the terrorizing grip that race had on America during Owens's childhood years. Segregation was a given. In the rural South, the issue was frequently survival more than opportunity. Owens's parents headed north in the early 1920s to Cleveland, which was prospering as a result of the industrial boom. There were few chances for advancement, but there were jobs, and day-to-day existence was measurably better than in the rural South.

Life for Owens, as for most working-class Negro children, revolved around the church and school. The boys played late afternoon stickball games. Everyone talked baseball, and everyone worshipped Leroy "Satchel" Paige, the fireball-throwing phenom who had begun his career on a Negro league team in Alabama. Desperate for heroes, the black press fawned over Paige, Jesse "Nip" Winters, Raleigh "Biz" Mackey, James "Cool Papa" Bell, and Josh Gibson, chronicling their every home run and trumpeting occasional exhibition triumphs against all-white teams.

The sudden emergence of national black superstar athletes presented a dilemma for the churchgoing black community. It had long made a point of downplaying athletic success, instead stressing schooling as a way to accelerate assimilation into white society and shake the image of black inferiority. That strategy had not opened many doors. Now sports offered a more promising path to acceptance.

"That the Negro was deficient in the qualities of which athletic champions are made," Elmer Cater wrote in *Opportunity* in 1933, "was long one of the accepted shibboleths of the American people. That rare combination—stamina, skill, and courage—it was commonly believed were seldom found under a black skin. Like many other myths concerning the Negro, this myth is being exploded, not by theory, nor argument, but by performance."[3]

THE EMERGENCE OF THE DOMINANT BLACK SPRINTER

The English in the late nineteenth century were the first to set up formal track competitions, eventually exporting their love of the sport to the United States and north to Scotland, Ireland, and Finland. For years, up until World War I, whites from these countries dominated running, although a handful of blacks who had gotten a chance to compete while in college regularly challenged for the unofficial title of "world's fastest runner."

After the war, which ever so slightly pried open the door of opportunity for blacks in the United States, the color of elite running began to change. Among the top black stars, Harvard's Ned Gourdin in 1921 became the first person to break the 25-foot barrier in the long jump. The *New York Telegram* called his 25-foot, 3-inch leap "almost impossible . . . the greatest feat in track and field in a generation."[4] Three years later he won a silver medal in the event at the 1924 Olympics. The next year, William DeHart Hubbard broke Gourdin's mark with a leap of 25 feet, 10⅞ inches. Hubbard also lowered the 100-yard dash record to 9.6 seconds, before graduating from the University of Michigan—one of only eight blacks in a class of 1,456.[5]

The black domination of the sprints began at the 1932 Los Angeles Olympics. Three of the four blacks on the team won their events, the first individual gold medals won by African Americans. In one of the most exciting moments, two Negro runners, Ralph Metcalfe and Thomas "Eddie" Tolan, Jr., battled neck-and-neck in the 100 meters before Tolan eked out a win in world-record time. Tolan went on to set the Olympic record in the 200 meters, and teammate Ed Gordon won the long jump.[6]

The medals were headline news. "Colored Boys Sports Threat: Athletic Prominence Grows Year After Year," screamed the *Los Angeles Times of Sunday*. "Two more Olympic Games—three at the most—and the black man will dominate American Olympic track and field teams," noted sports writer Paul Lowry. The key to black success, wrote Lowry, was inner focus, or a "natural" ability to stay relaxed:

[The Black athlete] has the ease and grace and natural ability without the white man's besetting sin—tension. No colored man is ever beaten because he ties up. The white athlete is temperamental. He strains and presses on the day of the big race and away go his chances. The Negro is emotional to a high degree, but he is equal to do big things in a relaxed manner. [Black boys] don't press when they try hard. . . . They are confident to the point of cockiness. . . .[7]

The same year that Germany's Weimar Republic formally gave way to Adolf Hitler's Nazi regime, 1933, the state Supreme Court upheld an Ohio State University decision to ban "colored girls" from living in close proximity to whites. That fall, James Cleveland Owens, nicknamed Jesse, entered OSU, much to the chagrin of many in the black community. "Why help advertise an institution that majors in prejudice?" editorialized the *Chicago Defender*.[8]

Although Owens faced prejudice every day—he and his black friends were forced to live in off-campus housing and weren't allowed in university restaurants—he flourished on the track. At the collegiate championships in 1935, in one of the most remarkable days in track history, Owens broke three world records—in the 220-

yard dash, the 220-yard low hurdles, and the long jump—and tied the 100-yard-dash record.

The black press was understandably unabashedly effusive. "Owens . . . is without doubt the greatest individual performer the world has ever known,"[9] enthused the *Norfolk Journal and Guide*. Sports writer Roi Ottley of New York's *Amsterdam News* wrote that "the Negro has lifted himself to a dominating position in track and field. The Negro is not only keeping pace, but he is frankly surpassing the efforts of his white brothers."[10]

This emergence of black sprinters spurred a change in public perceptions about black athletes. "A theory has been advanced," mused a *New York Times* writer, "that through some physical characteristic of the race involving the bone and muscle construction of the foot and leg, the Negro is ideally adapted to the sprints and jumping events."[11] After being dismissed for years as not having the proper physique, their athletic accomplishments were now being devalued by conjecture about their "natural" animal-like physiology.

The recent emergence of so many black stars had inspired a spate of speculation, including a prediction by E. Albert Kinley, a noted X-ray specialist, that blacks would go on to set world records in events that depended upon leverage because of an elongated heel bone special only to blacks.[12] Kinley turned out to be right about the records. What about the elongated heel?

The eugenics craze drew some distinguished black scientists into the debate, including William Montague Cobb, a former professor at Howard University and the only African American to hold a doctorate in physical anthropology until after World War II. Cobb convened a team from Case Western Reserve University in 1936 to measure preserved skeletons of blacks and whites to test the hypothesis that long heel bones, a high arch, flat feet, longer tendons in the calf muscles, and long lower limbs were keys to the success of black sprinters.

Cobb's team of investigators concluded that there was a range of facial and body-types among blacks that defied easy classification. "There is not one single physical feature, including skin color, which all our Negro champions have in common which would definitely identify them as Negroes," Cobb wrote. He contended that "split-second" differences in the performance of black and white sprinters were insignificant and found it unconvincing that "Negroid physical characters are anatomically concerned with the present dominance of Negro athletes in national competition."[13]

The researchers went on to compare Owens with the top white runner of the day, Frank Wykoff, who at that time shared the world record in the 100-yard dash with Owens (and would finish fourth at the Berlin Games). Cobb commented that Owens had what was commonly thought to be a typically Caucasian calf muscle, with a long belly and short tendon, while Wykoff had what was believed to be a classic "Negroid" musculature. In other words, he believed that any generalization about black and white body types would prove ridiculous. "The margins separating the performances of White and Negro stars," Cobb concluded, "have been insignificant from an anthropological standpoint" to explain "the present dominance of Negro athletes in national competition in the short dashes and the broad jump."[14]

Cobb also dismissed as "pseudo-scientific" a number of voguish ideas, including the notions that blacks possessed an "inward serenity," "thicker skin," or smaller "viscera" (heart, lungs, kidneys, liver, spleen).[15] By the end of his study he was thoroughly unimpressed by the theories that blacks were innately better athletes, or even significantly different.

Curiously, Cobb's own data were far more intriguing than his sweeping pronouncements might suggest. For instance, he administered a "tapping test" of Owens's reaction time. Many scientists believe, and tests have since suggested, that blacks of West African ancestry, such as African Americans, on average have quicker reflexes than whites. Cobb reported that Owens was "exceptionally fast with his right arm and above average with his left," but chose to draw no conclusion.[16] Three years later, with the public debate of racial aptitude raging and the place of the Negro in American society so unsettled, Cobb appeared to reverse himself in reporting the results of the reaction test. In the absence of any new evidence, he now declared that Owens's reflexes "were no speedier than those of the average person."[17]

Cobb's definitive conclusions did little to dent speculation. Dean Cromwell, the head coach of the US Olympic team at the Berlin Games, would come to extol the special anatomical and psychological advantages of black athletes. "The Negro excels in the events he does because he is closer to the primitive than the white man," he wrote in *Championship Technique in Track and Field* in 1941. "It was not long ago that his ability to sprint and jump was a life-and-death matter to him in the jungle. His muscles are pliable, and his easy-going disposition is a valuable aid to the mental and physical relaxation that a runner and jumper must have."[18]

As a result of the success of black sprinters, the former stereotype of the weak-stomached black malingerer who could tap-dance up a storm but was otherwise unemployable was reworked. "For years it had been said that Negroes can sing and dance," wrote Harry F.V. Edwards, a black sprinter on the 1920 British Olympic team. "From now on we will hear the platitude that all Negroes can run and jump."[19] He was correct.

Comments about black athletic superiority had a darker echo when it came to morality and intelligence. For example, London physician Francis Crookshank took it upon himself to figure out why blacks, whites, and Asians were so different in athletic ability and social behavior. In a widely disseminated theory, he proposed that the races were actually different species. The Negro evolved from the gorilla, the Mongolian from the orangutan, and Caucasians from the chimpanzee, he maintained. Crookshank thus concluded that whites were the most intelligent of the human races because chimps were the most intelligent of the anthropoids. Reflecting the popular polygenist perspective, he concluded that blacks therefore must be of a "lower race."[20]

THE RISE OF THE GERMAN SUPERMAN

The young Adolf Hitler developed an obsession with the concept of evolution, or at least his version of it. Whiling away the time in jail after his failed Beer Hall Putsch in 1924, he claims to have come upon an internationally recognized textbook on genetics, *Human Heredity*, written by German biologists Erwin Baur, Eugen Fischer, and Fritz Lenz. Hitler twisted eugenics to serve his political version of "survival of the fittest." By his measure, Germans were the obviously superior Aryans. The title of his autobiography, *Mein Kampf*, translated as *My Struggle*, is widely thought to be a play on Darwin's *On the Origin of Species*, which is subtitled "Struggle for Existence." Later Hitler would write that "environmental influences have never been known to bring about the formation of a new race. That is one more reason for our belief that a Jew remains a Jew, in Germany or in any other country. He can never change his race, even by centuries of residence among other people."[21]

Hitler was in step with German attitudes about race. Even before the end of World War I, the movement for racial hygiene had taken hold in Germany as it had in most Western countries, although it was embraced with a unique fervor, no doubt a reflection of the German romantic tradition. Eugenic science was institutionalized in 1918 with the creation of the Kaiser Wilhelm Institute for Research and Psychiatry. Nine years later, the government founded the Institute for Anthropology, Human Genetics, and Eugenics to research ways to help restore racial purity and strength to greater Germany. Fischer was named its first director.[22]

Yet even as late as the early 1930s, the German racial hygiene movement was not overtly anti-Semitic but was part of the mainstream international eugenics movement. It focused more on preserving the Aryan race, which German eugenicists believed was threatened by war and, ironically, modern medicine, which kept alive congenitally inferior people who then went on to have children. On the other hand, Lenz made no bones of the fact that he thought of Jewishness as indelible, writing that "Jews do not transform themselves into Germans by writing books on Goethe."[23] Although Jews were less than 1 percent of the German population, it was widely perceived that they had disproportionate influence in medicine and the arts.

Under Hitler's direction, and with widespread popular support from both liberals and rightists, Heinrich Himmler established the

Task Force of Hereditary Experts to begin drafting sterilization laws. The Law for the Prevention of Genetically Diseased Offspring set up "genetic health courts" to decide who should be sterilized because of genetic deficiencies. The courts originally targeted schizophrenics, psychotics, epileptics, and severe alcoholics, but they broadened their range over the years. The Hereditary Biology and Racial Research Institute was established at Frankfurt University to begin applying all of the new research on the mentally and racially "defective."

As his hold on German society tightened, Hitler showed no compunction about enlisting top German scientists to further his ambition of racial purification. For the most part there was eager complicity. "We geneticists and racial hygienists," said geneticist Otmar Baron von Verschuer with evident pride, "have been fortunate to have seen our quiet work in the scholar's study and the scientific laboratory find application in the life of the people."[24] Lenz, who later headed up the Kaiser Wilhelm Institute, which was transformed by the Nazis into a temple of racial science, would say that "National Socialism is nothing but applied biology."[25]

The subversion of Nazi science was complete. Articles appeared regularly in the Nazi anthropological and genetics journal *Volk und Raase* (People and Race) extolling the Nordic profile of a young athlete, tall, long-headed, with blue eyes and blond hair.[26] A Swiss anthropologist actually examined a sample of 250 draftees from three German-speaking cantons for evidence of racial purity. The Nordic stereotype was not found in a single individual.[27] "The ideal Aryan," it was later said with understandable sarcasm, "was as blond as Hitler, as long-headed as Göring, and as tall as Goebbels."[28]

THE BOYCOTT FIZZLES

The International Olympic Committee signaled in May 1931 that Germany was being welcomed back into the world community when it awarded the 1936 Games to Berlin. It was a coup for Hitler and his supporters, who viewed the Olympics as an opportunity to showcase National Socialism. Hitler was intent on rebuilding the romantic notion of the Aryan superman. Spectacle played a major role in Nazi folklore; the combination of sport, nationalism, and militarism offered a dramatic vehicle for the Aryan message of racial pride.

After being appointed chancellor in January 1933, Hitler launched his campaign called *Judenrein* (literally Jew-clean). He used the pretext of an arson fire at the Reichstag in February to assume emergency powers, suspending freedoms of speech, assembly, and press. The first concentration camp was opened at Dachau in March. On April 1, Jews were excluded from government employment, including teaching jobs. These internal crackdowns prompted calls for an international boycott of the Games. The Amateur Athletic Union, then the most powerful of American amateur sport bodies, passed a resolution in November declaring that the United States should not compete in the Games if the situation in Germany did not change for the better.[29]

But Avery Brundage, then president of the American Olympic Committee, was adamant in his opposition to any protest. He publicly argued that politics had no place in sports; privately he was scornful of the Jews, liberals, Catholics, and unionists, who were pressing the issue. He would speak of a "Jewish-Communist conspiracy" to keep the United States out of the Games and would write in the AOC paper, *American Athletes,* that America should steer clear of the "Jew-Nazi altercation."[30] His views were not uncommon.

In early 1934, Brundage finally bowed to public pressure and organized a high-profile but tightly managed visit by American Olympic officials to Germany. Much to the outrage of many Jews, he returned with effusive praise for the "new" Germany and its treatment of Jewish athletes.[31] "Certain Jews must now understand that they cannot use these Games as a weapon in their boycott against the Nazis," said Brundage.[32]

Although a few black organizations and newspapers such as the NAACP, the *New York Amsterdam News,* and the *Cleveland Gazette* supported a walkout—"Refusal to participate," ran an editorial in the *Gazette,* "would do untold good in helping Germany and the world to realize that racial bigotry must be opposed in its every manifestation"[33]—the black press in general was adamantly opposed. The *Pittsburgh Courier-Journal*, which was nationally circulated and considered the most influential black newspaper in the United States, published a series of editorials blasting the boycott sympathizers. Many blacks felt it hypocritical that so much attention was being paid to a minority in Germany while blacks in the United States still suffered so many inequities. Talk of a boycott was perceived by some African Americans as Jewish-inspired. Jews were occasionally tarred by blacks (and many whites) with a familiar stereotype of the money-grubbing shyster and blamed for a host of ills, among them the Depression.[34]

As the Olympics approached, most blacks eagerly anticipated the opportunity to show up the Nazis while exposing Jim Crow racism in America. In some aspects, race relations had begun to improve as a result of the social leveling caused by the Depression and the structural changes brought about by the New Deal and organized labor. A *Baltimore Afro-American* reporter would write that success in the Games offered an opportunity to raise up the "despised darker races and lower the prestige of the proud and arrogant Nordic."[35]

The discussion over what came to be called the Nuremberg Laws brought the boycott question to a head in the summer of 1935. "Neither Americans nor the representatives of other countries can take part in the Games in Nazi Germany without acquiescing in the contempt of the Nazis for fair play and their sordid exploitation of the Games," wrote International Olympic Committee member Ernest Lee Jahncke, a German American and a former assistant secretary of the Navy, in a letter to Count Henri Baillet-Latour, president of the IOC. But Brundage would have none of this public defiance. After maneuvering behind the scenes, Jahncke was forced to resign from the IOC in July, and Brundage was elected to take his place.[36]

That same summer, the president of the AAU, Judge Jeremiah Mahoney, adamantly backed a boycott, pointing out that Germany had already broken the Olympic rules forbidding discrimination based on race and religion. But Brundage would not give an inch, and President Franklin D. Roosevelt stood by the forty-year tradition of allowing the IOC to operate independent of government intervention.

Hitler poured more fuel on the fire when, over two nights in September, during the meeting of the Reichstag at the annual National Socialist Party rally, he and his top aides put the Nuremberg Laws into place. They would effectively exclude Jews from German life and mark the most conspicuous of Germany's "racial undesirables" as second-class citizens. The "Blood Protection Law," officially known as "For the Protection of German Blood and German Honour," made it illegal for "Aryans" and Jews to have sexual relations. These new laws were championed by some in the German science establishment as public health measures based on sound, scientific knowledge of the genetic defects of Jews and others.

In December, with Brundage pulling every string available, the AAU defeated the boycott resolution by two-and-a-half votes. The black press cheered the decision and even the few black papers who had voiced support for a boycott fell into line. Even after Hitler's army moved into the previously demilitarized Rhineland in the early spring of 1936, touching off renewed cries for a boycott, it was clear that the Nazi Olympics would not be derailed.

THE BERLIN GAMES

Berlin emerged as a grand battlefield not only between fascism and freedom, and Nordic purity versus the ethnic "melting pot" of America, but between propagandists for both the Nazis and the west. The emergence of the African American athlete did not escape the attention of Hitler, who was determined to restore the purity of the bloodlines. German propaganda portrayed blacks as "monstrosities halfway between man and ape." The official Nazi newspaper *Völkischer Beobachter* began editorializing that blacks should be excluded from the games or the "sacred grandeur of the Olympiad" might be destroyed.[37] These remarks fell on deaf ears in the United States.

In contrast, black newspapers celebrated the moment, for the
U.S. team had by far the largest number of African Americans ever,
sixteen men and two women. All of the athletes came from predominantly white universities, which provided fodder for black journalists who made much of the inferior facilities and training equipment
at mostly black colleges.

When the SS Manhattan, carrying the U.S. team arrived in Bre-
merhaven on August 24, friendly German autograph-seekers
mobbed Owens and his seventeen black teammates. There were
twelve track-and-field athletes, four boxers, and two weight lifters.
On opening day the anticipation of the battles to come between the
black American and the Nordic stars rippled through the crowd.
Hitler was in attendance. After watching two Germans and a Finn
win gold medals, he personally congratulated them at his stadium
box. As the afternoon wore on, it grew dark and rain began to fall.
Soon after, Cornelius Johnson, a black American, won the high jump
with his black teammate David Albritton winning the silver medal.
Before the playing of the U.S. national anthem, Hitler and his en-
tourage slipped out of the stadium.

The American press, particularly the tabloid newsreels which embraced the propaganda spin of the moment, wrote that Hitler had
"stormed" out of the stadium in a "tantrum." The *New York Times*
proclaimed, "Hitler greets all medalists except Americans," which
turned out not to be accurate. Owens did not actually compete until
the following day. By this time the original incident, which had become so distorted, was a cause célèbre and soon to be part of the
folklore of the Games. The adverse publicity led to an unusual rebuke of the Führer by the IOC, which asked that Hitler publicly
greet all or none of the winners. Hitler decided that thereafter he
would not personally greet any of the gold-medal winners.[38]

It was not until the second day of the Games that Owens began
his quest for a record four gold medals. At first, he denied having
been snubbed, but he soon gave in to the hyperbole as the event took
on a life of its own. Each day, the German spectators gave Owens
the warmest of receptions after every race, including the heats. According to his coach, Larry Snyder, one German coach stared in-

tently at Owens "like a scientist studying a rare species of fauna." The German athletes, rather than keeping their distance, gathered around him like awestruck teenagers.[39]

Owens flourished in the spotlight, out-jumping his German rival Carl "Luz" Long in the long jump, setting an Olympic mark at 200 meters, and running the leadoff leg in a win in the relays. Including his victory over teammate Metcalfe in the 100 meters, in a race that also included an East Asian and three whites, Owens racked up four gold medals in total. "The Führer was furious that his Nordics were unable to beat Owens," ran a newsreel playing at American movie houses.[40]

All told, American blacks won six individual gold medals, eight golds in all, and accounted for 83 of the U.S. team's 167 total points, all scored in track-and-field events. "Mack" Robinson, Jackie Robinson's older brother, took a silver in the 200-meter dash. The medal haul lit up the black community. The *Pittsburgh Courier-Journal* opined, "Hitler is an individual envious of talent, suspicious of high character, devoid of chivalry, bereft of culture, a cowardly effeminate, who proved incapable of being a gentleman even at the Olympic Games where prejudice and politics are traditionally taboo."[41]

Privately, minister of propaganda Goebbels called the victories by blacks a "disgrace." German reporters scrambled to turn around the embarrassment and shape it according to Nazi propaganda. They pumped up the myth of the invincible black athlete as an excuse. There were stories of a sorrowful "physical decline" in white American athletes that was so serious that the United States could not hope to compete in sports or war without its "black legion" of "differently bred" gladiators.[42] "If the American team had not brought along 'Black auxiliaries,' editorialized one Nazi paper, "one would have regarded the United States as the biggest disappointment of the Games."[43]

In truth, although Owens's wins may have dampened Hitler's spirit, the hurt was little more than a bruise. Hitler's new Germany dominated the Berlin Games, destroying the competition in many events and finishing far ahead of the United States in medals, with fascist Italy a close third. The victories by Owens and his teammates provided some cover for what otherwise was a stunning loss for the U.S. team, which had racked up the most gold medals and total medals at every Olympics since the 1908 Games.

In fact, master Nazi filmmaker Leni Riefenstahl used the Berlin Olympics as a backdrop to produce and direct *Olympia*, which idealized German athletes as übermenschen, or supermen, and is widely considered a classic work of propaganda. Rather than being humiliated as myth has it, Hitler and his minions made international hay out of the propaganda masterpiece and German Olympic *blitzkrieg*, foreshadowing what was to come across the far wider playing field of continental Europe.

Nevertheless, much of America was jubilant and united, at least briefly and if only superficially. Of course there was still the usual sports-writer hyperbole, with glowing references to our "Ethiopian phalanx."[44] But the triumphs of the black athletes were widely seen as an incentive for black Americans in general to work their way into the country's mainstream. For the first time, whites didn't just admire the singular skills of one anomalous overachiever, they celebrated their black countrymen. With the possible exception of the Joe Louis–Max Schmeling heavyweight boxing match in 1938, no sport event so captured the imagination of the black press as the 1936 Olympics.[45]

The victories at Berlin also provoked some American newspapers to highlight the hypocrisy of the fact that Negroes could be stars in Berlin and second-class citizens on their return home. The black press made noise over the fact that Owens could order a meal at any restaurant in Hitler's Berlin, but not in F.D.R.'s Washington, D.C. No one should underestimate the subtle effect these victories had on opening the minds of many whites who had never given racial issues much thought. But the stark reality remained: Owens's triumphs were a supernova in the life of black America. Few blacks were even allowed to participate in American sports, and all blacks, athletes and nonathletes, had to make their way in a society dominated economically by whites.

Within hours after winning his fourth gold medal, the AAU dispatched him and his teammates on a ten-day racing tour of Europe.

It was a huge public relations and financial bonanza, but it took a toll on the exhausted Owens. He raced eight times, losing eleven pounds in the process. When the AAU ordered him to Sweden for more exhibitions, he declined, asking to be allowed to go home. As a result, Owens was later suspended and thrown out of amateur sports.

Owens and his teammates were treated as war heroes when they finally arrived back on American shores after the exhibition meets. They were treated to a ticker tape parade by New York City Mayor La Guardia, who singled out Owens as an "American that all America should be proud of."[46] Owens was feted again soon after when he returned to his hometown of Cleveland.

The moment in the sun faded all too quickly. After the celebrations, Owens could line up only a fleeting job with the Atlantic Richfield Company. Although he would later be named "Athlete of the Half-Century" by the Associated Press, he was dismissed by some as more brawn than brains. Owens was soon reduced to vaudeville, racing against horses, trains, and motorcycles in Mexico and Reno. "People say that it was degrading for an Olympic champion to run against a horse," Owens remarked years later. "But what was I supposed to do? I had four gold medals, but you can't eat four gold medals. There was no television, no big advertising, no endorsements then. Not for a black man, anyway."[47]

Still, Owens and other blacks who ran to prominence between the two world wars had made a statement with their victories that no one could ignore. Unlike in the great American team sports of football, basketball, and baseball, in running (along with boxing), blacks could not be so easily dismissed as short on talent. "Perhaps because the judging of track races is so objective," wrote Arthur Ashe, Jr., "it was relatively difficult for white authorities to deny any talented runner his or her rightful place on the starting line."[48] Even though few blacks had the leisure time or the financial resources to compete in running, those who made it to the start line proved that this was a sport that blacks could dominate. In sprinting, at least, individual dedication and natural talent prevailed.

CHAPTER 14

A KNOCKOUT BLOW

TO RACE SCIENCE

Black America rode a roller coaster of emotions in the 1930s. Along with the tremendous success of Jesse Owens and his teammates in Berlin, and the revival of the Negro National League, which had collapsed in the early days of the Depression, there was the meteoric rise and fall and rise again of boxer Joe Louis. In 1935, Louis captured New York in a triumphant debut, when he buckled the "Italian Ox," Primo Carnera. That sixth-round knockout was particularly sweet for the black community with Mussolini's troops poised to conquer Ethiopia, an independent nation and another source of pride for many American blacks.

"When I walked into church" after beating Carnera, Louis marveled later, "you'd have thought I was the Second Coming of Christ. I was to uplift the spirit of my race. I must make the whole world know that Negro people were strong, fair and decent."[1]

The white press conferred star status on the young heavyweight for the fight was portrayed as a battle between Italian fascism and American democracy. The accolades were clouded by the usual array of racial stereotypes, however. Like Jesse Owens, Louis was hailed as a "role model" for young black children and a "credit to his race." While not necessarily submissive, he learned to play to type, adopting a compliant manner that would serve him well with the media, as long as he was winning. The lesson of Jack Johnson loomed large.

Joseph Louis Barrow was born in 1914 into poverty in a sharecropper's shack in Alabama, the seventh of eight children. When he was twelve, he moved to Detroit where his stepfather had gotten a job in the Ford auto factory. By the age of 17, he had quit school and was himself working in an auto plant. But he was also learning how to box on the side, using money that his mother had given him for violin lessons to join a recreation center.

Louis's boxing career almost ended before it started. In his first amateur fight, against Johnny Miller, a member of the 1932 Olympic team, he was floored seven times in two rounds before the fight was mercifully stopped. But he picked himself off the canvas and quit his job to devote himself to boxing full-time. He dropped the name Barrow and took on his mother's maiden name of Louis. He was soon storming his way through the light-heavyweight ranks. Over the next year he won 50 of 54 amateur fights, 43 by knockout.

Despite his great talent, Louis at first had found it almost impossible to break through the race wall that had been reinforced in the years since Jack Johnson had been driven out of the sport. He had realized that to succeed in America he would need the help of sympathetic whites. As it happened, his victory streak attracted the attention of two Chicago fight managers, John Roxborough and his partner, trainer Jack Blackburn. Blackburn knew he had a project on his hands when he first agreed to work with Louis in 1934. "You know, boy," he said, "the heavyweight division for a Negro is hardly likely. If you ain't gonna be another Jack Johnson, you got some hope. The white man hasn't forgotten that fool nigger with his white women."[2] Roxborough, warned the young fighter that his toughest battles would not be in the ring. "For God's sake," he said, "after you beat a white opponent, don't smile."[3]

It was a fractious time in the United States. The urban centers of the Northeast and Midwest swelled with poor blacks who had fled rural America for jobs in steel mills, motorcar factories, and other heavy industries. They clashed with working-class whites, who also suffered under the strains of a seemingly endless Depression. Enforced, legal segregation was as American as apple pie. Black and white America remained tense, separate, and unequal. The Ku Klux Klan and other hate groups flourished.

Even in the more sympathetic world of sports, racial stereotypes ran rampant. Descriptions of Louis ranged from benign to coarse.

Jungle metaphors abounded. Grantland Rice, one of the era's premier sports writers, called Louis a "bushmaster" and a "brown cobra" with the "instinctive speed of the wild." After the knockout of Carnera, wire service sports writer Davis Walsh led his story: "Something sly and sinister and perhaps not quite human came out of the African jungle last night to strike down and utterly demolish the huge hulk that had been Primo Carnera, the giant." "In Africa," read an editorial in the *New York Daily Mirror*, "there are tens of thousands of powerful, young savages that with a little teaching could annihilate Mr. Joe Louis."[5]

New York Daily News columnist Paul Gallico dubbed Louis the "jungle killer . . . a truly savage person, a man on whom civilization rested no more securely than a shawl thrown over one's shoulders." Gallico would later liken him to an escaped tiger, marauding and dangerous. "The magnificent animal," he wrote. "He eats. He sleeps. He fights. . . . Is he all instinct, all animal? Or have a hundred million years left a fold upon his brain? I see in this colored man something so cold, so hard, so cruel that I wonder as to his bravery. Courage in the animal is desperation. Courage in the human is something incalculable and divine."[6]

"THE WORLD'S MOST CONSPICUOUS NEGRO"

It was clear to everyone, including Louis, that he was fighting for a greater cause than his own career. With every victory, the pressure on him escalated immeasurably. In his ghostwritten autobiography, released in 1935, he wrote, "I realize the Negro people have placed a big trust in me. It is my duty to win the championship and prove to the world that, black or white, a man can become the best fighter and still be a gentleman."[7] Louis bent over backwards trying to please skeptical white America.

"His place in the limelight makes Joe Louis the world's most conspicuous Negro," wrote Theophilus Lewis, a writer for the *Amsterdam News*, the popular Harlem daily. "In the mind of the average white man, the personal qualities of the most conspicuous Negro are merely an enlargement of the racial traits of all Negroes. . . . Give [whites] the impression that Negro is a synonym for Joe Louis and race relations will change for the better."[8]

Louis found himself caught between the conflicted expectations of blacks and whites. The editors of the black magazine *Crisis*, published by the National Association for the Advancement of Colored People (NAACP), wrote that they were "ecstatic" after his knockout of Carnera but worried about the example it set. "We do not advise our race to hitch its wagon to a boxer," they wrote, "or base its judgements of achievement of the size of a black man's biceps of the speed and power of his left hook. . . . Those who maintain that a Negro historian or editor or philosopher or scientist or composer or singer or poet or painter is more important than a great athlete are on sound ground."[9] In the eyes of black intellectuals, the stereotype of the "black sports hero" offered a decidedly mixed message to black youth.

Well before black dominance of high-profile sports, both white and black Americans were coming to see the Negro athlete as the "defining symbol of African American talent."[10] That image intimidated many whites. In response, Louis was not about to present the defiant persona that had derailed Johnson. He and his handlers were careful to ensure that he dressed conservatively and was not seen with white women. He believed that if he kept up a public front as the pliant Negro and played by the white man's rules, he would get a shot at James Braddock's heavyweight crown. What appears today as feet-shuffling Uncle Tomism was a survival tactic in 1930s America.

In January 1936, Louis signed to fight one of the remaining top challengers, the German Max Schmeling, the champion in 1931 and 1932, and was immediately installed as an 8-to-1 favorite. The promoters realized that a Louis-Schmeling fight would be a huge event, soaked in nationalist and racial imagery. Both boxers signed a contract forbidding them to fight anyone else until their bout in June. In the interim, Louis took off for Hollywood. For the first time in his life he was making real money, having grossed hundreds of thousands of dollars. He lowered his guard, partied almost every night, and caroused with starlets, black and white, even though his wife was with him. He didn't return to training until May.

It was soon apparent that Louis had spent too much time on the golf course. When he entered the ring in Yankee Stadium on June 22, 1936, a cocky Louis had put on twenty-five pounds. Schmeling battered him. He knocked the startled fighter on his rump in the fourth round, the first time Louis had ever been decked in his professional career. Schmeling then stunned Louis with a savage blow just as the fifth round ended. After that, the German was never challenged. A thunderous right flattened Louis again in the twelfth, knocking him out cold.

An ecstatic Schmeling whisked home in the zeppelin *Hindenburg* to a hero's welcome. It was a sharp turnabout from his position before the fight, when he had been viewed with scorn after losing to Max Baer. Baer was considered Jewish because he wore a Star of David on his trunks (although his Jewish ancestry was limited to his paternal grandfather). Baer's victory over Schneling came as quite a blow to the Nazis, for it challenged one of the tenets of European race science, that Jews were biologically effeminate.[11] Before the bout, Hitler had said that "there seemed an excellent chance that having already been knocked out by a Jew, [Schmeling] would now be stretched in the resin at the feet of a cotton-field Negro."[12]

In its October issue, the NAACP magazine *Crisis* reprinted a chilling article translated from the Nazi magazine *Der Weltkampf*. "The Negro is of a slave nature," it wrote, "but woe unto us if this slave nature is unbridled, for then arrogance and cruelty show themselves in the most bestial way. . . . France, England and white North America cannot thank Schmeling enough for this victory, for he checked the arrogance of the Negro and clearly demonstrated to them the superiority of white intelligence."[13]

Schmeling, who surprised even himself, played the upset for all it was worth and reciprocated the Nazi propaganda outburst, bragging that he owed his success to Hitler's inspiration. Whereas the German champion received hundreds of telegrams and letters from grateful white fans in the United States, Louis slipped from being an "example" to his race to providing a renewed target for racial stereotyping, particularly by southern sports writers. He went from being the

"Brown Bomber" to the "Brown Bummer." *New York Journal* writer Bill Corum praised Louis for being "superbly built," then added that he was "born to listen to jazz music, eat a lot of fried chicken, play ball with the gang on the corner and never do a lick of heavy work he could escape."[14]

For a week Louis holed up in his Harlem apartment, nursing his swollen jaw, ashamed by his performance, before vowing a comeback. Humbled but resilient, he slipped off to Chicago to resume training. He was back in the protective hands of Mike Jacobs, the promoter who had orchestrated the publicity for the Carnera fight. Months later, he fought ex-champion Jack Sharkey. Louis knocked him out, then proceeded to make easy work of a half-dozen lesser boxers. The next step, a shot at the title, was out of his hands. Braddock, the reigning champion, had a choice between Louis or Schmeling, He chose the Brown Bomber.

On a June night in 1937, 45,000 people, half of them black, crammed into Chicago's Comiskey Park. It was the largest number of blacks ever to witness a live bout. Braddock stunned the crowd when he sent Louis onto his rump with a hard right. But the challenger quickly recovered. Within a few rounds, every blow delivered by Louis roused the crowd into a delirium of hugging and crying. When Braddock went down for good in round eight, Louis was crowned champion of the world.

Although thrilled by the victory, Louis and Jacobs, a Jew, had unfinished business. They itched for a rematch with Schmeling, who reveled in his role as Hitler's warrior. The German boxer had become a hulking symbol of Aryan supremacy. Jacobs understood that if the public were forced to choose between an American black man and a symbol of Nazism, the black man would win. In effect, Louis was cast as an American hero, or as much of one as white society would allow. It took months for Jacobs and Schmeling's camp to work out the details. Hitler was reportedly opposed to the fight, but the Nazi sports minister and the Schmeling team prevailed, confident of a repeat victory.

LOUIS VERSUS SCHMELING: THE REMATCH

The rematch between Louis and Schmeling, set for June of 1938, became fraught with surreal expectations. Germans and fascist sympathizers saw it as a chance to affirm once and for all the superiority of the Aryan race. Blacks sought redemption from Schmeling's unexpected win two years before. Jews around the world, horrified at reports of Nazi atrocities, viewed the battle in biblical terms, with Louis as a "black David." To many Americans it was truly a confrontation between good and evil. Jacobs arranged a meeting with Franklin D. Roosevelt. "Joe, we need muscles like yours to beat Germany," said the president.[15] Though the United States was reluctant to be drawn into another overseas war, it could do battle against the Nazi juggernaut in the world of sports.

Many older American blacks consider the second Louis-Schmeling fight a defining moment in their lives. "No political happening, no other sports occasion, no war, no imminent passing of any law could compare with the possibility of a Louis victory," wrote Arthur Ashe, Jr., in *A Hard Road to Glory*, his compelling history of blacks in sports. "Neither Jesse Owens's four Olympic gold medals nor Jackie Robinson's signing with the Brooklyn Dodgers equaled the elation of this night."[16] It was boxing's first million-dollar gate. Seventy thousand fans roared themselves hoarse at Yankee Stadium, with tens of millions more glued to their radios.

"The fight," wrote one reporter, "was short, swift, merciless and complete." Louis charged Schmeling at the opening bell and began landing stinging left jabs. Schmeling responded listlessly, trying to wrap his opponent in a clinch before Louis renewed his fury. Another series of lefts, and Schmeling dropped his guard. A stunning right just below the German's ear sent him reeling against the ropes, only to bounce back again toward Louis. The "Dusky David from Detroit," as he was called in the tabloid press, followed up with a right hand smash to Schmeling's body. Ringside spectators heard the German squeal "like a stuck pig."[17]

"It was no fight," wrote Jack Mahon of the *Daily News*. "It was slaughter." Schmeling sagged towards the center of the ring, but he made no further effort to defend himself. A quick right by Louis and he was down again, this time for a three-count. Schmeling rose to his feet, but before he could manage a punch, Louis connected with a combination to the head, sending him to his knees once again. Somewhere amidst this contained explosion, one Louis blow cracked Schmeling's spine in two places. Everyone feared that the German might face permanent injury. His handlers, preparing for the worst, cut the short-wave-radio wires that were being used to broadcast the fight back to Germany. Dazed and uncomprehending, Schmeling struggled back up. As the German challenger staggered around the ring, tens of thousands of blacks roared their approval. Redemption was at hand.

"What made Louis a unique figure was not simply his great talent as an athlete," wrote economist Thomas Sowell.

> He appeared at a time in American history when blacks were not only at a low economic ebb, but were also the butt of ridicule. In this kind of world, Joe Louis became the most famous man in America. What he did as a man could reinforce or counteract stereotypes that hurt and held back millions of people of his race. How he fared in the ring mattered more to black Americans than the fate of any other athlete in any other sport, before or since. He was all we had.[18]

Seemingly possessed, the champion made a final charge. Louis scored with yet another combination, finishing with a crushing right to the jaw. "Schmeling's Defeat Stings Nazis" read the banner head-line in a victory edition of a New York paper. "The Aryan idol, the unconquerable one had been beaten," read another. "The bright, shining symbol of race glory has been thumped in the dust. That noise you hear is Goebbels making for the storm cellar." The fight of the century officially came to an end little more than two minutes into round one. It was a knockout blow to the smug Nazis and their legion of Aryan-supremacist sympathizers around the world.

The first American triumph of the war was short-lived, however.

Negro sports stars in America never had the luxury, taken for granted by white athletes, of savoring the purely personal sense of achievement. In the twinkling of a moment one stereotype—the physically strong but plodding black—was permanently replaced by another, equally pernicious—the hard-punching, fleet-footed beast, fresh out of the African jungle. Thereafter, every athletic conquest by a black stood in danger of being subtly devalued as a product of his ancestry or a result of selective breeding of slaves. "It is a doubtful compliment to the Negro athlete," wrote Westbrook Pegler, "[to suggest] that he is still so close to the primitive that whenever he runs a foot-race . . . his civilization vanishes and he becomes again for the moment an African savage in breechcloth and nose-ring legging it through the jungle."[19]

Louis's knockout may have unleashed a wave of euphoria among blacks, but it played to mixed reviews in the middle-class black community, where some worried that such an intense focus on athletics would challenge the schoolhouse and the church as symbols of black achievement. "The black bourgeoisie," wrote historian Gerald Early, "rejected Louis at first, rejecting the idea of having the 'genius' of the Negro race represented by a mere prizefighter in much the same way that whites rejected him at first as representative of American manhood and masculinity."[20] Sports writer Edwin Bancroft Henderson went so far as to refer to Louis as "a human replica of Rodin's Thinker" in an attempt to elevate the new champion's physical accomplishments.*

After the destruction of Jack Johnson, black sport stars had felt compelled to become experts at humility, making themselves acceptable to whites without straining their links to the black community. As a result, they were viewed by some less as pioneers than as supplicants for the entertainment value of white America who had exchanged their black identities for fame and dollars.[21] But to the vast majority, Louis, Owens, and other African American athletes were super heroes who earned with their triumphs welcome scraps of dig-

---

*Henderson went on to hyperbolize: "In the ring he associates ideas and responds with lightning-like rapier thrusts about as rapidly through the medium of mind and muscle as an Einstein calculates cause and effect in cosmic theory."

nity in an otherwise difficult life. Whether the black establishment liked it or not, by the late 1930s the athlete was coming to supplant the scholar and even the entertainer as the role model and symbol of black achievement in the minds of most Americans.

CHAPTER 15

THE "SCHEMING, FLASHY TRICKINESS"

OF JEWS

T here are horrific parallels in the experiences of Jews and blacks in the first half of the twentieth century. Along with Africans and American blacks, Jews were considered by many to be morally inferior and physically infirm. These two beleaguered ethnic groups also shared another similarity: in defiance of previous stereotypes, both became prominent in sports, and for many of the same reasons. Like all oppressed minorities, they followed the opportunities.

"Basketball is a city game," notes Sonny Hill, a former college basketball player and an icon in Philadelphia, where the African American coach has run a summer league for high school kids for nearly forty years. "If you trace basketball back to the 1920s, '30s, and '40s, that's when the Jewish people were very dominant in the inner city. And they dominated basketball."[1]

For Jews at the turn of the century, urban life meant boxing and playing basketball. In its earliest years, basketball was a "white" game and a haven for scores of immigrants who flooded the cities of the Northeast at the turn of the century. With no gymnasiums and almost no equipment, few blacks took up the sport, although a handful did play for elite colleges or better equipped YMCAs. For a brief period before World War I, in a few Eastern cities, "colored athletes" on club teams were "thrown into competition with the whites" and did very well.[2] But for the most part, basketball was a gritty playground sport for blue-collar immigrants.

With so many immigrant Jews, New York City became a mecca of

Jewish basketball. It bred such stars as Nat Holman, the captain of the original New York Celtics, and the famed St. John's "wonder five," college basketball's best team from 1927–1930, when it won sixty-four out of sixty-eight games—with four Jews as starters. For sheer concentration of talent, however, even New York could not challenge the City of Brotherly Love, one hundred miles to the south.

From 1918 to 1950, the South Philadelphia Hebrew Association team, better known as the SPHAs, barnstormed across the East and Midwest, playing in a variety of semiprofessional leagues that were precursors to the modern game, although blacks were banned. In an incredible twenty-two-season stretch, the SPHAs played in eighteen championship series, losing only five. In the early years of the Depression, the popularity of the SPHAs even surpassed that of Philadelphia's baseball teams, the Athletics and Phillies.

Basketball was a magnet for inner city immigrants. "The Jews never got much into football or baseball. They were too crowded [with other players] then," said the late Harry Litwack, who starred for the SPHAs in the thirties, before going on to become one of college basketball's premier coaches in a twenty-one-year career with Temple University. "Every Jewish boy was playing basketball. Every phone pole had a peach basket on it. And every one of those Jewish kids dreamed of playing for the SPHAs."[3]

"It was absolutely a way out of the ghetto," added Dave Dabrow, a guard with the original SPHAs. The diminutive Dabrow, who has since passed away, spoke with the thick Yiddish accent so common among turn-of-the-century immigrant families. "It was where the young Jewish boy would never have been able to go to college if it wasn't for the amount of basketball playing and for the scholarship."[4] Familiar?

Baseball and football were far more popular in much of the country, but Philly was a basketball town. The first intercollegiate game in the East, a 6–4 shellacking of Temple University by Haverford College—offense was in short supply in the earliest iteration of basketball—took place in March 1894 at the Temple gymnasium. Basketball had a notorious reputation. The early rules provided for few fouls, making the game more like controlled assault and battery.

There was no out-of-bounds on many courts, which were often ringed with steel mesh. It was common practice to drive an opponent into the steel fence, and pile-ups were as frequent as at a hockey game today. Players paraded in and out of games with bandaged legs and bleeding heads. This offended the Victorian sensibilities of turn-of-the-century Philadelphia, leading to a gradual, although temporary, ban on the game at local YMCAs, which were fearful that their Christian boys would be forever tainted.

Not so in the Jewish, Irish, Polish, and Italian communities, which were filled with the sons of hard-scrabble immigrants, many recently off the boat. The two best high school squads, Southern High School and its scholastic rival, Central High, were stocked with first-generation Jews. It was here that future SPHAs Eddie Gottlieb, Harry "Chicky" Passon, Edwin "Hughie" Black, Mockie Bunnin, and Charlie Newman led Southern to three city high school titles in 1914, 1915, and 1916. According to the players, the Jews had a different style of play. "It was a quick-passing running game, as opposed to the bullying and fighting way which was popular other places," explained Litwack.[5]

For years the best graduates would go on to play for one of the church teams or at the YMCA, until that was forbidden as anti-Semitism heated up. A few played in the Eastern League, which included the original Celtics in New York. But there were far more talented players than opportunities to play. In 1918, Gottlieb and some of his former high school buddies convinced the local Young Man's Hebrew Association at Fourth and Reed to buy them some uniforms with Hebrew initials and the Magen David as team symbols.[6]

It was a nomadic existence, with the team either playing as an independent or as a member of the fledgling American Basketball League of Philadelphia. For the next few years, the SPHAs earned some decent pocket money, as much as $5 a game each, big bucks for ghetto kids. "Half the fans would come to see the Jews get killed and the other half were Jews coming to see our boys win," Gottlieb remembered.[7] Needless to say, there were a lot of brawls.

By the end of the 1921 season, their uniforms had become too ragged to wear, but the YMHA couldn't come up with the money for new ones. Gottlieb, Black, and Passon started a local sporting goods store, Passon's, which soon became a city landmark. With the uniform crisis solved, they ventured out on their own into the world of traveling semipro ball but kept their team name and Jewish identity. At times it was a brutal experience. The Jewish players faced incessant racial slurs and biased officials in the small Pennsylvania, New Jersey, and New York towns in which they played.

"The toughest place was Prospect Hall, the home of the Brooklyn Visitation," said Gottlieb. "They made the fans check their guns at the door. They used to have a balcony that hung over the court where the spectators sat, and they'd serve the fans bottle beer and sandwiches. Whenever something would happen down on the court that those Brooklyn fans didn't like, they'd send those bottles down at us."[8] Harry Litwack, the team's star defensive player in the 1930s, remembered having to be careful just going down the court. "There was a lady in the front row with hat pins," he recalled. "She used to jab you when you went by."[9]

Gottlieb was the player coach. He would remain in Philadelphia and in basketball into the 1950s, starting two professional leagues including the NBA, and coaching the Philadelphia Warriors to a Championship. He was affectionately nicknamed "the Mogul" and was inducted into the Hall-of-Fame. "In my time, I got involved in lots of things, lots of 'em," Gottlieb said shortly before his death in 1979. "But the SPHAs, that's what I loved."[10]

A regular stream of players flowed right from high school to the SPHAs. Enticed by the money and the challenge, Louis "Inky" Lautman lied his way onto the team in the early 1920s, when he was only sixteen and still attending Central High. The ambidextrous pivotman went on to play for seventeen years. Tuesday night doubleheaders at the YMHA on Broad and Pine Streets attracted crowds of 1,500 or more to watch Lautman, Passon, lady-killer Cy Kaselman, and Gottlieb display their ball-handling skills.

The SPHAs produced such legendary figures as Litwack, Herman "Red" Klotz, the former player and owner of the Washington Generals, the team that played the longtime patsy of the Harlem Globetrotters, and Max Patkin, who would become far better known as a baseball clown. During the height of their success in the late 1920s, the SPHAs were one of only three major teams in the country. Their competition came from the New York Celtics, a powerful team of mostly Jewish and Irish players, coached by Nat Holman, which lost but eleven games in one two hundred-game stretch, and the all-black New York Renaissance. The Rens were flashy in 1920s terms but methodical playmakers by any fair measure, and nearly unbeatable.

According to the late William "Pop" Gates, the star of the Renaissance, the SPHAs were renowned as a "thinking" team while the Rens were famous for their "quickness"[11]—stereotypes about Jews and blacks that endure even today. "Usually when the Renaissance would have you licked, the last three, four minutes of the game, they'd start passing the ball around, and the crowd would go crazy," recalled Gottlieb. In one 1935 exhibition game, the SPHAs became the only non–New York team to beat the Rens on their home court. The encounters between the "Yids" and the "niggers" were legendary, particularly at the marvelous Ballroom at Philadelphia's Broadwood Hotel, where tickets went for a lofty 65 cents and 2,500 spectators jammed the stands.

Jews starred in other basketball leagues. Hall-of-Famer Barney Sedran, all of 5 feet, 4 inches and weighing 118 pounds, was the superstar guard for his New York Whirlwind team of 1919–1921, thought by many to have been the greatest professional team of the first half of this century. His playing partner and fellow Hall-of-Famer Max Friedman moved on to star with the Cleveland Rosenblums, one of the top teams of the era. City College of New York turned out one Jewish star after another, including Morris "Moe" Spahn, the ABL Most Valuable Player in 1937–1938, William "Red" Holzman, one of the winningest coaches in NBA history, and Holman, who coached the college team from 1919 to 1960 while sometimes moonlighting as coach of the Celtics.

The predominance of Jewish players became the subject of "learned" scientific treatises, not unlike that those that have followed black athletic successes. Writers opined that Jews were genetically and culturally built to stand up under the strain and stamina of the hoop game. It was suggested that they had an advantage because short men have better balance and more foot speed. They were also thought to have sharper eyes, which of course cut against the other stereotype that they suffered from myopia and had to wear glasses. And it was said they were clever. "The reason, I suspect, that basketball appeals to the Hebrew with his Oriental background," wrote Paul Gallico, sports editor of the *New York Daily News* and one of the premier sports writers of the 1930s, "is that the game places a premium on an alert, scheming mind, flashy trickiness, artful dodging and general smart aleckness."[12]

Following the transformative experience of war, the new generation of Jews began moving on to other pursuits. By the late 1940s, the torch of urban athleticism was passed on to the newest immigrants, mostly blacks who had migrated north from dying southern plantations. In a few short years, the SPHAs were a team of the past, reduced to a supporting role, along with the Washington Generals, as the slow-footed white boys in one-night stands against the Harlem Globetrotters, which had evolved into a vaudeville act after the NBA began stealing its best players. It would not be long before the stereotype of the "scheming . . . trickiness" of the Jews was replaced by that of the "natural athleticism" of Negroes.

V

NATURE OR NURTURE?

CHAPTER 16

THE INTEGRATION OF SPORTS

hile Louis and Owens toiled in symbolic battles against Nazism, Hitler's Germany began its death march across Europe. Shortly before the Schmeling-Louis rematch, the first reports of German concentration camps were making their way into the Allied press. By August 1939, the madness of genocidal eugenics was officially, but secretly, put into place. Known as Project T4, it targeted "deformed new-borns" to age three, as well as retarded and handicapped children, and eventually adult psychiatric patients. The Nazis, known for their fanatical record-keeping, documented 70,273 Germans with "genetic illnesses" being put to death in the first years of the war, although most scholars believe that the number was actually higher.

It is now known that many, if not most of those killed, were German citizens, many of them healthy. Beginning in the fall of 1940, diplomats at the American consulate in Leipzig began noticing a number of strange death notices. Not everyone was old, and all died at the Grafeneck asylum in Württemberg for the mentally enfeebled. In every case, the relatives were not notified of their deaths until the deceased had been cremated. After some investigative digging by the local consulate, Vice Consul Paul H. Dutko cabled the U.S. Embassy in Berlin and the State Department in Washington that there was reason to believe that the Third Reich was killing people it deemed useless. The United States did nothing and in fact denied for nearly sixty years that it had any inkling of Germany's euthanasia program until at least mid-1941.[1]

Under cover of the international taboo about confronting Germany, on the eve of the United States entry into the war, Hitler escalated his scheme of "genetic cleansing," instituting Special Action 14f13, which expanded T4 to include "defectives" up to age sixteen, including those citizens deemed enemies of the state. Josef Mengele and other rising stars of Nazi science were soon plucking eyes from living Jews and blood samples from twins they had had infected with typhus, all in the name of improving humanity under the guiding policy of *rassenhygiene*.[2] The "final solution" was finally being implemented.

The Holocaust abruptly brought the era of race science to a close. Before World War II, anthropology centered on why and how humans were different; in the postwar rebuilding period, the focus shifted toward a search for our shared humanity. The egalitarian ethic of America became the operating ideology of the postwar world. And now that it had demonstrated its prowess in battle, the United States began addressing its moral responsibilities at home.

Many reforms were driven by the new economy. The insatiable demand to keep the war machine humming had drawn millions of rural whites and blacks to the factories and mills of the North and Midwest. After blacks and whites had worked, fought, and died side by side, the idea of white supremacy seemed ignorant and indefensible, especially in the early days of the Cold War when the United States and the Soviet Union were competing for the "hearts and minds" of the emerging, nonaligned countries of the developing world. In 1947, President Harry Truman created a civil rights commission to draft anti-lynching measures, end poll taxes, and fully integrate the military. Executive Order 9981, signed into law on July 26, 1948, called for "equality of treatment and opportunity for all persons in the armed services without regard to race, color, religion or national origin." Although it would be six more years before the Army disbanded its last all-black unit, change was in the air.[3]

THE REINTEGRATION
OF SPORTS IN AMERICA

Sports became a highly visible way to demonstrate to the world that Americans took their government's pronouncements on freedom and equality to heart. Even before the war officially ended, black and white integrationists were agitating for change. The NAACP launched its "Double V" campaign which linked victory over the racist doctrines of the Nazis to victory over white racism at home. Athletics became the primary new battleground.[4]

Although college sports had long been technically integrated, de facto segregation existed and was enforced vigorously when teams played in the South. "Southern politicians had attempted to make capital out of the fact that ... no Negro ever had played or ever would be allowed to play with or against a white team in the South," wrote historian Morris Bealle.[5] An attempt in 1946 to challenge the "blackout" blew up in everyone's face when a football game between all-white Mississippi State and the University of Nevada, which had two black players, was abruptly canceled for fear of a riot.

The very next year, the University of Virginia in Charlottesville was scheduled to host Harvard. Crimson senior Chester Pierce, a black, who later went on to become a distinguished psychiatrist and Harvard professor, started at tackle. "Some of our older players, who had been in the service during the war, contacted the Virginia team in an effort to head off trouble," remembered Jim Fenn, a Harvard lineman. "Their captain was Larry Baumann, and I had served with him in the Navy. He assured me there wouldn't be any trouble on the field. And there wasn't."

Virginia ended up trouncing Harvard 47–0, but the score is a footnote to history. Pierce survived ugly slurs from fans and a warm reception from hundreds of local blacks who cheered as he and his teammates made their way into the stadium. "It was no big deal and took no courage by me," said Pierce modestly. "Historically, the time was right, among all of America's changes after World War II. I just happened to be in the right place at the right time."[6]

Professional football, which had shut its doors to blacks only in

1934, quietly reintegrated in 1946. In the inaugural year of the All-America Football Conference, Cleveland Browns owner and coach Paul Brown signed Bill Willis, a hard-knock lineman, whom he had coached at Ohio State, and University of Nevada running back Marion Motley, whom he had seen play in high school. According to Jim Brown, who later signed with Cleveland and went on to become the premier fullback in football history, the signing of the two black athletes had little to do with symbolism. "[Paul Brown] was a person of his times and he had high standards and he believed people should be treated the same," he says. "Paul was a top business person who was driven to setting up an organization that would be the best in the world, utilizing the best personnel, developing the best devices to win. Color never came into his philosophy."[7]

It is easy to forget just how slowly change came to baseball. When Brooklyn Dodgers executive Branch Rickey signed Kansas City Monarchs infielder Jackie Robinson to a minor-league contract in 1945, the support for integration among the players and the press was hardly unanimous. "Robinson will not make the major leagues," wrote New York sports writer Jimmy Powers the following spring. "He is a thousand-to-one shot at best. The Negro players simply don't have the brains or the skill." Future Hall-of-Famer Bob Feller of the Cleveland Indians was equally dismissive. "He's tied up in the shoulders and can't hit an inside pitch to save his neck," he declared. "If he were a white man, I doubt they would even consider him big league material."[8]

However, the black and white establishments began to realize that it was in both of their interests to promote black athletes as symbols of American opportunity. Newspapers that had tacitly observed double standards for years began indulging in an orgy of cultural self-congratulation. The integration of sports, declared *The Cleveland Plain Dealer*, was "more spectacular and noble than all the [anti-discrimination] laws ever devised."[9] Yet it would take a dozen years after Robinson's major-league debut in 1947 before all sixteen teams would sign a black player.

Basketball integrated in fits and starts. Although the black college West Virginia State went 30–0 during the 1947–1948 season, it was not invited to play in the National Invitational Tournament or for the National Collegiate Athletic Association championship. The professional Basketball Association of America, whose star player was Minneapolis's hot shot rookie George Mikan, hired two former Harlem Renaissance stars, "Pop" Gates and William "Dolly" King, to play with the Tri-Cities Blackhawks, but they were given a rough welcome and were soon gone.[10]

The turning point came in 1950 during the annual draft of college seniors. "Boston takes Chuck Cooper of Duquesne," rang out the voice of Celtics owner Walter Brown when he announced his team's second pick. According to those present, the silence that followed lasted for what seemed like minutes until one of the owners finally piped up, "Walter, don't you know he's a colored boy?" Brown shot back, "I don't give a damn if he's striped, plaid, or polka-dot. Boston takes Chuck Cooper of Duquesne." After a few murmurs, the draft resumed. With that, basketball became the last of the major sports to break the color barrier.[11]

Boston's move could not have come at a more crucial juncture for the struggling sport of professional basketball. At the time, the NBA was in a deep funk. The game was slow, sometimes excruciatingly so. The league hit bottom on November 22, 1950, when the Minneapolis Lakers hosted the Fort Wayne Zollner Pistons (the team was owned by Fred Zollner, a local businessman). The Pistons took an early lead, then held the ball. Pass followed pass. The Lakers played in kind, choosing to stay in a group around star center George Mikan, who plopped down in the middle. Neither team budged out of its set positions, even after fans starting throwing garbage onto the court. The snoozing crowd had time to visit the washroom, buy a beer, and return to their seats without fear of missing a shot attempt. Fort Wayne won the embarrassment, 19–18.[12] Not surprisingly, several teams were facing insolvency, and owners were willing to try almost anything to rescue their sinking ship.

In 1954, the NBA made a fateful decision that would open the game to a grittier, urban style. Syracuse Nationals' owner Danny Biasone finally convinced the league to adopt his heretical idea of a 24-second clock, which limited how long a team could hold the ball before shooting. Purists fought it as a gimmick. It was certainly a last-gasp effort to save a game out-of-step with a faster-paced country running headlong into an era of unprecedented change. Little did the struggling NBA know that the move to a speedier pace would revolutionize the sport, and attract a different type of both player and fan.

The greatest boost to integration, however, came not on the court but in the courtroom. Topeka, Kansas, third-grader Linda Brown, who had been forced to walk a mile through a railroad switchyard to get to her segregated school, had sued to go to a nearby white school just a few blocks from her home. In a landmark 1954 ruling, *Brown v. Board of Education of Topeka, Kansas*, the Supreme Court declared "separate but equal," the legal justification for decades of enforced racial segregation, unconstitutional. The ruling signaled an end to *de jure* segregation in the South and began opening northern schools that were in fact segregated. More black players soon began appearing on sports teams in high schools and colleges.

UNIVERSAL EGALITARIANISM

In the aftermath of World War II, the emotional lure of the egalitarian ethic cannot be underestimated. This ideology resonated particularly loudly in the United States, where the idealism of the Enlightenment had been preserved like a flower in amber. The spirit of equality is one of the New World's most inspiring and enduring qualities. In the 1770s, the renegade colonies had petitioned for freedom in a direct challenge to the elitism of the Old World European order. The rebels embraced a new ethic that would be embodied in the Declaration of Independence: "all men are created equal." It was a more poignant and more complex sentiment than any of the founders could have imagined.

The post–war stirrings of integration mirrored a changing consciousness that unfolded throughout the western world. Europe bore the deep scars, psychological and structural, of the last war. Those who talked of "race" or "racial differences" were openly ridiculed as being Nazis. Universalism became the new ideology, with ethnic and racial antagonisms giving way, in theory at least, to a brief period of idealism. Britain and the nations of continental Europe began to dismantle their colonial empires in Africa and elsewhere.

The Allied powers, taken by a new spirit of universalism, resurrected the League of Nations as the United Nations and established its headquarters in New York City. One of its first undertakings was to come up with a new understanding of race. Charged to remake science in a more benign image, the UN Economic and Social Council (UNESCO) began drafting a "doctrine of the equality of man and races" and a "programme of disseminating scientific facts, designed to remove what is generally known as racial prejudice."[13]

This reform got a boost in 1950 with the convening of the Cold Spring Harbor Symposium on Quantitative Biology on the Origin and Evolution of Man, when the neo–Darwinist "modern synthesis" of genetic and environmental perspectives on evolution was forged. Genocide hung like a dark cloud over the proceedings. The scientists agreed to substitute the word "population" for the more charged "race."[14]

The following year, at the behest of UNESCO, a distinguished group of social scientists led by Ashley Montagu formulated a Statement of Race. "Scientists," it read, "have reached general agreement that mankind is one: that all men belong to the same species, *Homo sapiens*." UNESCO substituted "ethnic group" for "race," and declared its support for "the ethic of universal brotherhood."[15] Under the new definition, differences were defined by concentrations of population, not by popular racial types, although there remained a general agreement that there existed three biological groups, denoted as Mongoloid, Negroid, and Caucasoid. The scientists disconnected biology from the concept of mental and intellectual differences, and declared that genes were not a major factor in shaping human cultures.[16]

This new cultural perspective, though a necessary rebuke of Nazism, the Ku Klux Klan, and other virulent racist movements that had flourished between the world wars, carried with it a new set of ideological baggage. Although Montagu was the principal author of the UNESCO statement, its intellectual founding father was Columbia University's Franz Boas, a German-born physical anthropologist and revolutionary figure in the history of the social sciences.[17] Early in his career Boas had embraced the widely accepted belief that intelligence was genetically fixed, the cause and not the result of the wide gap between Africans and Europeans. "As we found clear evidence of differences of structure between races, so we must anticipate that differences in mental 'characteristics' will be found," he wrote in *The Mind of Primitive Man* in 1911.[18] At the time, only a few scientists such as American ethnologist Lewis Henry Morgan argued for a bio-cultural understanding of intelligence, contending that brains were not immutable and that biological intelligence could be improved.[19]

After years of witnessing the growing abuse of science, Boas gradually redirected anthropology from its measurement mania to refocus on the individual and society. When he reissued *The Mind of Primitive Man* in 1938, he edited out all mention of human biological disparities.[20] By this time, Boas was celebrated as an almost mythic figure carrying the torch of reason into an irrational racial darkness, a hero to a new generation of intellectuals.[21] Their new anthropological model—that people are born with blank slates and are shaped by personal experience and social conditioning—has since come to dominate intellectual and popular thinking.

Montagu had been one of Boas's most ambitious students. Born Israel Ehrenberg in London, he grew up in a working-class England rampant with anti-Semitism. While attending University College in London, Ehrenberg changed his name to Montague Francis Ashley Montagu, leaving behind most traces of his ethnicity. He took on the pretentious appellation from the English establishment of barons and dukes and far from his modest upbringing. Considered a dilettante by many who knew him, Montagu affected an upper-class British accent and manner. The newly christened Montagu later left college without finishing his degree, eventually ending up in Boas's graduate program at Columbia.[22]

Shortly after the death of his mentor in 1942, and determined to obliterate the mutant form of eugenics that he had come to believe was the intellectual backbone of fascism, Montagu published *Man's Most Dangerous Myth: The Fallacy of Race*.[23] By the end of the decade, he had come to a new understanding. "When one uses the term 'ethnic group,'" he wrote, "the question is immediately raised, 'What does it mean? What does the user have in mind?' And this at once affords an opportunity to discuss the facts and explore the meaning and falsities enshrined in the word 'race' and to explain the problems involved and the facts of the genetic situation as we know them."[24]

Montagu and his colleagues embraced the "nurture" argument with the zeal of fundamentalists. The human baby may be a product of nature, they said, but its soul amounted to a tabula rasa to be inscribed by life's experiences. Margaret Mead, another of Boas's pupils, propagated the cultural determinist line in her best-seller *Coming of Age in Samoa* (which has since been effectively discredited). "Human nature," declared Mead, "[is] the rawest, most undifferentiated of raw material."[25]

The UNESCO statement that Montagu helped craft was a reasonable observation about human cleverness, but it was flawed science. It implied the mutability and perfectibility of humankind. The inexorable forces of evolution and heredity receded into the background, to be replaced by a moral dimension: it was now suggested that prehistoric humans had adapted to austere climates through clever discoveries of fire, clothing, and artificial shelters, not as a consequence of chance, natural mutations, and the survival of the fittest. Shadowed by the racist ideologies of fascism, common sense was sacrificed to a new ideology: environmentalism.

THE BATTLE OVER
THE DEFINITION OF RACE

In the cautious postwar social climate, few hard scientists felt comfortable openly challenging the new paradigm that considered race and genetics dirty words. Although they appreciated the danger of romanticizing race science—the specter of genocide weighed on everyone—they continued to believe that the study of human biodiversity was a coherent, if politically flawed, model for understanding evolutionary development.

Their lobbying led to the convening of yet another international panel to push for a stronger biological component to refine the concept of race. Instead of Montagu's declaration that "mankind is one," the new team of geneticists and anthropologists stated matter-of-factly that "scientists are generally agreed that all men living today belong to a single species." Although the statement hinted that innate racial differences, including mental ones, were likely, it asserted that such differences were eclipsed by the range of biological variation that exists within groups.

The anthropological paradigm emerging out of these extraordinary sessions all but relegated intelligence research to the intellectual dustbin. Such a result did not sit well with many scientists who had no apparent ideological ax to grind. "Available scientific knowledge," said Sir Ronald A. Fisher, one of the founders of modern statistics and a brilliant synthesizer of evolutionary thought, "provides a firm basis for believing that the groups of mankind differ in their innate capacity for intellectual and emotional development, seeing that such groups do differ undoubtedly in a very large number of their genes."[24] Herman Muller, winner of the Nobel Prize for his research on mutations, would add his belief that, "in view of the conspicuous hereditary differences, it would be strange for there not to be similar mental ones between averages."[26]

But some of the opposition was driven by the same fervent belief in a racial hierarchy that the postwar synthesis was intended to dismantle. Former Nazi scientist Fritz Lenz, who had resurrected his career by getting himself appointed as professor of human genetics at the University of Göttingen, claimed that the latest advances in genetics had begun to destroy "the fallacious concept of the equality or similarity of all men and the current belief in the omnipotence of social influences." He went so far as to state that Africans, Eskimos, and Europeans were of different species.[27]

Die-hard race scientist Henry Garrett, past president of the American Psychological Association and chair of the psychology department at Columbia University, was so disgusted by what he considered the antiscience dogma of the Boas-influenced UNESCO panel that he set up a group, the International Association for the Advancement of Ethnology and Eugenics, to continue research on genetics and race. "No matter how low . . . an American white may be, his ancestors built the civilizations of Europe," Garrett wrote in the prestigious journal *Science* in a manifesto in opposition to social desegregation, "and no matter how high . . . a Negro may be, his ancestors were (and his kinsmen still are) savages in an African jungle. Free and general race mixture of Negrowhite groups in this country would inevitably be not only dysgenic but socially disastrous."[28] Garrett's new group became a magnet for avowed right-wingers of the time, among them the Liberty Lobby's Willis Carto, a major proponent of white racial superiority and Jewish conspiracy theories.[29]

Such extremists only pushed the more liberal environmentalists to the other extreme. That the new zeitgeist rested on scientific thin ice—an exaggerated belief in the power of the environment to determine, not just influence, human behavior—did not diminish its appeal to a world still licking the wounds of ethnic wars and racial bitterness. The tide had turned decisively against the science of race and human biodiversity. It was a popular message. A memorable exchange between Humphrey Bogart and Katherine Hepburn in *The African Queen*, awarded the Oscar for Best Picture in 1951, shows how quickly the new culture-based paradigm captured public consciousness. Hepburn, playing a missionary, pours Bogart's gin into the river, touching off a discussion about temptation. In effect, Bogart assumes the intellectual guise of a sociobiologist. He claims that controlling his surrender to temptation would be impossible: "Missy," he says, "it's just human nature."

"Nature," Hepburn responds, "is what we are put in this world to rise above."[30]

CHAPTER 17

THE SIXTIES

The civil rights movement took on a new head of steam with the election of President John Kennedy and an activist Democratic administration in 1960. While Martin Luther King, Jr., preached desegregation and accommodation, radical activists such as Stokely Carmichael and the defiant Black Panthers spoke with eloquent anger of their bitterness at growing up black in America. Racial differences were on everyone's mind, especially in the academic community, where they were becoming a taboo subject, yet one that was discussed endlessly.

The new generation of social scientists was determined to be part of the solution, not a source of the problem. "Race," with all its historical baggage, was gradually rubbed out of textbooks to be replaced by "ethnicity." How ironic that postwar anthropology, which strove to cleanse the field of politics and biological determinism, now sought to substitute a new ideology—the absolute belief that all individuals are created equal with no meaningful differences other than life experiences. Rather than reaching for a more balanced perspective—that science is both a product and producer of culture—environmentalists merely exchanged "culture" and "nurture" for biological "nature." The belief that theory in part influences reality morphed into the extremist view that theory determines reality. This new ethic was the core belief in a movement known as "postmodernism," which even today remains the dominant theology in the social sciences and popular culture.

The tipping point from the old dogma to the new came in 1962 with the explosive reaction to the theories of Carleton S. Coon, a preeminent physical anthropologist in the conservative Harvard tradition. His intellectual mentors, Harvard anthropologists Roland B. Dixon and Earnest A. Hooton, shared the once popular view that the races were different enough to be separate species.[1] Like the eugenicists before him, Hooton, a patrician New Englander, did not see his views as racist and in fact stood alone among American anthropologists of the 1930s, campaigning openly against racism. He would advocate such ideas as solving the "Jewish problem" through biological assimilation—the gentile gene pool would become smarter and Jews would become nicer—and not understand when people thought such proposals racist.[2]

Coon's work spanned a number of anthropological paradigms, including the postwar physical anthropological model, though he never fully embraced the synthesis which proclaimed that modern humanity was rooted in the evolution of a single lineage. Nor did he embrace the radical environmental perspective of Columbia University ethnologists Boas and Montagu. Coon considered those views simplistic and their followers, many of the top young anthropologists of the time, almost cult members who had swallowed an ideology rather than engaging in science. His personal animus and his political naïveté would ultimately lead to his self-destruction.

In his 1962 book, *The Origin of Races*, Coon argued that humanity developed along parallel but separate paths and took on different characteristics. Intent on capping his career by writing an evolutionary history of the races, he ended up provoking an ugly debate that laid bare the deep ideological divisions in the anthropological community. "Wherever *Homo* arose," he wrote, "and Africa is at present the likeliest continent, he soon dispersed, in very primitive form, throughout the warm regions of the Old World. . . . If Africa was the cradle of mankind, it was only an indifferent kindergarten. Europe and Asia were our principal schools."[3]

The various races, Coon insisted, adapted to their respective environments with the hardiest surviving and thriving to spread their seed. There was no escaping his implication that African, Native American, and indigenous Australian populations had developed more slowly than Caucasians and Asians. In support of his contention, he marshaled the latest fossil evidence available at the time, which included the oldest skull with a large braincase, found in China. Crania size, which was thought to correlate with brain size and intelligence, became his most significant indicator of how far along the evolutionary road each race had traveled, a yardstick commonly used by anthropologists throughout history and even today. By his measure, Asians likely crossed the *sapiens* threshold first, while Australian aboriginals and blacks lagged further behind.

Coon outlined his conclusions in his inaugural address in 1962, a challenging time for modern science, as president of the American Anthropological Association. The Scopes "monkey trial" in 1925 had sent a chill over science textbook designers who were not about to buck deep suspicions by conservatives about the "un-Godly" theory of evolution. That distrust only began to wane in earnest after October 4, 1957, when the Soviet Union startled the world with its launch of Sputnik, the first orbiting artificial satellite. The scare that followed prompted a renaissance in American science. By 1961, the National Science Foundation had finally helped craft a series of biology textbooks that asserted the preeminent role of evolutionary theory.[4]

Any threat to this emerging but fragile public consensus was viewed with alarm. And with the civil rights movement in full flower, Coon could not have been so naïve as to think that others would not read more into his findings than he intended. Nonetheless, by dint of his prominence, his challenge of what came to be known as the postwar synthesis elevating the role of culture over biology threatened to undermine support for evolution and plunge anthropology back into its century-long rift.

His book and speech ignited an academic battle worthy of Louis versus Schmeling. It was a fight Coon could never hope to win. Although his accounting of the fossil record then available was within reason, key elements of his theory verged on speculation. Most improbable was his belief that five different hominid populations, including two in Africa, in relative isolation from one another, evolved separately from *H. erectus* to *H. Neanderthalensis* to *H. sapiens*. The statistical improbability of "sapienization" occurring along relatively similar paths in insular populations suggests that Coon suffered from a basic misunderstanding of population genetics. "He never showed the commitment to the importance of variation that is the foundation of the new synthesis, the importance of understanding the *pattern of variation* within as well as between populations," wrote Wolpoff and Caspari, who portray Coon as well-intentioned but backward-looking, the epitome of the "colonial anthropologist."[5]

Pressed about whether there was a clear hierarchy of intelligence based on race, Coon remained adamantly agnostic, claiming there were not enough data. Nothing in his career had suggested an overt prejudice (and indeed, he appeared delighted years later, when skull remains unearthed by Richard Leakey raised doubts about his finding that blacks had smaller brain capacity).[6] Nonetheless, he faced a crescendo of criticism, much of it personal, the likes of which had not been seen in anthropology for decades.

Coon had few public allies. *Origin* was widely perceived as a racist book, especially by those who hadn't read it, for it had been so praised by the racist press and those opposed to the civil rights movement.[7] Carleton Putnam, an ex-chairman of the board of Delta Airlines and a distant relative of Coon, twisted *Origins* to support Putnam's campaign that scientific evidence of race differences proved *Brown v. Board of Education* was wrongly decided. Coon's critics used that connection to inflame the controversy. Some critics even circulated the rumor that Carleton Putnam was Coon's nom de plume.[8]

For whatever reasons, the debate over Coon's theories was perceived as a litmus test between socially progressive liberals and backward thinkers. His work would be caricatured by all sides, misused by racists and abused by political conformists. Ashley Montagu weighed in with critical comments. Henry Schwarzchild, a leader of the Anti-Defamation League, fired off a letter of protest that was published in the *New York Times*. Sherwood Washburn brutalized Coon in his presidential address at the annual meeting of the American Anthropological Association.[9] Sidney Mintz, a social anthropologist then at Yale, accused Coon of being "a racist of the worst sort, but extremely clever. He has left the dirty work to others."[10]

Theodosius Dobzhansky, a Christian evolutionist and one of the architects of the modern synthesis, became a vocal and devastating opponent. Like many of his colleagues, Dobzhansky was torn between the scientific evidence, his religious beliefs, and his social ideals. A few months before Coon's presentation, he had sharply rebuked a colleague for ridiculing the validity of the concept of race, warning that "to say that mankind has no races plays into the hands of race bigots," for it seemed to crudely deny common sense and a hundred years of research, as tainted as some of it may have been.[11] After struggling to establish public acceptance for the scientific legitimacy of genetics, Dobzhansky viewed environmental fundamentalism with some queasiness. But after reading Coon's book and hearing him speak, he believed it was the lesser of two evils. Although Dobzhansky was prepared to acknowledge the existence of races, he was aghast at Coon's suggestion of multiple evolutionary tracks. He thought Coon naïve at best for offering up "grist for racist mills." He "cannot disclaim all responsibility for such misuses," Dobzhansky wrote.[12]

Coon was shocked at the personal tenor of the critiques. Although he had counted Dobzhansky as a professional friend, he now found himself the subject of what Coon believed were zealous and vicious personal attacks. "Dobzhansky states that, 'It is the duty of a scientist to prevent misuse and prostitution of his findings,'" Coon wrote. "I disagree with him. It is the duty of a scientist to do his work conscientiously and to the best of his ability, which is exactly what I have done and will continue to do, and to reject publicly only the writings of those persons who, influenced by one cause or another, have misquoted him, as Dobzhansky repeatedly has done with my work, for reasons known to himself."[13]

As the Coon controversy began to fade, it was clear that few were left on the middle ground in anthropology. "Race" had become a dirty word in academic circles. Ostracized from the anthropological mainstream which declared that race did not exist, Coon's fifty-year career lay in shambles with the controversy over racial differences in no clearer focus.

SPORTS AND "RACE CONSCIOUSNESS"

For the most part, the popular view that athletics was a haven of racial tolerance was more illusion than not, at least into the 1960s. "With my gold medal actually hanging from my neck," said Cassius Clay (who would later change his name to Muhammad Ali) matter-of-factly after winning the Olympic heavyweight championship in 1960, "I couldn't get a cheeseburger served to me in Louisville."[14] Colleges and professional teams were notoriously slow in opening up their rosters. It wasn't until July 1959, when the Boston Red Sox brought up Pumpsie Green from the minors after protests from the NAACP, that every team in baseball had at least one black player.[15] The National Hockey League did not integrate until 1957, with the debut of Canadian Willie O'Ree.[16] The Professional Golfers Association kept a written "Caucasian clause" in its bylaws until 1961.[17] It wasn't until 1962, when the all-white Washington Redskins traded for Bobby Mitchell that every team in all of the major sports had at least one black player. By 1964, only 15 percent of NBA players were black, although they were already disproportionately the stars, led by Bill Russell, Wilt Chamberlain, and Oscar Robertson, among others.

As the pace of integration picked up, the color and style of all of the major sports began to reflect the urban rhythms of black America. The upset victory by Texas Western (now the University of Texas at El Paso) in the 1966 NCAA basketball championship finals brought the change home to the public. Texas Western dunked the all-white Kentucky Wildcats in the first game ever in the history of the tournament in which a team starting five black players beat an all-white team. In the view of many Americans of the time, "blacks weren't disciplined enough [to] defeat a well-coached talented white squad," wrote Frank Fitzpatrick in his book on the historic game. "They weren't mentally tough. They didn't have heart. If they fell behind, they'd quit. At least one white was required, the thinking went, to provide stability and discipline—the quarterback in football, the shortstop or catcher in baseball, the point guard in basketball."[18]

Ironically, the victory set much of the country abuzz with talk of the "natural superiority" of the black athlete, shuffling stereotypes.

Adolf Rupp, Kentucky's imperious coach, would later refer to the victors as "a bunch of crooks" (although four of the seven blacks on the team earned degrees and all moved on to middle-class careers).[19] It was also an inspiring and pivotal event, for it opened doors for aspiring black athletes all across the country who previously may not even have been recruited. In retrospect, Texas Western's victory has come to symbolize the passing of the torch from the methodical style of the white era to the more athletic elegance favored by many blacks.

By 1968, black stars were establishing new standards of excellence in any number of sports. That year, O. J. Simpson received the Heisman Trophy, Arthur Ashe, Jr., became the first black to win the U.S. Open, and Bill Russell was named Sportsman of the Year by *Sports Illustrated* after playing and coaching his team to yet another NBA title. The African American domination of the sprints and the emergence of Kip Keino in middle-distance running at the Mexico City Olympics marked the beginning of the end of racial diversity in track, a process that culminated in 1997 when the last major record held by a non-African, Sebastian Coe's 800-meter mark, fell to a Kenyan.

At the time, however, these accomplishments seemed like minor notes in an otherwise discordant tragic opera. A surprise Viet Cong offensive launched during the Tet holidays ripped an irreparable hole in the already tattered national support for the war and in President Lyndon Johnson's reelection hopes. By late February, Johnson had declared that he would not run for reelection but would devote all his efforts to ending the conflict; then the bombing escalated again. The new Democratic front-runner, Senator Robert Kennedy, would later be gunned down. While Dustin Hoffman was succumbing to the wiles of Anne Bancroft in the film *The Graduate*, Columbia University exploded. Martin Luther King, Jr., fell to a rifle shot in Memphis. For a second year in a row, a summer of riots turned sickly urban ghettoes into refugee camps. Only weeks before the Mexico City Olympics, the Democratic National Convention was serenaded by sirens of Chicago's riot police busy mashing the faces of protesters who had pelted them with rocks and flowers.

The 1968 Olympic protest grew out of a conviction that the civil rights movement had exhausted its energy, if not its idealism. Racism was so inbred, so structurally a part of our country, that the familiar forms of political engagement seemed to have lost their power. Harry Edwards, fresh out of Cornell University's Ph.D. program and a brash San Jose State University sociology instructor, hatched the idea of an Olympic boycott. Based on his personal experience—he had parlayed his athletic skills into a college scholarship—Edwards had come to believe that the country was fooling itself with the belief that it was making dramatic strides in race relations. Sports had been elevated into a false icon of racial harmony. The Olympics offered an inviting stage to provoke some international soul-searching.

"LET WHITEY RUN HIS OWN OLYMPICS"

If there is one image of the American black athlete in the sixties, etched into the public consciousness, it is that of a clenched fist held high, determined and dignified. In one dramatic moment at the 1968 Mexico City Olympics, sprinters Tommie Smith and John Carlos, two determined and frightened young men, turned the adulation of the crowd into hisses and boos. It was a troublesome and inspiring act that even today reminds us of the divide that separates blacks from whites. But it also helped speed the transformation of sports for the better.

All spring and summer of that year, while the nation shook with assassinations and riots, a group of Olympic hopefuls, including Smith and Carlos, trained in south San Francisco under Bud Winter, a white coach respected as tough by his mostly black runners. Winter's protégés would occasionally attend political gatherings organized by Edwards, who was noisily attracting notoriety at San Jose State. Edwards had befriended Carlos and Smith during the fiercest days of the Black Power movement. The Black Panthers, based in Oakland, were under twenty-four-hour surveillance. FBI director J. Edgar Hoover made it his personal mission to destroy the Panthers. Hoover's agents were eventually held responsible for gunning down dozens of black activists. Edwards would subsequently discover that he had been number six on the FBI list of "most subversive" Americans.[20]

An imposing and singular figure, Edwards stands 6 feet, 8 inches tall, with sculpted features, a goatee, wire-rimmed glasses, and a polished dome acquired well before Michael Jordan made that look fashionable. Although San Jose State was considered tolerant for the times, its few black students were forbidden to join fraternities, denied on-campus housing, and channeled into soft courses specifically designed for athletes imported to carry the university colors on the playing field. Edwards, who had become a campus guru to antiwar radicals and the few black students, most of whom were athletes, was incensed that college administrators viewed his charges as chattel or candidates for the penitentiary. The previous fall, he had persuaded every black member of the university football team to boycott the opening game. Fearing a bloody confrontation, university officials caved in and canceled the game.

Edwards was still steaming over the public humiliation of Muhammad Ali, who had been stripped of his heavyweight title in 1966 for following his Muslim beliefs and refusing to fight in Vietnam. Now, with the IOC on the verge of admitting apartheid South Africa to the upcoming Olympics, and no peep of concern from the U.S. government, Edwards organized a meeting of what he called the Olympic Project for Human Rights. It drew some of the most respected and successful black athletes of the time, including Ali, Bill Russell, and Jim Brown. Kareem Abdul-Jabbar, then known as Lew Alcindor, an All America basketball star at the University of California at Los Angeles, stirred the gathering when he explained why he supported the boycott of South Africa. "Everybody knows me," he said, towering over the crowd at 7 feet, 2 inches. "[But] last summer I was almost killed by a racist cop shooting at a black cat [himself] in Harlem. . . . Somewhere each of us has got to make a stand. . . . I take my stand here."[21]

The boycott caught a strong tail wind in December 1967 when Martin Luther King, Jr., joined with activist luminaries such as H.

Rap Brown and Stokely Carmichael to back the protest.[22] But boy-cott fever did not catch on until the New York Athletic Club meet, an annual indoor event held each February at New York's Madison Square Garden. The NYAC had become notorious for its all-white and anti-Jewish membership policies. Yet here it was, hosting the event's one hundredth anniversary, with black runners as the big draw.

Smith and Carlos; a raft of high-profile black track stars; college teams including Villanova, New York University, and Morgan State; and the Soviet national track team all honored the boycott. The NAACP, Urban League, and Anti-Defamation League praised the boycotters for highlighting the discriminatory practices of the NYAC. Nonviolent and idealistic, the boycott was a tremendous coup. It also catalyzed Edwards and his followers, who turned their focus to-ward a possible boycott of the upcoming Olympics, an idea that had been floated at the first national Black Power conference.

It was a long shot at best, and certain to rile the sports establish-ment. As if to hammer home that point, on the very day of the suc-cessful NYAC boycott, IOC Chairman Avery Brundage announced that the Olympic committee would definitely let South Africa's team compete. Edwards and his group were outraged. "They've virtually said 'the hell with us,'" Edwards said. "Now we'll have to reply, 'let Whitey run his own Olympics.'"[23]

Over the ensuing months, thirty-two countries threatened to pull their teams from the Games to protest the IOC's decision. Backed into a corner, Brundage appeared to give ground. In April, the IOC reinstated the boycott against South Africa. But instead of letting the issue die a natural death, Brundage clumsily reignited the militants by huffing that the black athletes were "ungrateful to attempt to boy-cott something which has given them such great opportunities."[24]

The mixed messages left the athletes unsure of how to react. Em-boldened, but not convinced that their grievances were being ad-dressed, they debated endlessly about whether to carry out their threat. Prominent track and field stars Ralph Boston, Bill Gaines, and Lee Evans agreed to go along if necessary. But considering that the most visible goal, keeping South Africa out of the Games, had been achieved, support for a symbolic protest faded. A poll in *Ebony* found that only 1 percent of black athletes supported a boycott.[25] Even many sympathetic white reporters felt that enough was enough. Citing the decision by Jesse Owens not to boycott the Berlin Games, Red Smith, the Pulitzer Prize-winning sports columnist for the *New York Times*, said that sports had been "the Negro's best friend."[26]

By the end of the summer it was clear that the boycott threat had petered out. Edwards, who had received ugly death threats, decided to skip the Olympics altogether, taking temporary refuge in Canada. Anxiety about their future and outright fear about what might happen if they carried out a boycott took its toll among the athletes. They were left to fend for themselves when the Games finally got underway.

Tommy Smith and Juan Carlos, two of the favorites in the 200 meters, had agonized over what they would do until the last minute. They were an unlikely pair—the taciturn Smith, twenty-four years old and still a student, and the outgoing, upbeat Carlos. They considered starting the race and then breaking into a trot. They thought of going all out then declining their medals. In the end, Smith simply told Carlos that he was going to "do something on the stand" and that he wanted support. Carlos promised it.[27]

Smith ended up winning the race easily, ignoring a strained thigh muscle, and setting a world record in the process. Carlos took the bronze medal. After the race they met under the stands to await the medal ceremony. Smith, wearing a black scarf, pulled from his bag two black gloves purchased by his and Evans's wives and gave the left one to Carlos, who wore a string of Mardi Gras beads. They slipped into sweat suits and removed their running shoes to reveal black socks underneath. On the spur of the moment they agreed on their gesture, which, according to Arthur Ashe, would "forever change the image of the black American athlete."[28]

The two black protesters, and the surprise silver medalist, Peter Norman of Australia, who is white, marched to the podium. All three wore buttons that read "The Olympic Project for Human Rights." As the anthem began to play, and two American flags rose into the sky, Smith and Carlos stared intently at the ground. Rather than graciously accepting their medals, they raised their fists in silent protest, offering themselves as a public sacrifice for African Americans, athletes and nonathletes, frustrated at being defined, limited, and ridiculed for the accident of skin color. Though revisionist historians now cite the protest as a dignified moment in the maturing of a melting-pot society, at the time Smith and Carlos were widely vilified. In a not-atypical comment, ABC's Brent Musberger, then a *Chicago American* columnist, labeled Smith and Carlos "a pair of dark-skinned storm troopers."[29]

There were other, more muted, protests. The three American medalists in the 400 meters, gold medal winner Lee Evans, silver medalist Larry James, and third-place finisher Ron Freeman, all wearing black berets, gave clenched fist salutes when they mounted the platform during the medal ceremony. They removed the berets only at the last minute and faced the three American flags when the Star Spangled Banner was played. After the long jump, which was won by Bob Beamon with Ralph Boston finishing third, neither medalist wore shoes to the podium. Beamon displayed black knee-length socks.

The Mexico City Olympics had been a triumph for African American athletes, who accounted for all eight Olympic running records set by the United States. "If not for the blacks," quipped one European coach not totally facetiously, "the U.S. team would finish somewhere behind Ecuador."[30] But the brouhaha over the salute swept aside much of the good feeling. Responding to a threat made by the IOC, the United States Olympic Committee issued an international apology for the incident, suspended the medal winners, and banished them from the Olympic village.[31] Jim Hines, who had set a world record that would stand for fifteen years when he won the gold medal in the 100 meters, believed it rolled back years of progress toward racial harmony because of the tensions it stirred. Smith eventually settled into a long career as a sociology teacher and athletic coach at Santa Monica College in California. Carlos went on to set a world record in the 100 the following year before his fortunes headed downward. He ultimately landed a job as a track coach at a Palm Springs, California high school. He's still reluctant to talk about the protest.[32]

The events of 1968 also exposed the rift among different generations of blacks. In one particularly caustic exchange, Jesse Owens
attacked Harry Edwards as a self-promoting opportunist who was
destroying for talented blacks the "all-important gift of opportunity."
Edwards saw a far less level playing field. While blacks were achiev-
ing parity and more so, racism still haunted the athletes once they
left the court or hung up their track shoes. He called Owens an
"Uncle Tom" with a "ridiculously naïve belief in the sanctity of athletics."*

It was a bitter volley that echoed the tensions within the black
community of the 1930s over the success of Owens and Joe Louis. It
also served a transformative purpose, for it brought to the surface
the long-suppressed anger of black athletes who had become among
the most successful of Americans, yet had accumulated so few of
the fruits that success usually brings. Once they stepped off the playing field, most black athletes still traveled figuratively at the back of
the bus.

"BLACK IS BEST"

During the height of the black power movement, an avalanche of
articles chronicled the changing color of sports. A five-part series
published by the *Los Angeles Times* in 1968 and an essay in *Sports Illustrated* in 1971 stirred the most controversy. Although the reports
drew similar conclusions—that blacks appeared to have some biological edge over white athletes—the reactions to the articles were as
different as black and white. The *Times*'s Charles Maher's articles,
"Blacks Physically Superior? Some Say They're Hungrier" and "Do
Blacks Have a Physical Advantage? Scientists Differ," focused on the
nature/nurture controversy, interviewing skeptics who questioned
the significance of the physiological differences between races.

---

*Vince Mathews, who participated in the proposed boycott of the Mexico City Olympics, recalled
a visit by Jesse Owens with black Olympians after the Smith–Carlos incident at the 1968 Games:
"When Jesse walked into the room, most of us tried to show him respect. But when he got up at
the meeting and said he didn't want the white athletes in the room to leave because 'these are my
brothers' and I want to talk to them, you could see the snickers on some of the faces."[33]

Thomas Cureton, a physical education professor who had published numerous studies of champion athletes, flat-out rejected the hereditary theory. "Because of years of training, yes," said Cureton. "Because of motivation, yes. Because of social goals, yes. Those make a difference. But not race."[34]

Basketball coach John Wooden, in the midst of his unparalleled success at UCLA in the 1960s and '70s, ascribed the rise of black athletes to their having "just a little more ambition" than whites. Los Angeles Lakers star Tommy Hawkins looked back over thirty years of success stories by black athletes and concluded, "You identify with people who have been successful. From a Negro standpoint, those people would be in sports and entertainment."[35]

However, not everyone agreed that the key ingredients for athletic success were individual drive and role models. Maher interviewed Carleton Coon and Edward E. Hunt, Jr., a Penn State anthropologist, coauthors of the 1950 book, *Races and Living Races of Man.* Coon and Hunt acknowledged the social factors that pushed blacks into sports, but both believed that the growing disparity in performance at the elite level could not be accounted for by differing cultural experiences. Blacks, they concluded, were more likely than whites to be born with a physique suitable for elite competitive sports.

Despite the controversial subject matter, Maher's articles created hardly a ripple. But three years later, when *Sports Illustrated* published its infamous article on the same subject, "An Assessment of 'Black is Best,'" a fierce public debate erupted. That report, by respected senior editor Martin Kane, was measured and in the best tradition of journalism, mixing anecdotes with available science. Yet the reaction was so vitriolic, and persisted for so many years, that no other magazine, popular or academic, would even touch the subject for more than fifteen years.

What had changed? The answer was "IQ."

CHAPTER 18

SPORTS AND IQ

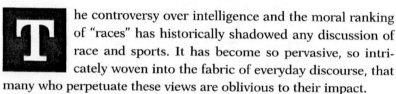

T he controversy over intelligence and the moral ranking of "races" has historically shadowed any discussion of race and sports. It has become so pervasive, so intricately woven into the fabric of everyday discourse, that many who perpetuate these views are oblivious to their impact.

In 1987, on the fortieth anniversary of the fall of the color barrier in baseball, long-time Los Angeles Dodgers executive Al Campanis was asked to appear on the ABC News program *Nightline* to talk about his old friend Jackie Robinson. Campanis had earned a reputation as a good baseball man with a big heart. Over four decades, he had worked himself up from a fringe minor-league player to one of the most respected general managers for one of the most successful teams in all of professional sports. More than most sports executives, Campanis was acutely aware of the hard road traveled by blacks in sports.

That evening on nationwide television, Campanis proceeded to make a number of links between black athletes and intelligence. The very public self-immolation that followed ended his career almost immediately. But the brouhaha had a far more profound impact. Campanis managed to touch every raw nerve of racial suspicions. To critics of race science, his inopportune comments epitomized all that was dangerous about breaking the taboo linking race and sports.

In many respects, Campanis was an unlikely figure to find himself in the middle of such a contentious debate. He was an American boot-strapper, born in Greece and raised in New York City. After

graduating from New York University, he tried to make it in baseball. Campanis had been toiling away at the Brooklyn Dodgers' top
farm club in Montreal in 1945 when Branch Rickey signed Jackie
Robinson. The two teammates had battled amicably all year for the
batting title, which Robinson ultimately won. They became friends
as Campanis, a second baseman and the better fielder, took to tutor-
ing Robinson. Their mutual respect grew when a rival player sliding
into second roughed up Robinson, prompting Campanis to throw
down his glove and challenge the player to a fight.[1] The friendly ri-
vals led Montreal to the Minor League World Series Championship.

Unlike Robinson, however, Campanis simply didn't have what it
took to be a major-league star. Abandoning the diamond for the back
office, he worked his way up through the Dodgers system, managing
in the minors and eventually becoming director of baseball's best
scouting system, which he expanded to Latin America. He would
sign many, many African Americans and Latinos while developing a
reputation for not caring a whit whether a player was black or
white. "I don't believe Campanis has a prejudiced bone in his body,"
said Don Newcombe, the great African American Dodgers pitcher.[2]
Campanis's only concern was whether a young player was prepared
to bleed Dodgers blue.

That evening on *Nightline*, Campanis was fondly reminiscing
about Robinson with host Ted Koppel when the discussion segued
into why there were so pitifully few blacks in management in baseball. "No, I don't believe it's prejudice," Campanis offered. He volunteered that blacks "may not have some of the necessities" to compete
with whites as managers or general managers. The words were particularly startling coming from Campanis. No one who knew him
could remember him ever before uttering anything that could be
even vaguely construed as racist. Taken aback, Koppel did all he
could to give Campanis an opportunity to recoup. "Do you really believe that?"

"Well, I don't say all of them, but they certainly are short in some
areas. How many quarterbacks do you have, how many pitchers do
you have that are black?" As if to underline his point that both on-
the-field performance and off-the-field aspirations are based mostly

on physiology, Campanis asserted that blacks couldn't swim "because they don't have buoyancy."

After a break for a commercial, the usually unflappable Koppel, visibly flapped, threw the Dodgers executive a soft one over the plate. "I'd like to give you another chance to dig yourself out," he said. Oblivious, and considering his statements matter-of-fact, Campanis dug an ever deeper professional grave with one ignorant-sounding comment after another. "I have never said that blacks aren't intelligent, but they may not have the desire to be in the front office. I know that they have wanted to manage, and many of them have managed. But they are outstanding athletes, very God-gifted and they're very wonderful people. . . . They are gifted with great musculature and various other things. They are fleet of foot, and this is why there are a number of black ballplayers in the major leagues."

"Oh, I get it, Al," interrupted flabbergasted fellow guest Roger Kahn. "Blacks have the ability to work in the cotton fields, but not to manage a baseball team."

Campanis looked stunned and confused. He was certainly not the prototypical aging white power broker who had consciously barred the door to black and Hispanic players. Just the opposite. Years earlier, before Roy Campanella became paralyzed and Jim Gilliam died, he had expressed high hopes that they would become big-league managers.[3] But minutes after the show ended, his insensitive burbling had sparked an uproar and threats of protests by black and white groups. Two days later, the still bewildered Campanis, after forty-four years with the Dodgers, was fired.

IQ REDUX

For two decades, scientists and social reformers had worked to disconnect the once accepted link between race and IQ. Almost overnight in 1969 it was restored, and in the process the long-whispered stereotype of the genetic seesaw, with physical ability on one end and smarts on the other, again became a public issue. After two decades in which intelligence research was viewed as an acade-

"I've checked everything, Sir . . . his bones, lungs, heart . . . there's nothing extra to make him run faster." This cartoon appeared in the *Sunday Nation*, Nairobi. Much to the bemusement of Kenyans, scientists from around the world have descended upon Kenya to try to unlock the mystery of the country's extraordinary road racing success.

Kenyans dominate the cross-country and road racing circuits, frequently sweeping all of the top places. It's reached the point where most of the world's best non-Kenyan men have all but given up contesting the middle distances in elite races.

Revered in his country, Kipchoge Keino and his wife have opened their family farm to hundreds of orphan children, many of them prospective distance runners. "We are natural runners," Keino asserts.

African American athletes were stars in many sports in the late nineteenth century before Jim Crow. At left, bare-handed catcher Moses "Fleetwood Walker, shown in 1881 (middle row) with his Oberlin College teammates, was the son of a physician who pursued his dream of playing professionally before being forced out of the game by threats of racial violence.

Jack Johnson, the first black heavyweight champion, feared no one and took to parading his very public affairs with white women. His less than submissive attitude cost him his title and eventually his liberty. Two years after beating boxing's first "great white hope," Jim Jeffries, he was convicted of crossing a state line to have sex with a white woman, who he later married.

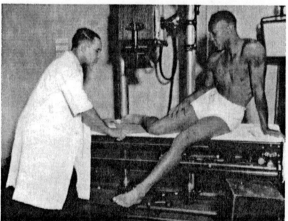

Famed anthropologist William Montague Cobb convened a team from Case Western Reserve University in 1936 to examine Jesse Owens and test the hypothesis that a distinctive anatomy was key to the success of black sprinters. The researchers found it unconvincing that "Negroid physical characters are anatomically concerned with the present dominance of Negro athletes."

"The reason . . . that basketball appeals to the Hebrew," wrote New York sportswriter Paul Gallico, "is that the game places a premium on an alert, scheming mind, flashy trickiness, artful dodging and general smart aleckness."

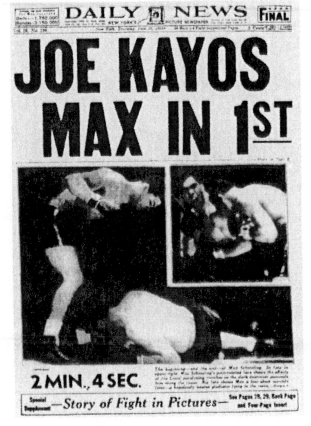

On June 22, 1938, "The Dusky David of Detroit" destroyed Hitler's Aryan superman, Max Schmeling. It was a stunning knockout blow against white supremacy and for black racial pride.

After she was accidently killed during a robbery in 1980, Stella Walsh (top), a champion sprinter and jumper for more than a quarter century until she retired in the 1950s, was found after an autopsy to be biologically a male. In contrast, long-legged Wilma Rudolph (bottom), dubbed "the black pearl," became the darling of the press while winning three gold medals in the 1960 Rome Olympics.

Texas Western (now the University of Texas at El Paso), with five black starters, dunked all-white Kentucky for the 1966 NCAA championship. Wildcat coach Adolph Rupp would later refer to the victors as "a bunch of crooks." All of the Miner's starters moved on to middle class careers.

One of the enduring and most controversial images of the 1960s is that of the clenched fists of Tommie Smith (center) and John Carlos at the Mexico City Olympics. (Australian silver medalist Peter Norman is at left). ABC's Brent Musberger, then a sports columnist, labeled them "a pair of dark-skinned storm troopers."

As with many black sprinters, aboriginal star Cathy Freeman of Australia, has faced questions about her "natural" athleticism.

Different regions of the world have become bio-cultural athletic hot-houses in specific sports. Whites such as John Godina, world shot-put champion, dominate field events, in part because of superior upper body strength. The world's best sumo wrestler, Konishiki is not from Japan, where body types tend to be short and squat, but from Samoa, where athletes are larger and quicker. The Tarahumara Indians from Mexico's Copper Canyons are among the best ultra-endurance runners—when they choose to compete.

Sports which demand quickness, speed, and jumping ability "naturally" attract blacks with West African ancestry. Herschel Walker was an all-American sprinter and football player at the University of Georgia before becoming a star in the NFL. He took time out in 1992 to make the US men's bobsled team as a "pusher," winning numerous World Cup runs and placing seventh in Lillehammer.

Like many black runners, Namibia's Frankie Fredericks, who has run more sub–10 second 100-meter runs than anyone else in sprinting history, is frequently compared to an animal. "That's where the indignity comes in," declares University of California-Berkeley professor Harry Edwards.

The mile has never been just a race but a romantic, almost heroic quest. In 1954, Roger Bannister did the "impossible" when he cracked the four-minute barrier, running 3:59:4. For years, the British and Irish dominated the mile and metric mile, 1500-meters, led by Sebastian Coe, who held both records for years. Hicham El Guerrouj of Morocco now holds the record of 3:43:13 after a scintillating win over Kenya's Noah Ngeny in Rome in 1999. Both the Moroccan and the Kenyan times would have left Roger Bannister in the dust, more than 120 yards behind.

mic graveyard and a taboo subject in general, an article in an unlikely place, the normally staid *Harvard Educational Review*, exploded like a forgotten land mine, scattering shards of racial controversy far and wide.

The title was innocuous enough: "How Much Can We Boost I.Q. and Scholastic Achievement?" Its author, Arthur Jensen, a respected psychologist at the University of California at Berkeley, contended that there was now enough evidence to resolve the question of whether nature or nurture most shapes intelligence. By his account, genetic factors account for 80 percent of the observed differences in intelligence. He wrote:

> Genetic differences are manifested in virtually every anatomical, physiological, and biochemical comparison one can make between representative samples of identifiable racial groups. There is no reason why the brain should be exempt from this generalization. Any groups which have been geographically or socially isolated from one another for many generations are practically certain to differ in their gene pools, and consequently are likely to show differences in any phenotypic characteristics having a high heritability.[4]

The understandable uproar over Jensen's article was so intense that in its very next issue the *Harvard Educational Review* reprinted the piece in its entirety along with a number of critiques. The controversy escalated yet again later in 1969 when the late William Shockley of Stanford, who had shared the Nobel Prize in physics in 1956, issued his ruminations on human differences. Although Jensen's theorizing had been explosive in implication, it had the virtue of being cautiously packaged and written by a careful academician with sterling credentials in that field.* Not so with Shockley, who was frequently reckless, seeking publicity for his views on what he termed "human quality problems."[5] He announced that he had donated his sperm to one of the first sperm banks, arguing that it

---

*Jensen has published more than four hundred papers in refereed journals and is author of, among many books, *The g Factor: The Science of Mental Ability* (Westport, Conn.: Praeger, 1998).

was a great way to ensure future geniuses. Naïve or callous, he proposed as a "thinking exercise" a scheme to pay those who had low
IQs who would agree to be sterilized.[6]

The press had a field day lumping the two writers together, although they were not colleagues and disagreed on many points. Harvard psychologist Richard Herrnstein, who would later coauthor *The
Bell Curve*, weighed in with an *Atlantic Monthly* piece entitled simply
"IQ."[7] He wrote that the form of intelligence that has since come to
be called general intelligence (or *g*) was substantially heritable. What
were the implications? According to Herrnstein, those who succeeded economically in life tended to have higher IQs. And because
social standing is largely a scorecard of economic success, therefore
status, economic success, and IQ are interrelated.[8] Media attacks
were loud and long.

"BLACK IS BETTER"

The 1971 piece in *Sports Illustrated* thus hit a public nerve already
rubbed raw. In writing the article, Martin Kane assembled a broad
range of informed scientists, coaches, and athletes. He cited research by the World Health Organization, reported in the British
medical journal *The Lancet*, that black Ugandan babies were more
physically developed and neuromuscularly alert than white babies
from infancy, despite nutritional deficiencies. He interviewed numerous athletes who believed that "slavery weeded out the weak."
And he reported on fitness tests of American black and white schoolchildren that purported to show that "Negro . . . fitness scores remained significantly higher with respect to pull-ups, standing broad
jump, 50-yard dash, softball throw, and 600-yard run-walk." He concluded, "Environmental factors have a great deal to do with excellence in sports, but so do physical differences and there is an
increasing body of scientific opinion which suggests that physical
differences in the races might well have enhanced the athletic potential of the Negro in certain sports."[9]

Despite the article's measured assertions, the speculative tone of
much of the reporting enraged many. "There are no differences that

make any difference," retorted Harry Edwards. "Athletic skills are essentially culturally linked capabilities. It is racism, not genes, that explains the domination of black athletes."[10] Edwards was motivated by more than just casual concern about sloppy thinking. As an outspoken black power advocate, he was especially struck by the *Sports Illustrated* piece. He had been taken aback by the rabidity of the reactions to Jensen's article on IQ and had come to fear that rising tide of intellectual racism might spill even more effluents into the nooks and crannies of American life. When Kane's article appeared, he pounced.

In "The Myth of the Racially Superior Athlete," a polemic in the guise of an academic article, Edwards dissected the airiness of some of the anthropometric evidence cited by Kane, challenged the Middle Passage theory that the hardiest slaves survived the Atlantic crossing to eventually breed super athletes, and ridiculed as "ludicrous as even a common sense assumption" the conjecture that blacks might be genetically primed to handle pressure better than whites.[11]

Edwards's real target was not sports but "creeping Jensenism" and the perceived inverse link between sports performance and intelligence. "By asserting that blacks are physically superior," he wrote, "whites at best reinforce some old stereotypes long held about Afro-Americans— to wit, that they are little removed from the apes in their evolutionary development. . . . It opens the door for at least an informal acceptance of the idea that whites are intellectually superior to blacks."[12] Edwards contended that whites give up little to endorse the idea of black athletic superiority. This spate of articles on blacks, IQ, and athletic superiority served little purpose other than to legitimize the racist symbols he had thought were buried.

IQ ÜBER ALLES?

Is intelligence a measurable entity? Can it be captured by IQ tests and boiled down to one statistic called *g*, for general intelligence? This concept is far more ambiguous than the dissection of athletic ability, where we have the luxury of easily identifying winners and losers. Scientists generally believe that *g* can be measured and can predict with some accuracy academic and even career success; the more hotly contested issue, which rages to this day, is to what degree it is genetically based, substantially heritable, and varies by population.

Overflowing with figures, tables, references, and regression analyses, *The Bell Curve*, written by the late Richard Herrnstein and Harvard- and MIT-trained political scientist Charles Murray, was widely commented upon but sparingly read when it was published in 1994. The focus of the book is on the importance of differences in IQ, its potential genetic make-up, and how and why this should be incorporated into the public policy debate. They based much of their conclusions on the fact that various racial and ethnic groups score significantly differently on intelligence tests and that those relative scores correlate with "racial" patterns of "success" and "deviant behavior." Although only one chapter is specifically on race, and there is very little mention of eugenics, the authors clearly sought to refurbish the scientific status of the concept of race and to destigmatize eugenic thinking.

Many, if not most, media outlets savaged *The Bell Curve*, sometimes by innuendo. For instance, in one of its reports on the controversy stirred by the book, ABC News superimposed a Nazi swastika over the cover of *The Bell Curve*. The scientific community was more divided, though the critics were certainly louder in making their views heard. Analogies were made with the tainted legacy of racial biology and genocide. One reviewer, Hampton (Virginia) University sociologist Steven J. Rosenthal labeled *The Bell Curve* "a vehicle of Nazi propaganda wrapped in a cover of pseudo-scientific respectability" and "an academic version of Adolf Hitler's *Mein Kampf*."[13] Some critics were actually harsher.

Harvard's Stephen Jay Gould wrote that though the data on brain size and behavior merit serious review, those who use such data and claim they are engaging in "objective" science, such as Murray and Herrnstein, are being disingenuous. According to Gould, *The Bell Curve* offered the pretense of being a study about IQ but it actually focused on race, sometimes disguised as class, and social policy. Gould also mocks *g* theorists for falling prey to what he calls reification: "the propensity to convert an abstract concept (like intelligence) into a hard entity (like an amount of quantifiable brain stuff).[14] Gould sees the belief in an entity called intelligence as a remnant of the nineteenth century, when it was assumed that we could assess brain function in much the same way that we measure cholesterol levels or compare the processing speed of computers.

Gould and other race science critics have focused much of their ire on some of the sources cited in *The Bell Curve*. One of the more controversial is J. Philippe Rushton, a Canadian psychologist, whose work is amply cited. Rushton subscribes to the out-of-Africa theory but believes that modern humans took sharply different evolutionary paths. Separate races of human beings evolved by relying on different reproductive strategies to cope with differing environments. Those who evolved in the warm but highly unpredictable environment of Africa adopted a strategy of high reproduction, whereas human beings who migrated to the moderate cold of Europe and the more hostile climes of northern Asia took to producing fewer children but nurturing them more carefully. These strategies led to physical differences in brain size, and hence in intelligence.[15]

Rushton classifies humankind into three major races, roughly Asian, white, and black in that order. He ranks the races in what he believes are related categories, topped by IQ scores and including the tendency toward violence and crime. Brains and brawn are inversely proportional. East Asians, who evolved in demanding colder climates that put a premium on intelligence and protection of the young, have the largest brains and the lowest sex drives; Africans have the lowest IQ and are the most sexual.

Whatever the intent of the researchers, the racial focus of much of this research is readily apparent. To contemporary race scientists, however, these views are not racist but are in the best tradition of science: objective and value-neutral conclusions. They do not believe they are responsible for hate groups using their data to support twisted ends. Some scholars of human biodiversity have adopted the phrase "race realism" to explain their belief in the innate hierarchy of intelligence; critics bash them as "scientific racists."

Rushton and other "race realists" do in fact draw upon substantial data documenting a relationship between brain size and race, cranial capacity and intelligence, and intelligence and career success or criminal behavior. As with the debate over athletic performance, the sticking point in all this is *why* such differences exist; whether they matter, to what degree they are genetically influenced; and to what extent they can be modified. For example, although magnetic resonance tests confirm disparities in average brain size between Asians, whites, and blacks, and between males and females,[16] whether that constitutes biological "proof" of differences in intelligence is another argument. As Arthur Jensen has noted in his research, women have proportionately smaller brains then do men, even after adjusting for body weight, yet they score the same as men on intelligence tests. Separating the environmental from the biological is frequently more problematic than those who make sweeping claims about human differences admit.

Gould and other critics make a lot of noise about the supposed links between some contemporary scientists and eugenicists of the 1930s. The controversial Pioneer Fund has provided millions of dollars to bankroll research on intelligence at more than sixty institutions in eight countries. It was chartered in 1937 by Wickliffe Draper, a textile magnate, to improve "the character of the American people" by encouraging "white persons who settled in the original thirteen colonies prior to the adoption of the constitution and/or from related stocks" to increase their reproductive rates. It bankrolled numerous U.S. and German scientists, including the biologist Harry H. Laughlin, who drew up a model sterilization law that was used by many countries, including Germany, in drafting the Nazi Law for the Prevention of Hereditary Ill Progeny, National Socialism's cover for genocide.[17] The fund embraced "race betterment" and the forced sterilization of "inferior stock" reflecting the tenets of the most extreme elements of the American eugenics movement.* Yet such beliefs were mainstream enough to receive the blessing of John Marshall Harlan II, a prominent New York attorney who would later be appointed to the Supreme Court (and would later vote for the NAACP in *Brown v. Board of Education*), and President Roosevelt's secretary of war, Harry I. Woodring.[18]

---

*Pioneer Fund Certificates of Incorporation, on file with the New York Department of State.

Though eugenic thinking appears extreme to today's sensibilities, it was certainly considered within the boundaries of reasonable policy in the thirties and forties.

After the war the Pioneer Fund became a fund for antisegregation activists based on Draper's belief that the mixing of races would not close the black-white achievement gap in schools. He also privately espoused sending blacks, on a voluntary basis, back to their African "homeland."[19] Columbia University anthropologist Henry Garrett, an outspoken opponent of integration, consulted with the Pioneer Fund to bolster his research on the intelligence differences between races. Garrett and his colleagues launched two controversial magazines that are now considered the intellectual digests of extremist hereditarian theories of intelligence, *The Mankind Quarterly* in Britain and a more recent German off-shoot, *Neue Anthropologie*. Although *Mankind Quarterly's* original board included some eminent scientists such as paleoanthropologist Henri Valois, who helped draw up the UNESCO statement, it became a haven for hard-line eugenicists.[20]

Since 1978, *Mankind Quarterly* has been edited by Roger Pearson, a controversial British anthropologist. He founded the Northern League (also called the Pan-Nordic Cultural Society) in 1957, which recycled the pre-World War II belief in the natural superiority of northern Europeans. According to Pearson, humanity could only be preserved if we preserved "an aristocracy of mankind" by selective breeding of "ideal" types. That was a code word for the Nordic race.[21]

Over the years, the Pioneer Fund has backed a virtual Who's Who of scientists who study "racial characteristics," many brilliant, who have published more than two hundred books and two thousand scholarly papers, many with the view that inferior groups are "dumbing down" society by disseminating inferior seeds.[22] Although Murray and Herrnstein accepted no money from the Pioneer Fund, critics are quick to point out that they cite in *The Bell Curve* work by thirteen scholars who have benefited from grants in the last two decades. The grants total more than $4 million.[23]

The Pioneer Fund continues to funnel money to dozens of academics, including such respected researchers as Thomas Bouchard, who has pioneered twin studies at the University of Minnesota, and Berkeley professor Arthur Jensen. Though almost all hold professorships at distinguished universities, it is not uncommon for them to be vilified as "professors of hate."[24] Yet Robert Sternberg, a Yale professor of Education and Psychology, who has been critical of the hereditarian concept of intelligence, has included articles from fund-supported scientists in his *Encyclopedia of Intelligence*. "The fact that it funded it doesn't mean that the work is therefore invalid," says Sternberg. "Work stands or falls on its own. It just makes me think twice about what they say."[25]

In fact some recipients of sizable Pioneer Fund grants have demonstrated what might be called questionable judgment. For instance, Florida State University professor of psychology and neuroscience Glayde Whitney, an otherwise competent scholar, wrote a glowing foreword to former Ku Klux Klan leader David Duke's 1998 autobiography, *My Awakening* (which however was not funded by the Pioneer Fund), calling it an "academically excellent" work that could "change the very course of history."[26] Let's not speculate on "how."

There is little question that the Pioneer Fund has become a magnet for white supremacists. Neo-Nazis regularly pay homage to the intellectual rationalizations provided, unwittingly, by the fund and *Mankind Quarterly*, giving their poisonous ravings a patina of academic respectability. Any number of avowedly racist websites have a link to *Mankind Quarterly* side-by-side with links to such sites as the White Pride World Network, Afrikaner Resistance Movement, White Nationalist New Agency, the Ku Klux Klan, and the (not-to-be-missed) Aryan Dating Page.[27] Eugenics and intelligence research continue to be a lightning rod.

THE NATURE OF INTELLIGENCE

If as Gould and others claim, IQ does not measure intelligence, what might the concept of intelligence mean? To do justice to the complexity and elusiveness of what the average person means by intelligence, Yale's Sternberg postulates a triarchic model: *analytic in-*

telligence similar to what is measured by IQ tests; *creative* intelligence; and *practical* intelligence, or what is popularly called street smarts. He offers the example of Kenyan children who are great at identifying medicinal herbs, indicating high practical intelligence, and can be quite creative, but score low on IQ tests. The reverse sometimes holds true in Asian populations.[28]

Harvard Ph.D. and science writer Daniel Goleman, bowdlerizing the far more subtle ideas of John Mayer of the University of New Hampshire and Yale University's Peter Salovey, argues that empathy, self-awareness, persistence, and other social skills—essentially anything that is not analytic IQ—represent a form of intelligence at least as important in life as intelligence.[29] Ironically, Goleman calls this second concept EQ for "emotional intelligence," in effect reaffirming the distinctiveness and primacy of IQ.[30]

Harvard education professor Howard Gardner suggests even more forms of intelligence—at least eight including *linguistic, musical, logical/mathematical, spatial, bodily/kinesthetic, intrapersonal, interpersonal*, and *naturalist*.[31] For illustration, let's apply Gardner's bodily/kinesthetic form of intelligence to a basketball superstar such as Michael Jordan. Like many great athletes, Jordan has thought a lot about the upcoming game and is conversant with the styles of the opposition players. In that sense, any game decisions draw upon the cognitive skills usually associated with measured intelligence, or *g*. But Jordan also can make split-second decisions on the court that translate into truly special physical feats that have no analogy outside athletics. Though no one could call these "decisions" traditional intelligence, they do draw on considerable spatial aptitude. Gardner, however, mucks up an intriguing theory by lumping athletes who demonstrate "sports intelligence" with those who have obviously different skills, such as car mechanics who work with their hands. And as many researchers have pointed out, the various forms of supposedly noncognitive intelligence all show strong correlation with traditional measures of IQ.

The concept of multiple intelligences is more than just idle speculation. There is intriguing evidence that the human brain may grow modularly with separate development of language, cognition, and other forms of mental processing. This process of development might explain the so-called idiot savant syndrome, depicted in the movie *Rainman*, in which people with depressed IQs demonstrate a genius-level ability in a limited area, such as remembering or making mathematical calculations or patients who suffer from Williams-Beuren syndrome, who have an average of IQ of 60 and poor logic thinking yet have highly developed language and music skills.[32]

Some evolutionary theorists have postulated what they call the "Machiavellian intelligence hypothesis" to explain the varied nature of intelligence. It proposes a bio-social perspective that links intelligence to the competition of everyday life, with roots in "social manipulation, deceit and cunning cooperation." Unlike g theorists, these scholars consider intelligence unmeasurable and IQ less than meaningful. "It is even possible," conclude some such exponents, "that disparate pressures, social and nonsocial, have resulted in a legacy of separate 'intelligences' within one brain at the same time."[33]

If the brain does employ varied intelligence modules, then we would indeed expect to find differing degrees of its expression in different populations. Even conventional g theorists such as Arthur Jensen, while forcefully arguing that the concept of general intelligence makes scientific sense, believe that it can take a variety of forms. But most psychologists, and g theorists in particular, take a dim view of the idea that there is a conceptually distinct form of intelligence that represents our emotional life or other noncognitive qualities. It would require, they contend, a redefinition of what we mean by intelligence as a problem-solving cognitive ability. In a detailed critique, University of Sydney psychologist Lazar Stankov suggests that the concept of "emotional intelligence" is little more than slapping a new label on unmeasurable personality traits. "Speculation must be replaced with hard, empirical evidence," wrote Stankov with his coauthors, student Michaela Davies and Richard Roberts of the National Research Council and Armstrong Laboratory at Brooks Air Force Base, San Antonio, Texas. Their tests didn't find much.[34] "Like psychoanalysis, [emotional intelligence] can provide a nice topic for after-dinner conversation but nothing more," Stankov says.[35]

Those who do subscribe to the multiple intelligence hypothesis appear to do so for political and ideological reasons as much as any-

thing else. Dinesh D'Souza of the American Enterprise Institute believes that different races may express mental aptitude in distinct,
genetically determined ways. "It stands to reason that groups that
are unlike each other in some respects may also differ in other respects," wrote D'Souza.

> Why should groups with different skin color, head shape, and
> other visible characteristics prove identical in reasoning ability or
> the ability to construct advanced civilization? If blacks have cer-
> tain inherited abilities, such as improvisational decision making,
> that could explain why they predominate in certain fields such as
> jazz, rap, and basketball, and not in other fields, such as classical
> music, chess and astronomy.[36]

But just as early eugenicists considered themselves progressives,
there is a dangerous side to those who propose speculative theories
of multiple intelligences. Although they may be well motivated and
incorporate the latest research, implicit in their argument is that ag-
grieved and culturally vulnerable segments of society—women and
minority populations most prominently—express their "intelligence"
not through traditional means such as logic or verbal skills but
through body and soul—emotions, sports, music, dance, thinking-
on-one's-feet. For both D'Souza on the right and the avowed liberal
Gould, the skill of making a jump shot may be metaphorically, if not
functionally, the equivalent of solving a math problem. The implicit
suggestion, of course, is that athletes are less mentally capable than
those who do well in math—but heck, that doesn't matter, since each
group is as intelligent in its own special way.

Dare I suggest that this perspective may be seen as patronizing and
could even be construed as racist? It cannot be stated too strongly that
the data that conclusively links our ancestry to athletic skills have little
or anything to say about intelligence. It must be remembered that the
human brain is the product of about 40,000 genes, or almost half the
human genome. It is far, far more complex than the genetics of reaction time or endurance. Differences on the track or basketball court do
not necessarily mean differences between the ears.

CHAPTER 19

WINNING THE GENETIC LOTTERY

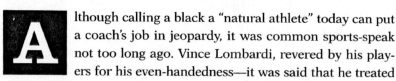lthough calling a black a "natural athlete" today can put a coach's job in jeopardy, it was common sports-speak not too long ago. Vince Lombardi, revered by his players for his even-handedness—it was said that he treated everyone the same, like dogs—used the compliment freely. "I think Negroes are more naturally endowed. I think physique has a great deal to do with it. They're built differently. Their muscular development is longer. Their muscles are not as bunched. They have a longer type of muscle. This gives them greater spring and more quickness."[1]

With but a few notable exceptions,[2] athletes, white and black, talk openly about the "natural" differences between the races in style and stature. "We generally carry less fat, the athletes. I can look at [our bodies] and tell that. We have long levers. And those are the two things that help us sprint better," observed Carl Lewis, who is known for his frankness.[3] "We are built a little differently," noted O. J. Simpson in 1977, when he was starring for the Buffalo Bills, "built for speed—skinny calves, long legs, high asses are all characteristics of blacks."[4] According to Hall-of-Fame second baseman Joe Morgan, "blacks, for physiological reasons, have better speed, quickness, and ability. Baseball, football, and basketball put a premium on these skills."[5]

The public has been fascinated by these apparent differences for well over a century. In the 1890s, scientists took a fancy to Peter Jackson, the great black Australian boxer, from whom the legendary John L. Sullivan turned tail and refused to fight. Jackson was portrayed as "a human fighting animal," the very "idea of some splendid glossy-coated thoroughbred horse," in the words of the English boxing expert W. S. Doherty. Of course, he was also thought to suffer the alleged Negro infirmity, an Achilles' stomach—it was assumed that brutish blacks had no guts and little stamina, so they would invariably fall to a crafty white fighter.

By the turn of the century, the fascination had become more clinical. While racing in eugenics-minded Europe in 1901, the great Negro bicyclist Marshall "Major" Taylor was asked by physicians at the Academy of Sciences in Bordeaux, France, to undergo a variety of tests. They examined his heart, took X-rays, and checked his body measurements before concluding he was an "absolutely perfect" physical specimen.[6] John Dayer "Doc" Taylor agreed to be prodded and probed after he becoming the first black to win a gold medal at the Olympics when he ran the third leg in the 4x400 meters in London in 1908.[7] The emergence of every new black sports celebrity sent scientists scrambling for calipers to measure limbs, skin folds, heel length, and the like and then generalizing, often speciously. "The negro's proficiency in athletics," ran an article in the *New York Times* in 1914 after a spate of victories by black sprinters, "has become a source of much speculation and discussion in athletic clubs."[8]

The fascination with measuring and comparing athletes, which mirrored the rise of eugenics fever, applied not just to blacks. After a day of anthropometric measurements at Columbia University during his record-breaking 1921 season, when he cracked fifty-nine home runs, Babe Ruth was declared fully 50 percent more "efficient" than the average human and smarter to boot.[9] Determined to find the "ideal athlete," a team of Swiss anthropologists undertook in the 1920s what is believed to be the first of dozens of studies comparing the physiques of Olympians. They found that Japanese male skiers measured considerably shorter and lighter than the German skiers, who had slightly different physiques than did the Romanians and Norwegians.[10]

The emergence of so many black star athletes in the 1930s sparked a number of studies, including the one by Cobb of Jesse Owens and another by Iowa State University physical educator Eleanor Metheny. In 1939, Metheny conducted extensive body measurements of 102 students, with the group split evenly by race. The whites were of varied ethnic backgrounds; almost all of the blacks could trace their ancestry to West Africa. Metheny's results were in line with other studies before and since; she documented smaller lung capacity, longer arms and legs, shorter trunks, narrower hips, and heavier bones in blacks.[11]

Metheny mused about the implications for sports performance, the question that had prompted her study. Longer limbs, she suggested, allowed for greater momentum to develop, contributing to an advantage in jumping and throwing. Blacks, on average, could take longer strides with less angular reaction to the forward stride. Lower breathing capacity would mean that blacks with a West African heritage would do less well in endurance activities. A cautious scientist, she did note that her findings were tentative and that the physical qualities she had evaluated were only a piece of a far more complex puzzle.

Over the years there have been more than two hundred studies comparing the physique and body composition of athletes.[12] The seminal modern work, by British physician James M. Tanner, *The Physique of the Olympic Athlete*, published in 1960 after the Rome Olympics, detailed the height, weight, muscle width in arm, and calf and thigh length of 137 athletes.[13] Tanner noted that there appeared to be an ideal physique for each sport, although he found considerable overlap in body types—a classic bell curve. Sprinters were the most muscular. Muscularity progressively decreased the longer the run. Marathoners were generally small, short-legged, narrow-shouldered, and ectomorphic, or lacking in muscle.

These body types correlate loosely with population categories. "Amongst competitors in both track and field events there are large significant racial differences," Tanner wrote.[14] Blacks with West African ancestry had a range of anatomical characteristics that contributed to their excellence in jumping and sprinting while hindering them in endurance events such as the marathon.[15] Although his conclusions matched racial studies done both before and since, it should be noted that Tanner only studied fifteen black athletes, twelve of whom traced their ancestry to West Africa. Asians were generally smaller, with relatively short extremities and long torsos.

Of course, the vast continent of Africa contains a multitude of genetically diverse tribes. West Africans have the most mesomorphic physiques, which means they have bigger, more visible muscles, including a larger chest. This anatomical package apparently translates into more explosive energy.[16] East Africans have a genetic diversity between that of Africans and non-Africans and slender body types, a perfect package for endurance sports.[17] But with their ectomorphic physiques, Kenyans will never compete for the title of "world's fastest human," no matter how diligently they may train. The converse holds true for West Africans. It's genetically improbable to expect to find any elite marathoners coming out of Cameroon, Nigeria, or Senegal.

Tanner's findings have been confirmed again and again. As nature would have it, different populations are better suited to excel at anaerobic activities such as sprinting, jumping, and lifting, than at aerobic sports such as distance running, cycling, and swimming. We see these differences on the playing field, but they are apparent at the micro level as well. In the mitochondria of cells, the body's powerhouse, oxygen combines with the glucose released by carbohydrates and, eventually, fats to produce sustained energy. When the body demands quick bursts, it breaks down carbohydrates quickly, if incompletely. At roughly 400 meters, about 40–50 seconds of running (equivalent to about 50 meters of swimming), the body has depleted much of its anaerobic capacity. That is the point at which anaerobic athletes experience an accumulation of lactic acid, the waste product of the muscles. If physical activity continues past this bio-physiological divide, the body begins to process energy more deliberately.

SEPARATED AT BIRTH?

Anatomical differences are apparent at birth. Black babies are born a week earlier than white or Asian babies, yet they are already more mature as measured by amniotic fluid, bone development, and other indices.[18] "The most remarkable finding was the precocity of the younger infants," wrote French physician Marcelle Geber in a 1957 study of Ugandan children, noting that the black infants stood earlier and were more dexterous. "The motor development was greatly in advance of that of European infants of the same age. It was paralleled by advanced adaptivity, language, and personal social behaviour."[19]

"On average . . . the black infant is somewhat more mature biologically speaking than the white infant," says Michigan State's Robert Malina, editor of the *American Journal of Human Biology*, who has tracked the issue since the 1960s. "Black infants tend to have somewhat advanced skeletal development. They also tend to be somewhat more neurologically, or what we call neuromuscularly, alert."[20] The faster maturation of black babies continues throughout life even when blacks are poorer and eat a less healthy diet.[21] They demonstrate superior eye-hand coordination, hold their necks erect earlier by a couple of weeks, walk earlier by about a month, and enter puberty earlier by about a year.[22]

"I think the reason [for precocity in black infants] may be partially biological," agrees William Frankenburg, a professor of pediatrics and preventive medicine at the University of Colorado. In the mid-1960s Frankenburg and fellow researcher Joe Dodds developed a standardized measure of thirty gross motor skills of infants, including throwing, jumping, kicking, and coordination, that is now used in more than fifty countries. The researchers were intrigued to find that black children as young as six months developed significantly more quickly than the white infants.[23]

"When I first looked at the data I thought, 'Those were interesting but maybe not replicable kind of findings, perhaps chance findings,'" says Dodds.[24] The researchers, who have worked together for more than twenty years, then crunched the numbers on thousands more children. Once again, they were flabbergasted. "There were no items that the white children were doing earlier than the black children in the first year of life," Dodds notes. Even by age four, blacks had an edge in fifteen categories while whites bested blacks in only three. "These are two studies removed by years and totally different samples of kids. To come up with some of the same trends, I didn't believe that we would find that."

Can environmental factors account for such significant differences? "Biological factors are major determinants of how the child seems to be developing during the first few months of life," states Frankenburg. "There are people who suggest that you should provide lots of exercises and buy special toys and things for children to help them mature motorwise. But those who have experience with those kinds of activities have shown that it doesn't make any difference in how the child develops." Time and again researchers have found that participation in sports and physical training cannot significantly alter the endowed physiology of children (although it may improve their ability to fulfill their genetic potential).[25]

Although black children appear more physically precocious, are they more likely to become better athletes? The researchers are understandably uncomfortable about making such a leap of judgment. "We haven't a shred of evidence that there's any connection between what's going on in the development of the first year of life and performance on the basketball court or the swimming pool at age eighteen," explains Dodds nervously, very aware of the controversy.

It's hardly an irrational leap to suspect that precocious infants will end up as athletically skilled adults, however. Blacks and whites do develop different body types at an early age.[26] Numerous studies have found that by age five or six black children consistently excel in the dash, the long jump, and the high jump, all of which require a short power burst.[27] Racial differences become more pronounced over time.[28] By the time boys are teenagers, blacks demonstrate a significantly faster patellar tendon reflex time—the knee jerk response—and an edge in reaction time over whites.[29]

One test frequently cited by critics to rebuff evidence of West African superiority in sprinting and jumping was conducted in 1988 by Hampton University's David Hunter, then a graduate student at Ohio State University. He compared laboratory and "real-world" performance of seventy-four blacks and sixty-two whites. The athletes were not statistically different in age, height, weight, lean body weight, and body mass, although the blacks had a significantly lower percentage of body fat, which is to be expected based on physiological profiles of African Americans as compared to whites. Although he found no difference in anaerobic power in the lab, black subjects performed significantly better at the vertical jump and 40-yard dash. Then Hunter performed a statistical manipulation called Analysis of Covariance (ANCOVA), which he used to adjust the data based on the higher amount of body fat of the white subjects. Hunter found that it "washed away" the difference in the dash, in effect washing away the case for a black anaerobic advantage along with it.[30]

Did Hunter reach the right conclusion? Even after adjusting for fat, blacks still had a faster dash time, about a tenth of a second, not quite statistically significant. All Hunter really "proved" was that when you equate blacks and whites for percentage of fat, there is little difference in sprint performance. But in reality, otherwise identical black and white athletes do not have equal body measurements—blacks *naturally* have much less fat, a tiny physiological advantage that can translate into a huge on-the-field advantage. This difference may be one key variable that provides black males with an advantage in running.

Scientists evaluating jumping ability frequently test for vertical leap—the ability to jump into the air without a run-up. A jump of one-third of an athlete's height is considered impressive. White members of a U.S. Olympic men's volleyball team, known for their terrific vertical leap, max out at 50 percent.[31] Black basketball players commonly exceed that figure. The greatest vertical leap ever recorded in a jump-and-reach, called a Sargent test, is 48 inches by former Utah Jazz star Darrell Griffith (a.k.a. Dr. Dunkenstein). That's more than 63 percent of his 6-foot, 4-inch height. Former Atlanta Hawk guard Spud Webb, all of 135 pounds and 5 feet, 7 inches, regularly wowed crowds with his one-handed dunks. "I can't believe this," quipped sports columnist Peter Vecsey after Webb leaped away with the NBA slam-dunk championship. "Somebody get God on the phone." Given an unofficial vertical jumping test while in college, Webb once soared 42 inches, a stunning 66 percent of his height.[32]

"If you want to be a great jumper," observes San Diego State University biomechanist Peter Francis, "the first thing you've got to do is choose your mother and father very carefully."[33] Francis dissected a videotape of a Webb dunk in his laboratory. "It looks as though he's going to use a backwards takeoff." Jumps require a flexion, followed by a simultaneous extension of the hip, knee, and ankle joints so rapid and forceful that the center of gravity is propelled upward, causing the body to leave the ground. "That uses the gluteals and the hip extensor muscles more effectively," he continued. "[Webb] would probably be upset if I pointed it out to him, but he's got the synchrony of a great ballet dancer." Francis noted that the thigh segment of the leg, the femur that runs from hip to knee, tends to be longer and the muscles better developed in blacks.

THE MYSTERY AND MYTHS OF MUSCLES

"Is the composition of muscle tissue of blacks different from that of whites?" asks a reader in a letter to *Muscle & Fitness* magazine. "To me, the muscle definition of black bodybuilders . . . looks better than that of their white counterparts."[34] It certainly seems that *something* is going on. But is it a projection of white insecurities or something more substantive?

For years it was axiomatic that performance differences were linked to muscle composition. It was long believed that muscles have two types of fibers—Type I, or slow-twitch, fibers contribute to endurance; Type II, or fast-twitch, are constructed for power movements, such as leaping or sprinting. Sprint athletes may have 75 percent or more fast-twitch fibers, whereas distance runners usually have 75 percent or more slow-twitch fibers. Whites on average have a higher percentage of slow-twitch fibers than West African blacks, who generally have more fast-twitch fibers. So what is the significance of these differences?

Studies have shown that fiber distribution is determined more by genetics than the environment. It's estimated that 40 percent of the phenotypic variance of fiber type is due to environmental influences such as exercise, whereas 45 percent is associated with genetic factors (the remaining 15 percent is due to sampling error). Although physical activity can improve fitness, it cannot alter a person's biological endowment.

But scientists have also come to understand that the fast-twitch/slow-twitch model is too simplistic. There are in fact two types of fast-twitch fibers, one more metabolically efficient. Training can convert the less metabolically efficient fibers into more efficient ones—for instance, when trained athletes run so fast that they go into severe oxygen debt, forcing the muscles to use oxygen more efficiently. However, training cannot significantly convert fast-twitch fibers to slow-twitch ones, or vice versa,* although people do gradually and permanently lose fast-twitch muscles as a result of aging.

Just how crucial is endowed fiber type in athletics? Geneticist and exercise physiologist Claude Bouchard, known as a guru on muscles and metabolism, and exercise biochemist Jean-Aimé Simoneau, long time colleagues at Laval University in Quebec City, addressed that issue in comparing two populations, French-Canadian and West African students. Using long needles inserted into the thighs of test subjects, the Canadain team extracted tiny sections of fibers, which look to the naked eye like pieces of raw meat. They were chemically treated to reveal metabolic differences, put on a glass slide, and slipped under a high-power microscope, where they appeared as a collage of tiny red and white crocodile scales. The African subjects, by a ratio of approximately two to one, had more of the larger fast-twitch fibers.[35] The researchers concluded that the force generating capacity of Type II fast-twitch fibers at high velocity, the speed and tempo of movements, and the capacity of an individual to adapt to exercise training are all genetically influenced.[36] (See Figure 19.1.)

Scientists studying the debilitating effects of muscular dystrophy may even have stumbled upon a "smoking gun" that bolsters the genetic case for population-linked differences in sprinting capacity. While searching for a gene responsible for muscle weakness caused by the disease, researchers at a Sydney, Australia, hospital found that 20 percent of people of Caucasian and Asian background have what they affectionately called a "wimp gene," a defective gene that blocks the body from producing a-actinin-3, which provides the explosive power in fast-twitch muscles. However, samples drawn from African Bantus, specifically Zulu tribal members, showed that only 3 percent had the wimp gene.[37] The discovery could explain why "some people train for ages but remain eighty-pound weaklings,

*Scientists have converted Type I slow-twitch fibers to Type II fibers with the use of long-term electrically induced contractions.

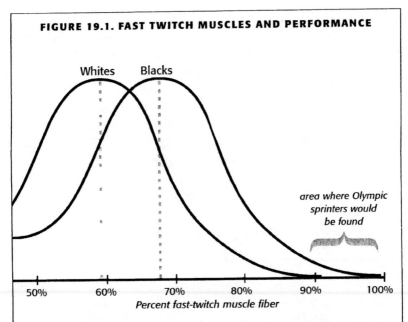

FIGURE 19.1. FAST TWITCH MUSCLES AND PERFORMANCE

Whites   Blacks

area where Olympic sprinters would be found

50%   60%   70%   80%   90%   100%

Percent fast-twitch muscle fiber

On average West African blacks have 67.5 percent fast-twitch muscle fiber and French Canadian whites 59 percent. Given a normal distribution curve, there should be more black individuals than whites at the far end of the curve where Olympic sprinters would be found. Adapted from P.F.M. Ama et al., "Skeletal Muscle Characteristics in Sedentary Black and Caucasian Males," *Journal of Applied Physiology*, 1986.

while others develop muscles very quickly," said the team leader, Dr. Kathryn North, head of the Neurogenetics Research Unit at the New Children's Hospital. She and her colleagues speculate that the need for the "speed gene" is dying out because the speed to hunt animals or flee from enemies is no longer necessary for our survival—although it certainly helps in sprinting.[38]

The genetic evidence underscores what we find in athletes. Even though fiber composition can significantly affect physical performance, a favorable composition is not sufficient by itself to ensure high performance. Since endurance is only about 25 percent inherited, training plays an integral role—but more so in blacks than whites.[39] Experiments show that with only a modest amount of training, blacks can experience an explosive rise in exercise capacity, while even with far more effort whites don't improve nearly as much.[40] In contrast, it appears that no amount of training can break through genetically imposed, inherited limits on anaerobic capacity—the ability to sprint and jump. Thus, although fiber type alone does not itself guarantee a champion, if an athlete does not have a certain proportion of fast-twitch muscles, he or she can't hope to be a champion sprinter or jumper.[41] In practical terms, this suggests that sprinters are born, not made.

How might these lab results translate into on-field performance? That's tricky. It appears that for blacks from West Africa, innate ability may be more critical than training in turning out great leapers and sprinters.[42] Even team sports such as soccer and basketball that require some aerobic ability place a premium on anaerobic skills. Consider soccer, which is known as football outside North America. "Football is an intermittent-intensity activity dominated energetically by aerobic processes," noted Stephen Seiler, a physiologist at the Institute for Sport in Norway, in an e-mail message.

> However, the capacity of individual athletes to develop repeated high-power outputs for brief periods is decisive for achieving success. In a given match, an attacker may attempt thirty or more rushes on the goal each at [high] intensity. . . for 3 to 10 seconds. He will succeed or fail based on his ability to develop (1) brief periods of explosive power while (2) simultaneously exhibiting brilliantly creative yet precise ball-handling skills. As I write this I am having visions of Brazil's Ronaldo dancing, then exploding through three defenders, then firing the ball left-footed past a helpless and pissed-off goalie. Now, a pure attacker like Ronaldo actually spends a reasonable amount of time doing nothing more than walking, while the ball is at the other goal. He is the 100-meter dash man of the soccer world, having almost no defensive responsibilities.[43]

As we would expect, there are relatively more blacks—almost all of West African heritage—in the speed positions in soccer, basketball, and football and relatively fewer at positions in which short-burst activity is less critical than strength: center in basketball, center and guard in football, and defense in soccer.

THE SCIENCE OF ENDURANCE

The human body can sustain anaerobic activity such as sprinting and jumping for only a short time. It requires explosive energy and burns mostly sugar. As we run longer distances, as the aerobic process kicks in, the body uses carbohydrates differently. If genetics and race really do matter in athletic performance, then we might expect to find noticeable differences in the ways different population groups sustain anaerobic and aerobic functioning. Sure enough, by applying population genetics to athletic performance and examining the aerobic/anaerobic energy cycle, scientists are beginning to understand the racial pattern in sports.

Timothy Noakes, the longtime director of the Sport Science Center at the University of Cape Town Medical School, is one of those rare individuals who has blended his personal and professional passions. He has competed in more than seventy marathons and ultramarathons, including South Africa's famed 54-mile Comrades run. He is also the author of many scholarly papers and books, including *Lore of Running*, a scientific and medical guide that is to long distance-running what the New Testament is to Christianity.

Noakes has observed that black South Africans, who share much of their genetic ancestry with East Africans, sweep more than 90 percent of the top places in endurance races held in South Africa, despite the fact that blacks represent no more than one-quarter of the country's active running population. Based on the available research, Noakes is convinced that black South Africans are genetically privileged as athletes. "I'm not sure that it's physically measurable, but it's so obvious. The problem is that there are so few white runners who compete at the levels of the great black middle- and long-distance athletes. We don't have the white athletes to study the differences."[44]

Nevertheless, Noakes has attempted to test his thesis in the laboratory. In a treadmill study black marathoners consistently bested whites.[45] In a subsequent study of middle-distance runners, university researchers found that the blacks were significantly shorter and lighter and had considerably smaller and leaner muscle mass, less skin folds, and less subcutaneous fat. Although white runners matched or exceeded the black runners at distances up to 5,000 meters, blacks were "clearly superior at distances greater than 5km."[46] Again, this finding conforms to what we have found time and again. Blacks from East Africa, and South African blacks who have a similar genetic footprint, are superb endurance runners.

The fine print in the data was particularly revealing. There was a dramatic difference in the ability of the blacks to run at a higher maximum oxygen capacity. In the case of the marathoners, blacks performed at 89 percent of the maximum oxygen capacity, while whites lagged by nearly 10 percent. The muscles of the black athletes also showed far fewer signs of fatigue as measured by lactic acid.

Noakes noted a link between his lab findings and the training habits of well-known Kenyan runners who report favoring low-mileage, high-intensity workouts. This presents a nurture/nature conundrum: Does hard training lead to a change in oxidative capacity and fatigue resistance, or does it merely reflect a genetically well-endowed athletic machine?

The answer can be found in the wild card in performance: muscle efficiency. David Costill, longtime head of the Human Performance Laboratory at Ball State in Muncie, Indiana, has shown that the adaptability of the muscle fiber for aerobic metabolism—its oxidative potential—is more important than the basic composition of the muscle.[47] More aerobically efficient fibers produce fewer fatigue-producing lactate toxins, resulting in better performance. And although fiber composition is genetically fixed, which effectively limits the pool of possible successful athletes in each event, exercise can help muscles better utilize oxygen.[48]

A team from South Africa and Australia, headed by Adele Weston, an exercise physiologist at the School of Exercise and Sport Science at the University of Sydney, and including Noakes, has found an apparent link between oxidative capacity, resistance to fatigue, and race. The researchers measured "running economy"—the amount of metabolic work (and therefore oxygen consumption) that is required to run at a given speed, much like the fuel economy of a car. Running economy can be affected by a variety of factors both environmental, such as running technique, and physiological, such as body-mass distribution and muscle elasticity.

"We've shown that the oxidative enzyme capacity of the [black] athletes we looked at was one and a half times higher on average than the white runners," reports Kathy Myburgh, a coauthor of the report and senior lecturer at the University of Stellenbosch in South Africa.[49] Comparing black and white athletes with nearly identical race times, the researchers found that blacks were both more efficient runners and able to utilize a considerably higher percentage of their maximum oxygen potential—a decided advantage if two athletes otherwise have the same capacity.

"Whilst the current study does not elucidate the origins of these differences," the authors concluded, "the findings may partially explain the success of African runners at the elite level."[50] A subsequent study determined that the superior fatigue resistance during high-intensity endurance exercise is partially related to the higher skeletal-muscle oxidative capacity and lower plasma lactate accumulation found more commonly in blacks.[51]

COMPARING KENYANS AND SCANDINAVIANS

Noakes's fascination with endurance running is matched by the allure that cross-country skiing holds for Bengt Saltin, director of the Copenhagen Muscle Research Center. Saltin believes that certain population groups, including Northern Europeans, who are notable endurance runners and cross-country skiers, may have superior fatigue resistance encoded in their genes. He has found that Scandinavian distance runners, Kenyans, and South African blacks all have consistently lower blood-lactate levels and perform more efficiently than athletes from other regions, the likely result of their having evolved in mountainous regions. Population genetics—ancestry—is the key determinant.

Saltin also suspected that East Africans might have an edge over Scandinavians in endurance running. To test that theory, he brought a half-dozen established Swedish national class runners to St. Patrick's High in Iten, Kenya, in 1990 to see how they might match up against up-and-coming East African schoolboys. It was a demoralizing experience for the Swedes. National champion after national champion was soundly trounced in races from 800 meters to the 10 kilometers. Stunned, Saltin estimated that in this one tiny area of the Rift Valley there were at least five hundred school boys who could best his national champions at 2,000 meters.[52]

In a subsequent study, Saltin returned to Stockholm and arranged to bring several groups of Kenyans to the Karolinska labs, where he was then headquartered. Muscle-fiber distribution was similar for the Kenyans and Swedes. But biopsies of the quadricep muscles in the thighs indicated that the Kenyans had more blood-carrying capillaries surrounding the muscle fibers and more mitochondria within the fibers. That's important because mitochondria act a little like power stations, processing the glucose with oxygen brought in by breathing into energy. The Kenyans also were found to have relatively smaller muscle fibers than the Swedes, which Saltin speculated might serve to bring the mitochondria closer to the surrounding capillaries. This process aids in oxidation, bringing more "fuel" to the mitochondria, the engine of the muscles.

The Kenyans also showed little ammonia accumulation in their muscles from protein combustion and less lactic-acid buildup. They have more of the muscle enzymes that burn fat and their glycogen reserves are not burned as quickly, which improves endurance. Most impressively, they are able to take months off from regular training and then regain their old form quickly. When they do train, more than half of their total mileage occurs at heart rates of 90 percent of maximum, far higher than the rate for Europeans or Americans—a 5 to 15 percent greater running economy at far less mileage, but a higher intensity.[53] Saltin characterizes Kenyans as the most perfect aerobic *potential* measured so far on earth. "The basis for the success of black runners is in the genes," Saltin states flatly.[54]

Although there is no one genetically consistent African population, the environment appears to have resulted in some characteristics shared across the sub-Saharan populations. Claude Bouchard is persuaded that a large fraction of *both* West and East African blacks enjoy biological advantages for power or sprint events and endurance activities, respectively. "West Africans have more of the key anaerobic enzymes in their skeletal muscle, those enzymes being responsible for regenerating the energy in the muscle cell through anaerobic pathways," wrote Bouchard.

> We are talking here about a two-fold difference between a significant fraction of blacks from West Africa and whites from North America. East Africans, on the other hand, seem to have more ability to mobilize the energy stored in adipose tissue in other body depots and to use that energy for prolonged periods of exercise. The key point is that these biological characteristics are not unique to either West or East African blacks. These characteristics are seen in all populations, including whites. However, based on the limited number of studies available, there seems to be more African Blacks with such characteristics than there are in other populations.[55]

WAS JIMMY "THE GREEK" RIGHT?

What are we to make of claims that "blacks have been bred" to be great athletes—the very claim that abruptly ended Jimmy "the Greek" Snyder's career? There is some relevant research in this area.

The slave trade dates back to the fifteenth century, when Portuguese adventurers began exploring the African coast. Many returned home with enslaved Africans, who fetched a handsome price. By the early 1700s, almost every country in Europe was trafficking in slaves, with England the preeminent trader and some African kings as willing accomplices. It was reported that the king of Congo and the royal family of Dahomey bartered kidnapped humans for muskets, alcohol, cloth, and even horses offered by the Europeans. By the end of the century, it is believed that some 70,000 slaves a year were being exported from Africa, mostly by the British. Many were ticketed for the New World to work the mines in Peru and Mexico and the sugar and coffee plantations in Brazil, the Caribbean, and Central America.[56]

Until the late seventeenth century, most slaves in North America were not black but Amerindian. Although some blacks were present in the tobacco fields of Virginia as early as 1620, it was really the Treaty of Utrecht in 1714, which terminated the War of Spanish succession, that started the mass importation of slaves from Africa to North America. Estimates of the number of Africans who started on the Middle Passage to the Americas range from 10 to as high as 18 million.

Slaves who reached the auction blocks in Savannah and Charleston netted traders a fabulous profit of more than 100 percent. It has long been speculated that the slaves who survived were strong but subject to all kinds of diseases. However, few generalizations can be made about the millions brought forcibly to America. They were rounded up across a broad swath of central West Africa and represented hundreds of different tribes, each with different cultures, health standards, and genetic dispositions. They had no common language, only the color of their skin to bind them together.

Despite revisionist stories of slaves being kept in home—like security, their living conditions for the most part were brutal. Approximately one in four died in forced marches to the west coast of Africa or the long period in camps awaiting embarkation. The harsh trip, which could take as long as nine months, claimed another 12 to 15 percent. A third of those brought over succumbed within three years. Half of all the offspring of new arrivals died.[57] As a consequence of this death machine, more and more slaves were required to keep the plantation industry stable. It was a monstrous but incredibly lucrative process.

Growing ethical concerns, the gradual industrialization that displaced agriculture, and a number of bloody slave uprisings gradually eroded public support for slavery. By 1807, both the British Parliament and the U.S. Congress voted to outlaw the transatlantic trade, and France followed in 1818. But the ban did not touch the flourishing internal market in the United States, which made homegrown slaves even more critical to maintain the Southern "way of life."

There were in fact crude attempts to cultivate hardier slaves. Virginia became a veritable breeding ground, exporting slave offspring to other states and taking on the nickname of the "Negro raising state," according to Thomas Dew, a historian at the College of William and Mary.[58] In *Narrative*, an autobiographical account of slave life, Frederick Douglass recounted his shock at discovering that humans were bought and sold to be "breeders." He told the story of how a young plantation master, who could afford only one slave, purchased Caroline, "a large able-bodied woman about twenty-years old." The slave lord then turned around and rented a physically powerful male slave. "And him he used to fasten up with Caroline every night!" wrote Douglass. "The result was that at the end of the year, the miserable woman gave birth to twins."[59]

Could the slave experience, from the hellish Middle Passage to toiling in the tobacco and cotton fields of the South, have acted as a kind of genetic bottleneck or winnowing process that turned out hardier workers and perhaps, centuries later, better athletes? Such a conclusion is questionable on both historical and scientific grounds. Historian Philip Curtin noted that the slave experience varied greatly in diet and the availability of medical treatment.[60] George Washington University historian James Horton claimed that planned mating was only "scattered." Howard University anthropologist Michael Blakey believes it was more extensive, but he too discounts it. "It was pure and simple a matter of reproducing large numbers [of slaves] rather than body types. That kind of breeding couldn't possibly lead to any difference in athletic ability," Blakey has written.[61]

OVERSTATING THE GENETIC CASE?

Scientists who are convinced that innate differences exist between races unavoidably walk a very slippery slope of exaggeration and conjecture. It is important to remind ourselves that genes set parameters, but it is life experiences that "express" biological capabilities.

Consider the controversy that erupted in 1970 when two psychologists, Morgan Worthy and Allen Markle, wrote an article suggesting that blacks were better at what they called "reactive" sport skills, whereas whites excelled at "self-paced" activities.[62] They asserted that blacks seemed more adept at hitting in baseball, jump-shooting in basketball, or quick-burst running in an array of sports. Whites, they contended, were better at more deliberative tasks such as baseball pitching or shooting free throws in basketball.

Worthy subsequently reported that he had found a significant association between the proportion of blacks at a given position in professional football and the eye color of whites at those same positions.[63] By his measure, whites playing traditionally reactive "black" positions such as defensive back, wide receiver, and running back were found to have dark eyes, whereas white players in predominantly self-paced "white" positions such as quarterback, linebacker, and offensive line tended to have light-colored eyes. In fact, studies have since shown that those with dark eyes do have slightly faster reaction times than light-eyed people.[64]

The plausibility of these theories underscores the problem with surface logic. The reaction study was flawed from beginning to end. There was no direct measure of reactivity or controlled experiments, and the scientists used pseudoscientific questionnaires and categories of reactive and self-paced skills that were too arbitrary to be convincing (for instance, the basketball shooting average does not account for the myriad types of shots—stuff, layup, tip-in, etc.—and probably reflects an enigmatic blend of skills). Moreover, the theory has not panned out in other research.[65]

As for the eye-color hypothesis and its meaningfulness, the jury is still out. Though there is certainly some science to support elements of these theories, sports demand so many unique skills, both reactive and self-paced, that any generalization is all but unprovable. The danger is quite real, however: such sweeping suppositions feed the stereotype that blacks are more naturally athletic than whites, who are considered more intelligent and better strategists.

Speculation fever has also infected the unresolvable debate over whether blacks can handle pressure better than whites. As far back as

1941 the renowned track-and-field coach Dean Cromwell advanced the notion that "[the black athlete's] ability to sprint and jump was a life-and-death matter to him in the jungle. His muscles are pliable, and his easy-going disposition is a valuable aid to the mental and physical relaxation that a runner and jumper must have."[66] "The black athletes have an ability to let their bodies go—you know, they hang everything loose," agreed Stan Dowell, who coached many top black athletes in the 1960s and 1970s. "They walk loose, they dance loose, they *are* loose."[67] Coaches have long invoked folk science to explain this phenomenon. "As a class, the black athletes that have trained with me are far ahead of the whites in that one factor—relaxation under pressure," once commented track coach Bud Winter. "It is their secret. I remember one of my quarter-milers, Thelmo Knowles. I kept saying to him, automatically, to stay loose. One day Thelmo answered, 'Coach, if I relax any more, I'm going to fall asleep.'"[68]

This romanticized belief that blacks are rhythmically better attuned to sports has circulated for more than a century and is embraced even by blacks.[69] These observations, far-fetched to some, have been made time and time again. "You know, the black athlete—you can almost tell in their walk that they're athletes," comments Philadelphia's Hall-of-Fame third baseman Mike Schmidt, a white, who was liked and respected by his African American teammates.[70] It is now axiomatic that there is indeed a black athletic aesthetic so pervasive that it defines superstars from the urban ghetto as much as upper-middle-class blacks such as Grant Hill, who grew up in affluent suburbia.

Yet the compliments "relaxed" and "naturally gifted" can be found along the same continuum as "indolent" and "lazy," familiar code words used to subtly denigrate black athletes. After Howard Porter Drew staked claim to the title as world's fastest human title in 1910, his ability to "relax under pressure," became the stuff of legend. It was noted that he didn't train very much, and maybe didn't need to. Reflecting the racial stereotypes of the times, the press mistook the University of Southern California star's quiet self-confidence for indifference or laziness.

There are actually intriguing data in support of the stereotype that blacks *are* more relaxed than whites, who are in turn less anxious than Asians.[71] If substantiated, would this trait translate into on-the-field benefits? Peter Cavanagh, director of the Center for Locomotion Studies at Penn State University, who has compared the biomechanics of black and white athletes using stop-action photography and computer analysis, is convinced that African Americans have a naturally more relaxed gait.[72] Years ago Carleton Coon referred to this appearance of "loose-jointedness" in black athletes, noting that it was characteristic of "swift living things [humans as well as fast animals] known for their speed and leaping ability."[73] Robert Malina has reached a similar conclusion.

It certainly makes logical sense that there may be some genotypic basis for various functional psychological and physiological stylistic differences. If we grant, for example, that tens of thousands of years of evolution has left a genetic imprint on sharply different lung capacities of East and West Africans, then it may well have also influenced different populations' gait and the ability to relax under pressure. But such stereotypes are clearly filtered through a cultural prism cut by centuries of racism. While a white might believe it is a compliment to call a black a natural athlete, a black may see it as a denigration of years of personal sacrifice and hard work. "This appreciative testimonial to the eloquence of black body language . . . reflexively juxtapose[s] the mind of the white with the instinct of the black," observes sociologist John Hoberman. "Such naively well intended comments testify to the sheer tenacity of the original 'lazy' African stereotype."[74]

Hoberman's point is well taken. However, the echo of cultural bias does not necessarily mean that such observations are wrong or racist. Stereotypes, after all, often contain at least a factual nugget, though it is frequently exaggerated or distorted. It's the exaggeration, not the core of truth, that stirs the ire. The difficulty, of course, is sorting out how much of a trait is genetically inbred, how much may be shaped by the environment, and what is just plain poppycock.

IN OUR GENES

Of course evolution does not work to isolate individual traits, such as sprinting, leaping, or tallness. Rather, it "chooses" species that evidence a conglomeration of traits that help them survive or thrive in particular environments. So it is naïve of both critics and proponents of the "Darwin's athletes" hypothesis to focus on specific traits instead of on broad skills sets. That's as close as we can expect to get to a smoking gun.

New research offers tantalizing genetic evidence that may help identify the genetic contribution of some traits that may be associated with athletic success. For instance, geneticists have found that trunk flexibility can be as high as 66 percent inherited, lung capacity approximately 27 percent, and reaction time 15 percent.[75] "Since we find these differences at what we call the phenotypic level, and we know they probably exist at the gene level, we're looking at the DNA to try to find the primary causes," said Bouchard.[76]

Bouchard and his former team at Laval are leaders in such research. One study of sedentary whites concluded that environmental and genetic factors about equally determine a person's oxygen processing capability.[77] In a study of muscle fiber types, also of whites, they determined that the total variance in the proportion of Type I or slow-twitch fibers is approximately 45 percent inherited.[78] In one recent genetic study, the Canadians found that individual differences in physical trainability can be directly correlated to specific gene sequences.[79] A similar study by scientists at the University College of London has isolated what they have dubbed "high-performance genes," a stretch of DNA that helps regulate metabolic efficiency. Those who had this gene variant more efficiently transferred nutrients and oxygen to the muscles—they were able to work harder with less fuel, showed greater endurance, and responded to physical-fitness training far better than those who did not.[80] The British scientists believe that 90 percent of the performance of athletes could be determined by their genetic makeup, although no research has yet been done on which population groups might be lucky enough to have high-performance genes.[81]

These are intriguing, if controversial, findings. "The problem is that the gene may be a marker of something else and not the cause of the superior performance," wrote Tim Noakes in an analysis of the British study.

> There will be different genes [that determine] different abilities. In running, genes will relate to skeletal muscle function (in my view especially to components of the elastic elements in skeletal muscles). In sports like baseball and cricket, they will relate to visual abilities (and hand-eye coordination) predominantly. But then again, as sports become more and more competitive, [elite athletes] have to have all the athletic genes for physical ability—endurance, speed, etc.—plus the specific skills emphasized by the different sports. There will not be one gene, just one that is perhaps dominant when all the others are also there.[82]

Whether or not genes confer a competitive advantage on blacks when it comes to stealing bases, running with the football, shooting hoops, or jumping hurdles remains the $64,000 question. Since the first known study of differences between black and white athletes in 1928,[83] the data have been remarkably consistent: in most sports, African-descended athletes have the capacity to do better with their raw skills than whites. Let's summarize the physical and physiological differences known to date. Blacks with a West African ancestry generally have:

- relatively less subcutaneous fat on arms and legs and proportionately more lean body and muscle mass, broader shoulders, larger quadriceps, and bigger, more developed musculature in general;[84]
- smaller chest cavities;
- a higher center of gravity, generally shorter sitting height, narrower hips, and lighter calves;
- a longer arm span and "distal elongation of segments"—the hand is relatively longer than the forearm, which in turn is relatively longer than the upper arm; the foot is relatively longer than the tibia (leg), which is relatively longer than the thigh;

- faster patellar tendon reflex;[85]
- greater body density, which is likely due to higher bone mineral density and heavier bone mass at all stages in life, including infancy (despite evidence of lower calcium intake and a higher prevalence of lactose intolerance, which prevents consumption of dairy products);[86]
- modest, but significantly higher, levels of plasma testosterone (3 to 19 percent), which is anabolic, theoretically contributing to greater muscle mass, lower fat, and the ability to perform at a higher level of intensity with quicker recovery;[87]
- a higher percentage of fast-twitch muscles and more anaerobic enzymes, which can translate into more explosive energy.

Relative advantages in these physiological and biomechanical characteristics are a gold mine for athletes who compete in such anaerobic activities as football, basketball, and sprinting, sports in which West African blacks clearly excel. However, they also pose problems for athletes who might want to compete as swimmers (heavier skeletons, smaller chest cavities, and a performance of fast-twitch muscle fibers could be drags on performance) or in cold-weather and endurance sports. West African athletes are more susceptible to fatigue than whites and East Africans, in effect making them relatively poor candidates for aerobic sports.

East Africa produces the world's best aerobic athletes because of a variety of bio-physiological attributes. Blacks from this region in Africa have more energy-producing enzymes in the muscles and an apparent ability to process oxygen more efficiently, resulting in less susceptibility to fatigue; they have a slighter body profile and a larger lung capacity than whites or West Africans, which translates into great endurance.

White athletes appear to have a physique between West Africans and East Africans. They have more endurance but less explosive running and jumping ability than West Africans; they tend to be quicker than East Africans but have less endurance. "From a biomechanical perspective, the answer is 'yes,' race and ethnicity do matter," says Lindsay Carter, assessing the wide array of black/white bio-physical differences. "All of the large-scale studies show it, and the data go back more than a hundred years." But he adds a critical caveat. "These are tendencies, only tendencies. There are far too many variables to make blanket statements. An average advantage, 'yes,' but that says nothing about any individual competitor."[88]

This politicized question may never be answered with the kind of bullet-proof evidence demanded by ideologically driven skeptics. The code of life is enormously complex. For instance, a fruit fly has at least fifty genes that work together to produce so simple a feature as the red color of the eye.[89] Yet science puzzles, like crimes, are rarely solved by indisputable eyewitness evidence. The key is to assemble the pieces and use deductive logic, the backbone of critical thinking, to see if a picture emerges. That we cannot yet definitively prove beyond a shadow of a doubt the persuasiveness of the theory of relativity or that a white man will never again be considered the fastest runner on the planet doesn't automatically render judgments about those phenomena irresponsible. Such genetic definitiveness may remain elusive for some time, although the research pace has increased enormously in this area and these genes will likely be identified early in the next millennium.

In the cross fire of warring factions, many lose sight of the fact that the historical dichotomy between nature and nurture does not do this controversy justice. Both biology and society inform our humanity no less than our athletic capabilities. "Whether these physical differences contribute significantly to the dominance of blacks in sports remains an elusive subject," notes Indiana University kinesiologist Gary Sailes. "The research appears to support the contention that the Black athlete may enjoy some physical advantages over his White counterpart. . . . [But] these advantages are insignificant unless they are fully developed through vigorous training and by participating in a nurturing and competitive environment that creates an opportunity for athletic success."[90]

"You've got to be very careful generalizing from the athletic population to the broader population," agrees Robert Malina. "A big part of sport is not only having ability but being identified as having ability and receiving good coaching. Economic circumstances influence whether or not you are successful in them to some extent." But that is simply an argument for why whites monopolize sports with high economic and social barriers, not for why blacks have a lock on the most accessible sports such as track, basketball, and football.

However elusive may be the secrets of athletic success, the emperical and scientific evidence strongly suggests that functional differences can have a genetic basis. With dramatic advances in quantitative genetics, it is now possible to calculate the genetic and environmental effects on any number of phenotypes from schizophrenia to obesity to sprinting—and many of these differences do break out by populations. We have identified the environmental factors that interact with genes in the case of sports—for instance, career channeling and cultural traditions. Now scientists are on the verge of locating and identifying the genes themselves.

"Elite athletes are by definition rarities; they are statistically aberrant," says Malina. "There are consistent differences in body physique and body composition [between black and white athletes]. And perhaps in some physiological characteristics. There are also differences in genetic markers in the blood—the classic one of course is the sickle cell trait. If people deny the existence of that, I'm not sure what there is to say. I just don't think we can make the kind of measurements that will end this debate once and for all for those committed to being skeptical."

Like almost all scientists who have studied this explosive subject, Malina is acutely aware of the political bombshells he may be setting off. "Are there sports for which we would predict success for a white more so than for a black on a purely physical or physiological basis," Malina asks rhetorically. He pauses, almost reluctant to answer. "I don't think there is right now, given the available data."[91]

Let's never forget, however, that exceptional athletes are extraordinary individuals. The late Ernst Jokl, who for years headed the Physiology of Exercise Research Laboratories at the University of Kentucky, once remarked that blacks have an innate *capacity*, not an innate *ability*, for athletic excellence.[92] Perhaps that comment says it best. Still, all the hard work in the world will go for naught if the roulette wheel of genetics doesn't land on your number. And the unassailable truth is that the genetic pool of potential champions is a lot wider and deeper in Africa than anywhere else.

CHAPTER 20

THE ENVIRONMENTALIST CASE AGAINST

INNATE BLACK SUPERIORITY IN SPORTS

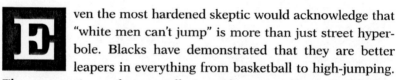ven the most hardened skeptic would acknowledge that "white men can't jump" is more than just street hyperbole. Blacks have demonstrated that they are better leapers in everything from basketball to high-jumping. The provocative and potentially incendiary question is "why"? For many athletes and coaches, particularly whites who know what it is like to be overmatched, the sociological explanations offered for white under-representation in some sports are less than convincing.

"I work camps in the summer time with white kids," says NBA forward Christian Laettner. "The white kids are still trying as hard as they've ever tried. They're probably trying now harder. The players who tend to be really athletic and really good once you get to the higher levels, more and more it seems to be the black group. That's just the way it is."

"The black players are superior. No doubt," says Lebanese-born Rony Seikaly, also a forward. "I go to Lebanon in the summer, and we have pickup games, and there's this one eighteen-year-old Nigerian playing in the Lebanese league who can touch his head to the rim. It's amazing, [blacks'] athletic ability. They're built, they're buffed. We work out to get a body like that, and they come out just naturally gifted."[1]

Such facile theories run smack against environmentalist dogma. "It's genetic hocus-pocus," fumes zoologist Owen Anderson, a former columnist for *Runner's World*. "Superior and elite runners have worked unbelievably hard, and their extreme physical travail and motivation—not their genes—have played the key roles in getting them to the front of the pack!"[2]

"Not in our genes"—that's the acceptable explanation, with the taboo on this issue firmly in place. It's said that black athletic superiority results from hard work, a dearth of nonsport role models in the black community, and racism. "Discrimination curtails black access to alternative high-prestige occupations," notes Harry Edwards. "We are channeling disproportionately high numbers [of young blacks] toward athletic participation."[3] According to Dennis Rodman, an under-sized power forward who became one of the most effective rebounders in NBA history, "A black player knows he can go out on a court and kick a white player's ass." Why? "[Because] the black player is conditioned to think he can take the white guy whenever he needs to."[4] In other words, athletic ability is not in the blood, it's in our culture.[5]

And let's not forget that whites still dominate the "country-club" sports of tennis, golf, and swimming; sports that require expensive equipment or facilities such as hockey, skiing, bicycling, and gymnastics; Olympic-type sports such as fencing, polo, archery, and rowing which attract only a limited number of competitors. Whites also predominate in certain field events, most notably the discus, shotput, javelin, and pole vault.

Like many academicians, University of the Pacific sociologist John Phillips has suggested that the historical monopoly by whites in these activities is *prima facie* proof that dominance by blacks is a myth. "Black athletes are concentrated in those sports to which Blacks in general have access (in terms of coaching, facilities, and competitions). For sports in which Blacks are rare, the best facilities, coaching, and competition are found in private clubs. If blacks were dispersed across all sports," he has concluded, "their apparent superiority would largely disappear."[6]

But would it? There is merit to the argument that racial attitudes have shaped expectations and opportunities. Elite level sprinting, basketball, and even football to a degree are seen as increasingly black sports. It is also true that blacks have faced systematic discrimination that limits career choices, which makes professional sports, however much a long-shot, an enticing dream. But can the breadth and depth of black athletic accomplishments be so easily explained away as a product of the "white establishment" directing blacks toward basketball, while whites are encouraged to pursue less "black" sports?

Nurture theories assume that the very existence of the pattern proves racism is at work. That runs smack up against a catch-22: Do blacks dominate sports because of racial stereotyping or have some of the stereotypes emerged because of genetic factors and then exaggerated and enhanced by culture? Why do such patterns exist in the first place? This chicken-or-egg dilemma has long bedeviled scientists.

STACKING

In high school, whites who compete in baseball, football, basketball, and even in track, far outnumber black athletes. Yet as the competitive funnel winnows the athletes with less drive or talent, at the college and professional levels, blacks show their dominance. Why? "Basketball coaches look to fill their teams with black athletes because they believe blacks can jump higher, run faster and are more explosive," says former University of California guard Monica Wiley, an African American and three-time All-Academic selection. "A lot of coaches and recruiters do stereotype players," agrees Stanford University and former women's Olympic coach Tara VanDerveer, who is white. "They talk about their slow white players and their quick black players. I think it's harmful to both."[7] Miki Turner, an African American who is a sports columnist for the *Oakland Tribune*, says she ended up running track at her predominantly white Cincinnati high school even though her first love was softball. "You're wasting your time in this sport [softball]," she remembers being told by the track coach, who was white. "You'll have more opportunities in track-and-field."[8] And he was right. She ended up as the fastest runner on the team.

Many athletes and coaches believe that athletes are pushed into certain sports and away from others primarily because of their race. Sociologists call this the "anglocentric hypothesis," which holds that the racial patterns in sports are the product of structural inequalities and discrimination against minorities.[9] That theory has also been used to explain why minorities—blacks in most cases but also Aborigines, Maoris, and Pacific Islanders in other sports such as rugby, Australian rules football, and New Zealand netball—are over-represented at certain positions. In the world of academia, this pattern is referred to as stacking.

It doesn't take a rocket scientist to recognize that African Americans are concentrated in sports and positions that demand speed and quickness, the "reactive" positions. Whites, on the other hand, are over-represented at so-called strategic positions were long thought to demand decision-making skills. In baseball, blacks dominate at the outfield positions, whites at pitcher and catcher. In football, white defensive backs, receivers, and running backs (there are a number of white fullbacks whose main responsibility is to block and hang back as a safety-valve option receiver) are rare, yet whites dominate so-called central positions such as quarterback and center.

Academicians who first studied these patterns in the early seventies assumed that they were a legacy of racial discrimination. They invented phrases soaked in pre-judgment such as "position discrimination" and "positional segregation" to describe these phenomena.[10] After all, for years there had been no black quarterbacks and few black point guards—the leadership positions in football and basketball. The prevailing racist belief was that blacks were not intelligent enough to command the respect of their mostly white teammates. The handful of graduating black college quarterbacks were either ignored altogether or when offered an opportunity, got one shot. If they didn't become a star overnight, and quarterbacks rarely do, black or white, they were shuffled off to traditionally "black positions" such as running back, defensive back, or wide receiver, where their "natural athleticism" would presumably serve them better.[11]

"As a black QB they are constantly trying to switch you to another position," said James Harris to *Ebony* magazine in 1974, when he was the lone African American NFL quarterback, playing for the Los

Angeles Rams. He blamed his limited success at least in part on racism. "Blacks get two types of opportunities to play quarterback in the NFL: A chance and a 'nigger chance.'"[12]

The prejudice that whites would only reluctantly accept blacks as leaders, though dogged, has all but disappeared. Sociologists acknowledge that the stacking phenomenon faded in basketball decades ago as African Americans literally took over the sport, point guard included Blacks now dominate at every position save center, for which the most important "skill" is height, giving whites a better shot. Even at the center position, however, blacks are over-represented and are almost exclusively the stars

The stacking argument appears to fall short on any number of grounds. Sociologists have created the artificial distinction between "central" positions that demand strategic thinking and "noncentral" positions that are defined by instinct. Are linebackers and receivers really less "central" positions than center or guard as sociologists claim? That's doubtful in this day of Manhattan telephone book-sized playbooks. In this day, most positions demand fearlessness and an ability to quickly assess the opponent's offense or defense—in other words, courage and intelligence, which have historically been associated with whites.

Lingering racism may account for at least some of the whiteness of quarterbacking in professional football. Some 30 percent of NFL quarterbacks as of the 2000 season are African American. The position not only demands refined physical skills, including mobility, arm strength, and great peripheral vision, it requires a host of other intangible but critical qualities such as character, leadership ability, and "football intelligence." Those are highly subjective qualities. But the sport of football, and with it the skill profile of successful quarterback, has undergone a fundamental change over the past decade.

"For a long time, the NFL had a mold that quarterbacks had to fit," says Tony Dungy, coach of the Tampa Bay Buccaneers and one-time college quarterback who shifted to defensive back to get a shot in the NFL. "Everyone was looking for a drop back passer with a cannon arm who was relatively tall. If you didn't fit that mold, black or white, you didn't get much of a look. The few blacks who got a chance, like Doug Williams, fit that prototype."[13] Indeed, white quarterbacks who didn't fit the mold, such as Doug Flutie, didn't get much of a chance either and were forced, like black collegiate stars, to try their hand in the more wide-open Canadian Football League.

Today's quarterbacks need to be both strong and fast. Ironically, one of the best white quarterbacks of all time, Joe Montana, is credited with helping to bring down the white wall in the NFL. His ability to scramble changed what *quarterback* meant, and the days when a classic drop-back passer like Sonny Jurgensen—or Doug Williams for that matter—could sit in the pocket were over. All the coaches now look for "athleticism." Not too many years ago, that was a word that echoed assumptions of limited black intelligence. "That used to be a code word to describe a black quarterback who a coach wanted to shift to receiver or defensive back," says Dennis Green, the Minnesota Viking head coach. "Now with the speed and strength in the game, we all need athletic quarterbacks. Every coach is looking for mobility. Good strong arms that can run. That fits Tim Couch, Daunte Culpepper, Donovan McNabb, Akili Smith, Cade McNown. It's just not a black-white thing anymore."[14]

Except at the quarterback position, racial patterns in North American sports have remained remarkably consistent over the past quarter century, once opportunities for blacks increased and after most professional leagues were fully integrated. McNabb, Smith, and Culpepper, all African Americans, were selected in the first round of the 1999 draft, equaling the number of black first rounders over the entire history of the draft. The percentage of black quarterbacks on rosters is now more than twice as large as their percentage of the population.

So, while racial stereotyping goes a way toward explaining why, until recently, there have been so few blacks quarterbacks, racism seems less and less a plausible explanation for the domination of most positions in football other sports by African Americans (though it continues to help explain the relative lack of blacks in "country club" sports). Certainly, an athletic black can expect a warmer reception trying out for track or basketball than for the swim or golf team—or for the biology club for that matter—based purely on racial stereotyping. But the playing field is awfully level these days and talent quickly comes to the fore.

A BIO-CULTURAL EXPLANATION
FOR SOME SPORTS STEREOTYPES

Although stereotypes—blacks can't swim or whites can't jump—can indeed be limiting, the fact that they are stereotypes does not mean that they are necessarily fallacious. It is certainly plausible that the stereotype that blacks are quicker and better jumpers than whites is neither racist nor wrong. African Americans and other blacks with West African roots may gravitate to positions in which they may have some phenotypic and genotypic advantages. Wide receiver, running back, and defensive back require athletes with football smarts, above-average speed, excellent coordination, jumping ability, quick instincts, and great reaction time. That's the classic biomechanical profile of an athlete of West African descent.

In baseball, outfielders are traditionally the quickest athletes on the field. One recent study by two University of Wisconsin researchers, Benjamin Margolis and Jane A. Piliavin, actually attempted to prove that racial stereotyping could explain the domination of the outfield positions by blacks. What did they find? "African Americans were predominantly faster by our measure than white or Latino players," the sociologists wrote, "and their speed accounted for part of the reason they were assigned to the outfield." As for the preponderance of Latin infielders, the researchers noted the stereotype that Latin players are considered better infielders because they are relatively short, more agile, have better hands, but lack the speed of black outfielders. "The fact remains," they wrote, "that in our sample, Latinos *are* shorter and lighter than white or African American players."[15]

Taken aback by their own findings that the stereotypes about black, white, and Latin differences may correspond with innate abilities, Margolis and Piliavin scurried for cover. "We do not intend to raise here the issue of race-linked physical differences," they stated, after which they devoted four pages to the issue of race-linked physical differences. As for the crowd of Latin players at second base and shortstop, they wrote that "managers appear to be acting *both* on their expectations regarding the appropriate placement of Latinos . . . and on their prejudices." Yet once again, as with most analyses of "racial stacking," the researchers never presented any evidence of prejudice, only of genuine differences of physique and skills. A far more plausible explanation for black domination of the outfield positions is the reality that blacks are naturally faster than whites.

What did Margolis and Piliavin finally conclude after presenting data that destroyed the popular belief that stacking could be explained by racial stereotyping? They ignored their own findings and jumped to the wholly speculative conclusion that the predominance of blacks in positions that require speed is *by definition* racist. "It is only by understanding how apparent discrimination occurs that we can hope to combat it,"[16] they opined. That's an admirable sentiment but one without any link to the evidence that they proffered.

A classic nature/nurture feedback loop appears to be in place. West African-descended blacks are naturally faster and better jumpers than whites. Black success attracts other talented blacks to certain positions and sports—who would not want to play sports at which we are most likely to do best. That discourages whites from even trying to compete. In other words, cultural conditions exaggerate the small but meaningful differences that led to the athletic edge. Black athletic success reflects bio-cultural factors.

It's becoming increasingly apparent that nature and nurture are separable only as semantic concepts and not in the real world. There is no way to control for all of the environmental influences to determine whether behavior, temperament, or skills are genetic or are shaped by the environment. Science is just beginning to decipher how genes and culture interact, and whether the small but noticeable functional differences we can identify in population groups underlay what we have come to think of as cultural patterns.

CONSIDER CANINES

The "not in our genes" dogma also caricatures what we know about the powerful role of genetics. Consider canines. In 1998, the American Kennel Club was forced to withdraw its nineteenth edition of *The Complete Dog Book* after charges of perpetuating "pernicious stereotypes" about dog breeds. Each year, U.S. insurance companies pay out an estimated $250 million in claims from dog attacks, with overall costs to society estimated at $1 billion a year.[17] In response to these mushrooming, injury statistics, the AKC reclassified some forty breeds as not good for children. Like pit bulls. The reaction?

"To say that all these dogs are 'this' and all these dogs are 'that,' that's racism, canine racism," barked Roger Caras, ABC News reporter and president emeritus of the American Society for the Prevention of Cruelty to Animals. Outraged owners of those breeds that have a penchant for tangling with young children's ears and fingers raised the specter of "breed cleansing." "You just can't make such a blanket statement about dachshunds. Each one is an individual," growled Carl Holder, the outraged secretary of the Dachshund Club of America, ignoring the unquestioned reality that these yappers are not exactly worry-proof pets.

The belief that dog breeds do not have stereotypical personalities is as intuitively ridiculous as claiming that there are no meaningful differences between human populations. More than 100,000 years as "man's best friend," with all but a century of that time free of sometimes rigidly directed breeding, has left some pretty distinctive functional differences. Basset hounds are sweet and stubborn; Mastiffs are sluggish; Border collies may be great at herding the family together, but if a young child falls into the pool, pray that you own a Newfoundland. Though any individual Chihuahua may be a lovable, taco-loving, Godzilla-catching hombre, the product of lucky genes and diligent owner, Chihuahuas as a breed are frequently snappish.

Like in humans, some dog diseases are "breed specific." For instance, shepherds are subject to hip dysplasia, Irish setters to degenerative blindness, poodles to epilepsy, Scottish terriers to sudden muscle rigidity. Every one of the twenty inborn diseases in dogs have been traced to specific defective genes that have also been found in humans.[18] These are functional, genetically linked differences, as any geneticist participating in the modestly financed Dog Genome Project will acknowledge. Nonetheless, despite an overwhelming belief that canine stereotypes are both reasonably accurate and critical information for pet-shopping parents, the AKC caved to the criticism, recalling more than 10,000 copies of its book at a cost of $800,000.[19]

Now, the breeding of dogs does not equate with the evolution of races. Although canine genes flowed as freely as human genes for almost all of evolutionary history, more recent breeds are exaggerated by rigorously controlling gene flow. Humans, in contrast, intermarry widely, exchanging genes far more randomly. But there are similarities: We are both polymorphic—we have individual differences like height, weight, strength, etc.; and we are extremely polytypic—there are many types, whether "races" or "breeds." To suggest that there are no functional differences is its own form of pseudo-science, a religious and not a scientific argument. And while no one expects to find a gene for dog loyalty any more than we should expect to find a gene for 100-meter running, it is not far-fetched to assume we will soon locate alleles for herding or guarding in dogs, as well as faster reflexes or more efficient energy processing in humans.

Now it is certainly true that genes alone don't make a champion, as many a Kentucky breeder has learned after mortgaging the horse farm to buy the prized sperm of yesterday's Triple Crown winner. Even the most gifted alchemist cannot mold clay into marble. The most successful performers invariably have the temperament and intelligence to match their prodigious talents. Although any one athlete may bootstrap himself to stardom, the overall pattern remains circumscribed by the biology of human evolution.

ATHLETIC BIO-CULTURAL "HOT POCKETS"

"While sociologists can attack the flaws and failures of the physiological and psychological literature," acknowledges sports sociologist John Phillips, "we can offer little empirical or theoretical work as an alternative."[20] Such an admission hasn't stopped some sociologists from trying. Rather than challenge the evidence, however, they end up attacking the concept of science itself to justify an unqualified dismissal of the formative role of genetics.

"Whites appear to be threatened by black success in sport, and the common-sense preoccupation with the question of racially linked genetic differences between black and white athletes reflects this racist fear," argues Laurel Davis, citing absolutely nothing but her opinion. "Belief in the scientific notion of objectivity directs attention away from the social structure of science itself and from the sociopolitical contexts that encapsulate science. . . . The effect of reports that purport to show black genetic advantages in sports [is] built upon racist assumptions [and reinforces] white power structures."[21] In typical postmodernist fashion, Davis never gets beyond a jargon-soaked attack to actually address the evidence which devastates her claim.

The problem of course is that the "culture-explains-everything" sociologists are wedded to the simplistic cant that "race is a *only* a social construct." The environment has become the default explanation and biology is often ignored completely. Yet science has long since passed that notion by. The more refined biocultural explanation is intuitively and scientifically more plausible and squares with the anecdotal evidence. It is testable, predictive, and elegant in its simplicity, meeting the key elements of good science. Most critically, it helps us to make sense of patterns we see around us.

Indeed, there are persuasive physiological and genetic reasons that explain why blacks don't do well in some sports and why whites, Asians, and Amerindians dominate in others.

Blacks have never excelled in swimming or diving, for example. Until 2000, no black has ever qualified for the Olympic swim or diving teams. Indeed, despite a number of special programs and considerable funding that have attracted thousands of aspiring black Olympians, there were only seven blacks who could even qualify to compete against the 455 swimmers at the 1996 U.S. Olympic trials. The only black swimmer to win an Olympic championship is Anthony Nesty of Suriname, who touched out Matt Biondi for the gold in 1988 in the 100-meter butterfly, a swimming equivalent of a long sprint.

Chris Martin of the University of Florida, one of a handful of top black swim coaches, is convinced that swimming presents just one more barrier for blacks to crash through. "Until 1968, people said blacks couldn't run distance races," Martin said. "Now look. Inclusion of all people has come to all sports. I sometimes think swimming is an inch on the yardstick of sports history. Soon it will be practiced by many people all over the world."[22] Certainly it requires training and pools, which are in short supply in many rural areas and inner city neighborhoods, to become a champion swimmer. But if some scientists are correct, there are genetically-linked physical and physiological restraints to competing at the Olympic level.

In colloquial terms, blacks are considered "sinkers." Numerous studies over many decades have consistently shown that blacks have denser skeletons and that elite black male athletes have lower levels of body fat than whites or Asians.[23] Perhaps more important, the advantages that African Americans possess in short burst, anaerobic sports such as sprinting, translate into a disadvantage in swimming events longer than 100 meters, which require considerable endurance. Those of West African ancestry fare as poorly in aerobic swimming races in middle and long distance running. Swimming also places a premium on upper body strength, wich generally favors whites. Yet even the mere suggestion that genetics may play a part is frequently dismissed out of hand. For example, an *Atlanta Journal–Constitution* profile of one black Olympic swimming hopeful referred to the "deeply segregated" American swim team and "the ridiculous myth that blacks have no buoyancy."[24]

It's also possible that other racial patterns in sports cavalierly dismissed as myths may have a biological as well as a sociological basis. It is well established that athletes from different countries, populations, or ethnic groups sometimes have different physical characteristics.[25] These differences are not huge, certainly not on the order of the differences between Laurel and Hardy or Abbott and Costello, but they show up time and again and have a demonstrable effect on the performance patterns in elite sports.

For example, studies show that on average, Asians are generally smaller, with relatively short extremities and long torsos, not as fast, and less strong than whites or blacks. They are more flexible and have the quickest reaction time. Although there are certainly cultural factors at work, it is not surprising that Asians are the world's best at Ping-Pong and are among the best in ice-skating, wrestling and gymnastics (hence the term "Chinese splits").

In a few rare cases, nature has conspired with the environment to produce athletic "biocultural hot spots." The Dominican Republic, home of Sammy Sosa, with only 8 million people, is the world's greatest per capita producer of baseball talent, turning out six times as many major leaguers as baseball-mad Mexico (12 percent as compared to 2 percent), yet with a population only one-tenth the size of Mexico's.[26]

The cluster of Pacific islands that straddle the international date line in the South Pacific, including Somoa and American Somoa, have funneled hundreds of players into American football and Australian rugby. Since the early 1970s, these tiny islands have produced no less than fifty NFL players, beginning with the "Throwin' Somoan," all-American quarterback Jack Thompson from Washington State University in 1976. "[Football] is like legalized village warfare," explains Thompson. "There's an innate competitiveness in the warrior sense in Polynesian culture."[27] It doesn't hurt that Pacific Islanders tend to be both large and explosively fast.

The rugged mountains and canyons of Mexico's Copper Canyon in north-central Mexico, the "Grand Canyon of Mexico," is home to another athletic hot spot. The 4,000 or so Native Americans who live in and around the town of Creel produce some of the world's most remarkable endurance runners. Like the Nandi tribe in Kenya, the Tarahumara Indians subsist by herding, growing crops, and hunting. At the urging of American anthropologists and running aficionados, they have become a fixture at one of the world's most grueling sporting events, the 100-mile Leadville, Colorado race that tops out at 11,000 feet in elevation. With no formal running experience and wearing traditional *huarache* sandals instead of running shoes for most of the race, fifty-five year old Victoriano Churro won the 1993 race. Tarahumara Indians went on in later years to eclipse the course record.[28]

Perhaps the most persuasive *prima facie* case suggesting that sports success is not a purely environmental phenomena may be found in the real-life laboratory of the Nandi Hills. Kenya, and more specifically the Kalenjin, represent a mind-boggling concentration of athletic talent. The Kalenjin represent roughly three-quarters of Kenya's world-class runners (half of whom are from one tribe, the Nandi). Hundreds of years ago, what African historians refer to as a proto-Kalenjin population migrated from the Nilotic core area northwest of Lake Turkana to the Mt. Elgon area, where the group fragmented and moved to its present locations in the highlands.

The past concentration of top runners among the Nandi, and the more recent emergence of top runners in the more northerly groups such as the Keiyo, Marakwet, and Tugen, could understandably be linked to the influence of the internationally renowned running program at St. Patrick's in Iten, which is close to those three groups. However, these trends only reconfirm overall Kalenjin dominance. There certainly appears to be a common genetic thread that runs through the amorphous Kalenjin population. According to John Manners, there is an inseparable link between population genetics and East African culture:

> Intriguingly, one of the few non-Kalenjin tribes to make a mark on the international running scene is the Kisii, with whom the Kalenjin have had especially intense interaction over the past several centuries. The Datooga (also called the Dadog) in Tanzania, who speak Southern Nilotic, a language very close to that of the Kalenjin, are one of two small tribes in that country to turn out world-class distance runners in any numbers. The Sabei in Uganda, who are Kalenjin (they live adjacent to their Kalenjin cousins on the other side of the border), dominate Uganda's increasingly successful international cross-country teams, even though they constitute a tiny proportion of the country's population. And on a much broader, less meaningful scale, the Eastern Cushitic speakers who dominate the formidable distance running corps of Ethiopia have some distant connection to the Kalenjin, according to anthropologists.[29]

There is little doubt that for many centuries the Kalenjin have been a substantially stable population group, however mixed in origin, not just unrelated peoples who have come to speak the same language. "The fact that this tribe of about 3 million is able to dominate world distance running is so astonishing as to beggar purely cultural or environmental explanations," writes Manners. "That the various Kalenjin groups originated independently and somehow adopted the same language and customs is both counterintuitive and contrary to the evidence. The only reason I can think for propounding such a theory is essentially a political one—to try to undercut potentially divisive notions of ancient ethnic or blood ties—an admirable sentiment, maybe, but bad history."[30]

SMOKING GUNS?

"Since the word *race* causes such discomfort, *ethnic groups* is often substituted, but it is inappropriate," Theresa Overfield, University of Utah professor of anthropology and expert on the biology of health and illness, has written. "Race is a characteristic used most effectively to describe, rather than explain, health difference. . . . Ignoring the differences between humans is at least shortsighted and can be medically harmful."[31]

"We are keenly aware that [race] has its limitations and that it has been abused in the past," Claude Bouchard wrote in response to attack on research in the *American Journal of Human Biology* by Barry Bogin, professor of anthropology at the University of Michigan at Dearborn. Bogin had accused Bouchard and his Canadian research team of violating the political guidelines of mainstream anthropologists and of "inviting abusive and offensive generalizations." Race "has no usefulness in human biology, " he declared, all but charging them of racism.

Bouchard's reply? "In human biology and clinical studies, as well as in epidemiological research, it is important to understand if age, gender, race, and other population characteristics contribute to the phenotype variation. Only by confronting these enormous public health issues head-on, and not by circumventing them in the guise of political correctness, do we stand a chance to evaluate the discriminating agendas and devise appropriate interventions. To disregard monumental public health issues is to be morally bankrupt."[32]

In other words, race may matter. Even as some critics dogmatically insist that research linking race to disease has yielded few new insights and may contribute to the stereotype that ethnic minorities are less healthy than or inferior to whites,[33] new genetic studies documenting racial differences in rates of diabetes, kidney disorder, cardiovascular disease, and other pathologies appear daily. The continued study of biodiversity is critical if we hope to decipher the archeology of diseases. By finding the genetic underpinnings of long-term health and various diseases, 3,000 to 4,000 of which are believed to be hereditary, researchers are developing treatments for those not yet sick but who, because of their genetic history, have a higher risk of falling ill.[34]

Scientists now know that genetically linked, highly heritable characteristics such as skeletal structure or the ability to use energy more efficiently are not evenly distributed across racial groups. There are plenty of alleles (strings of DNA) that are unique to Europeans, West Africans, Amerindians, as well as smaller population groups. Genetically similar groups, such as Scots and French Canadians, may cluster somewhat differently in some aspects, such as the likelihood of developing cystic fibrosis, indicating different evolutionary histories. Certain blood types, such as ABO, show up within defined populations. Type II diabetes has been linked to a gene found commonly in various North American Indians. Almost 90 percent of Native Americans, Orientals, and blacks are lactose-enzyme deficient.

Several different mutations including defective genes that lead to breast cancer and diseases such as Tay-Sachs, Gaucher's, and Niemann-Pick are common to Ashkenazi Jews, who trace their ancestry to Central Europe. Beta-thalassemia is most prevalent in populations in Mediterranean countries, the Middle East, and Southeast Asia. American Indians are far more likely than other groups to carry an enzyme that makes it harder to metabolize alcohol, increasing the vulnerability to alcoholism. Geneticists have even isolated a gene that causes a form of progressive hearing loss by studying eight generations of one Costa Rican family.[35]

A number of diseases specifically target sub-Saharan Africans. Colorectal cancer for one is far more common among those of West African descent. Blacks are more susceptible to Alzheimer's. Black and other equitorial populations are ten times more likely than whites to be born with sickle cell disease, which has been traced to the race-related sickle cell gene, which protects native carriers in equatorial Africa from getting malaria.[36] There are significant black-white differences in the prevalence of genetically based hypertension, cerebrovascular diseases, and Type II diabetes.[37]

So why do we so readily accept the idea that evolution has turned out Jews with a genetic predisposition to the degenerative mental disease Tay-Sachs and that blacks are more susceptible to sickle cell anemia, yet find it racist to suggest that West Africans may have evolved into the world's best sprinters?

CHALLENGING SKEPTICS

What *would* satisfy skeptics? "For me to be convinced," states Owen Anderson, "[geneticists] would simply have to identify the genes that are important for endurance performance and show that those genes are more prevalent among Kenyan runners. Since we don't know which genes are important, it's impossible to measure the relative frequencies of performance-enhancing genes in different groups of runners."[38] Since specific genes cannot yet be directly linked to specific sport skills, Anderson refuses to even consider that there may be population-linked athletic talents. By demanding a "smoking gun," he has set up a straw man.

Evolutionary biologist Jonathan Marks has erected his own nearly impossible standard. Marks asserts that only an airtight experiment would convince him that there are meaningful differences between populations—yet he knows that airtight experiments are impossible. A scientist can test the patellar tendon reflex, measure muscle fiber types, or evaluate endurance in a laboratory, but sports demand the messy reality of a playing field. "If no scientific experiments are possible, than what are we to conclude?" he nonetheless writes. "That discussing innate abilities is the scientific equivalent of discussing properties of angels."[39]

Ironically, the arguments advanced by Marks and Anderson echo the creationist attack on evolution. "The evidence for evolution is far less compelling than we have been led to believe," the Creation Legal Research Fund represented in a legal brief argued (unsuccessfully) before the Supreme Court. "[Macro-] evolution is not a scientific 'fact,' since it cannot actually be observed in a laboratory. . . . The scientific problems with evolution are so serious that it could accurately be termed a 'myth.'"[40] In other words, since no one was present at earth's beginning, and the creation of life cannot be replicated in an experiment, any statement about the origin of life is "the scientific equivalent of discussing properties of angels," to borrow Marks's phrase.

If scientific theories depend only upon observable evidence or laboratory experiments then everything from the theory of relativity to the certainty that the earth revolves around the sun could be written off as speculative. Geneticists may never isolate the particular strands of DNA that resolve what little ambiguity remains in the debate about race and athletics, "but that is not the same as saying that there is not a genetic basis for the racial patterns we see in sports," asserts Bengt Saltin. There is an incredibly complex relationship among genes, culture, potential, and performance. "Identifying genes will not and cannot expect to resolve the issue."[41]

Genetic and behavioral research has shown that genetics and the environment are part of an endless loop, each reinforcing and reshaping the other. At the end of the nineteenth century, J. M. Baldwin observed that when a species learns a useful new skill—for argument sake, say, sprinting or jumping—the addition to its behavioral repertoire may reshape its biology. Over time, natural selection blesses the ensuing generations whose limbs and brains are suited to this learned maneuver and culls out those whose anatomy is ill suited to the innovation.

Are Kalenjin great long distance runners because of a genetic advantage or because their high-altitude lifestyle serves as a lifelong training program? Studies of children who grow up at high altitudes show that they have lungs with greater oxygen capacity and a greater proportion of red blood cells than children of similar genetic background raised at low altitudes. This relationship between hypoxia—a deficiency in the amount of oxygen reaching the tissues—and its effects on physique has been termed plasticity. Although these changes appear to be environmentally induced, they are not always reversible. Unlike what happens with acclimatization, with plasticity a high-altitude child would retain these characteristics even if she were to relocate to sea level.

Although it smacks of Lamarckism, this so-called Baldwin Effect, which has many adherents, suggests that over the course of evolution, some advantages may have yielded to other more advantageous survival skills, physical or intellectual. Some gene-linked advantageous behaviors, if passed along to future generations, may gradually reshape the genes of the species, resulting in biological pre-programming—an instinct.[42]

So we're back to a chicken-and-egg dilemma: Did the altitude reconfigure the lungs of Kenyan endurance runners or was a genetic predisposition induced by the altitude? Is that nature or nurture . . . or both?

Such scientific conundrums do not lend themselves to "smoking guns" and absolute certainty. The fact that geneticists cannot yet isolate the DNA that contributes to hip-shifting, breakaway running doesn't automatically undermine the fact that such skills are genetically based. As Vincent Sarich notes, science may never identify a gene that ensures that we grow five fingers, but we can be assured there is one, or a set of genes. We have yet to find a gene for tallness, yet we can be quite certain that if one exists, men will be more likely to have it than women. Most theories, including those in genetics, rely on emperical evidence tested against common sense, known science, and the course of history. That scientists may yet not be able to identify the chromosomes that contribute to specific athletic skills does not mean that genes don't play a defining role—any more than the lack of an eyewitness at a crime is "proof" that the crime never happened.

In sports a minuscule advantage in body type or firing muscle fibers can make a dramatic difference on the playing field. Though small differences may mean nothing when comparing average people, at the elite level, an infinitesimally small advantage can be decisive. "Differences among athletes of elite caliber are so small," notes physical anthropologist Robert Malina, "that if you have an advantage that might be genetically based . . . it might be very, very significant. The fraction of a second is the difference between the gold medal and fourth place."[43] And that is not genetic hocus-pocus.

VI

WHAT ABOUT WOMEN?

CHAPTER 21

THE SUPERIORITY OF

WHITE FEMALE ATHLETES

omen's sports is coming of age. To newly converted devotees, it is symbolized by the now famous photograph of Brandi Chastain, who, in exultation after scoring the winning penalty kick for the United States in the 1999 World Cup, whipped off her jersey to reveal sculpted biceps and sinewy shoulders: now *that's* a world-class athlete. Such triumphal images are now commonplace: Chamique Holdsclaw spinning past a defender for an impossible lay-up; a blistering backhand by Venus Williams (or was it Serena?), Tegla Loroupe taking the victory lap, draped in a Kenyan flag, after yet another marathon victory; the blur of sprinter Marion Jones of the United States crossing the finish line yards ahead of her nearest competitor.

These empowering pictures are a far cry from the schizophrenic images that have traditionally been associated with women's sports. On one extreme is the icon of the prepubescent gymnast or skater. The celebration of the pixie-as-athlete was in part an understandable reaction to the more brutish image that, fairly or not, had come to symbolize female athleticism—an overmuscled female East European weight-lifter, field athlete, or swimmer, her body seemingly twisted out of all natural proportion by drug use. Although that legacy can be linked to the rusting, drug-addled sports machines of the former Soviet Union and its East-bloc allies, it actually has roots that go back many years earlier.

Born Stanislawa Walasiewicz in 1911 in Wierzchowina, Poland, Stella Walsh is considered by many to be the greatest woman athlete ever. When only nineteen in 1930, she rocketed to fame, setting records at 50 yards and 100 meters, marks that would stand for twenty-six and twenty-five years, respectively. She was also a champion in the long jump, discus, and pentathlon, and would collect sixteen Polish national championships. Walsh began her Olympic career representing Poland at the 1932 Games in Los Angeles, where she won the 100-meter race, and retired twenty-six years later, competing as a naturalized U.S. citizen at age forty-seven. By then, she had amassed forty-one AAU championships, including eleven each in the 200 meters and the long jump. Some of her world records held into the 1960s, a remarkable three-decade span.

By any measure, Walsh was among the best athletes of the twentieth century. But for years she raced in a swirl of rumors. When she competed in her first Olympics, officials were taken aback by her awesome performance and her "long, manlike strides." In 1936, one Polish journalist took the scuttlebutt public and accused her of *being* a man. In response, Berlin Olympic officials released a statement that they had given her a thorough physical and determined that she was indeed female.

On December 4, 1980, Stella Walsh had the misfortune of being in the wrong place at the wrong time. Living out her retirement in her adopted home of Cleveland, she had just emerged from buying decorations for a Polish American dance when she wandered into cross fire from gunmen attempting a robbery. An autopsy performed by the Medical Examiner's office revealed that Walsh had ambiguous sexual organs but was biologically a male.[1]

The revelation, shocking only to those unfamiliar with Walsh's exploits, highlights one of the enduring controversies in female athletics: the issue of sexuality. Her amazing story underscores the seemingly baffling fact that over the past seventy-five years, elite white female athletes have performed better than white males in competition against blacks. How could this be so if genetics plays such a defining role in athletic performance?

DOUBLE INDEMNITY

It is axiomatic that women have had far fewer opportunities than men to test their mettle in most fields, sports included. There are relatively few female professional leagues, and prejudice against female athleticism remains strong, particularly in less-developed countries. In the West social opprobrium has waxed and waned over the century and has been applied differently at different eras to different sports. As a result of these social factors, it is far more difficult to make meaningful comparisons between black and white female athletes than between black and white men.

Female black athletes have had to overcome a double taboo: racism overlain by the belief that sports and femininity are incompatible. In the black community success in sports has long been a symbol of pride, empowerment, and achievement—for males. Jack Johnson not only beat his opponents silly, for a time he also beat the system that denied blacks a fair shake. Owens, Robinson, Louis, and many other black sports stars saw themselves as proto-males and role models for all of black America. Their manhood was a chip that could be played in the game for racial pride and civil rights. To the degree that successful women athletes might be seen as overshadowing the achievements of men, the black community has historically been less than supportive of its female stars.

Linda Williams, an African American historian, contends that the "white press" has systematically downplayed stories of black female athletes to concentrate on the accomplishments of black men, which has skewed public perceptions. She also attacks what she calls the chauvinist penchant for black writers to hold that "blacks are men" and "African American athletes are men," as if women didn't exist. Her prime example is Arthur Ashe. In his award-winning history of blacks in sports, *A Hard Road to Glory*, Ashe does not even mention the tradition of black women in basketball and running, which dates back to the early part of the century.[2] "Most black women spent very little time engaged in competitive organized sport," he wrote, as if to justify why so little of his mammoth work focused on African American women.[3] It was an uncharacteristic oversight by a man rightly admired for his sensitivity.

But race, not gender bias, remains the most formidable barrier. As with men, the most familiar prejudice is the intelligence issue. As far back as the late nineteenth century it was suspected that tennis was "too sophisticated and intellectual" for young blacks, women in particular.[4] But even though there have been relatively few African American women tennis players, black women have been among the sport's greatest stars. Lucy Slowe was national champion in 1917 and 1925, before segregation prevented competition against whites. Althea Gibson's emergence as a star in the 1950s led to the re-entrance of African Americans into white tournaments.[5]

The brouhaha that has greeted the Williams sisters in tennis has made it transparent that race remains a prickly issue. "I'm tall, I'm black, everything's different about me," said Venus Williams after her run in her first try at the 1997 U.S. Open title. "Just face the facts."[6] Her father Richard who protectively and provocatively manages Venus and her sister Serena, literally phoned in to the media charges of racism as that tournament progressed. The racial undertones subsided considerably by the U.S. Open in 1999, in which Serena upset Martina Hingis, and with Venus's 2000 win.

Whites also have dominated swimming, another "country club" sport (although the relatively lighter bone density of whites and Asians compared to blacks may also provide an edge). In the early part of the century, swimming was one of the few sports considered appropriate for young females, perhaps because of its association with beauty contests and ultimately the Miss America pageant, celebrations of "white American beauty" which became wildly popular. After World War I, women's rights activists successfully lobbied to open more Olympic events to female athletes. That movement triggered a backlash. Although female swimmers were described as "queens" or "nymphs" and were invariably white and middle-class, track-and-field participants, far more likely to be black or working-class whites, were tagged with unflattering put-downs about their flat chests and muscular proportions.

These social crosscurrents came to a head during the 1928 Olympics. At the "long" distance of 800 meters, several female runners fell to the ground in emotional and physical exhaustion as they crossed the finish line. Although hardly unusual in the men's competition, the "collapse," as it came to be called, ignited a cause célèbre. Critics waiting for an opportunity to pounce proffered this incident as proof that females were unfit for such activities. One of the fiercest of the old guard, Frederick Rand Rogers, alleged that track-and-field events were "profoundly unnatural" for women because they stressed unfeminine qualities such as brute strength and endurance. According to Rogers, the Olympics were "essentially masculine in nature and develop wholly masculine physiques and behavior traits." Competition would severely wound womanhood, for it would sacrifice "health, physical beauty, and social attractiveness." Conjuring up a master eugenic plan, Rogers suggested ominously that such athletic women "may constitute nature's greatest failures, which should perhaps, be corrected by as drastic means as those by which the most hideous deformities are treated."[7]

Besieged by such tripe disguised as social conservatism, and in the wake of the 1928 incident, the Olympic Congress, after briefly considering a total ban on women's running, eliminated all medium- and long-distance races. The ambivalence about women in sports only increased with the exploits of Walsh; "bobbed-haired, flat-chested" Missouri farm girl Helen Stephens; Babe Didrikson; and other muscular females who didn't fit the bathing-beauty stereotype. Didrikson captured three medals at the 1932 Games and managed for a brief time to become a press favorite. Standing but 5 feet, 4 inches and weighing 110 pounds, she appeared anything but the rugged warrior-princess ridiculed by social conservatives—that is, until she gave interviews. Then she became a target of both gender and class prejudices.

Didrikson was a working-class girl from Port Arthur, Texas. She had little time for feminine niceties, cut her hair short, wore loose-fitting sweatsuits, and played basketball, football, and baseball when she wasn't running track or throwing the javelin. When asked whether there was anything at all that she didn't play, she parried, "yeah, dolls."[8] Her language was, shall we say, colorful. The public recoiled at this unfeminine display, and by the mid-1930s much of America had lost patience with what was perceived as the fad of females in sports. Social pressures forced many ambitious young white women to abandon their athletic dreams.

WHITE AMERICA'S LOSS, BLACK AMERICA'S GAIN

At first, the cultural antipathy to sports did not bite nearly as deeply among blacks, who were attuned to welcoming opportunity in whatever form it was offered. Black female runners moved to fill the vacuum created by the withdrawal of support for women's track and field, although not without some concerns within the black community, which shared the popular prejudice that the sport was too "mannish."*[9] As Susan Kahn observed in *Coming on Strong*, "at the precise moment when the majority of white women and the white public rejected the sport as undignified for women . . . African American interest . . . toward women's athletics set the stage for the emergence of black women's track."[10]

It was never easy. Black female athletes encountered all of the barriers faced by their male counterparts and then some. The few men who cracked the color barrier in track, football, and basketball were from primarily white universities—not one black athlete on the 1936 Olympic team was from a black school. Black women had few such opportunities.

It fell to the southern black colleges such as the Tuskegee Institute to nurture the future stars. Young hopefuls focused on track and field because it was cheap, requiring no great investment in equipment. Athletic budgets at black schools were tiny; college administrators were generally far more interested in men's team sports and track; and the white press, particularly in the South, all but ignored competitions at black colleges except when the Olympics neared. But despite crushing poverty and a dearth of opportunities, the years between the World Wars were a golden age of sorts for black women in sports.

Tuskegee Institute pioneered women's track in the late 1920s un-

---

*The noted physical educator E. B. Henderson would take pains to contrast "effeminate . . . colored girl" runners with white runners who "are more man than woman," an apparent swipe at Stella Walsh.

der the sure hand of Major Cleveland Abbott, the college's director of physical education. Abbott had founded a "running carnival" to provide an outlet for teenaged boys in Alabama and across the Deep South who were shut out from competitions with whites in track, golf, and tennis. Its instant success led him to tap basketball coach Amelia Roberts to introduce competition for young girls. By 1936, Tuskegee was inviting the best of the best female stars to a special summer camp, where they got to practice side by side with the men.[11]

Abbott's precious gem in the rough was Alice Coachman, the pride of Albany, Georgia. Life in the rural South was strictly segregated: whites and blacks sipped from separate water fountains, ate in different restaurants, went to one-race schools, and never mixed socially. Little Alice was one of nine siblings who spent any spare time picking cotton for 50 cents for every 100 pounds plucked. She was fast as a whip, a quality her mother exploited by sending her into town on errands. By the time she was nine, she was making a game out of jumping.

"We'd tie rags together and have somebody hold onto it on each side and jump over it," she recalled.[12] Alice wanted to go to the Olympics, her dreams fired by the exploits of Eddie Tolan, Ralph Metcalfe, Archie Williams, Cornelius Johnson, and Jesse Owens. But she faced the treble burden of being black, dirt poor, and female. "In my time, most of the girls didn't worry about participating in sports," Coachman said. "They had to be ladylike. All the people would say, 'There goes Alice, that crazy fool playing with them boys.' But I didn't care."[13]

Determined to learn a trade, Alice left home in 1938 at age fifteen and headed for Tuskegee in neighboring Alabama. The school had already begun its twenty-year run as the dominant college in women's track. With loads of talent but without sneakers, Alice became an immediate star on a star-studded team. "It felt good," she chuckled, thinking back to when she competed in bare feet. Coachman broke the Alabama high school and college high-jump records before upgrading to tennis sneakers and then to regulation track spikes.

The following year, Coachman won the national amateur high-jump competition, the first of ten consecutive championships. She emerged as one of the few athletes who could hold her own against Stella Walsh, who was the 100-meter champion in 1943 and 1944. Coachman won in 1945 and 1946. By 1948, when Coachman won the high-jump title at the London Olympics and became the first black woman to win a gold medal, she had edged past the aging Walsh as the reigning queen of track.

The athletic program at Tuskegee's chief rival, Tennessee Agriculture and Industrial, prospered under the direction of Jessie Abbott, daughter of Tuskegee's Clive Abbott. From 1936 until the early 1970s, almost all African American female Olympians were products of either Tuskegee or Tennessee A&I, later renamed Tennessee State.[14]

Even with such widespread success, the small but influential black middle-class vacillated between pride at the achievements of its best and brightest and concern over negative stereotypes. To short-circuit potential backlash, Tennessee A&I instituted a strict dress code and would not allow photographers to snap postrace pictures until the girls had washed up and added some makeup. The coach "wanted to show them that we were ladies—respectable ladies," commented sprinter Martha Hudson.[15]

THE "WORLD'S FASTEST FEMALES"

The first postwar U.S. Olympic team, in 1948, included eleven female track-and-field athletes, nine of them black. The only two whites competed in the field events. Since the London Games, blacks have never represented less than a majority of a U.S. Olympic track-and-field team, male or female.[16] "American [white] women have been so thoroughly licked over so many years by the Booker T. Washington Girls," wrote E. B. Henderson in trying to explain the ascension of the black female track star, "that they have almost given up track-and-field competition."[17] Some twenty years after African American men had decisively emerged as the elite sprinters in the world, their female counterparts had scaled even higher racial, class, and gender barriers to become the best in their sport.

By the eve of the Helsinki Games in 1952, in the early stages of the Cold War, black American athletes, particularly the female running contingent, were tying the world in knots. *Ebony's* pre-Olympic profile was headlined, "Can Negro Athletes Stop the Russians?"[18] They frequently did, in Finland and around the world, which posed serious public relations problems for the Eastern bloc, where rockets and runners were symbols of the virtues of communism.

By this time, the center of women's sprinting had shifted to Tennessee State University. Under the firm hand of Eddie Temple, some forty TSU women made the national track-and-field teams over the next three decades, winning thirteen gold medals, six silver, and four bronze. And for anyone who doubted that brains and brawn can go together, thirty-nine of the forty graduated and twenty-eight earned master's degrees.[19]

TSU's brightest star was willowy Wilma Rudolph, who earned a spot as a fifteen-year old on the 1956 Olympic team in Melbourne. Growing up in the Tennessee backwater of Clarksville, Rudolph had had no childhood dreams of swim meets, there were no golfing outings, no dance lessons or gymnastics competitions, no taking a turn as an ice princess. The seventeenth of nineteen children, she lived with her family in a ramshackle red-framed house that bedded eleven other half-brothers and -sisters. At no point did her parents' combined yearly income exceed $2,500.[20] For the skinny, pint-sized Rudolph, who had barely survived childhood bouts with polio, double pneumonia, and scarlet fever, there were few options except to attempt to run her way out of poverty.

At Rome, four years later, Skeeter (as she became known) so enthralled the world that Cassius Clay, her teammate and dashing gold-medal boxer, was the second banana. Rudolph became the first American woman to win a gold medal in the sprints since Helen Stephens in 1936, taking the 100 meters in a wind-aided 11 seconds. She also set a world record in the 200 meters and anchored the gold-medal winning 400-meter relay squad, which edged out the Soviets. Her gold heist marked the first time since Psaumis of Camarina in the ancient games in Greece that a woman athlete had won three Olympic events.

"If there is a single common denominator about her 'secret' of success, it is hard, aching poverty, so much so that at the height of her popularity in Rome, Wilma Rudolph did not have three coins of her own to throw into the Trevi fountain," wrote sports historian Michael Davis. "Certainly it is not any physical characteristics attributable to race. All of these canards have since been proven false by scientists." [21]

Canards or not, Rudolph proved a revelation for women's track. She had sex appeal. Not yet twenty-one, this long-legged beauty challenged the existing stereotype of women sports stars. "Unlike many American female athletes," opined *Newsweek*, "she looks feminine."[22] The Italian press called her La Perla Nera (The black pearl); the French nicknamed her La Gazelle Noire (The black gazelle).[23] She was also married and had a child, which muffled whispers of lesbianism, which had stalked women's sports for decades. Modest as well as elegant, she was seen as a refreshing change from other track stars who "have often been characterized by overdeveloped muscles and underdeveloped glands," wrote *Time*.[24]

Every year from 1955, beginning with Mae Faggs, to Wyomia Tyus in 1968, a black woman was the U.S. national champion at 100 and 200 meters. Tyus won the 100 meters at Tokyo in 1964 and set a new world record of 11.8 seconds four years later in Mexico City, becoming the first female sprinter to win gold medals at consecutive Olympics. African American women earned three gold medals and one silver medal in 1968.[25] It would mark the end of an era for black women track stars. By the next Olympics, the Eastern bloc sports machines, with a boost from modern chemistry, would begin manufacturing a new breed of female athlete.

CHAPTER 22

EAST GERMANY'S

SPORTS MACHINE

Fairly or not, Wilma Rudolph and other great African American athletes of the 1950s and 1960s were seen to have none of the dominatrix swagger associated with female athletes from the then communist bloc. In a mixture of Cold War fever and racial pride, *Ebony* magazine would mock Soviet-bloc athletes as "short on beauty but long on brawn."[1] Columnist William Barry Furlong likened Soviet braggadocio about their broad-waisted, muscle-armed female Olympians to bragging about the best-looking automobile wreck. "Venus wasn't a shot-putter," he wrote.[2]

The stereotype got so insidious that for a brief time in the early 1960s Olympic officials debated whether to eliminate several events considered not truly feminine. To make his point, one official sarcastically proposed creating a special competition for "hermaphrodites," who would invariably defeat "normal . . . child-bearing" women handicapped by "largish breasts" and "wide hips." In 1966, the IOC announced it was instituting biological checks. (Since the rules were introduced, an estimated one in every five hundred athletes tested has been refused permission to compete.[3]) After the announcement, six Eastern bloc females pulled out of the European championships in Budapest and two of the top field athletes of this era, the sisters Irene and Tamara Press of the Soviet Union, immediately retired. The next year, the Polish sprinter, Eva Klobkowska, failed the Barr Sex Test after she was found to have an excess of male hormones, a consequence it was determined of having internal testicles.[4] Needless to say, speculation raged, tarring all female athletes with the brush of suspicion.

The cross-gender issue initially masked a far more serious problem: the abuse of performance-enhancing drugs. For decades, until the late 1960s, black women runners, like their male counterparts, had all but owned the sprints. Then almost overnight, a phalanx of females from the Soviet Union, the German Democratic Republic (GDR), and the rest of the Eastern bloc suddenly became competitive, even dominant. Over the following two decades they accounted for seventy-one of the eighty-four running records set at distances from 100 meters to 1,500 meters, including a remarkable thirty-four world records in the 100-meter dash alone.[5]

It has long been assumed that blacks had excelled for the same reasons that Jews were the early stars in basketball, Canadians dominated hockey, and Japanese made the best sumo wrestlers: blood, sweat, and tears. At first this sudden rise to sports excellence by the communist bloc, East Germany in particular, was seen in much the same light: a showcase for the environmentalist argument that athletes are made and not born. They were touted as products of efficient sports machines: raw diamonds were identified and polished to perfection by a system dedicated to turning out the best that hard work and money could create. If that were the only explanation.

With the Soviet satellites slow to revive economically after World War II, the fragile governments recognized that sports provided a diversion for an increasingly disenchanted populace. Money that could have been spent rebuilding roads or establishing schools was funneled into constructing sports complexes. The latest five-year plan might be in disarray, but sports offered something in which to believe in a soul-less state. The vaunted sports machines were one of the few success stories in the dismal history of postwar Eastern Europe. Propagandized as a stunning example of the virtues of communism, they were in fact something far more malignant. These apparent sports utopias would never have been possible without wide and systematic exploitation of illegal drugs.

Recently released KGB documents reveal that Soviet officials began experimenting with steroids in the 1950s in response to the dramatic success of American black athletes, who were emerging as the new stars of international sport. At first, they focused on weightlifters and field athletes, particularly women. At the Tokyo Olympics in 1964, fortified by an elaborate bureaucracy that coddled the best young athletes, the once ragtag Soviet squad waltzed off with the most medals. It was a propaganda coup. "To the failures of U.S. policy in international affairs," boasted the Soviet journal *Theory and Practice of Physical Culture*, "to the loss of its influence in several Asian, African and Latin-American countries have been added the defeats of American sportsmen in the international arena."[6]

The Soviets' success spawned similar experiments throughout the Eastern countries. By the end of the decade, steroid use was popular in communist countries and the west, including the United States, where, for the most part, it amounted to dabbling by individual athletes. But for the Eastern bloc, it was a state enterprise. Drugs became the secret tool that would transform the communist countries into dominant sports superpowers. Although the Soviet sports machine was by far the best financed, the East German version emerged as the gold standard of efficiency, productivity—and corruption.

SPORTS AS RELIGION

The truth of the unloved German Democratic Republic can be found in the rubble of the rebuilding effort in East Berlin, Jena, and other formerly dingy cities where Paleozoic construction sites swarm with dinosaur-like cranes. Yet, Easterners still speak with awe and pride of their sports accomplishments. The GDR's massive gold collection managed to irk even the Soviets, embarrass the West Germans, and drive the Americans to defensive apologies. In a country where a rusting, fuel-snorting, two-stroke Trabant automobile that needed to be cranked to start became emblematic of the nation's problems, the state-controlled athletic system resembled a BMW. It churned out Olympic-class widgets with relentless German precision, an invaluable achievement for a country hungry for recognition.

Created by partition in 1947, East Germany was never the better half. Seventeen million people, one-third the population of the Fed-

eral Republic of Germany to the west, crowded into a land the size
of Virginia that had been laid destitute by war. While western invest-
ments poured into West Germany, sparking a postwar economic
boom, the East remained a dour and crumpled mess, a pariah. East
Germany's first leader, Walter Ulbricht, settled on sports to galvanize
national pride and forge a distinct identity separate from that of the
West. Declaring that "athletes were ambassadors in gym clothes," he
drew upon a German tradition of sports and fitness stretching back
more than three hundred years.[7]

In the early days, the official government sports complex was one
room in a tiny brick building in a bombed-out neighborhood, a mere
bullet shot from where the Berlin wall would later rise. Milking his
political connections, Manfred Ewald quickly emerged as the sports
power in the new country. He had been recruited for the job by the
future communist party chief Erich Honecker, who had just taken
over the leadership of the Free German Youth after spending twelve
years in concentration camps for his opposition to Hitler. "We
needed high performances to demonstrate and underline the existence of our sports system," said Ewald.[8]

Ewald was quick to grasp the historic opportunity. He created the
Deutscher Turn und Sports Bund (DTSB), or German Gymnastics
and Sports Union. He begged, borrowed, and squeezed bone-dry
budgets to piece together a vast system of sports clubs and schools.
A sports college was built on the cheap in Leipzig. While the nearby
city remained a living corpse of shattered, bomb-pocked buildings,
the DTSB spent lavishly on a 100,000-seat stadium, tartan tracks,
numerous indoor and outdoor Olympic-sized pools, modern rowing
and canoeing facilities, and dozens of laboratories and lecture halls.
The Research Institute for Physical Culture became the official heart
of the sports machine. Training centers sprouted like dandelions.[9]
The government even reserved the most up-to-date medical facilities
for athletes. The West had nothing comparable to the long-secret
Baro-chamber in a suburb of East Berlin, where select elite athletes
would spend days or weeks training underground at simulated altitudes.

For the most part, however, the trumpeted machine was decidedly low tech. Even the best workout facilities, such as the vast government gymnasium in Berlin or Katarina Witt's nearby ice rink, looked like industrial eyesores. The system relied on a mind-boggling number of dedicated volunteers, scouts, coaches, and scientists. The winnowing process began with a form of Olympics for toddlers: children were measured, weighed, timed, and psychologically evaluated not long after they learned to walk. The results were matched against a "superior toddler" model for each and every sport.

"In East Germany, what mattered was not the individual but the collective," observed Manfred Hoppner, once East Germany's top sports physician. The most promising children were steered into the appropriate state-supported maze of sports programs and schools. The rest were summarily discarded, their careers over before puberty.[10]

By the time grade schoolers turned into teenagers, the eye of the needle had narrowed considerably. "The government did everything for me," said sprinter Katrin Krabbe, who, like many former East German stars, recalls the old days with fondness. "I started training professionally at thirteen. I went to a sports school in Neubrandenburg. All the training, everything, cost my parents [very little]."

The best young athletes were channeled into the country's 2,000 training centers. The survivors shuttled into the elite residential sports schools, where they were catered to by thousands of full-time trainers as well as doctors, masseurs, and cooks. "You lived in barracks," recalled former champion Heidi Krieger, who was recruited into the sports program at the Dynamo sporting club in East Berlin. "You get up, have breakfast, go to school, then train. You have lunch, go to school, then training. Everything revolved around sport."[11] Some 2,000 of the country's top athletes were housed at any given time at the College of Sports and Physical Culture in Leipzig. Tens of thousands more toiled at satellite sports colleges.

Success in the GDR was a product of quantity as much as quality. "If there was one expert in the United States per athlete, there were fifty in the East," noted Helmut Digel, president of the German track and field federation. Hans Georg Hermann, former deputy rector at Leipzig, said that the GDR once had more than 7,000 certified professional coaches, 10,000 schools, and 8,000 workers' sports clubs.[12] Today, there are only some 400 high-performance coaches in all of unified Germany.

"Yes, there was a lot of pressure to win," said Volker Mai, a triple jumper from the golden age. "But people were proud of the athletes. I could go through my hometown and everybody would know me. In East Germany, everybody felt they were a part of it because they financed it and they worked in a whole society. Now, everybody makes their own money and no one really cares."[13] Those who made it through the grueling gauntlet were amply rewarded with special privileges, such as a car, an apartment, and travel. It was a Faustian bargain.

STATE PLAN 14.25

If Kenya is nature's sports laboratory, the German Democratic Republic proved to be a creation of Dr. Frankenstein. Although there had been rumors for years, the details of the vast corruption long remained hidden behind the stolid facades of former top GDR officials. But many German athletes, including former West German Olympic discus thrower Brigitte Berendonk, author of *Doping Documents* and a competitor in the relatively drug-free 1960s, campaigned relentlessly after the fall of the Berlin Wall for a full-scale investigation. Provoked by the publicity, the German parliament authorized a limited probe by Berendonk's husband, Heidelberg University biologist Werner Franke. During a search of an army library, Franke stumbled across a trove of damning documents detailing the GDR's Marshall Plan to create super-athletes through drugs. It was known as State Planning Theme 14.25.

According to the plan, East German scientists figured out how to increase the strength of female athletes by artificially raising the levels of two naturally occurring hormones, testosterone and epitestosterone. The normal ratio of testosterone to epitestosterone in women is between 1 to 1 and 1 to 2. Because the level can fluctuate fairly widely owing to women's hormonal cycles, officials have set the allowable cut off at 6 to 1 to avoid false positives. But East German scientists perfected a way to load up the athletes and disguise the doping without appearing to exceed the limit.[14] Two years later the ruling party's Central Committee expanded its doping authority. Athletes in every Olympic sport except sailing and female gymnastics were soon being force-fed drugs.[15]

The effects were spectacular. Before 1968, Australia and the United States had dominated women's swimming; Britain, Scandinavia, and the United States set the pace in running. Then, boom, record times went into a free fall in event after event, with almost all of the new records set by Eastern bloc athletes. This crash in times, induced by sudden massive drug use, is what some now call an "anabolic break."[16] From 1968, when the sports machine first kicked into gear, through the 1988 Seoul Games, shortly before the collapse of Eastern European communism, the Soviets and East Germany were the top Olympic medal earners, the best athletes that chemistry could buy.

One of the first guinea pigs, in 1970, was a female skater. But runners and swimmers were among the first groups of athletes to be systematically used as test-tube babies. The East German secret police files document a full-scale doping effort in the run up to the 1972 Olympics in Germany. Doctors reportedly administered steroids to gold-medal winners Renate Meissner, a sprinter, and pole vaulter Wolfgang Nordwig, among others. The GDR lifted its medal count from thirty in 1968 to eighty only four years later. Not one East German female swimmer had won a gold medal in 1972, but East Germany would sweep eleven of thirteen events at Munich. The team from the mighty United States, with a population twelve times as large, won thirty-four gold.

At the Montreal Olympics in 1976, the East German's scooped up a startling 109 medals, including forty gold. Built like granite, Kornelia Ender won four gold medals and became the poster girl for communism. "I remember [US Olympian] Kathy Heddy running up to me, saying 'There are men in the ladies' locker room!'" recalled Jack Nelson, coach of the women's swim team. "I said, 'No, dear, those are the East Germans.' It's sad people didn't realize we truly had the greatest women's team in history. I don't count the East German team as a women's team because they had so much testosterone in their bodies."[17]

East German officials conceded nothing, however. "Our athletes have come here to swim not sing," said one swim coach.[18] Documents prepared by Stasi, the GDR's infamous secret police, would later shed light on the swimmers' secret weapon—drugs. "They were not allowed to approach a microphone because their voices were so deep" from steroids, discovered Brigitte Berendonk. After watching the awesome performance of the fräuleins of swimming, GDR coaches in other sports began clamoring for anabolic cocktails. The tentacles of the doping program would eventually extend to the universities and the sporting schools, all under the watchful eye of the Stasi. As many as 1,500 of the country's premier scientists, physicians, and trainers were actively involved.[19]

To what degree the athletes were victims or accomplices is not entirely clear. Walther Troeger, head of the German National Olympic Committee, believes few were aware, at least in the early stages, that they were taking illegal drugs. "They were given injections during training and didn't even know what they took," he claimed. "They were told they were just vitamins, and they believed it. They didn't ask questions."[20] Though the younger athletes were certainly unaware that the "vitamins" were anabolic steroids, the bodily changes were so severe and the improvement in performance so significant that it is hard to believe that over time they didn't suspect something fishy was going on. "When, at fifteen or sixteen years old, you suddenly have a deep voice, need to shave your legs and look fattened up, then naturally you talk to one another about it," said Christiane Knacke-Sommer, a former world-record holder in swimming.[21]

UPPING THE DOSAGE

It was 1981. Sixteen biologists, physiologists, physicians, and university research professors—the scientific cream of East Germany—

nervously gathered around a table at the top research institute in Leipzig to discuss the crisis. This was serious business: not the threat of biological warfare or a health crisis but sports. More than a decade after East Germany had ramped up its doping program, the country's cover was in danger and General Secretary Honecker was furious.

Soviet Olympic shot-put champion Ilona Slupianek had recently been nabbed for doping. The bust inflamed the sports world and caused consternation in East Germany, which had been self-righteously denying rumors of massive doping for years. The international sports community was awash in rumors and threats of increased surveillance by the dreaded doping police. Honecker demanded that the scientists devise a chemical shield to ensure that no East German athletes would fail international screening tests.

Anticipating this day of reckoning, several top scientists had been experimenting with a new steroid delivery method that might survive scrutiny. After reviewing the predicament, Michael Oettel, then research director at the GDR-owned pharmaceutical company Jenapharm, focused on androstenedione, a synthetic form of a male hormone that occurs naturally in the body and is converted to testosterone. Andro, which Mark McGwire has made wildly popular among baseball players and in the gym, was not yet banned by the IOC. The researchers found that andro could prolong the effects of the more powerful anabolic steroids that competitors would stop taking weeks before major events to avoid positive tests.

Jenapharm developed a nasal spray that could be used immediately before competition and would deliver an immediate explosion of aggressive energy, yet still be masked from drug testers. German doctors said in a patent application for andro at the time that it would raise the testosterone levels of experienced elite athletes by 237 percent in just fifteen minutes. "It felt like a volcanic eruption," remembered swimmer Raik Hannemann, who was not fully aware of the implications of what he was taking.[22]

It was certainly a breakthrough drug, however, and it provided an immediate resolution of the crisis. But it was not without severe side effects. Hannemann for one reported that "it tore up my nasal membranes and made me retch," forcing him to withdraw from the Seoul games in 1988.[23] Sure, it had problems but it worked. The delivery system made the drug undetectable, perhaps explaining why not one East German athlete was nabbed during the 1980s despite a massive doping dragnet.

Although few East German athletes were caught by the drug police, their drug use did catch up with them. There are reportedly numerous instances of ambiguous sexuality in athletes, either from birth disorders or steroid use, most notably Heidi Krieger, an East German shot-putter. GDR sports authorities identified her as an elite prospect when she was a young teenager. At age sixteen, she was put on little blue "vitamin" pills. "The trainer took me to one side and said there was the possibility of increasing my performances with supportive measures," Krieger recalled him saying. "Supportive measures" was code for steroids. "He gave me the blue pills in a small packet of silver paper. He said it was normal here. I was told that the only thing I shouldn't do was get pregnant."[24]

The GDR's notorious drug program focused mostly on female athletes, and for good reason. Although steroids promote tissue growth and repair in both men and women, their relative effect is far more dramatic on females, who have far less testosterone naturally. Even a moderate intake of testosterone can significantly masculinize the female musculature (along with increasing facial hair and sexual libido), converting competitive female athletes into champions. On the other hand, a man, whose own natural production of testosterone shuts down when he takes supplemental drugs, needs to take much larger doses to boost performance.[25]

As Krieger's annual intake of the steroid Oral-Turinabol soared, the effects were explosive. At sixteen, she was throwing 14.08 meters (46.2 feet). Three years later she broke the 20-meter (65.6-foot) barrier, and in 1986 she was European champion. "It felt fantastic," she said of the victory. "It was the happiest moment of my life. You are so proud. You hear the national anthem, see the flag. There's a patriotic feeling and real pride that you finally made it."[26] According to recently unearthed documents, East German researchers nicknamed her Hormone Heidi. The changes were so pronounced, claimed Krieger, that she not only began looking more like a man, she also began feeling like one. Today, after sex-change surgery, the former champion shot-putter lives in Berlin as Andreas Krieger (although scientists doubt that hormones, even if taken in extremely high doses, could alone "turn" someone's gender identity).

During his investigation, Werner Franke uncovered a list, written in felt-tip pen, of 143 athletes, many of whom were later proven to have taken performance-enhancing drugs. Other documents indicate the doping of more than 10,000 athletes, most of them female.[27] The doping operation continued in East Germany and the Soviet Union until Communism's final hours. *Zmena*, a former publication of the Communist Party of the USSR, published an admission in 1989 that the state had had an industrial-strength doping program in place as recently as the Seoul Olympics. Soviet helicopters had ferried athletes to the $2.5 million testing facility housed on the ship *Mikhail Shalokhov*, which sat forty miles off the coast of Korea. Athletes who tested positive were scratched from events, although injury or illness were given as the official explanations.[28] East Germany finished the 1988 Games in Calgary and Seoul with 127 medals, second only to the Soviets. The United States, with more than twice the number of athletes entered, placed third in both gold medals and total medals. A little more than a year later, the Berlin Wall would begin to crumble, and with it would spill forth the drug-drenched secrets of the greatest sports machine in history.

These bizarre tales help resolve one critical controversy about racial differences and athletic performance. For years sociologists have cited the success of East German athletes as proof that success in sports is purely a cultural phenomenon. "Any sports fan knows why East Germans have been good in sports," wrote John Phillips five years after the collapse of the dictatorship, "sophisticated selection and training of the available talent. Curiously, many people tend to favor explanations of black success in sports that parallel the easily refuted "natural ability" arguments just made regarding East Germans."[29] Of course, the only "easily refuted" explanation is the belief that "sophisticated selection and training" were the essential ingredients of the GDR success story.

No drug or scientifically tuned training program can craft an unbeatable athlete if the raw talent is not there. Ukrainian sprinter Valeriy Borzov, a gold medalist in the 100 meters at the 1972 Olympics, is often cited as the prototypical machine-made athlete. He was selected as a child and given every edge the Soviet state could muster. Yet his 10.14 second time in Munich was far off the world's best and doesn't even rank among the top one thousand all-time performances. Despite state-financed and -controlled sports systems, and even with the persistent use of steroids, elite athletes from the East-bloc barely held their own against tinier contingents of African and African Americans in competitions such as running in which naked ability matters most. With a level playing field, it certainly would have been no contest: runners of African ancestry are simply better. Naturally.

CHAPTER 23

THE RENAISSANCE OF
THE BLACK FEMALE ATHLETE

Not too many years ago, at the height of feminist ortho-doxy in the 1970s and 1980s, while the drug-sopped fräuleins of East Germany atomized record after record in swimming and track and field, some theorists boldly asserted that it was only a matter of time before women would com-pete on equal terms against men. For two decades during the doping era, women's running times escalated spectacularly. Knowing schol-ars trotted out graphs purportedly demonstrating that the perfor-mance curves of male and female athletes were destined to intersect before the millennium. In a letter published in the January 1992 is-sue of the venerable journal *Nature*, physiologists Susan Ward and Brian Whipp compared the average rate of improvement in world records for men and women since the 1920s, projected those trends into the future, and predicted that women would match men in the marathon by 1998 and at other distances early in the next century.[1]

The reality check: it didn't happen, won't happen, and can't hap-pen. Such pie-in-the-sky predictions extrapolate on data hopelessly tainted by drug use. Historically, track records have fallen on a regu-lar basis as training and techniques have improved. But whereas every men's record has been broken since the Eastern-bloc sports powers collapsed, most many times over, today's female athletes still cannot crack some records set a decade or more ago when drug use was at its peak.

During the 1990s, in the ten Olympic events in which men and women run, only six female world records have been broken, one-

sixth the number of male records. The oldest of the female individual records, Jarmila Kratochvilová's 800-meter win at the 1983
World Championships, remains unsurpassed and maybe unsurpass-
able. Today her body is bent into a male-like weightlifter's physique
by years of drug use—yet Kratochvilová, dubbed the "Wonder
Woman" of Czechoslovakia, was never caught by the Swiss-cheese
drug tests of her day.

Still, some sociologists are determined not to give up the equality fantasy that women are closing the gender gap in sports. Ellis
Cashmore, a professor at Staffordshire University in Stoke-on-
Trent, England, claimed that although "women cannot close the
strength gap entirely . . . they can get to within 5 percent of an
equivalent male body-strength."[2] It's not at all clear what he means
(what is "equivalent body strength"?). Scientists scoff at predictions that females can close the strength gap even after adjusting
for weight.

Since the collapse of the Eastern-bloc drug-peddling machine, the
gender gap has widened significantly. The difference in times between men and women runners at the 1996 Olympics was the greatest since 1972, the last mostly pre-anabolic Olympics. The average
disparity at all running distances has actually increased from 10.2
percent in 1989 to 11.2 percent, after factoring out dubious Chinese
records.[3] And contrary to assumptions that women may actually
equal men in endurance, the gender gap is slightly greater in the distance races than in the sprints.

Although many individual women can beat most men and the average man can best the average woman, in head-to-head competition between elite athletes, men will prevail (except occasionally in a
few extreme events such as ultra-marathons, the Iditarod, and
marathon swimming, in which women's naturally higher fat levels
turn from a liability to an asset).[4] This does not mean that Marion
Jones cannot beat most men; it just means that genetic differences
dictate that she will always be a relative slowpoke against the fastest
men. The disparity between blacks and whites in sports is at least as
pronounced.

The public caught a glimpse of the distortions wrought by past drug abuse when, in 1998, nineteen former top athletes related their personal horror stories of being pumped full of steroids by East German sport officials. Jane Lang and Kerstin Olm testified that they had been forced-fed "blue pills" that contained male hormones. "At the age of fourteen my voice suddenly went deep," said Olm, who said she was told she was being given vitamins. The teenagers all suffered from unnatural body hair, out-of-proportion muscles, and severe acne, as well as voice changes. "We couldn't really blow the whistle on what was happening, but our music teacher was very unhappy," Olm added, not cracking a smile.[5]

For others the effects were more than temporary. Petra Kind-Schneider, a gold-medal swimmer in 1980, revealed that she was slowly dying of liver and heart problems, which she blamed on the forced steroid use that began when she was fourteen.[6] Gold medalist Rica Reinisch blamed steroids, which she began receiving at age twelve, for her ovarian cysts. Birgit Hekie Matz, a top junior swimmer, developed a liver tumor.[7]

Asked to speculate on how many of the GDR's track-team members would have been involved in doping, German track coach Frank Hensel replied, "All of them."[8] Investigators have found detailed diagrams and charts documenting the drug regimen of more than two hundred elite athletes, including such former world champion sprinters as Heike Drechsler and Kerstin Behrendt.[9] "You haven't seen a single athlete in a blue GDR shirt who wasn't on drugs," maintained Werner Franke. "You name them."[10]

Since the fall of communism, East European female athletes are no longer the dominant superstars. For instance, in 1984, thirty-eight women ran the 1,500-meters under 4:05, most from Eastern-bloc countries. Yet by 1991, after a boom in women's running and improved training techniques, the number had fallen to only nine. The only plausible explanation is a decrease in the use of steroids.

Even with their secret weapon, the best East German women were always hard pressed to beat the best African Americans. Consider Evelyn Ashford, who was only nineteen years old when she surprised everyone, including herself, with a stunning fifth place finish in the 100 meters at the Montreal Olympics in 1976. Three years later, she upset the reigning world-record holder, East Germany's Marlies Göhr, in the World Championships. In 1982, she bested Göhr, Marita Koch, and two-time Olympic 200-meter champion Barbwel Wockel. Then, after taking a year off to have a child, she returned to running at the 1986 Goodwill Games to defeat Heike Drechsler, the GDR's newest sprinting sensation.[11] Along the way Ashford twice broke the 100-meter record.

Unfortunately, the specter of drugs throws a cloud over many top performances by innocent athletes. In 1987, the year before Ben Johnson was nabbed at the Seoul Games, the notoriously porous IOC tests found some 521 cases of illegal steroid use. Former Olympic silver medalist David Jenkins, who was convicted of trading in steroids, estimated that as many as 50 percent of active track and field athletes had used performance enhancing drugs at some time.[12] The problem is particularly acute in women's running, where facts and rumors swirl together to create a dust storm of questions.

For instance, it has long been whispered that Florence Griffith-Joyner used drugs in preparation for her startling four-medal, three-gold performance at the 1988 Olympics. Before obliterating the 100- and 200-meter records, Joyner had been a solid but not a brilliant sprinter. Her best time over 100 meters did not rank in the top forty marks of all time and her previous best at 200 was not in the all-time top twenty. Then she turned up in Seoul with a new sleek, muscular physique and promptly ran times that would have challenged Jesse Owens.

Keenly aware of the limitations of the human body, athletes at Olympic Village began speculating on her redefined body and extraordinary performances. Griffith-Joyner angrily dismissed the allegations and volunteered to take a drug test "any–time, anywhere," but it was an empty promise. There would be no more races, no more tests. Months later, at the peak of her abilities, she abruptly retired. The story got more complicated the following year when Darrell Robinson, a former national quarter-mile champion, claimed that shortly before the Seoul Games, Griffith-Joyner had paid him $2,000 for 10 cubic centimeters of human growth hormone, which would not have been picked up in any drug test. She dismissed Robinson as a "crazy, lying lunatic," but she never raced again.[13]

By the 1992 Olympics, with the East German sports system in collapse, the unified German team won nine women's swimming medals, and only one gold. Four years later, Germany would win not even one gold medal. Its track team was now decidedly second rate, no longer a match for the black stars from West Africa, North America, the Caribbean, France, and the United Kingdom. For the first time in decades, for a brief time, athletes in many Olympic sports actually competed mostly on merit.

THE EAST GERMAN LEGACY

The drug bugaboo still haunts sports. Doping scandals in Australia, Spain, and China in particular indicate that countries desperate for Olympic success seem perfectly willing to put former drug peddlers in charge of their young athletes. "[Drug users] are still out there today," said Franke, "the coaches, the physicians, the technology, the functionaries. It's global. The legacy of the GDR doping system is the know-how and recognition of what can be achieved by anabolic steroids and the application of scientific methods to avoid detection by controls."[14]

Except for China, the remaining problem appears to be renegade coaches and athletes, not state-sponsored drugging. Yet many believe drug use is returning to past levels. "We are in the same situation as before Seoul" when Ben Johnson was stripped of the gold medal and the 100-meter world record after testing positive for steroids, said the German athletics federation's chief doctor, Karl-heinz Graff. "Then there were many signs that there was widespread doping: a lot of positive tests and an explosion of performances, especially among women. The system of testing does not work in many countries. Things are taking off again."[15]

The problem is not likely to disappear soon; just look at the cascade of scandals that has threatened to destroy the credibility of international biking and the recurring scandals involving Chinese athletes. The magnitude of the problem is anyone's guess. Among top females, sprinters Katrin Krabbe and Grit Breuer of Germany, Jamaican sprinter Merlene Ottey, middle-distance runner Mary Decker Slaney of the United States, and Dominican high jumper Juana Arrendel have been cited for possible drug violations. Among the men, sprinters Linford Christie of the United Kingdom and Butch Reynolds and Dennis Mitchell of the United States, as well as high jump great Javier Sotomayor of Cuba, all have faced accusations of drug use.

"Obviously, something that constitutes cheating is going on," said running coach John Babington of Boston. "This is especially damaging because it messes things up at the highest level, at the world-record level. It alters everybody's frame of reference in a confusing and frustrating way."[16] The sad lesson learned from these escapades appears to be that many athletes believe they cannot compete against the world's best without a superhuman, drug-aided effort.

SPRINTING

Even the massive drug use by the former Communist-bloc in the seventies and eighties was never able to dent the domination by blacks in the 100 and 200 meters in which natural abilities such as reaction time and speed matter most. However, performance-enhancing drugs have had a distorting impact in longer sprints. To gauge the impact of drugs, it's instructive to compare the top all-time one hundred times against the best times over the past decade, when presumably drug use was less prevalent. (See Table 23.1.)* White female runners appear to have come down with a collective case of lead feet over the past decade. The percentage of top times by whites, all from Eastern Europe, drops from 18 to 10 percent at the 100 meters and 35 to 10 percent over 200 meters. At a distance of 400 meters, the body begins to draw on the energy from slower contracting muscle fibers, making natural speed less decisive and the effect of drug use potentially more

---

*Based on top 100 times in 1990s and excluding performances by Chinese athletes in races in China where international drug testing standards were not in effect.

TABLE 23.1

**TOP 100 PERFORMANCES IN WOMEN'S SPRINTING
ALL-TIME VS. 1900–2000**

Distance	White	W. African	Asian	Ab*	Other*
100 meters					
no drug filter	18	81	1		
with drug filter	15	85			
200 meters					
no drug filter	35	64	1		
with drug filter	10	90			
400 meters					
no drug filter	73	22		3	
with drug filter	16	65		13	3

*Ab reflects performances of Australian Aboriginal Cathy Freeman; other reflects runs by a Colombian and Mexican.

critical. It's hardly suprising that the percentage of top times by whites collapes from 73 to 16 percent. Female runners who trace their ancestry to West Africa now sweep upwards of 85 percent of sprint races.

This extraordinary statistical reversal dramatically underscores the natural ability gap between black and white sprinters. When stripped of the drug factor, what appears in the history books as a decades-long duel between European and African American female sprinters has been a fraud. Black female sprinters are a cut above, much like their male counterparts.

Marion Jones is the world's indisputable top female sprinter—the "other MJ," as her coach and friends call her. She is the epitome of an elite athlete: hard driving, smart, disciplined, and gifted with the explosive speed and jumping ability that mark the prototypical athlete with West African ancestry. One hundred meters? In recent years, only a few whites have cracked the 11-second barrier; Marion Jones managed it twenty times in 1998 alone. Two hundred meters? Jones regularly cracks 22 seconds, the high mark of excellence for women, and often wins by 10 yards or more. Only Florence-Griffith Joyner has run either distance faster. Only in the long jump, in which she is also ranked number one in the world, do competitors entertain even being competitive.

In 1998, Jones became the first woman since newly Americanized Stella Walsh in 1938 to win simultaneous U.S. national championships in all three events. And that's not the headline. During a remarkable string, Jones won *every* final in the long jump and at 60, 100, 200, and 400 meters—thirty-six straight. Sprinting experts, including her coach Trevor Graham, are enthralled by her naturally fluid motion, her Zen-like calm, and her responsiveness to training.[17] After adding the 4x100- and 4x400-meter relays to her repertoire, she won five medals at Sydney in the 2000 Olympics, including three gold and she is now near her prime.

Although she now trains feverishly, Jones is as close to being a born athlete as exists in sprinting. "When I was six or seven," she said, "I wrote on my chalkboard that I wanted to be an Olympic champion. Seeing the way people compete and the feeling that they seemed to get when they won, that it was something I wanted to be a part of, and that I wanted to experience."[18] By the time she was fifteen, she had demolished the high school 100-meter record, running 11.17 seconds. She also set the national prep record for the 200 five times and long-jumped the second-best mark ever by an American schoolgirl.

Jones's mother, who emigrated to America from Belize and raised her alone, encouraged her to try every sport. She was terrific at almost everything else she tried, particularly basketball. And though she would go on to qualify in sprinting as an alternate for the U.S. Olympic team (but did not go to Barcelona), her love of basketball prevailed, at least for a time. Jones packed off to the University of North Carolina. As a 5-foot–10-inch, 140-pound point guard converted from star forward, she led the Tar Heels to the 1994 national basketball championship while only a freshman.

Jones remained in a constant quandary over what sport she should pursue. On her ankle, she had carved a tattoo of a basketball with a thunderbolt passing through it, held aloft by little white wings; the thunderbolt signifies speed and the wings her grace at track and basketball. For three seasons, she did both, spectacularly. Then, in March 1996, after scoring 1,716 points in her career, she marched into her coach Sylvia Hatchell's office and announced she was giving up basketball for good. Hatchell was stunned, but not surprised. "She said she wanted to be the fastest woman in the world," her coach recalled. "And . . . she did that."[19] Four months after beginning serious training, Jones won the world track and field 100-meter championship.

ENDURANCE RUNNING

The ranks of African American females and other runners of West African origin falls off dramatically at the middle distances and dwindles to zero in the longer races. Although East and North African men have come to dominate middle and long distance running, until recently social stigmas have all but prevented African women from competing. East Africans, Asians, and whites are all competitive in endurance events, although the most notable newcomers are from East Africa, Ethiopia, and Kenya in particular.

Fatuma Roba of Ethiopia, another hothouse along the Great Rift Valley, closed out the 1990s with three straight victories in the Boston Marathon. Roba vies for the honor of world's best female endurance runner with Kenya's Tegla Loroupe, who smashed Ingrid Kristiansen's thirteen-year-old world mark in the marathon in 1998, then broke her own record in 1999 running 2:20:43 at Berlin. Loroupe's toughest opponent, Uta Pippig of Germany, who won at New York in 1993 and swept Boston three times, was suspended in 1998 for two years after being nabbed for abnormally high levels of testosterone by drug police using a new carbon isotope test.[20]

Loroupe, who hails from a poor farming community, is one of a new generation of female trailblazers in Kenya. She had to face down the disapproval of her father and the ridicule of boys who were not used to seeing a girl pursue her dreams, let alone her athletic dreams. "They don't want me to do sports," she said. "But I didn't give up."[21] Deceptively frail at just 4 feet, 11 inches and 86 pounds, Tegla stood her ground. She toughened herself physically by running back and forth six miles each way to school when she was thirteen.

Loroupe eventually became so dominant in local races, even beating most boys, that she went on to earn a scholarship to boarding school. She credits her mother and her devout Baptist faith. "God has given me a plan," she said. "Man cannot close my door." After graduation, she was given a job at the Kenyan Post and Telecommunications Corporation, where many up-and-coming athletes are placed. "Other women have come out of Kenya and run before Tegla," said Ann Roberts, who spotted her when she was just a teenager and encouraged her to race in the United States. "But all were very careful not to rock the boat. She is the first to have the courage to say something and to continue to say it emphatically until someone listened."[22]

A surprise entry at the Advil 10-kilometer race in New York in 1993 when she was only 20, Loroupe demolished the favorite, Lisa Ondeiki. She made her marathon debut the next year, in New York, winning in an impressive 2:27. Remarkably, she ran the back half of the 26.2-mile race faster than the first half. The victory was a first for a black African woman in such a high-profile marathon (Kenyans Angelina Kanana and Pascaline Wangui had previously won less prestigious marathons). Loroupe has gotten better each racing season. After taking a year off for the birth of her daughter in 1997, she returned with a vengeance. She smashed the world best held by her idol, Sweden's Ingrid Kristiansen and burned up the U.S. circuit in winning fourteen of fifteen races on the way to being named runner of the year in 1998.

Loroupe, who regularly trains 140 miles per week before major marathons, has been an inspiration for other young Kenyans, most notably Catherine Ndereba, a top female road racer. "I am very proud of our women," said Godfrey Kiprotich, a former Olympian. "I used to feel it was too bad to see only the men dominating outside of Kenya because I knew there were many women back home who were just as talented, only they did not have the opportunity."[23] As the saying goes in Swahili, *Mambo baadu*—"The best is yet to come."

AFRICAN AMERICAN DOMINATION OF WOMEN'S BASKETBALL

Long after African Americans came to dominate men's basketball, women's basketball remained predominantly white. That changed rapidly in the wake of Title IX as schools were forced to introduce women's programs. Today, black females dominate professional basketball almost as overwhelmingly as African American males. More than 75 percent of the players in the Women's National Basketball Association are black as are eight of the ten players selected to the all-WNBA teams in 1999 and 2000.

The most celebrated up-and-coming female star, Chamique Holdsclaw, nicknamed "Mique," appears poised to elevate the athleticism of women's professional basketball in ways that echo the transformative impact on the men's game by Elgin Baylor, Connie Hawkins, and Julius Erving. Her quickness sets her apart from most other players. She demonstrated an unprecedented virtuosity while leading the University of Tennessee Lady Volunteers to three consecutive national championships. Holdsclaw led *every* team she had played on since the eighth grade to a title until an upset loss in the 1999 NCAA playoffs. Selected to the All-America team four times, she was the overwhelming choice as the best woman player in college basketball and was named winner of the Sullivan award as the nation's top amateur athlete.

At 6 feet, 2 inches, Holdsclaw can play center as effectively as point guard. She drives repeatedly to the basket, shifting the ball dexterously from one hand to the other, floating near the rim for a double-pump hook shot or silky layup. "She's awesome. She, she plays just like a guy!" skeptical announcers are known to shout in their enthusiasm.[24] It was no surprise that she won the rookie-of-the-year award in her first professional season while reviving a moribund Washington Mystics franchise. The future mega-superstar of women's professional basketball wears Michael's Jordan's retired number 23.

How is it that black women now dominate basketball and running at levels approaching that of black men? It is far-fetched to believe that social and cultural forces explain all. Certainly young white female athletes, like their male counterparts, are channeled away from basketball and track. But why? Are these sports so culturally "black" that it is socially uncomfortable for whites to play them, or, as seems more likely, do athletes regardless of their ancestry pursue sports in which they excel and therefore are amply rewarded, socially and perhaps financially? Obviously, both factors are at work. Slight genetic advantages spawn cultural stereotypes—blacks are "naturally better sprinters"—that form an endless feedback loop. Culture exaggerates biology. A dispassionate inquirer would have to suspect that there are a host of *intertwined* cultural and genetic explanations for black athletic success. And the dispassionate observer would be right.

VII

FINAL THOUGHTS

CHAPTER 24

A GENTEEL WAY TO SAY "NIGGER"?

"Even today, few scientists dare to study racial origins, lest they
be branded racists just for being interested in the subject."[1]

Jared Diamond
Professor of Physiology, UCLA Medical School

lack domination of sports is so pronounced that a kind
of reverse racism has set in. Consider the media attention that has greeted Jason Sehorn, the star cornerback
for the New York Giants. Sehorn is the first white to
start at that position in many years and one of only a handful of his
race in a quarter century to play defensive back with any degree of
success at the professional level. "Cornerback has been a position
overrun by black men," said Thomas Randolph, the African American former teammate whom Sehorn replaced when Randolph was
injured at training camp a few years ago. "He'll probably help a lot
of other white guys now who want to play the position. There
weren't too many coaches who would give a white guy a chance at
corner."

Sehorn and a handful of other "Great White Hopes" are curiosi-
ties who have earned admission into the 'hood. One of the NBA's few
young white stars, New Jersey's Keith Van Horn, is described by a
teammate as "a very light-skinned black," the quip delivered with a
wink and a smile about the ultrapale Utah native who regularly
lights up the Meadowlands.[2] The flashy play of Sacramento's Jason
Williams has earned him the affectionate nicknames "White Choco-

late" and "The Thrilla in Vanilla." Their catlike play has stirred considerable gee-whizzing from sportscasters and fans as in, "Wow, *some* white guys really can jump and run." But only some.

"If you can believe that individuals of recent African ancestry are not genetically advantaged over those of European and Asian ancestry in certain athletic endeavors," lectures Berkeley biological anthropolgist Vincent Sarich to undergraduates taking his introductory course in anthropology, "then you probably could be led to believe just about anything."[3]

Why, as the quip goes, has there never been a *white* Michael Jordan? Such comments send environmentalists into overdrive. "Well, until recently there was no *black* Michael Jordan either,[4] retorts Jonathan Marks.* Indeed, though the best athletes are genetic mutants, far more than superior genes go into creating sports stars. The hardwood floors of America echo with the broken dreams of all-star wanna-bees with Michael Jordan-like talent and less-than-all-star ambition, dedication, and intelligence. Every sport requires psychological focus and training to complement innate ability. But the mere suggestion that population genetics—race—could be a factor in the changing color of sports evokes charges of racism and pseudo-science.[5]

This debate resonates not of civil discourse but of civil war. Are these bitterly opposed models of human potential reconcilable? Is this a war worth fighting? In a word, yes. At stake is the role of science in society, for the deep suspicions about genetics put aspects of science itself on trial. That is exactly what some hardened critics intend to do, however reasonable their intentions.

SCIENCE ON TRIAL

"The obsession with the natural superiority of the black male athlete is an attempt to demean all of us," writes African American sports writer Ralph Wiley. "The search for genetic explanations would deny black athletes the right to dream, to aspire, to strive. It

*Sarich response in an e-mail: "There are a lot more black guys coming a lot closer than any white ever has."

suggests that black men cannot set goals, which implies the struggle to survive, to triumph. That is the crux of the question. Our answer should be obvious."[6]

"We state that the 'natural' argument is seductive, destructive, and unjustified," argues Carole Oglesby in the introduction of a book she edited on black women athletes. "[It] undermines the importance of training, access, early exposure, social reinforcement and the like." She went on to quote Eldridge Cleaver: "White man = brain in the front office while the black man = muscle/body out in the field."[7]

Richard Lapchick, founder of Northeastern University's Center for the Study of Sport in Society, dismisses claims of innate black athletic superiority as "pseudo-scientific prattle. . . . Isn't it strange," he wrote sarcastically in the *New York Times*, "that no one feels very compelled to look for physical reasons for white dominance in sports?"[8]

In the most cynical of views, there is a racist continuum from a curiosity about human differences, in sports or in any other aspect of life, to the prejudice that blacks are innately more primitive than whites. Sociologist Donald E. Muir contends that those who see no harm in what he calls "race biology" are nothing more than "kind racists." By legitimizing race, they aid the "mean racists" who wish to do harm. Those who assert that there are "natural" differences between athletes from different populations are undoubtedly kind racists at best. British writer Kenan Malik goes so far as to blast not only contemporary academic "race realists" but supporters of multiculturalism—both are obsessed with what divides humanity not what unites us. "In recent years, the goal for antiracists has not so much been the right of people to be treated equally, as the right of every group to have their differences acknowledged and respected," he wrote. "But the notion of difference has always been at the heart, not of the antiracist programme, but of the racist agenda. . . . By emphasizing differences rather than equality, antiracists are resorting to the same philosophies as gave rise to racial thinking itself."[9]

This perspective is not all paranoia. The notion that racial biology determines the fortunes of humanity was rejected after World War II, in a reaction against mass genocide rationalized by racist ideology. The existence of innate differences has been invoked for hundreds of years to rationalize the established social order. Richard Lewontin and Stephen Jay Gould deride such thinking as "Panglossian adaptationism" after Voltaire's character Dr. Pangloss, a professor of "metaphysico-theology-cosmolonigology" who believed that all is best in the best of all possible worlds.[10] For those on the lower rungs of the racial or ethnic ladder, this is certainly not the best of all possible worlds. The contemporary fascination with race is, in its most extreme expression, an ember of racism that has not been entirely extinguished.

DOUBLE CONSCIOUSNESS

Black athleticism has bedeviled the black community for much of the past century. It's a classic double bind: success in sports may unwittingly devalue intellectual achievements.[11] In the 1930s, when integration was still a distant dream in America, churchgoing blacks fretted that every Joe Louis victory reinforced white stereotypes of the brutal warrior. Athletic success comes with a price, both for the individual and for the community as a whole. As a result of the celebrity status of black athletic stars—Michael Jordan, Tiger Woods, and Muhammad Ali are among the best-known people in the world—impressionable youths are enticed into believing that becoming an athlete is the only viable path to success.

Black intellectuals from W.E.B. DuBois to Harry Edwards have warned that the black community's historical romance with athleticism is like an affair with a succubus.* "Far from being a positive force in the development of the black masses," Edwards has written, "integrated big-time sport in its present form is perhaps a negative influence."[13] Edwards has campaigned over many years with eloquence and anger that big-time sports is a "form of cultural exhibitionism" with black athletes acting as minstrel actors who were

*"The average Negro undergraduate has swallowed hook, line, and sinker, the dead bait of the white undergraduate, who, born in an industrial machine, does not have to think, and does not think," said Du Bois in his commencement address at Howard University in 1930.[12]

shuffled from the "cotton fields to the playing fields" for the enter-tainment value of white America. Sports, he asserts, exerts a "novo-cain" effect on the "black masses" and provides the black fan with the illusion of spiritual reinforcement in his own life struggles.[14] "The only difference between the black man shining shoes in the ghetto and the champion black sprinter," Edwards has charged, "is that the shoe shine man is a nigger, while the sprinter is a fast nig-ger."[15] Although written in the seventies, when there were far fewer opportunities for blacks outside sports, no one should be fooled into thinking the opportunity gap has disappeared entirely. Even today, despite a remarkable surge in the salaries of all athletes, there re-mains a plantation-like imbalance between the dominance of blacks on the field and their dearth in the executive suite. As a conse-quence, says Harvard University scholar Henry Louis Gates, Jr., black pride has become more or less "tethered to the stereotype of innate physical superiority."[16]

Race, with all of its racist echoes, remains one of the most deli-cate social issues of our times. It is not outlandish to suggest that all of us, of all races, harbor some irrational prejudices—including blacks who are understandably skeptical that they will get a fair shake in a society in which they are a conspicuous minority. In its most simple sense, racism is an accusation that strips people of their humanity and reduces them to an exaggerated group stereotype. Ex-plorations of human biodiversity by their very nature cannot be stripped of racist undertones. That is a genuine and heartfelt fear.

It's one sign of the explosiveness of the subject that when a white sociologist, John Hoberman, advanced many of the same concerns as Du Bois, Edwards, and Gates about the outsized role that sports plays in the African America community, he was attacked by some African Americans as being racist. "The cult of the black athlete," he wrote in his searing polemic *Darwin's Athletes*, "exacerbated the dis-astrous spread of anti-intellectual attitudes among African American youth," thus creating a "spectacle of black athleticism" that in-evitably resulted in "a highly public image of black retardation."[17]

Hoberman's mistake, it turns out, was not in identifying this so-cial pathology but in apportioning responsibility, and slamming black intellectuals for their complicity in iconizing athletic success. While arguing that the doubled-edged icon of "black athlete as hero" was a product of sometimes shoddy science, the legacy of slavery, and persistent cultural biases, he laid part of the responsibility squarely on the backs of the black community. "Whereas white intellectuals tend to romanticize or elegize athletes as symbols of the past or for their sheer animal vitality, African American writers romanticize athletes because they seem to incarnate the blood, sweat, and tears of black life itself.[18]

Darwin's Athletes touched a raw nerve in many blacks. "Hoberman feels that African American intellectuals have failed the African American community for not speaking up about the harmful aspects of sport," fumed Wake Forest University sociology department chairman Earl Smith and Kenneth Shropshire of the Wharton Business School.[19] Reacting as much to Hoberman's frequently patronizing style, the two African American professors accused him of an unconscious form of white intellectual superiority.

If anything, the taboo that limits reasonable discussion about human diversity is in part responsible for such vituperation. Ironically, sports does offer a path out of this mess. "One of the great ironies Hoberman misses," Smith and Shropshire added, "is that many African Americans, like Whites, participate in sports not for some 'hoop dream' of professional success but rather for a simple love of the game."[20]

"Sometimes a baseball player is just a baseball player and sometimes an observation about racial difference is just an observation about racial difference," observed Malcolm Gladwell, a black Canadian writer, striking a note of balance in a notable piece in *The New Yorker*. "Black America has paid a high and largely unacknowledged price for a long list of things, and having great athletes is far from the top of the list."[21]

DECOUPLING MIND FROM BODY

Of course, we all know what is behind this contentiousness. The elephant in the living room is intelligence. In the familiar if erroneous calculus, IQ and athleticism are inversely proportional. Jocks are dense, so the stereotype goes, whether we are talking about a lean black power forward or a beefy white offensive lineman. Like a barnacle to a boat, this stereotype has attached itself to blacks, particularly African Americans, because blacks are starring in disproportionate numbers in almost all sports.

It's time to decouple intelligence and physicality. It's time to move from censorship to careful debate. After all, the issue of whether there are meaningful differences between populations *has all but been resolved*. The evolutionary crucible has left population groups with measuredly different physique, musculature, testosterone levels, metabolic efficiency, reaction time, and a slew of other characteristics. Soon we will have maps pinpointing the genes responsible for many traits. And though the earth may have become a much smaller place over the past few centuries—humans are notorious for "sleeping around"—our mobility has not yet erased what nature has forged. Human variation still congeals in fuzzy population groups: if you land in Nairobi, Shanghai, or Delhi, you certainly know you are not in Kansas.

Is the environment a factor? Of course, both in determining our genetic heritage and in setting the limits for any individual athlete. Human potential at birth may not be akin to a proverbial blank slate but we are far from a fully written book. Athletic success is certainly more complicated than environmental determinists might have us believe. Consider Michael Jordan, who grew up in the security of a two-parent home in comfortable circumstances. Or Grant Hill, son of a Yale-educated father and a Wellesley graduate. Or one of the world's top sprinters, Donovan Bailey who was certainly not motivated by a desperate need to escape destitution—he already owned his own house and a Porsche, and traded life as a successful stockbroker to pursue his dream of Olympic gold. More and more top black athletes are from the middle class. The classic argument that blacks pursue sports to escape desperate poverty is less and less plausible every day.

The nature/nurture split is a false dichotomy. Ultimately there is no real separation between the environment and biology, just a constant loop of experience passed through the genes and back around again. Today basketball is a "black sport" both genetically and culturally, with no clear separation. But don't expect ideological skeptics to agree that genetics matter. "Such dominance will never convince those whose minds are made up that genetics plays no role in shaping the racial patterns we see in sports," says Vincent Sarich. "When we discuss issues such as race, it pushes buttons and the cortex just shuts down."[22]

Acknowledging human differences, whether they are biologically or culturally defined, can be empowering or pernicious, depending on who is doing the analysis and for what end. Yes, we must guard against the slippery slope of racism, for such attitudes can harden into something far worse. Yet it is no solution to replace reasoned debate with fears that imagine a racist under every rock. The "censor it, don't test it" attitude, rooted in the never-never land of postmodernism, where everything is a social construct, is distressingly rampant. "Some sports sociologists have voluntarily assumed the burden of telling others what they ought to think and what subjects they should or should not investigate," John Phillips, himself a sociologist, notes with some consternation. "In science, good ideas are separated from bad ideas by reason and investigation, not by self-appointed censors or moral arbiters."[23]

The anthropological community, historically suspicious of the very concept of race, finally appears to be recognizing that it must join the debate over human biodiversity or risk being left without a voice. There has been a resurgence of race-focused scholarship in anthropology, including the founding of two new journals, *Identities* and *Transforming Anthropology*, devoted specifically to the issue. In 1997, Yolanda Moses, then president of the American Anthropological Association, and her colleague Carol Mukhopadyay, argued that it was reckless to ignore the issue in light of new insights about the way genetics shapes our humanity. "It is time to once again make race a central theme of anthropological inquiry," they wrote."[24] A year later, in September 1998, *American Anthropologist* devoted an entire issue to exploring race from a range of perspectives, genetic and cultural.

The hard truth is that we cannot avoid confronting our human biodiversity. The science of genetics and the quest to solve medical and scientific problems is barreling into the future, particularly in the arena of gene therapy, a key focus of the Human Genome Project. Limiting the rhetorical use of folk categories such as race, an admirable goal, is not going to make the patterned biological variation on which they are based disappear. The question is no longer *whether* these inquiries will continue but in what *manner* and to what *end*. Caricaturing population genetics as pseudo-science just devalues legitimate concerns about how this information will be put to use. If we do not welcome the impending onslaught of genetic and anthropological data with open minds, if we are scared to ask and to answer difficult questions, if we lose faith in science, then there is no winner; we all lose. It's impossible to reason with sweeping denunciations couched as moral virtue.

SPORTS AS METAPHOR

Using sports to reflect on human biodiversity offers some advantages. Despite considerable off-the-field disparities, professional athletics remains one of the most racially and ethnically diverse professions in the world. Individual athletes earn respect on the field, not by the privilege of their birth. Sports offer a unique definitiveness: there is one high scorer, one top rebounder, one leading rusher—and only one winner.

Unfortunately, ideology can sometimes overwhelm common sense. Consider the November 1998 gathering in Las Vegas of the North American Society for the Sociology of Sport. The attendees, mostly sociologists, listened to a variety of presentations, including a panel discussion on *Taboo*, but the centerpiece of the conference was a session on "position stacking." On hand was the team of sociologists who had authored the first detailed study on the subject, in 1970. The assumption this day was that except in basketball, where blacks dominate at every position, little had changed—positions in the major sports were filled based in large measure on racial stereotypes.

In the midst of this discussion, a massive black hand shot up from the rear. Sitting by himself was a man the size of an offensive linemen. "I've been listening to this nonsense going on half an hour," he said evenly. "I've been a coach at Ohio State. I can tell you that there is no way we would let stacking go on. This is just bull. At Division I or in the pros, to survive, coaches have to recruit the best players and we damn well better play them at the optimal positions. We don't care if a player is white, black, or striped. The pressure to win is immense. If we don't win, we will be out on our collective ass."[25]

The audience, about equally split between blacks and whites, was startled. Do racial patterns in themselves prove that there is racist stereotyping? Until the African American voiced his skepticism, that question was considered taboo at this conference supposedly dedicated to unfettered discourse. Yet maybe, just maybe, the world *had* changed. Maybe, but it says something of the subject's explosiveness that the one-time Ohio State University assistant coach asked not to be identified.

Earl Smith was one African American scholar willing to challenge the taboo. "Maybe he's not wrong," Smith mused after the session. "Maybe we are just too quick to automatically think that the answers that might have been accurate thirty years ago are correct today. I want to know why every man at the start line of the Olympic 100-meters is black." Smith heaved a deep sigh, clearly exasperated at the reticence of the public and those in his profession to even broach such heretical questions. "I've looked at the sociological explanations and they don't fully convince me," Smith added. "Maybe there are other explanations. Let's look at the science. We have to be willing to go where the evidence takes us."[26]

Indeed. Science is a method of interrogating reality, a cumulative process of testing new and more refined explanations, not an assertion of dry, inalterable facts. It is a way of asking questions, not of imposing answers. Scientific theories are testable and can be disproved in part or in whole if they do not explain the evidence. Although it is certainly true that all ideas are filtered through the prism of personal beliefs and cultural biases, it's bunk to hyperbolize that if conclusions make some uncomfortable, they should not be expressed. This is not just saber-rattling; look at the hoops evolution-ary biologists have had to jump through in their unending battle with "creation science."

In this case, the scientific evidence for black athletic superiority is overwhelming and in accord with what we see on the playing field. By and large, athletes who rely on the ability to sprint and jump trace their ancestry to West Africa; East and North Africans are best at endurance sports, particularly distance running; whites fall some-where in the middle. Certainly no individual athlete can succeed without considerable dedication and sport smarts, but the pool of potential success stories is far larger among certain populations. Cultural explanations do not, cannot, account for the magnitude of this phenomena. But the interaction of science and culture can. The evidence speaks for itself. Humans are different. No amount of rhetoric, however well-motivated, can undermine the intriguing kaleidoscope of humanity. It's time to acknowledge and even cele-brate the obvious: It's neither racist nor wrong to say that "white men can't jump."

ACKNOWLEDGMENTS

Books are not a project for the faint-hearted or those who insist on going it alone. Writing is a collaborative process which, in this case, drew on the good will of dozens of people. A few people deserve special mention, including brother-in-law Keith Turner, who took time out from his career as a graphic artist to shape many of the illustrations. My in-laws, Ken and Ada Lou Turner, offered continuous encouragement. Special thanks goes to Larry Bennett, a generous friend, who should quit his day job and become a full-time editor, and my agent Basil Kane, who shares my passion for running and stood by this book even when it appeared it was too hot a subject to ever see the light of day.

In recognition of the complexity and sensitivity of the issues addressed in *Taboo*, the evolving manuscript was submitted for review by experts drawn from a range of races, professional expertise, and countries. Even before the writing began, I set up a "board of advisors" who provided invaluable suggestions at every stage of the process: Gideon Ariel, a former Olympic athlete and former director of Computer Science and Biomechanics for the US Olympic Committee; Gaston Beunen, director of the Center for Physical Development Research and chair of the Department of Kinesiology, Catholic University, Belgium; J. E. Lindsay Carter, professor emeritus of exercise and nutritional sciences, San Diego State University; Michael Crawford, professor of biological anthropology and genetics, University of Kansas; David Hunter, chairman of the Department of Health and Physical Education, Hampton University, VA; Jay T. Kearney, Sport Science and Technology Division of the United States Olympic

Committee; Richard Majors, fellow with the Department of Social Policy and Social Work, University of Manchester, England; Gary Sailes, associate professor of kinesiology, Indiana University; Earl Smith, Chair of the Department of Sociology at Wake Forest University; and Michael Speirs, associate professor of anthropology and sociology, Swarthmore College and the University of Pennsylvania Medical School.

Earl Smith, who wrote the provocative introduction, became a friend during the writing and helped deepen my appreciation of the fact that few issues are black and white. John Manners, hands down the foremost expert on Kenyan running and author of two books on the subject, was more than generous in his insights. John Bale, a professor of geography and an expert on world sports, helped with research and offered a gracious introduction into the sports academic community. Steve Sailer, suffering Chicago Cubs fan, columnist and founder of the incredibly insightful Human Biodiversity e-mail list, was an intellectual guiding light. Timothy Noakes, one of the world's running gurus, put his own reputation on the line numerous times to ensure that the book would be published. Berkeley biological anthropolgist Vincent Sarich and Frank Miele, an editor at my favorite magazine, *Skeptic*, were generous enough to review the manuscript in detail, offering up dozens of critical editorial suggestions.

Numerous others offered support and analysis, including: Owen Anderson, David Andrews, Daniel Blackburn, Claude Bouchard, Chris Brand, Amby Burfoot, Ranajit Chakraborty, Duncan Chaplin, Jay Coakley, David Costill, Langley and Apollo Entine, Tom Farrey, Christopher Hallinan, Keith Harrison, Billy Hawkins, Debbie Henderson, John Hoberman, Nancy Hogshead, Steven Jackson, David Jones, Michael Joyner, Roger Kaufman, Marek Kohn, Kenneth Kidd, Wib Leonard, Dale Lick, Donna Lyons, Robin McConnell, Robert Malina, Jonathan Marks, Kathy Myburgh, John Phillips, Larry Proctor, Susan Rayl, Phil Rushton, Bengt Saltin, Stephen Seiler, Lee Smith, John Sutton, and Adele Weston.

This book would never have been written if not for Tom Brokaw's willingness to take risks in the name of truth-telling (and my lucky break of being his producer when we undertook what became the 1989 NBC News "Black Athletes: Fact and Fiction"). I will be forever grateful for Rick Wolff, now an executive editor at Warner Books, for originally seeing merit in this idea when he was at Macmillan. As many times happens in the publishing world, the book traveled a rocky path before ending up at PublicAffairs. It was a stroke of good fortune, starting at the top with publisher Peter Osnos. Editor Geoff Shandler, now executive editor at Little, Brown, has reshaped what was an intriguing manuscript into a thoughtful book. Everyone on the PublicAffairs staff has made a critical contribution, particularly publicist Gene Taft, managing editor Robert Kimzey, and his assistant Mary-Claire Flynn; you have given new meaning to the word patience.

Most of all, I'd like to thank my toughest critic and most supportive fan, my wife Ellen, who endured any number of eruptions of writer's angst and lived to beat me in yet another Sunday morning run. She offered many insightful editorial suggestions and was a great source of strength throughout. Thanks honey.

NOTES

1. BREAKING THE TABOO ON RACE AND SPORTS

1. Gideon Ariel interview, September 1998.
2. Harry Edwards interview, January 1989.
3. Carl Lewis interview, December 1988.
4. William C. Rhoden, "Searching to Bridge Racial Divide in Athletics," *New York Times*, January 5, 1998, S2.
5. Bob Herbert, "Throwing a Curve," *New York Times*, February 1994, A17.
6. See Richard Lapchick and Kevin J. Matthews, "1998 Racial and Gender Report Card," Center for the Study of Sport in Society, Northeastern University, http://www.sportinsociety.org; and Kenneth L. Shropshire, *In Black and White: Race and Sports in America* (New York: New York University, 1996).
7. Faye V. Harrison, "Expanding the Discourse on Race," *American Anthropologist* 100, September 1998, 619.
8. Quoted in Michael Sokolove, "The Greatest Race?" *Hartford Courant Northeast*, September 18, 1988, 14.
9. Quoted in Leonard Shapiro, "Nicklaus Clarifies Remarks on Blacks; Says He was 'Misinterpreted,'" *Washington Post*, August 10, 1994, C6.
10. Tom Brokaw interview, June 7, 1996.
11. Buddy Martin, "NBC Scores Slam Dunk," *Denver Post*, April 28, 1989.
12. Stan Isaacs, "NBC Tackles Touchy Issue," *Newsday*, April 25, 1989.
13. Les Payne, "Why Do Blacks Dunk Better? Why Ask?," *Newsday*, April 30, 1989.
14. Ralph Wiley, "The Fixation on Black Athletic 'Superiority': An Idea Whose Time Has Gone," *Emerge*, October 1989, 34–38.
15. Sybil Smith, "Why the Obsession with Race?" *Sports Illustrated*, May 8, 1989, 12.
16. Quoted in "Then and Now: A Symbol for All Time," *New York Times*, October 17, 1993, 23.

2. THE EDUCATION OF SIR ROGER

1. Roger G. Bannister, *The First Four Minutes* (London: Putnam, 1955), 121.
2. Quoted in Roger Highfield, Adrian Berry, and Toby Harnden, "Get Set for the 3-1/2-Minute Mile," *Manchester Guardian*, September 14, 1995.
3. Quoted in Peter Martin, "Blacks: Faster Than Whites. And Cleverer," *Observer*, August 3, 1997.
4. Kostya Kennedy and Jack McCallum, "Scorecard: A Different Race for Roger," *Sports Illustrated*, September 25, 1995, 15.
5. Roger Bannister interview, December 5, 1995.

3. BY THE NUMBERS

1. Brooks Johnson interview, November 1988.
2. Harry Edwards, *The Sociology of Sport* (Homewood, Ill.: Dorsey Press, 1973), 197.
3. Scott Ostler, "White Athletes: Fact and Fiction—Destroying Myths," *Los Angeles Times*, April 27, 1989, III3.
4. Center for the Study of Sport in Society, Northeastern University.
5. Terry Pluto and Bob Ryan, *48 Minutes: A Night in the Life of the NBA* (New York: Macmillan, 1987).
6. Spud Webb, interview, November 1988.
7. Jon Barry, interview, August 1996.
8. Hal Bock, "Pushing the Boundaries," *Associated Press Newswire*, March 12, 1998.
9. Christopher P. Winner, "Teams Still Feel Europe's Racial Tension," *USA Today*, July 7, 1998, C10.
10. Ellis Cashmore, *Making Sense of Sports* (New York: Routledge, 1998), 99.
11. Brent Staples, "A White Man's Place to Be," *New York Times*, April 8, 1997, 18.
12. Steve Sailer, "Making Sense of 'Race': A Race is an Extremely Extended Family," http://www.isteve.com.
13. Chuck Johnson, "The Best of the Best," *USA Today*, July 8, 1997, A1.
14. Bill James, *Bill James Historical Baseball Abstract*, (New York: Random House, 1987), 55–71.
15. Geoff Calkins, "Men in Middle Have Hopes, Too," *Scripps Howard News Service*, 1998, http://archive.espn.go.com.

4. THE MOST LEVEL PLAYING FIELD

1. Dave McCauley, "Kenyans Dominate as Course Records Fall!" http://www. RunMichigan.com, August 24, 1996.
2. Amby Burfoot, "White Men Can't Run," *Runner's World* (August 1992), 89–95.
3. All running statistics as of October 2000, from http://www.algonet.se.
4. Adapted from analysis by Steven Sailer, journalist and president of the Human Biodiversity Institute.
5. Ian Chadband, "Contrite Bailey Ready for Action," *Sunday Times* (UK), June 29, 1997.
6. S. Sailer, "The Words Don't Match the Pictures: Why the Polite Lies We Tell About Race and Sex are Undermined by What We See on ESPN," *National Review* Online, August 27, 1997, http://www.nationalreview.com.
7. Amby Burfoot, "A Real Head-Turner," *Runner's World* (November 1996), 72.
8. John Hoberman, *Darwin's Athletes: How Sports has Damaged Black America and Preserved the Myth of Race* (New York: Houghton Mifflin, 1998), 134.
9. For a discussion of the Afro-Asiatic ancestry of far southern Europeans and northern Africans, see, for example, Jared Diamond, "Guns, Germs and Steel."
10. Quoted in Jere Longman, "Reluctant Competitor Makes Stunning Debut in Chicago," *New York Times*, October 12, 1998, D10.
10. Quoted in Dick Patrick, "1996 Champion Makes it Eight in a Row for Kenyans," *USA Today*, March 21, 1998, 3C.

11. Burfoot, "White Men Can't Run," 91.
12. John Manners email, May 28, 1999.
13. Manners, "Kenya's Running Tribe," address to the British Society of Sports History annual conference, Keele University, April 12, 1997.
14. John Bale and Joe Sang, *Kenyan Running* (London: Frank Cass, 1996), 148.
15. John Manners email, June 4, 1999.
16. Marc Bloom, "Kenyan Runners in the US Face Bitter Taste of Success," *New York Times*, April 16, 1998, A1.
17. Quoted in ibid., C24.
18. Quoted in Hoberman, 136.
19. Quoted in *Runner's World*, October 1993, 15.
20. Marty Post, "Prince of Times," *Runner's World*, December 1993, 55.
21. Marc Bloom, "Africans are Making Their Mark in the Record Book," *New York Times*, September 16, 1997, C24.

5. NATURE'S EXPERIMENT: THE "KENYAN MIRACLE"

1. Interview with John Velzian, November 1988.
2. Interview with Fred Hardy, November 1988.
3. Interview with Ibrahim Hussein, November 1988.
4. Manners, email to author, June 4, 1999.
5. Kenny Moore, "Sons of the Wind," *Sports Illustrated*, February 26, 1990, 77.
6. John Manners, e-mail, May and June 1999.
7. Christopher Ehret, *Southern Nilotic History: Linguistic Approaches to the Study of the Past* (Evanston: Northwestern University Press, 1971).
8. Moore, 77.
9. Manners, "Kenya's Running Tribe."
10. Quoted in Moore, 77.
11. Ibid., 78.
12. Interview with Kipchoge Keino, November 1988.
13. Joe Drape, "Keino Remains a Hero," *Atlanta Journal-Constitution*, http://atlantagames.com.
14. Toby Tanser, *Train Hard, Win Easy: The Kenyan Way* (Mountain View: Tafnews, 1997), 55–59.
15. "Keino: Going the Distance," ESPNET SportsZone, http://espn.go.com.
16. "The Road to Seoul," *Weekly Review* (Kenya), August 19, 1988, 29-30.
17. E.J. Kahn, Jr., "II-The Olympics," *New Yorker*, October 26, 1968, 189-199.
18. Jim Murray, "A Charger From Kenya," *Los Angeles Times*, September 8, 1972, III-1.
19. Ibid.
20. Tanser, 95–97.
21. Interview with Colm O'Connell, November 1988.
22. Quoted in Linda Villarosa, "The Other Kenyans," *Runner's World*, August 1992, 102.
23. Brian Cazeneuve, "A Mysterious Warrior," *Sports Illustrated*, August 23, 1999, R6.
24. Tanser, 109-111.
25. Quoted in Villarosa, 98-99.
26. Quoted in Moore, 78.

27. Quoted in Jere Longman, "Runner's Victory Also Cultural," *New York Times*, April 17, 1995, B9.
28. Quoted in Villarosa, 101.
29. Dick Patrick, "800 is Kipketer's to Win, Set Record," *USA Today*, July 31, 1997, C1.
30. Quoted in Tom Ratcliffe, "Camp Kenya," *Runner's World*, March 1994, 65.
31. Tanser, 66–71.
32. Ratcliffe, 66.
33. Dick Patrick, "Kenyan Wins Despite Untied Shoe," *USA Today*, October 3, 1997, C1.
34. John Manners, "A World of Their Own," *Runner's World*, June 1998, 94-95.
35. Manners, "Kenya's Running Tribe."
36. Paul Ereng interview, November 1988.
37. Quoted in Moore, 83.
38. Quoted in Jere Longman, "Difficult to Know, Tough to Catch," *New York Times*, August 8, 1997.
39. Edward Zuckerman, "The Kenyan Connection," *Special Report* (April 1989).
40. Ibid.
41. Interview with Kipchoge Keino, November 1988.

6. "MORE BRAINS OR MORE. . . "

1. Quoted in Jonathan Rowe, "The Greek Chorus," *Washington Monthly*, April 1988, 32.
2. Quoted in David K. Wiggins, *Glory Bound: Black Athletes in a White World* (Syracuse: Syracuse University, 1997), 194.
3. Leonard Shapiro, "'Jimmy the Greek' Says Blacks are 'Bred' for Sports," *Washington Post*, January 16, 1988, A10.
4. Ibid.
5. Quoted in Martin Kane, "An Assessment of 'Black is Best,'" *Sports Illustrated*, January 18, 1971, 80.
6. Quoted in Elliott Almond, "Debate over Whether Black Athletes Are Superior to Whites is Not a New One," *Los Angeles Times*, III 9.
7. Kane, 76, 9.
8. W. Montague Cobb, "The Negro as Biological Element in the American Population," *Journal of Negro Education* 8 (1939), 342, 336.
9. Quoted in Shapiro, A10.
10. Richard C. Lewontin, Steven Rose, and Leon J. Kamin, *Not in Our Genes* (New York: Pantheon Books, 1984).
11. Quoted in Mark Williams, "A White Professor Argues that Today's Cult of Black Athleticism is Part of a Long Tradition of Racism," http://www.herring.com.
12. Cashmore, 75–76.
13. Lesley Thomas, "Why Do Blacks Dominate Sprinting but Make Few Waves in Swimming?" *Financial Times*, September 21, 1995.
14. Tom Hyde, "White Men Can't Jump," *Metro: Essentially Auckland*, September 1993, 63 69.
15. Christopher J. Hallinan, "Aborigines and Positional Segregation in Australian Rugby League," *International Review for the Sociology of Sport* 26, (1991), 69–78.

16. Wiley, 38.
17. Interview with Brooks Johnson.
18. Richard E. Lapchick, "Pseudo-Scientific Prattle About Athletics," *New York Times*, April 29, 1989, 15.
19. Hoberman, 193–195.
20. Laurel R. Davis, "The Articulation of Difference: White Preoccupation With the Question of Racially Linked Genetic Differences Among Athletes," *Sociology of Sport Journal* 7 (1990), 179–187.
21. Leon Jaroff, "Teaching Reverse Racism," *Time*, April 4, 1994, 74._
22. Quoted in Sokolove, 2.
23. "Bias-Free Interracial Comparisons," *Nature*, 377, September 21, 1995, 183–184.
24. Thomas.
25. Claude Bouchard interview with Tom Brokaw on the NBC News Special: *Black Athletes: Fact and Fiction–Live Forum*, April 25, 1989.
26. Interview with Kathy Myburgh, May 31, 1996.
27. Quoted in S. L. Price, "Is It in the Genes?" *Sports Illustrated*, December 8, 1997, 53–55.
28. Arthur Ashe, Jr. interview with Tom Brokaw, on *Black Athletes*, April 25, 1989.

7. EVOLUTION (OF GREAT ATHLETES)

1. Jean–Jacques Hublin, "The Quest for Adam," *Archaeology*, July/August 1999, 28.
2. Stephen Jay Gould, "Honorable Men and Women," *Natural History* 97 (1988), 16–20.
3. See Christopher Stringer and Robin McKie, *African Exodus: The Origins of Modern Humanity* (New York: Henry Holt), 1997.
4. Milton Wolpoff e-mail, September 1998.
5. See I. Hannaford, *Race: The History of an Idea in the West* (Baltimore: Johns Hopkins University, 1966).
6. Ruth Flanagan, "Out-of-Africa," *Earth*, February 1996.
7. Julian S. Huxley, *We Europeans* (London: Jonathan Cape, 1935).
8. Daniel C. Dennett, *Darwin's Dangerous Idea* (New York: Touchstone, 1995), 20.
9. Ian Tattersall, "Rethinking Human Evolution," *Archaeology* 52 (July/August 1999), 24.
10. Ibid.
11. Michael D. Lemonick, "How Man Began," *Time*, March 14, 1994.
12. Christopher B. Stringer and P. Andrews, "Genetic and Fossil Evidence for the Origin of Modern Humans," *Science* 239 (1988), 1263–1268.
13. Alan G. Thorne and Milford H. Wolpoff, "The Multiregional Evolution of Humans," *Scientific American* 266, (1992), 76–83.
14. Milford Wolpoff and Rachel Caspari, *Race and Human Evolution: A Fatal Attraction* (New York: Simon and Schuster, 1997), 32.
15. Lemonick.
16. R.L. Cann, M. Stoneking, and AC Wilson, "Mitochondrial DNA and Human Evolution," *Nature* 325 (1987), 31–36.
17. For a summary of the hullabaloo surrounding the Eve Theory, see M.H. Brown, *The Search for Eve* (New York: Harper and Row), 1990.

18. See Luigi Luca Cavalli-Sforza and Francesco Cavalli-Sforza, *The Great Human Diasporas: The History of Diversity and Evolution* (Reading: Addison-Wesley), 1995.
19. "Human Origins: A Million Year Old Relative," *Discover* 18, October, 1998, 26–27.
20. Evelyn Strauss, "Can Mitochondrial Clocks Keep Time," *Science*, March 5, 1999, 1435.
21. N. Eldredge and S. J. Gould, "Punctuated Equilibria: An Alternative to Phyletic Gradualism," in T.J.M. Schopf (ed.), *Models in Paleobiology* (San Francisco: Freeman, Cooper, 1972), 82–115.
22. Eugene E. Harris and Jody Hey, "X chromosome Evidence for Ancient Human Histories," *Proceedings of the National Academy of Sciences*, 96, March 16, 1999, 3320–3324.
23. Elizabeth Pennisi, "Genetic Study Shakes Up Out of Africa Theory," *Science*, March 19, 1999.
24. Henry C. Harpending et al., "Genetic Structure of Ancient Human Populations," *Current Anthropology* 34 (1993), 483–496.
25. Quoted in Wolpoff and Caspari, 306.
26. J. H. Relethford and H. C. Harpending, "Ancient Differences in Population Size Can Mimic a Recent African Origin of Modern Humans, "*Current Anthropology* 36 (1995), 667–674.
27. C. Duarte et al., *Proceedings of the National Academy of Sciences USA* 96 (1999), 7604-7609.
28. Quoted in Scott Norris, "Family Secrets," *New Scientist* 162, June 19, 1999, 44.
29. Erik Trinkaus et al., "Long Bone Shaft Robusticity and Body Proportions of the Saint-Césaire 1 Châtelperronian Neanderthal," *Journal of Archaeological Science*, 26 (1999), 753–773.
30. Quoted in John Noble Wilford, "Discovery Suggests Man Is a Big Neanderthal," *New York Times*, April 25, 1999, 1,19.
31. Erik Trinkaus and Pat Shipman, *The Neanderthals: Changing the Image of Mankind* (New York: Knopf), 1993.
32. Michael D. Lemonick and Andrea Dorfman, "Up From Apes," *Time*, August 23, 1999, http://www.pathfinder.com/time/magazine.
33. Dan Vergano, "Sizing up Neanderthals and Human Heritage," *USA Today*, September 21, 1999, 9D.
34. Matthias Krings, Helga Geisert, Falf W. Schmitz, Heike Krainitzki, and Svante Pääbo, "DNA Sequence of the Mitchondrial Hypervariable Region II From the Neandertal Type Specimen," *Proceedings of the National Academy of Sciences USA* 96 (1999), 5581–5585; Krings et al., "Neanderthal DNA Sequences and the Origin of Modern Humans," *Cell* 90 (1997), 19.
35. Milford Wolpoff, "Letters", *Science* 282, December 11, 1998.
36. Robert Kunzig, "Learning to Love Neanderthals," *Discover* 20 August 1999, 68–75.
37. Norris, 44, 43, 46.

8. RACE WITHOUT COLOR:
THE HISTORY OF HUMAN DIFFERENCES

1. Harry Edwards, "The Myth of the Racially Superior Athlete," *Intellectual Digest* 2 (March 1972), 59.

2. Scott Shane, "Genetics Research Increasingly Finds 'Race' a Null Concept," *Baltimore Sun*, April 4, 1999, 1.
3. Jared Diamond, *The Third Chimpanzee: Evolution and the Future of the Human Animal* (New York: HarperCollins, 1992), 111.
4. Edwards's comments during panel following NBC News documentary *Black Athletes: Fact and Fiction–Live Forum*, April 25, 1989.
5. Esteban J. Parra et al. "Estimating African American Admixture Proportions by Use of Population-Specific Alleles," *American Journal of Human Genetics* 63 (1998), 1839–1851; also see T. E. Reed, "Caucasian Genes in American Negroes," *Science* 165 (1969), 762–768.
6. *Skeptic* 4, (1996), 28.
7. J. L. Myres, *Geographical History in Greek Lands* (Oxford: Clarendon Press, 1953).
8. Quoted in L. Luca Cavalli-Sforza, P. Menozzi, and A. Piazza, *The History and Geography of Human Genes* (Princeton: Princeton University Press, 1994), 16.
9. Sharon Begley, "Three is Not Enough," *Newsweek*, February 13, 1995, 67.
10. Audrey Smedly, "'Race' and the Construction of Human Identity," *American Anthropologist* 100, September 1998, 695.
11. Jonathan Marks, *Human Biodiversity: Genes, Race, and History*, (New York: Aldine de Gruyter, 1995), 49, 5–7.
12. Carolus Linnaeus, *Systema Naturae*, First Edition (Amsterdam: Nieuwkoop, 1964), 22.
13. Marks, *Human Biodiversity: Genes, Race, and History*, 50.
14. Quoted in S.J. Gould, "The Geometer of Race," *Discover* 15, November 1994, 68.
15. Quoted in Marek Kohn, The Race Gallery: The Return of Racial Science (London: Jonathan Cape, 1995), 20.
16. Quoted in Cavalli-Sforza et al., *The History and Geography of Human Genes*, 17.
17. Quoted in Gould, *The Mismeasure of Man*, 71.
18. Quoted in Ibid., 411.
19. Quoted in Jonathan Marks, "Black, White Other: Racial Categories are Cultural Constructs Masquerading as Biology," *Natural History* 103, December 1994, 34.
20. Quoted in Gould, *The Mismeasure of Man*, 412.
21. Quoted in Marks, 234.
22. Quoted in George W. Stocking, Jr., *Race, Culture, and Evolution: Essays in the History of Anthropology* (Chicago: University of Chicago, 1982), 31–32.
23. Quoted in Gould, "The Geometer of Race," 67.
24. Jim Myers, "Examining the Races: Experts Scoff at Myths," *USA Today*, 1994, 3C.
25. Jack E. White, "Of Mandingo and Jimmy 'the Greek,'" *Time*, February 1, 1989, 48.
26. Jared Diamond, "Race Without Color," *Discover* 15, November 1994, 83–89.
27. Ibid., 89.
28. Richard Lewontin, "The Apportionment of Human Diversity," *Evolutionary Biology* 6 (1972), 381–398.
29. See M. L. Baba and L. L. Darga, "The Genetic Myth of Racial Classification," In: *Science and the Question of Human Equality*, edited by M. S.

Collins, A. W. Wainter, and T.A. Bremner (Boulder, Co.: Westview, 1981), 5–19; Alice M. Brues, *People and Races* (New York: Macmillan, 1977); E. S. Watts, "The Biological Race Concept and Diseases of Modern Man," in *Bicultural Aspects of Disease*, H. R. Rothschild (ed.) (New York: Academic, 1981), 3–23.

30. M. Nei and A. K. Roychoudhury, "Genetic Relationship and Evolution of Human Races," *Evolutionary Biology* 14 (1982), 51.

31. Diamond, *The Third Chimpanzee*, 28.

32. Nicholas Wade, "Human Or Chimp? 50 Genes Are the Key," *New York Times*, October 20, 1998, C1.

33. Michele Cargill, "Characterization of Single-Nucleotide Polymorphisms in Coding Regions of Human Genes," *Nature Genetics* 22, July 1999, 231–238.

34. Quoted in Cavalli-Sforza et al. *The History and Geography of Human Genes*, 17.

35. M. Nei and A. K. Roychoudhury, "Gene Differences Between Caucasian, Negro, and Japanese Populations," *Sciences* 177 (1972), 434–436; "Genic Variation Within and Between the Three Major Races of Man, Caucasians, Negroids, and Mongoloids," *American Journal of Human Genetics* 26 (1974), 421–443; "Genetic Relationship and Evolution of Human Races," *Human Polymorphic Genes: World Distribution* (New York: Oxford University, 1988); M. Nei, "The Theory of Genetic Distance and Evolution of Human Races, *Japanese Journal of Human Genetics* 23 (1978), 341–369.

36. L. B. Jorde et al., "Origins and Affinities of Modern Humans: A Comparison of Mitochondrial and Nuclear Genetic Data," *American Journal of Human Genetics* 57 (1992), 523–538.

37. W. H. Brown, "Polymorphism in Mitochondrial DNA of Humans as Revealed by Restriction Endonuclease Analysis," *Proceedings of the Natural Academy of Science USA* 77, 3605–3609.

38. Ranajit Chakraborty, "Allocation Versus Variation: The Issue of Genetic Differences Between Human Racial Groups," *American Naturalist* 120 (1982), 403–404; also see P. E. Smouse, R. S. Spielman, M. H. Park, "Multiple-Locus Allocation of Individuals to Groups as a Function of the Genetic Variation Within and Differences Among Human Populations," *American Naturalist* 119 (1982), 445–463.

39. See S. M. Garn, *Human Races 3* (Springfield, Ill.: Charles C. Thomas, 1971).

40. Li Jin et al., "Distribution of Haplotypes From a Chromosome 21 Region Distinguishes Multiple Prehistoric Human Migrations," *Proceedings of the National Academy of Sciences* 96, 7, March 30, 1999, 3796–3800.

41. J. Y. Chut et al., "Chinese Research Reveals Main Human Races," *Proceedings of the Natural Academy of Sciences* 95 (1998), 11763–11768,

42. Cavalli-Sforza,et al., *The History and Geography of Human Genes*, 19.

43. Ibid., 19.

44. Ibid., 79.

45. Ibid., 83.

46. Nicholas Wade, "DNA Backs a Tribe's Tradition of Early Descent From the Jews," *New York Times*, May 9, 1999, A1.

47. Vincent Sarich e-mail to the Human Biodiversity Mailing List, May 24, 1999.

48. Stanley Ambrose, "Late Pleistocene Human Population Bottlenecks, Vol-

canic Winter, and Differentiation of Modern Humans," *Journal of Human Evolution* 33, June 1998, 623–651.

49. "A Global Winter's Tale," *Discover*, December 30, 1998, 30.
50. Quoted in Andrea Lynn, "Ancient 'Volcanic Winter' Tied to Rapid Genetic Divergence in Humans," University of Illinois at Urbana-Champaign News Release, September 1998.
51. A. DiRienzo and A. C. Wilson, "Branching Pattern in the Evolutionary Tree for Human Mitochondrial DNA," *Proceedings of the National Academy of Sciences USA* 88 (1991), 1597–1601.
52. Peter Frost e-mail to the Human Biodiversity Mailing List, April 7, 1999.
53. Vincent Sarich, "In Defense of the Bell Curve," *Skeptic* 3 (1995), 84–93.
54. Claude Bouchard, "Genetic Basis of Racial Differences," *Canadian Journal of Sports Science* 13 (1988), 104–108.
55. Hjalti Gudmundsson, et. al, manuscript supplied by Hakon Gudbjartsson (hakon@decode.is) from the Duke University Institute of Statistics and Decision Sciences, July 26, 1999 e-mail.
56. Analysis by John Derbyshire [http://www.olimu.com] and others on the Human Biodiversity Mailing List.
57. Cavalli-Sforza et al., *The History and Geography of Human Genes*, 193.
58. Jared Diamond, "Bantu Banter and African Roots," *Nature* 398 (April 8, 1999), 477–478.
59. See G. Passarino, O. Semino, L. Quintana-Murci, L. Excoffier, M. Hammer, and A. S. Santachiara-Benerecetti, "Different Genetic Components in the Ethiopian Population, Identified by mtDNA and Y-Chromosome Polymorphisms," *American Journal of Human Genetics* 62 (1998), 420–434.
60. Wolpoff and Caspari, 302.
61. Peter Martin, "Blacks: Faster than Whites. And Cleverer," *The Observer*, August 3, 1997.
62. Henry Harpending, e-mails to the Human Biodiversity Mailing List, March 19 and May 4, 1999.

9. THE ORIGINS OF RACE SCIENCE

1. Nicholas Wade, "Finch DNA Shows Darwin was Right," *New York Times*, May 11, 1999, D5.
2. Cavalli-Sforza et al., *The History and Geography of Human Genes*, 17.
3. See Pat Shipman, *The Evolution of Racism: Human Differences and the Use and Abuse of Science* (New York: Simon and Schuster, 1994), 21.
4. See Marks, *Human Biodiversity*, 12–19.
5. Quoted in Shipman, 58.
6. Quoted in ibid., 59–60.
7. Ibid., 68.
8. For a detailed account of this issue, see Stephen Jay Gould, *The Mismeasure of Man*; for a contrary view and a critique of Gould, see J. Phillipe Rushton, "Race, Intelligence, and the Brain: The Errors and Omissions of the Revised Edition of S. J. Gould's *The Mismeasure of Man*," *Personality and Individual Differences* 23, July 1997, 169–180.
9. Gould, *The Mismeasure of Man*, 68.
10. Stocking, 29–35.
11. "How Mental Health Has Been Treated," *The Random House Encyclopedia* (New York: Random House, 1977), 762–763.

12. Cavalli-Sforza et al., *The History and Geography of Human Genes*, 17.
13. Kohn, 31.
14. Quoted in Gould, *The Mismeasure of Man*, 115.
15. Quoted in Stocking, *Race, Culture, and Evolution*, 48–49.
16. Michael Banton, *Racial Theories* (second ed.) (Cambridge: Cambridge University, 1998), 68–69.
17. Banton, 76.
18. J. S. Michael, "A New Look at Morton's Craniological Research," *Current Anthropology* 29 (1988), 349–354.
19. T. F. Gossett, *Race: The History of an Idea in America* (New York: Schocken, 1965), 44.
20. Banton, 76.
21. Ibid., 88–90.
22. Quoted in Kohn, 31.
23. Quoted in Gould, *The Mismeasure of Man*, 383.
24. Shipman, 107–8.
25. Quoted in Stocking, 41.
26. Daniel J. Kevles, *In the Name of Eugenics: Genetics and the Uses of Human Heredity* (Cambridge, Mass.: Harvard University, 1985), 6.
27. Ibid., 8.
28. See D. W. Forrest, *Francis Galton: The Life and Work of a Victorian Genius* (New York: Taplinger, 1974).
29. Quoted in Marks, 78, 65–66.
30. Charles Darwin, *The Descent of Man, and Selection in Relation to Sex* (Princeton, N.J.: Princeton University, 1981), 156, 170–171.
31. Shipman, 111.
32. Stocking, 167.
33. *Encyclopædia Britannica*, American Edition 17, (New York, 1895), 316–320.
34. Robert Bean, "Social Racial Peculiarities of the Negro Brain," *American Journal of Anatomy* 5 (1906), 379.
35. Cavalli-Sforza et al., *The History and Geography of Human Genes*, 17.
36. Shipman, 116–119.
37. Stocking, 60–61.
38. Wolpoff and Caspari, 135.
39. Ibid., 110.
40. John M Efron, *Defenders of the Faith: Jewish Doctors and Race Selection in Fin-de-Siècle Europe* (New Haven: Yale University Press, 1994), 9.
41. Quoted in Shipman, 136; Wolpoff and Caspari, 135, 102.
42. For an informative discussion about these rival German theorists, see Shipman, 73–103.
43. Houston Stewart Chamberlain, *Political Ideals* (London: National Vanguard Books, 1996).
44. Efron, 18–19.

10. THE SUPERIORITY OF WHITE ATHLETES

1. Charles H. Johnson, "Murphy and Salvator," *Turf and Sports Digest*, January 1957, 29.
2. David K. Wiggins, "Isaac Murphy: Black Hero in Nineteenth-Century American Sport, 1861–1896," *Canadian Journal of History of Sport and Physical Education*, May 1979, 15–33.

3. Arthur Ashe, Jr., *A Hard Road to Glory: Track and Field* (New York: Amistad, 1988), 3–4.
4. Wiggins, "Isaac Murphy."
5. Quoted in ibid.
6. Ashe, *A Hard Road to Glory: Track and Field*, xiii.
7. Stephen Fox, *Big Leagues: Professional Baseball, Football, and Basketball in National Memory* (New York: William Morrow, 1994), 216.
8. Ibid., 181.
9. Ashe, *A Hard Road to Glory: Football*, 3–6.
10. Benjamin G. Rader, *American Sports: From the Age of Folk Games to the Age of Spectators*, (Englewood Cliffs: Prentice-Hall, 1983), 35.
11. Fox, 300.
12. Ibid.
13. Ibid., 303.
14. Quoted in David K. Wiggins, "The Play of Slave Children in the Plantation Communities of the Old South, 1820–1860," *Journal of Sports History* 7, (Summer 1980), 32.
15. Rader, 35.
16. Quoted in Wiggins, *Glory Bound*, 178–179.
17. Quoted in Nelson George, *Elevating the Game: Black Men and Basketball* (New York: HarperCollins, 1992), 15–16.
18. Ashe, *A Hard Road to Glory: Track and Field*, 6–7.
19. Ibid., 8.
20. Ibid.
21. Fox, 216.
22. Ashe, *A Hard Road to Glory: Football*, 3.
23. Ibid., 3–4.
24. Ibid., 12–15.
25. Courtland Milloy, "In Recognition of the Complete Person," *Washington Post*, April 12, 1992, B1.
26. Ashe, *A Hard Road to Glory: Baseball*, 1.
27. Robert Peterson, *Only the Ball Was White: A History of Legendary Black Players and All-Black Professional Teams* (New York: Prentice-Hall, 1970), 16.
28. Quoted in Ashe, *A Hard Road to Glory: Baseball*, 3.
29. Quoted in Fox, 304.
30. Jules Tygiel, "Nineteenth Century Black Baseball," http://www.totalbaseball.com, 1996.
31. Ibid.
32. Ashe, *A Hard Road to Glory: Baseball*, 7.
33. Ibid., 8.
34. See Andrew Ritchie, Major Taylor: *The Extraordinary Career of a Champion Bicycle Racer* (San Francisco: Bicycle Books, 1988); and C. Grant Williams, "Marshall White Taylor: The World Famous Bicycle Rider," *Colored American Magazine* 5, (1902), 338–342.
35. Marshall W. "Major" Taylor, *The Fastest Bicycle Rider in the World, An Autobiography* (Worcester: Wormley, 1928; reprint, Brattleboro: Green-Stephens Press, 1971), 21.
36. Ibid., 259, 271
37. Dahn Shaulis, "Fred Hirchborn: 'Black Dan' Was a Pedestrian Hero of the 1800s," *Ultramarathon World*, http://www.fox.nstn.ca; see also Jerome Zuckerman et al., "The Black Athlete in Post-Bellum 19th Century," *Physical Educator* 29, October 1972, 142–146.

11. JACK JOHNSON IN THE RING AGAINST JIM CROW

1. Quoted in Hoberman, 152.
2. Quoted in Gwendolyn Captain, "Enter Ladies and Gentlemen of Color: Gender, Sport, and the Ideal of African American Manhood During the Late Nineteenth and Early Twentieth Centuries," *Journal of Sport History* (Spring 1991), 84.
3. Quoted in Hoberman, 68.
4. David Herbert Donald, *Lincoln* (New York: Simon and Schuster, 1995), 221
5. Quoted in Hoberman, 161.
6. B. A. Botkin, *A Treasury of American Folklore* (New York: Crown Publishers, 1944).
7. W.E.B. Du Bois, "The Problem of Amusement," *On Sociology* (1897), 236.
8. Robert Jakoubek, *Jack Johnson* (New York: Chelsea House, 1990), 43.
9. Quoted in Murray Phillips, "Sport and Race," outline for course taught at University of Canberra, Australia.
10. Jakoubek, 53.
11. Quoted in Hoberman, 13.
12. Quoted in Ashe, *A Hard Road to Glory: Boxing*, 24.
13. *Chicago Defender*, July 30, 1910, 1.
14. Quoted in Almond, III3.
15. Ashe, *A Hard Road to Glory: Boxing*, 24–25.
16. Quoted in Hoberman, 13.
17. Ashe, *A Hard Road to Glory: Boxing*, 25.
18. Cashmore, 101.
19. Ibid., 26.

12. AMERICAN EUGENICS

1. Daniel J. Kevles and Leroy Hood, *The Code: Scientific and Social Issues in the Human Genome Project*, (Cambridge: Harvard University Press, 1992), 40–41.
2. Quoted in Shipman, 124–6.
3. Kevles, 46–47.
4. Quoted in Stocking, 188.
5. Ibid., 127–128.
6. Charles Davenport, *Heredity in Relation to Genetics* (New York: Henry Holt, 1911), 4.
7. Marks, 82–83.
8. Quoted in Gould, *The Mismeasure of Man*, 182.
9. R. E. Fancher, "Henry Goddard and the Kallikak Family Photographs," *American Psychologist* 42 (1987), 585–590.
10. Quoted in Lewontin, Rose, and Kamin, 86.
11. Gould, *The Mismeasure of Man*, 226–227, 230.
12. Lothrop Stoddard, *The Rising Tide of Color Against White World Supremacy* (New York: Scribner's, 1920).
13. Madison Grant, *The Passing of the Great Race*, (New York: Scribner's, 1916), 16.
14. Stocking, 288–290.
15. Quoted in Kevles, *In the Name of Eugenics*, 76.
16. Madison Grant, *The Racial Basis of European History* (New York: Scribner's, 1923), 90.

17. Grant, *The Passing of the Great Race*, 47.
18. Shipman, 127–8.
19. Quoted in Marks, 84.
20. Ibid., 140.
21. Kevles, *In the Name of Eugenics*, 106–107,
22. Quoted in ibid., 62–63.
23. Ibid., 64.
24. Charles Valenza, "Was Margaret Sanger a Racist?" *Family Planning Perspectives* (January/February 1985).
25. Quoted in Kevles, 175.
26. Quoted in ibid., 174.
27. Quoted in ibid., 170–172, 164.
28. Ibid., 75.
29. Ibid., 137.
30. Quoted in ibid., 61.
31. R. G. Weisbord, *Genocide: Birth Control and the Black American* (Westport.: Greenwood, 1975), 41–42.
32. W.E.B. Du Bois, "Black Folks and Birth Control," *Birth Control Review* (June 1932), 166.

13. JESSE OWENS AND THE GERMAN RACE

1. Roger Thurow, "Fleeting Fame," *Wall Street Journal*, June 7, 1996, A1.
2. Ibid., A6.
3. Elmer A. Cater, "The Negro in College Athletics," *Opportunity*, July 1933, 208.
4. Quoted in Ashe, *A Hard Road to Glory: Track and Field*, 18.
5. Ibid., 27–28.
6. Ibid., 18–20.
7. Paul Lowry, "Colored Boys Sports Threat," *Times of Sunday*, July 31, 1932.
8. William J. Baker, *Jesse Owens: An American Life* (New York: Free Press, 1986), 35.
9. *Norfolk (Virginia) Journal and Guide*, June 8, 1935.
10. Roi Ottley, *Amsterdam News*, July 18, 1936.
11. *New York Times*, June 2, 1935.
12. Patrick B. Miller, "Anatomy of Scientific Racism: Racialist Responses to Black Athletic Achievement," *Journal of Sport History* 25 (1993), 129.
13. W. Montague Cobb, "Race and Runners," *Journal of Health and Physical Education* (January 1936), 54.
14. Ibid., 3–7, 52–56.
15. Hoberman, 167.
16. Cobb, "Race and Runners," 6, 7, 54.
17. Cobb, "The Negro as a Biological Element in the American Population," *Journal of Negro Education* 8 (1939), 343.
18. Dean B. Cromwell, *Championship Technique in Track and Field* (New York: Whittlesey House/McGraw-Hill, 1941), 6.
19. Harry F. V. Edwards, *Amsterdam News*, August 29, 1936.
20. Baker.
21. Shipman, 133.
22. Ibid., 135.

23. Quoted in Efron, 19.
24. Quoted in Kohn, 36.
25. Quoted in ibid., 28.
26. Benno Müller–Hill, *Murderous Science: Elimination by Scientific Selection of Jews, Gypsies, and Others, Germany 1933–1945* (Oxford: Oxford University, 1988), 10.
27. Wolpoff and Caspari, 207.
28. Quoted in Kohn, 34.
29. *New York Times*, November 21, 1933.
30. U.S. Holocaust Museum exhibit, "African-American Athletes," 1997.
31. Ashe, *A Hard Road to Glory: Track and Field*, 22.
32. Quoted in P. Hain, "The Politics of Sport and Apartheid," in J. Hargreaves (ed.) *Sport, Culture and Ideology* (London: Routledge and Kegan Paul, 1982), 233.
33. Quoted in Wiggins, *Glory Bound*, 86–87.
34. David K. Wiggins, "The 1936 Olympic Games in Berlin: The Response of America's Black Press," *Research Quarterly for Exercise and Sport* 54, September 1983, 285–286.
35. Quoted in Wiggins, *Glory Bound*, 87.
36. Ibid.
37. Wiggins, "The 1936 Olympic Games in Berlin," 282.
38. Arnd Kruger, "The 1936 Olympic Games–Berlin," in Peter J. Graham and Norst Veberhorst (eds.), *The Modern Olympics* (West Point, N.Y.: Leisure Press, 1976), 173–186.
39. Baker.
40. Excerpted from "Black Athletes: Fact and Fiction," NBC News documentary, April 25, 1989.
41. Quoted in *Pittsburgh Courier-Journal*, October 16, 1937.
42. Raspberry, 20.
43. U.S. Holocaust Museum Exhibit.
44. Chris Mead, *Champion: Joe Louis, Black Hero in White America* (New York: Penguin, 1986), 92.
45. Wiggins, "The 1936 Olympic Games in Berlin," 278–279.
46. Quoted in *Amsterdam News*, September 5, 1936.
47. Quoted in *Boulder Daily Camera*, February 26, 1995.
48. Quoted in Ashe, *A Hard Road to Glory: Track and Field*, 28.

14. A KNOCKOUT BLOW TO RACE SCIENCE

1. Quoted in Ashe, *A Hard Road to Glory: Boxing*, 34.
2. Chris Mead, "Black Hero in a White Land," *Sports Illustrated*, August 16, 1985, 82.
3. Gerald Astor, *And a Credit to His Race: The Hard Life and Times of Joseph Louis Barrow* (New York: Saturday Review Press, 1974), 27.
4. Mead, *Champion*, 62.
5. Quotes from Mead, "Black Hero in a White Land," 91.
6. Ibid., 91–92.
7. Ibid., 90.
8. Ibid., 98.
9. "Joe Louis and Jesse Owens," *The Crisis*, August 1935, 241.

10. Hoberman, 75.
11. See Nancy Stepan, *The Idea of Race in Science: Great Britain, 1800–1960* (London: Macmillan, 1982).
12. Mead, *Champion*, 84.
13. Mead, *Champion*, 98.
14. Ibid., 91.
15. Astor, 69.
16. Ashe, *A Hard Road to Glory: Boxing*, 36.
17. Joe Louis, *My Life Story* (New York: Duell, Sloan and Pearce, 1947), 101.
18. Thomas Sowell quoted in Richard Bak, "Joe Louis: The Great White Hope," 1966, http://www.hgs.11.net.
19. Mead, *Champion*, 105.
20. Quoted in Hoberman, 92.
21. Quoted in Vince Mathews with Neil Amdur, *My Race Be Won* (New York: Chaterhouse, 1974), 194.

15. THE "SCHEMING, FLASHY, TRICKINESS" OF JEWS

1. Interview with Sonny Hill, November 1988.
2. *Interscholastic Athletic Association Handbook* (1910), 41.
3. Interview with Harry Litwack, November 1988.
4. Interview with Dave Dabrow, December 1988.
5. Robert Strauss, "Oy, How They Played the Game," *PhillySport*, February 1989, 42.
6. Bill Ordine, "A Better Team Than Money Could Buy...," *Today Magazine (Philadelphia Inquirer)*, April 17, 1977, 33–34.
7. Quoted in Ron Avery, "The SPHAs: Basketball Champions Shined...When Stars Were Jewish," *Jewish Exponent*, June 25, 1982, 48–49.
8. Frank Dolson, "Old SPHAs Were Giants But Got Paid Like Pygmies," *Philadelphia Inquirer*, June 11, 1974, 1D.
9. Quoted in Strauss, 40.
10. Interview with William Gates, November 1988.
11. Quoted in Harold U. Ribalow, *The Jew in American Sports* (New York: Block, 1951), 223–224.
12. Quoted in Bernard Postal, Jesse Silver, and Roy Silver, *Encyclopedia of Jews in Sport* (New York: Bloch Sports, 1965), 78.

16. THE INTEGRATION OF SPORTS

1. David Stout, "U.S. Knew Early of Nazi Killings in Asylums, Official Documents Show," *New York Times*, July 29, 1999, A14.
2. Shipman, 138.
3. Andrea Stone, "Politics Mixed With Principles," *USA Today*, July 26, 1998, A12.
4. Ashe, *A Hard Road to Glory: Baseball*, 43.
5. Quoted in George Sullivan, "Another Barrier That Fell 50 Years Ago is Recalled," *New York Times*, October 5, 1997, C29.
6. Pierce related quotes in ibid.
7. William C. Rhoden, "When Paul Brown Broke Color Barrier," *New York Times*, September 25, 1997, C26.

8. Larry Lester, "Does History Make the Man or Does Man Make History," *New York Times*, April 14, 1997.
9. Quoted in Jules Tygiel, *Baseball's Great Experiment: Jackie Robinson and His Legacy* (New York: Vintage, 1984), 239.
10. Ashe, *A Hard Road to Glory: Basketball*, 22.
11. George, 95–96.
12. Fox, 298.
13. Kohn, 40–41.
14. Wolpoff and Caspari, 249.
15. Kohn, 41.
16. Ibid.
17. For one commentary of Boas's life and work, see Stocking, 133–233.
18. For selected readings, see Franz Boas and George W. Stocking, Jr., *A Franz Boas Reader: The Shaping of American Anthropology, 1883–1911* (Chicago: University of Chicago, 1989).
19. Wolpoff and Caspari, 79.
20. Quoted in Stocking, 193–194.
21. As an example, see T. F. Gossett, *Race: The History of an Idea in America* (New York: Oxford University, 1997); also George W. Stocking, Jr., "Review of *Race: The History of an Idea in America*," *Journal of the History of the Behavioral Sciences* 1 (1965), 294–296.
22. Shipman, 160–161.
23. Ashley Montagu, *Man's Most Dangerous Myth: The Fallacy of Race* (New York: Columbia University, 1942).
24. Ashley Montagu, "Redefining Race: The Potential Demise of a Concept in Physical Anthropology," *Current Anthropology* 23 (1982) 641–655.
25. See Derek Freeman, "Paradigms in Collision: Margaret Mead's Mistake and What it Has Done to Anthropology," *Skeptic* 5 (1997), 66–73.
26. Quoted in William B. Provine, "Geneticists and Race," *American Zoologist* 26, (1986), 857–887.
27. Quoted in Kohn, 46.
28. Provine, 860.
29. H. E. Garrett, "Racial Differences and Witch Hunting," *Science* 135 (1962), 982–983.
30. Andrew S. Winston, "The Context of Correctness: A Comment on Rushton," *Journal of Social Distress and the Homeless* 5 (1996), 231–250.
31. Quoted in Frank Miele, "The (Im)moral Animal: A Quick and Dirty Guide to Evolutionary Psychology and the Nature of Human Nature," *Skeptic* 4 (1966), 42–49.

17. THE SIXTIES

1. Wolpoff and Caspari, 143.
2. Ibid., 148.
3. Carleton S. Coon, *The Origin of Races* (New York: Alfred A. Knopf, 1962), 656.
4. Michael Shermer, *Why People Believe Weird Things* (New York: W. H. Freeman, 1997), 158.
5. Wolpoff and Caspari, 159, 155.
6. Shipman, 205, 286 n11.
7. Wolpoff and Caspari, 165.
8. Shipman, 199–200.

9. Ibid., 212, 210.
10. Sidney Mintz letter to Carey Williams, November 30, 1964, quoted in Ashley Montagu, *New York Times*, August 29, 1992, 18.
11. Sandra Harding (ed.), *The "Racial" Economy of Science: Towards a Democratic Future* (Bloomington: Indiana University, 1993).
12. Theodosius Dobzhansky, "A Debatable Account of the Origin of Races," *Scientific American* 208 (1963), 172.
13. Quoted in Theodosius Dobzhansky, "More Bogus 'Science' of Race Prejudice," *Journal of Heredity* 59 (1968).
14. Quoted in Giles Whittell, "Running for Their Lives," *The Times Magazine* (UK), July 6, 1996, 32.
15. Tom Weir, "Racial Integration was Slow," *USA Today*, April 16, 1999, 6C.
16. Ed Willes, "Belated Credit for a Goal: After 40 Years, the NHL Recognizes Its First Black Player," *New York Times*, January 19, 1998, C12.
17. Clifton Brown, "Strong-Willed Sifford Earned Place, Not Footnote, in History," *New York Times*, March 1, 1998, C23.
18. Frank Fitzpatrick, *And The Walls Came Tumbling Down: Kentucky, Texas Western and the Game That Changed American Sports* (New York: Simon and Schuster, 1998).
19. Christopher Lehmann–Haupt, "A Basketball Upset That Made a Lasting Impression," *New York Times*, March 15, 1999, E8.
20. Whittell, 33.
21. Quoted in Ashe, *A Hard Road to Glory: Track and Field*, 41.
22. Douglas Hartmann, "The Politics of Race and Sport: Resistance and Domination in the 1968 African American Olympic Protest Movement," *Ethnic and Racial Studies* (July 1996), 54–56.
23. Quoted in Wiggins, *Glory Bound*, 108–110.
24. Quoted in *Newsweek*, July 15, 1968, 57D.
25. *Ebony*, March 1968, 112.
26. Quoted in Ashe, *A Hard Road to Glory: Track and Field*, 42.
27. Whittell, 33.
28. Ibid., 44.
29. Quoted in Dick Patrick, "Athletes Left Mark on Sport, Culture," *USA Today*, June 18, 1998, 11C.
30. Quoted in Kane, 74.
31. "Black Power Show Causes Banishment," *Chicago Tribune* wire services, October 19, 1968.
32. Whittell, 30, 33.
33. Quoted in Wiggins, *Glory Bound*, 117–119.
34. Quoted in Kane.
35. Wiggins, *Glory Bound*, 185–186.
36. Kane.

18. SPORTS AND IQ

1. Richard Goldstein, "Al Campanis is Dead at 81; Ignited Baseball Over Race," *New York Times*, June 22, 1998, C11.
2. Quoted in Ross Newhan, "A Lifetime Destroyed by Own Words," *Los Angeles Times*, June 22, 1998, C8.
3. George Vecsey, "A Good Man Who Had a Very Bad Moment," *New York Times*, August 1998, 28.

4. Arthur R. Jensen, "How Much Can We Boost I.Q. and Scholastic Achievement?" *Harvard Educational Review* 39 (Winter 1969), 1–123.
5. See *"Playboy* Interview: William Shockley," (1974), 67–99.
6. Richard J. Herrnstein and Charles Murray, *The Bell Curve* (New York: Free Press, 1994), 10.
7. Richard J. Herrnstein, "IQ," *Atlantic Monthly*, September 1971, 43–64.
8. Herrnstein and Murray, 10.
9. Kane, 72–83.
10. Edwards interview.
11. Harry Edwards, "The Sources of Black Athletic Superiority," *Black Scholar*, November 1971, 38.
12. Ibid., 38–39.
13. Steven J. Rosenthal, "Academic Nazism," 1994, at http://www.shss.montclair.edu.
14. Gould, *The Mismeasure of Man*, 27.
15. J. Philippe Rushton, *Race, Evolution, and Behavior: A Life History Perspective* (New Brunswick: Transaction [Rutgers–The State University], 1997).
16. N. C. Andreasen et al., "Intelligence and Brain Structure in Normal Individuals," *American Journal of Psychiatry*, 150 (1993), 130–134.
17. Daniel Seligman, *A Question of Intelligence: The IQ Debate in America* (New York: Citadel, 1994).
18. Douglas A. Blackmon, "Silent Partner: How the South's Fight to Uphold Segregation Was Funded Up North," *Wall Street Journal*, June 11, 1999, A8.
19. Charles Lane, "Letter to the Editor," *Wall Street Journal*, December 2, 1994.
20. Winston, 220.
21. Kohn, 54.
22. Harry F. Weyher (President, The Pioneer Fund), "Letter to the Editor," *Wall Street Journal*, February 2, 1995.
23. Charles Lane, "The Tainted Sources of 'The Bell Curve,'" *New York Review of Books*, December 1, 1994.
24. Adam Miller, "Academia's Dirty Secret: Professors of Hate," *Rolling Stone*, October 20, 1994, 106–114.
25. Frank Miele interview with Robert Sternberg, *Skeptic* 3 (1995), 72–80.
26. David E. Duke, *My Awakening: A Path to Racial Understanding* (Monroe: Free Speech Books, 1998).
27. See for example *Stormfront: White Pride World-Wide* at http://www3.stormfront.org.
28. George Johnson, "Nobody's Smart About Intelligence," *New York Times*, March 1, 1998, C1.
29. Daniel Goleman, *Emotional Intelligence* (New York: Bantam Books), 1996.
30. Annie Murphy Paul, "Promotional Intelligence," http://www.Salon.com, June 28, 1999.
31. See Howard Gardner, *Frames of Mind: Theory of Multiple Intelligences* (New York: Basic Books, 1983).
32. "Medizin: Ich denke Musik," *Der Spiegel* 34 (1999), 174–176.
33. Andrew Whiten and Richard W. Byrne (eds.), *Machiavellian Intelligence II: Extensions and Evaluations* (Cambridge: Cambridge University, 1997), 1, 17.
34. M. Davies, L. Stankov, R. Roberts, "Emotional Intelligence: In Search of an Elusive Construct," *Journal of Personality and Social Psychology*, 75 (1998), 989–1015.

35. Quoted in J. D. Mayer and P. Salovey, "The Intelligence of Emotional Intelligence" *Intelligence* 17 (1999) 443–450.
36. Dinesh D'Souza, *The End of Racism* (New York: Free Press, 1995), 440–441.

19. WINNING THE GENETIC LOTTERY

1. Quoted in Almond, III 9.
2. Bill Russell and Jim Brown are two prominent African American former athletes who have sharply challenged suggestions that blacks are naturally gifted athletes.
3. Carl Lewis interview, December 1988.
4. Quoted in "Black Dominance," *Time*, May 9, 1977, 57–60.
5. Quoted in William C. Rhoden, "Are Black Athletes Naturally Superior?" *Ebony*, December 2, 1974, 136–8.
6. Peter Nye, *Hearts of Lions* (New York: W.W. Norton, 1988).
7. Ashe, *A Hard Road to Glory: Track and Field*, 6–7.
8. Quoted in A. S. Young, *Negro Firsts in Sports* (New York: Johnson Publishing, 1963), 82.
9. Hugh S. Fullerton, *Popular Science Monthly*, October 1921.
10. J. E. Lindsay. Carter, "Ethnic Variations in Human Performance: Morphological and Compositional Characteristics," *American College of Sports Medicine Symposium*, May 31, 1991.
11. Eleanor Metheny, "Some Differences in Bodily Proportions Between American Negro and White Male College Students as Related to Athletic Performance," *Research Quarterly* 10, December 1939, 41–53.
12. J. Borms and M. Hebbelinck, "Review of Studies of Olympic Athletes," in J. E. L. Carter (ed.), *Physical Structure of Olympic Athletes, Part II: Kinanthropometry of Olympic Athletes*, (Basel, Switzerland: S. Karger, 1984).
13. James M. Tanner, *The Physique of the Olympic Athlete: A Study of 137 Track and Field Athletes at the XIV Olympic Games, Rome, 1960* (London: G. Allen and Unwin, 1964).
14. Quoted in Hoberman, 194.
15. L. Xia, D. Gallagher, J. Wang, J.C. Thornton, and R.N. Pearson, "Appendicular Skeletal Muscle Mass (ASM) is Lower in Asian Males (AM) Than in White Males," *FASEB* 10 (1996), A733.
16. A. Damon et al., "Predicting Somatotype From Body Measurements," *American Journal of Physical Anthropology* 20 (1962), 461–471.
17. Himes; see also D. F. Roberts, and D. R. Bainbridge, "Nilotic Physique," *American Journal of Physical Anthropology* 21 (1977), 341–370.
18. Holly M. Cintas, "Cross-Cultural Variation in Infant Motor Development," *Physical and Occupational Therapy in Pediatrics* 8 (1988), 1–20; J. R. Williams and R. B. Scott, "Growth and Development of Negro Infants: Motor Development and Its Relationship to Child Rearing Practices in Two Groups of Negro Infants," *Child Development* 24 (1953), 103–121.
19. Marcelle Geber and R.F.A. Dean, "Gesell Tests on African Children," *Pediatrics* 20 (1957), 1061–1064.
20. Quoted in Frank I. Katch and Victor I. Katch, "Physiology: Is Black Beautiful," *Muscle & Fitness* 29 (April 1985), 160–161.
21. Kathryn Greaves et al., "Ethnic Differences in Anthropometric Character-

istics of Young Children and Their Parents, *Human Biology* 61 (1989), 459–477.

22. J. E. Kilbride et al., "The Comparative Motor Development of Baganda, American White, and American Black Infants," *An Anthropologist* 72 (1970), 1422–1428.

23. William K. Frankenburg and Josiah B. Dodds, "The Denver Developmental Screening Test," *Journal of Pediatrics* 71 (August 1967), 181–191; W. K. Frankenburg, Nathan P. Dick, and James Carland, "Development of Preschool-Aged Children of Different Social and Ethnic Groups: Implications for Developmental Screening," *Journal of Pediatrics* 87 (July 1975), 125–132.

24. Interview with William Frankenburg and Joe Dodds, December 1988.

25. Gaston P. Beunen, Robert M. Malina, Roland Renson, Jan Simons, Michel Ostyn, and Johan Lefevre, "Physical Activity and Growth, Maturation and Performance: A Longitudinal Study," *Medicine and Science in Sports and Exercise* 24 (1992), 576–585.

26. R. M. Malina, "Growth and Physical Performance of American Negro and White Children," *Clinical Pediatrics*, 8 (1969), 476–483.

27. R. M. Malina, "Racial/Ethnic Variation in the Motor Development and Performance of American Children," *Canadian Journal of Sports Science* 13 (1988), 136–143; Malina, "Growth and Physical Performance of American Negro and White Children," *Clinical Pediatrics* 8 (1969), 9–38; James M. Dinucci and David A. Shows, "A Comparison of the Motor Performance of Black and Caucasian Girls Age 6–8," *Research Quarterly* 48 (December 1977), 680–684.

28. R. M. Malina, "Genetics of Motor Development and Performance," in R. M. Malina and C. Bouchard (eds.), *Sport and Human Genetics* (Champaign: Human Kinetics Publishers), 23–58.

29. J. Dunn and M. Lupfer, "A Comparison of Black and White Boys' Performance in Self-Paced and Reactive Sports Activities," *Journal of Applied Social Psychology* 4 (1974), 24–35.

30. David W. Hunter, "A Comparison of Anaerobic Power Between Black and White Adolescent Males," Ph.D. dissertation, Ohio State University, 1988.

31. John Capouya, "The Art and Science of Jumping," *Sport*, June 1986, 61.

32. Ibid.

33. Quoted in ibid. 59.

34. Katch and Katch, 160–161.

35. Pierre F.M. Ama, J. M Simoneau, M. R. Boulay, O. Serresse, G. Thériault, and C. Bouchard, "Skeletal Muscle Characteristics in Sedentary Black and Caucasian Males," *Journal of Applied Physiology* 61 (1986), 1758–1761.

36. J. M Simoneau and C. Bouchard in E. Van Praagh (ed.), *Paediatric Anaerobic Performance* (Champaign, Ill.: Human Kinetics Publishers, 1998), 5–21; Blacks appear to possess a "slightly greater type II proportion" and the "extreme fibre type differences between sprinters and endurance athletes are probably more attributable to genetics than training," according to W. J. Duey, D. R. Bassett, Jr., D. J. Toronok, E. T. Howley, V. Bond, P. Mancuso and R. Trudell, "Skeletal Muscle Fibre Type and Capillary Density in College-Aged Blacks and Whites," *Annals of Human Biology* 24 (1997) 323–221.

37. Kathryn N. North et al., "A Common Nonsense Mutation Results in --actinin-3 Deficiency in the General Population, *Nature Genetics* 21 (April 1999), 353–354.

38. Deborah Smith, "We Can't Run So Fast With Our Genes Falling Down," *Sydney Morning Herald*, http://www.smh.com.au.

39. J. M Simoneau and C. Bouchard, "Genetic Determinism of Fiber Type Proportion in Human Skeletal Muscle," *FASEB Journal* 9 (1995), 1091–1095.

40. Martin Levesque, M. R. Boulay, G. Thériault, C. Bouchard, J. M. Simoneau, "Training-Induced Changes in Maximal Exercise of Short Duration and Skeletal Muscle Characteristics of Black African and Caucasian Men," unpublished manuscript, 1995; see also J. A. Simoneau, C. K. Allah, M. Giroux, M. R. Boulay, P. Lagassé, G. Thériault, C. Bouchard, "Metabolic Plasticity of Skeletal Muscle in Black and White Males Subjected to High-Intensity Intermittent Training, *Medical Science Sports and Exercise* 23 (1991), S149; and M. Levesque, , M. R. Boulay, J. A. Simoneau, "Muscle Fiber Type Characteristics in Black African and White Males Before and After 12 Weeks of Sprint Training, *Canadian Journal of Applied Physiology* 19 (1994), Supplement 25P.

41. See Bengt Saltin, "Metabolic Fundamentals in Exercise," *Medicine and Science in Sports* 5 (1973), 137–146.

42. Pierre F. M. Ama et al., "Anaerobic Performances in Black and White Subjects," *Medicine and Science in Sports and Exercise* 22 (1990), 508–511.

43. Excerpts from Stephen Seiler e-mail to Sportscience Listserve, December 29, 1998; based on Seiler, "Energy Contributions in Field Sports," http://www.endureplus.com.

44. Interview with Timothy Noakes, May 31, 1996.

45. Burfoot, "White Men Can't Run," 94.

46. Pieter Coetzer, T. D. Noakes, B. Sanders, M. I. Lambert, A. N. Bosch, T. Wiggins, and S. C. Dennis, "Superior Fatigue Resistance of Elite Black South African Distance Runners," *Journal of Applied Physiology* 75 (1993), 1822–1827.

47. P. D. Gollnick, R. B. Armstrong, C. W. Saubert IV, K. Piehl, and B. Saltin, "Enzyme Activity and Fiber Composition in Skeletal Muscle of Untrained and Trained Men," *Journal of Applied Physiology* 33 September 1972, 312–319.

48. David L. Costill, J. Daniels, W. Evans, W. Fink, G. Krahenbuhl, and B. Saltin, "Skeletal Muscle Enzymes and Fiber Composition in Male and Female Track Athletes," *Journal of Applied Physiology* 40, 2 (1976) 149–154.

49. Interview with Kathy Myburgh.

50. A. R. Weston, Z. Mbambo, and K. H. Myburgh, "Running Economy of African and Caucasian Distance Runners." *Medicine and Science in Sports, Exercise*, April 2000.

51. A. Weston, O. Karamizrak, A. Smith, T. D. Noakes, and K. H. Myburgh, "African Distance Runners Exhibit Greater Fatigue Resistance, Lower Lactate Accumulation and Higher Oxidative Enzyme Activity," *Journal of Applied Physiology* 86 March 1999, 915–923.

52. Burfoot, "White Man Can't Run," 94; B. Saltin, H. Larsen, N. Terrados, C. K. Kim, J. Svedenhag, C. J. Rolf, "Aerobic Exercise Capacity at Sea Level and at Altitude in Kenyan Boys, Junior and Senior Runners Compared with Scandinavian Runners," *Scandinavian Journal of Medical Science and Sports* 5 (1995), 209–221.

53. B. Saltin, C. K. Kim, N. Terrados, H. Larsen, J. Svedenhag, and C. J. Rolf, "Morphology, Enzyme Activities and Buffer Capacity in Leg Muscles of Kenyan and Scandinavian Runners," *Scandinavian Journal of Medical Science and Sports* 5 (1995), 222–230.

54. Interview with Bengt Saltin, December 1995.
55. Claude Bouchard, e-mail to author, March 3, 1999. Saltin interviewed on "Black Britian," BBC2 documentary, September 7, 2000.
56. Hugh Thomas, *The Slave Trade: The Story of Atlantic Slave Trade: 1440–1870* (New York: Simon and Schuster, 1997).
57. Kohn, 267–8.
58. Quoted in Rowe, 33.
59. Quoted in ibid., 32.
60. Quoted in Kohn, 270.
61. Quoted in Rowe, 33.
62. M. Worthy and A. Markle, "Racial Differences in Reactive Versus Self-Paced Sports Activities," *Journal of Personality and Social Psychology* 16 (1970), 439–443.
63. M. Worthy, *Eye Color, Sex and Race* (Anderson: Drake House/Hallux, 1977).
64. D. M. Landers et al., "The Influence of External Stimuli and Eye Color on Reactive Motor Behavior" in R. W. Christina and D. M. Landers (eds.), *Psychology of Motor Behavior and Sport–1976* 11 (Champaign: Human Kinetics, 94–112).
65. See J. M. Jones and A. R. Hochner, "Racial Differences in Sport Activities: A Look at the Self-Paced Versus Reactive Hypothesis", *Journal of Personal and Social Psychology* 27 (1973), 86–95.
66. Dean Cromwell and Al Wesson, *Championship Techniques in Track and Field* (New York, 1941).
67. Quoted in Kane, 75–76.
68. Quoted in ibid., 80.
69. See Richard Majors and Janet Mancini Bilson, *Cool Pose: The Dilemmas of Black Manhood in America* (New York: Lexington Books, 1992).
70. Mike Schmidt interview, January 1989.
71. Edward Miller, "Paternal Provisioning versus Mate Seeking in Human Populations," *Personality and Individual Differences* 17, (August 1994), 227-255.
72. John Underwood, "Troubling Thoughts About Top Athletes–and Too Much Success On the Playground," *Life*, Spring 1988, 107.
73. Quoted in Wiggins, "Great Speed but Little Stamina," 185.
74. Hoberman, 200.
75. Michael Crawford letter, August 25, 1998.
76. Claude Bouchard interview, December 1988.
77. C. Bouchard, E. W. Daw, T. Rice, L. Pérusse, J. Gagnon, M. A. Province, A. S. Leon, D. C. Rao, J. Skinner, J. H. Wilmore, "Familial Resemblance for $VO2_{max}$ in the Sedentary State: the Heritage Family Study," *Medicine and Science in Sports and Exercise* (1998), 252–258.
78. J. A. Simoneau and C. Bouchard, "Genetic Determinism of Fiber Type Proportion in Human Skeletal Muscle," *FASEB Journal* 9 (August 1995), 1091–1095.
79. Miguel A. Rivera, F. T. Dionne, J. A. Simoneau, L. Pérusse, M. Chagnon, Y. Chagnon, J. Gagnon, A. S. Leon, D. C. Rao, J. Skinner, J. H. Wilmore, and C. Bouchard, "Muscle-Specific Creative Kinase Gene Polymorphism and $VO2_{max}$ in the Heritage Family Study," *Medicine and Science in Sports and Exercise* (1997), 1311–1317, see also M. A. Rivera, L. Perusse, J.A. Simoneau, J. Gagnon, F. T. Dionne, A. S. Leon, J. Skinner, J. H. Wilmore, M. Province, D.C. Rao, and C. Bouchard, "Linkage Between a Muscle-Specific CK Gne Marker and $VO2_{max}$ in the Heritage Family Study," *Medicine and Science in Sports and Exercise* 31, (May 1999), 698–701.
80. Josie Glausiusz, "The Genes of 1998," *Discover* 20, January 1999, 33.

81. Paul Nuki, "Top Athletes Born With 'Go Faster' Gene," *Sunday Times* (UK), May 17, 1998.
82. Tim Noakes, "Trainability gene; and is there a "g" factor for athleticism?" e-mail to author, May 22, 1998.
83. T. Todd and A. Lindala, "Dimensions of the Body: White and American Negroes of Both Sexes," *American Journal of Physical Anthropology* 12 (1928), 35–119.
84. Stanley M. Garn, "Human Biology and Research in Body Composition," *Annals of the New York Academy of Sciences* 110 (1963), 429–446; J. Jordan, "Physiological and Anthropometric Comparisons of Negroes and Whites," *Journal of Health, Physical Education, and Recreation* 40 (November-December 1969), 93–99.
85. Jacques Samson and Magdeleine Yerlès, "Racial Differences in Sports Performance," *Canadian Journal of Sports Science* 13 (1988), 110–111.
86. Robert P. Heaney, "Bone Mass, the Mechanostat, and Ethnic Differences," *Journal of Clinical Endocrinology and Metabolism* 80, (1995), 2289–2290; D. A. Nelson, "Ethnic Differences in Regional Bone Density, Hip Axis Length, and Lifestyle Variables Among Healthy Black and White Men," *Human Biology* 58 (1986), 379–390; W. S. Pollitzer and J. Anderson, "Ethnic and Genetic Differences in Bone Mass: A Review with a Hereditary vs. Environmental Perspective," *American Journal of Clinical Nutrition* 52 (July 1990), 1244–1259.
87. J. A. Cauley et al., "Black-White Differences in Serum Sex Hormones and Bone Mineral Density," *American Journal of Epidemiology* 139 (1994), 1035–1046; William H. James, "Causes of Racial Differences in Testosterone Levels of Men," *Journal of Clinical Endocrinology and Metabolism* 80 (1995), 2289–2290; and Lee Ellis and Nyborg Helmuth, "Racial/Ethnic Variations in Male Testosterone Levels: A Probable Contributor to Group Differences in Health," *Steroids* 57 (1992), 72–75.
88. J. E. Lindsay Carter interview, September 1988.
89. Kevles, 146.
90. Gary A. Sailes, "the Myth of Black Sports Supremacy," *Journal of Black Studies* 21, June 1991, 482.
91. Robert Malina interview, January 1989.
92. Rhoden, "Are Black Athletes Naturally Superior?" 138.

20. THE ENVIRONMENTALIST CASE AGAINST INNATE BLACK SUPERIORITY IN SPORTS

1. Laettner and Seikaly quoted in S.L. Price, "What Ever Happened to the White Athlete," *Sports Illustrated*, December 9, 1997, 38.
2. Owen Anderson, "Dad, Mom, and You: Do Your Genes Determine Your Performances?" *Running Research* (October 1995), 1.
3. Edwards interview.
4. Dennis Rodman with Tim Keown, *Bad As I Want to Be* (New York: Delacorte Press, 1996).
5. For a cross-section of sociological explanations of athletic differences, see Sailes, "The Myth of Black Sports Supremacy."; Barry D. McPherson, "Minority Group Involvement in Sport" in: R. Wilmore (ed.) *Exercise and Sports Science Reviews* (New York: Academic Press, 1983), 71–101; and Jay

J. Coakley, *Sport in Society: Issues and Controversies*, (St. Louis: C. V. Mosby, 1982).

6. Phillips, "Toward an Explanation of Racial Variations in Top-Level Sports Participation," *International Review of Sports Science* 11 (1976), 49.

7. Ibid., 50.

8. Miki Turner, "White Girls Can't Jump," *Women's Sports & Fitness*, October 1992, 62.

9. Christopher J. Hallinan, "Aborigines and Positional Segregation in Australian Rugby League," *International Review for the Sociology of Sport* 26 (1991), 69–78.

10. The classic study of "racial stacking" is considered to be J. W. Loy and J. F. McElvogue, "Racial Segregation in American Sport," *International Review of Sport Sociology* 5 (1970), 5–23; for a discussion of the controversy about quarterbacking in football, see Jon Entine, "The Chattering Class: Dark Thoughts," *Gentlemen's Quarterly*, September 1999, 251–258.

11. Entine.

12. *Ebony*, December 1974, 134.

13. Interview with Tony Dungy, May 1999.

14. Interview with Dennis Green, May 1999.

15. B. Margolis and J. A. Piliavin, "'Stacking' in Major League Baseball: A Multivariate Analysis," *Sociology of Sport Journal* 16 (1999), 16–34.

16. Ibid., 30.

17. Stephen Budiansky, "The Truth About Dogs," *The Atlantic Monthly* 284, July 1999, 39.

18. Ibid., 41, 52.

19. Jonah Goldberg, "Mau-Mauing the Dogcatcher: Is it Racist to Dislike a Dachshund?" *National Review*, March 10, 1999.

20. J. Phillips, "Toward an Explanation of Racial Variations in Top–Level Sports Participation," 51.

21. Laurel R. Davis, "The Articulation of Difference: White Preoccupation With the Question of Racially Linked Genetic Differences Among Athletes," *Sociology of Sport Journal* 7 (1990), 179–187.

22. Jere Longman, "Black Swimmers Making a Bid for the Olympics," *New York Times*, March 10, 1996, C22.

23. For a sampling, see M. Cunningham, "Blacks in Competitive Swimming," *Swimming Technique* 9, January 1973, 107–108; and A. L. de Garay, L. Levine, and J.E.L. Carter, *Genetic and Anthropological Studies of Olympic Athletes* (New York: Academic Press), 1974.

24. Karen Rosen, "Long on Talent," *Atlanta Journal–Constitution*, October 6, 1995.

25. See J. E. L. Carter (ed.), *Physical Structure of Olympic Athletes, Part I: The Montreal Olympic Games Anthropological Project* (Basel, Switzerland: S. Karger, 1982); P. B. Eveleth and J. M. Tanner, *Worldwide Variation in Human Growth* second edition (Cambridge: Cambridge University, 1990); R. Martin and K. Saller, *Lehrbuch der Anthropologie II*, (Stuttgart: Fischer, 1959); John H. Himes, "Racial Variation in Physique and Body Composition," *Canadian Journal of Sports Science*, 13 (1988), 117–126; Albert R. Behnke, *Evaluation and Regulation of Body Build and Composition* (Englewood Cliffs: Prentice Hall: 1974), 359–386; K. I. Hirata and K. Kaku, *The Evaluating Method of Physique and Physical Fitness and its Practical Application*, Gifu City (Japan: Hirata Institute of Health, 1968); and K. I. Hirata,

Selection of Olympic Champions Vols. I and II (Toyota, Japan: Chukyo University, 1979).

26. Murray Chase, "A New Baseball Strategy: Latin-American Bargains," *New York Times*, March 22, 1998, 1.

27. Mark Adams, "Sons and Lavas," *Gentlemen's Quarterly*, September 1999, 445.

28. Peter Severance, "The Legend of the Tarahumara," *Runner's World*, December 1993, 74–80.

29. John Manners e-mail to author, May 1999; and Manners, *The Running Tribe* (New York: Praeger, 2000).

30. Manners e-mail, June 1999.

31. Theresa Overfield, *Biologic Variation in Health and Illness* second ed. (Boca Raton: CRC, 1995), 1–2.

32. Barry Bogin, "Letter to the Editor," and C. Bouchard, A. S. Leon, D. C. Rao, J. S. Skinner, and J. H. Wilmore, "Response," *American Journal of Human Biology* 10 (1988), 279–280.

33. Raj Bhopal, "Is Research into Ethnicity and Health Racist, Unsound, or Important Science?" *British Medical Journal* 314, June 14, 1997, 1751.

34. For a discussion of the bio-cultural aspects of race and disease, see Matt Cartmill, "The Status of the Race Concept in Physical Anthropology," *American Anthropologist* 100, September 1988, 651–660; and Ranajit Chakraborty, Ranjan Deka, and Robert Ferrell, "Letter to the Editor: Reply to Baer," *American Journal of Human Genetics* 53 (1993), 531.

35. Michael Waldholz, "Gene That Causes a Form of Deafness is Discovered in 20-Year Study of Family," *Wall Street Journal*, November 14, 1997.

36. Kangpu Xu et al., "First Unaffected Pregnancy Using Preimplantation Genetic Diagnosis for Sickle Cell Anemia," *Journal of the American Medical Association* 281, May 12, 1999, 1701–1706; Thomas H. Maugh II, "In Vitro Technique Averts Family's Sickle Cell Risk," *Los Angeles Times*, May 12, 1999, A1, A12.

37. C. Bouchard et. al., "Response," 280.

38. Owen Anderson, "What Research Tells Us About African Runners: Are They Really Genetically Gifted?" *Running Research* 11 (October 1995), 1, 4–7.

39. Jonathan Marks e-mail to the author, January 29, 1999.

40. Quoted in Shermer, 171.

41. Bengt Saltin interview December 1995.

42. N. Behera and V. Nanjundiah, "An Investigation into the Role of Phenotypic Plasticity in Evolution," *Journal of Theoretical Biology* 172 (1995), 225–234.

43. Robert Malina interview with Tom Brokaw, *Black Athletes: Fact and Fiction–Live Forum*, April 25, 1989.

21. THE SUPERIORITY OF WHITE FEMALE ATHLETES

1. Michael D. Davis, *Black American Women in Olympic Track-and-Field* (Jefferson, N.C.: McFarland and Company, 1992), 158.

2. Linda D. Williams, "Sportswomen in Black and White," in Pamela J. Cree-

don (ed.), *Women, Media and Sport: Challenging Gender Values* (Thousand Oaks: Sage Publications, 1994), 49–51.

3. Ashe, *A Hard Road to Glory: Basketball*, 75.
4. William C. Rhoden, "A Fruitful Past, But a Shaky Future" *Ebony* (1977), 32.
5. Cindy Himes Gissendanner, "African American Women and Competitive Sport, 1920–1960," in Susan Birrell and Cheryl L. Cole (eds.), *Women, Sport, and Culture*, (Champaign, Ill.: Human Kinetics, 1994), 85.
6. Quoted in Selena Roberts, "Williams Comes of Age, Emphatically," *New York Times*, August 31, 1997, 31.
7. Quoted in Susan K. Cahn, *Coming On Strong: Gender and Sexuality in Twentieth–Century Women's Sports* (New York: The Free Press, 1994), 114–115.
8. Ibid., 115–116.
9. Ibid.
10. Ibid., 118.
11. Nolan Thaxton, "A Documentary Analysis of Competitive Track-and-Field for Women at Tuskegee Institute and Tennessee State University," Ph.d. Dissertation, Springfield College, Springfield, Mass., 1970.
12. Quoted in Sam McManis, *Knight-Ridder Newspapers*, July 16, 1996.
13. Quoted in Paul Newberry, "Alice Coachman: First Black Woman to Win Olympic Gold," *Associated Press Newswire*, June 1, 1996.
14. Mechikoff, 118–119.
15. Cahn, 117.
16. Quoted in Davis, *Black American Women in Olympic Track-and-Field*, 49.
17. Mechikoff, 120.
18. Cindy Himes Gissendanner, "African American Women Olympians: The Impact of Race, Gender, and Class Ideologies, 1932–1968," *Research Quarterly for Exercise and Sport* (June 1996), 172–182.
19. Earl Smith, "Hope Via Basketball: The Ticket Out of the Ghetto?" *Journal of Sport and Social Issues* 19, 3, August 1995, 313.
20. Davis, *Black American Women in Olympic Track-and-Field*, 110–111.
21. Ibid., xvii.
22. "Girl on the Run," *Newsweek*, February 6, 1961, 54.
23. Davis, *Black American Women in Olympic Track-and-Field*, xiii.
24. "The Fastest Female," *Time*, September 19, 1960, 74.
25. Ibid., 143–149.

22. EAST GERMANY'S SPORTS MACHINE

1. "Fastest Women in the World," *Ebony*, June 1955, 67.
2. Davis, 148.
3. "The Gender Unbenders," *Economist*, February 1, 1992, 95.
4. Cashmore, 127.
5. Steve Sailer, "Track and Battlefield," *National Review* 49, December 31, 1997, 44.
6. Quoted in Davis, *Black American Women in Olympic Track-and-Field*, 148.
7. Greg Steinmetz, "An Old Race Opens Some New Wounds: East German Doping Prods U.S. Marathon Runner to Seek a 1976 Bronze," *Wall Street Journal*, October 21, 1998, A1.

8. Quoted in Michael Janofsky, "Born of Need for Recognition," *New York Times*, April 15, 1990, C4.
9. For more details of the first decades of the GDR system, see Doug Gilbert, *The Miracle Machine* (New York: Coward, McCann, and Geoghegan, 1980).
10. Alan Cowell, "Little Blue Pills and a Lot of Gold," *New York Times*, April 5, 1998, S29.
11. Both quoted in Andrew Phillips, "A Haunted Past," *Maclean's*, July 27, 1992, 29.
12. Gilbert, 65.
13. Quoted in Jeff Schultz, "Freedom Had Downside for German Athletes," *Atlanta-Journal Constitution*, www.atlantagames.com.
14. Linda Robertson, "Duped and Doped," *The Herald* (Jacksonville, Fla.), August 2, 1998, C2.
15. Steinmetz, A10.
16. Karen Helmstaedt, "Abnormal Evolution: Drug Use Has Shaped Women's Events," *Swim Canada Magazine*, 1996, www.swimnews.com.
17. Quoted in Robertson, C1.
18. Quoted in Alan Freeman, "East Germans Dumped Drugs into River After Montreal Olympics," *Toronto Globe and Mail*, November 9, 1996.
19. Steven Dickman, "East Germany: Science in the Disservice of the State," *Science* 254, October 4, 1991, 26–27.
20. Quoted in Schultz.
21. Quoted in Robertson, C2.
22. Quoted in Bill Pennington and Jack Curry, "Andro Hangs in the Balance," *New York Times*, July 11, 1999, S26.
23. Quoted in Robertson, C2.
24. Quoted in Cowell.
25. Pat Connolly, "Removing the Essence of Man for Women's Athletics," *New York Times*, October 2, 1994, 13.
26. Quoted in Cowell.
27. Robertson, C1, C2.
28. Sailer, "Track and Battlefield," 44
29. John C. Phillips, *Sociology of Sport* (Needham, Masssachusetts: Allyn and Bacon, 1993), 154–155.

23. THE RENAISSANCE
OF THE BLACK FEMALE ATHLETE

1. B. J. Whipp and S. A. Ward, "Will Women Soon Outrun Men?" *Nature* 355 (1992), 25.
2. Quoted in Mary Duffy, "Frailty Myth Haunts Women in Sports," *New York Times*, April 27, 1999.
3. Analysis by Steve Sailer, with contributions from Stephen Seiler, "The Fall and Rise of the 'Gender Gap in World Class Running,'" December 12, 1996, http://www.isteve.com.
4. For a complete discussion of male/female biological differences in health and illness, see Overfield.
5. Quoted in "Swimmers Reveal Doping Tactics," *Dispatch Online*, http://www.dispatch.co.za.

6. Neil Admur, "The Drug-Use Genie is Out of the Vial," *New York Times*, January 11, 1998, C26.
7. Robertson, C2.
8. Schultz.
9. "Researcher says East German Doping Methods Still Popular," *Associated Press Newswire*, September 17, 1997.
10. Ibid.
11. Adrianne Blue, *Grace Under Pressure: The Emergence of Women in Sports* (London: Sidgwick and Jackson, 1987), 82.
12. Cashmore, 144.
13. Randy Harvey, "In This Tragic End to the Life of an Olympic Gold Medalist and Beloved Wife, There May Be a Message as Yet Untold," *Los Angeles Times*, September 22, 1998, C11.
14. Quoted in ibid.
15. "Germany Hit by Sports Drug Scandal," *Reuters Newswire*, September 21, 1997.
16. Quoted in D. Patrick, "Athletes Left Mark on Sports, Culture."
17. Kirk Johnson, "Don't Blink, Next Sprinting Star is Within View," *New York Times*, July 19, 1998, A1.
18. John Brant, "Sights Set on Sydney," *Runner's World*, September 1998, 88.
19. Quoted in D. Patrick, "Bound for History," *USA Today*, August 5, 1999, 3E.
20. Quoted in J. Longman, "Pippig Suspended After Failing Drug Test," *New York Times*, October 9, 1998, C22; "Pippig Suspension for Drugs Upheld," *Associated Press*, July 16, 1999, 55.
21. Quoted in J. Longman, "Victory Also Cultural", *New York Times*, April 17, 1995, B9.
22. Quoted in ibid.
23. Quoted in Gordon Bakoulis, "Coming Into Her Own," *Running*, October, 1997, 18–23.
24. W. C. Rhoden, "The Game is Now Bigger For Women," *New York Times*, December 11, 1994, 32

24. A GENTEEL WAY TO SAY "NIGGER?"

1. Diamond, *The Third Chimpanzee*, 111.
2. John Feinstein, "This is a Player," *New York Times Magazine*, February 22, 1998, 40.
3. Vincent Sarich interview, January 28, 1997.
4. Marks, 237.
5. For a recent polemic, see Patrick B. Miller, "Anatomy of Scientific Racism: Racialist Responses to Black Athletic Achievement," *Journal of Sport History* 25 (1998), 119–151.
6. Wiley.
7. Carole. A. Oglesby (ed.), *Black Women in Sports* (Reston, Va.: American Alliance for Health, Physical Education, Recreation and Dance, 1981), 11.
8. Richard Lapchick, "Pseudo-Scientific Prattle About Athletes," *New York Times*, April 29, 1989, 19.
9. Kenan Malik, *The Meaning of Race: Race, History and Culture in Western Society* (New York: New York University, 1996).

10. Melvin Konner, "Darwin's Truth, Jefferson's Vision: Sociobiology and the Politics of Human Nature," *American Prospect*, July–August 1999.
11. See Majors and Billson; and Gary A. Sailes, "Sport Socialization Comparisons Among Black and White Adult Male Athletes and Nonathletes." Ph.d. dissertation, University of Minnesota, 1984.
12. Quoted in Patrick Miller, "To 'Bring the Race Along Rapidly': Sport, Student Culture, and Educational Mission at Historically Black Colleges During the Interwar Years," *History of Education Quarterly* 35 (1995), 128.
13. Harry Edwards, "The Black Athletes: 20th-Century Gladiators for White America," *Psychology Today* 7, November 1973, 44.
14. Ibid., 45.
15. Harry Edwards, *The Revolt of the Black Athlete* (New York: Free Press, 1970), 20.
16. Henry Louis Gates, Jr., "Delusions of Grandeur," *Sports Illustrated*, August 19, 1991, 78.
17. Hoberman, xiii.
18. Hoberman, 77.
19. See Kenneth Shropshire and Earl Smith, "The Tarzan Syndrome: John Hoberman and His Quarrels with African American Athletes and Intellectuals," *Journal of Sport and Social Issues* 22, February 1998, 103–112.
20. For Hoberman's response, see "Darwin's Athletes and Its Critics: A Response to Ishmael Reed," *The Black Family World Today*, http://www.tbwt.com.
21. Malcolm Gladwell, "The Sports Taboo," *New Yorker*, May 19, 1997, 51
22. Interview with Vincent Sarich, May, 1999.
23. J. Phillips, *Sociology of Sport*, 151, 169.
24. Y. Moses and C. Mukhopadhyay, "Reestablishing 'Race' in Anthropological Discourse," *American Anthropologist* 99 (September 1997), 521.
25. NASSS convention attended by author, Las Vegas, November 1998.
26. Interview with Earl Smith, June 1999.

INDEX

Aaron, Hank, 24
Abbate, Ernesto, 90
Abbott, Jessie, 302
Abbott, Major Cleveland, 301
Abdul-Jabbar, Kareem, 27, 226
Adams, Will, 140
Aerobic activity, 256, 257–259
Africa
  genetic variability in, 115–116
  racial classification in, 100, 113–116
  See also East African athletes; West African athletes
African Americans
  Berlin Olympic Games and, 183–187
  "breeder" theory of, 71–73, 263
  domination of sprint events by, 34–35, 174–176, 185
  early sports participation by, 139–145
  female athletes as, 297, 300–304, 322–328
  Mexico City Olympics protest by, 225–230
  professional sports ban on, 145–150
  racial mixing among, 98–99
  See also Blacks
African Queen, The (film), 217
Afrocentrism, 77–78
Albritton, David, 184
Ali, Muhammad, 9, 157, 223, 226, 334
Allen, Bernie, 24
Allison, Bob, 23–24
Amateur Athletic Union, 181, 187
Ambrose, Stanley, 110–111
American Anthropological Association, 96, 220, 221, 338
American Anthropologist (journal), 338
American Enterprise Institute, 245
American Eugenics Society, 168
American Journal of Human Biology, 286
American Samoa, 284
America's Cup yacht race, 25
Amsterdam News, 176, 181, 190
Anaerobic activity, 256, 257

Analysis of Covariance (ANCOVA), 252
Analytic intelligence, 242–243
Anatomy
  athletic ability and, 176–178, 246–249, 251–253, 256–261
  genetic traits and, 267–271
  musculature and, 253–257
  racial differences in, 176–178, 246–261, 268–269, 283–284
Anatomy and Physiology of the Nervous System in General, and of the Brain in Particular, The (Gall), 122
Anderson, Madame, 149
Anderson, Owen, 272, 288
Anglocentric hypothesis, 275
Anson, Adrian "Cap," 147
Anthropology, 123, 166, 216, 218–222, 338–339
Anti-semitism, 132, 133–134
Aouita, Said, 63
Ariel, Gideon, 3
Arrendel, Juana, 322
Aryan ideal, 133, 158, 179–180, 195
Ashe, Arthur, Jr., 80, 138, 160, 187, 194, 224, 229
Ashford, Evelyn, 319–320
Asia
  running performance of athletes from, 34
  sports suited for athletes from, 21, 283–284
Assimilationism, 134
Athletic ability
  anatomical characteristics and, 176–178, 246–249, 251–253, 256–261, 268–269
  black female athletes and, 298, 300–304, 319–321, 322–328
  drug doping and improvement of, 310–316, 319, 320, 322–323
  environmental factors and, 274–278, 337–338
  genetics and, 74, 76–80, 236–237, 264, 267–271, 288–289, 338

Athletic ability *(cont.)*
  intelligence and, 75–76, 139, 237,
    243, 245, 336–339
  racism based on, 230–231, 236–237,
    334–336
  relaxation ability and, 265–266
  women and, 297–300, 317–318,
    322–328
  See also Sports
Atlanta Journal-Constitution, 283
Atlantic Monthly, 236
Attwood, Paul Jason, 28

Babington, John, 322
Baer, Max, 192
Bailey, Donovan, 34, 337
Baillet-Latour, Henri, 182
Baker, Henry, 145
Baldwin, James, 289
Baltimore Afro-American, 182
Banks, Ernie, 24
Banks, Ted, 54
Bannister, Sir Roger, 11–13
Baptiste, Sheridon, 27
Barr Sex Test, 305
Barry, Jon, 20
Barry, Rick, 20
Baseball
  banning of black players from,
    147–148
  black players in, 21–25, 145–148
  historical origins of, 139
  position stereotypes in, 278–279
  racial proportion of athletes in, 19,
    21, 284
  reintegration of, 210
Basketball
  black domination in, 276
  integration of, 210–211, 223
  Jewish prominence in, 198–203
  racial proportion of athletes in,
    19–20
  women's participation in, 327–328
Baumann, Dieter, 41
Baumann, Larry, 209
Baur, Erwin, 179
Bealle, Morris, 209
Beamon, Bob, 229
Bean, Robert Bennett, 129, 162–163
Beddoe, John, 124
Behrendt, Kerstin, 319
Bell, Gus, 24
Bell, James "Cool Papa," 173

Bell Curve, The (Herrnstein and Mur-
    ray), 8, 236, 238–239, 241
ben-Jochannan, Yosef A.A., 77
Berendonk, Brigitte, 310, 312
Berlin Olympics, 183–187
Biasone, Danny, 212
Bicycling, 149
Bikila, Abebe, 30
Binet, Alfred, 127, 163–164
Biometrics, 122
Biondi, Matt, 282
Bismarck, Otto von, 131–132
Black, Edwin "Hughie," 200
Black Athletes: Fact and Fiction (TV doc-
    umentary), 6–7
Blackburn, Jack, 189
Blacks
  anatomical characteristics of,
    246–261, 268–269
  early sports participation by, 139–145
  female athletes as, 297, 300–304,
    322–328
  infirmity stereotype of, 152–154
  intelligence studies on, 165–167,
    170–171, 234–236, 238–239
  pseudo-scientific research on,
    123–125, 176–178
  racism based on athleticism of,
    230–231, 334–336
  relaxation studies of, 265–266
  Social Darwinism and, 127–130
  See also African Americans
Black Sports magazine, 142
Blakey, Michael, 263
Black Panthers, 218, 225
Blassingame, John, 145
Blumenbach, Johann Friedrich, 101,
    102
Boas, Franz, 214
Bobsledding, 25–28
Bogin, Barry, 286
Bogues, Mugsy, 20
Boit, Mike, 54, 58
Boston, Ralph, 227, 229
Boston Globe, 71
Boston Marathon, 38–39, 46–47
Botkin, B. A., 153
Bouchard, Claude, 79, 254, 261, 267,
    286
Bouchard, Thomas, 241–242
Boxing, 140, 151, 154–160, 188–197
Brace, C. Loring, 100
Braddock, James, 191, 193

Brain
  cranial size and, 123–124, 128–129,
    220
  pseudo-scientific studies of, 122–123,
    133
Brantly, Keith, 38
Brasher, Chris, 11
Brauer, Gunter, 88
Breeding
  eugenics movement and, 166,
    168–169, 170–171
  racial interbreeding, 98–99, 115
Breuer, Grit, 322
British Association for the Advance-
    ment of Science, 11, 119
Broca, Paul, 123
Brock, Lou, 9
Brokaw, Tom, 6, 7
Brooks, Scott, 20
Brown, H. Rap, 226–227
Brown, Jim, 210, 226
Brown, Linda, 211
Brown, Paul, 210
Brown, Ron, 7
Brown, Walter, 211
Brown v. Board of Education, 212, 221,
    240
Brundage, Avery, 181, 182–183, 227
Buffon, George Louis Leclerc de,
    101–102
Bunnin, Mockie, 200
Burfoot, Amby, 29–30
Burns, Tommy, 155–156
Burt, W. J., 152
Burundi, 36

Cable, Ted, 142
Campanella, Roy, 234
Campanis, Al, 232–234
Camper, Petrus, 121
Canine stereotypes, 280–281
Cann, Rebecca, 89–90
Caras, Roger, 280
Carlos, John, 225, 228–229
Carmichael, Stokely, 218, 227
Carnegie, Andrew, 162
Carnera, Primo, 188, 190
Carter, Lindsay, 269
Carto, Willis, 217
Cartwright, Samuel, 152
Casey, Bernie, 72
Cashmore, Ellis, 318
Caspari, Rachel, 82, 88

Cater, Elmer, 174
Cavalli-Sforza, Luca, 108
Cavanagh, Peter, 266
Chakraborty, Ranajit, 107
Chamberlain, Houston Stewart, 133
Chamberlain, Wilt, 223
*Championship Technique in Track and
    Field* (Cromwell), 178
Chastain, Brandi, 295
Chataway, Chris, 11
Chebet, Joseph, 61
Chemweno, Mary, 45
Chepyator, Rose, 58
Cheruiyot, Rose, 58
Chicago Defender, 157, 159, 175
Christianity, 83, 119–120
Christie, Linford, 322
Churro, Victoriano, 284
Circumcision ritual, 50
Civil Rights Act of 1875, 147
Civil rights movement, 218, 225
Cleaver, Eldridge, 333
Cleveland Gazette, 181–182
Cleveland Plain Dealer, 210
Clitoral extirpation, 50
Coachman, Alice, 301–302
Cobb, William Montague, 73, 176–178,
    247
Coe, Sebastian, 31, 37, 224
Coleman, Henry, 140
Colored Intercollegiate Athletic Associa-
    tion, 144
Columbus, Christopher, 100
Coming on Strong (Kahn), 300
Complete Dog Book (American Kennel
    Club), 280
Cool Runnings (film), 26
Coon, Carleton S., 219, 231, 266
Cooper, Chuck, 211
Copper Canyon, 284
Corum, Bill, 192–193
Costill, David, 258
Couch, Tom, 277
Craniology, 121, 122–125
Creationism, 83
Creative intelligence, 243
Crisis magazine, 157, 191, 192
Cro-Magnons, 94
Cromwell, Dean, 178, 265
Crooks, Garth, 12
Crookshank, Francis, 178
Cross-country skiing, 259–261
Cruz, Joaquim Carvalho, 36

Culpepper, Daunte, 277
Cureton, Thomas, 231
Curley, Jack, 159
Curtin, Philip, 263
Cuvier, Georges, 122

Dabrow, Dave, 199
Danney, Ian, 27
Darwin, Charles, 106, 117–119, 123,
    126, 131
Darwin's Athletes (Hoberman), 335–336
Davenport, Charles, 162, 163, 167, 168
Davies, Michaela, 244
Davis, Laurel, 77, 282
Davis, Michael, 304
Declaration of Independence, 212
Deford, Frank, 5
Denver Post, 6
Desailly, Marcel, 21
*Descent of Man and Selection in Rela-
    tion to Sex, The* (Darwin), 123, 128
Dew, Thomas, 263
Diamond, Jared, 96, 104, 105, 331
Didrikson, Babe, 299
Digel, Helmut, 309
DiRienzo, Anna, 111
Discover magazine, 104
Discrimination
    banning of blacks from professional
        sports, 145–150
    position stacking in football, 275–277
    See also Prejudice; Racism
Disease genetics, 287–288
Diving, 282–283
Dixon, Roland B., 219
DNA research, 88–90
Dobzhansky, Theodosius, 84, 86, 222
Dodds, Joe, 250, 251
Dog stereotypes, 280–281
Doherty, W. S., 247
Dominican Republic, 22, 284
Doping Documents (Berendonk), 310
Douglas, Stephen, 153
Douglass, Frederick, 140, 263
Dowell, Stan, 265
Draper, Wickliffe, 240, 241
Drechsler, Heike, 319, 320
Drew, Howard Porter, 142–143, 265
Drug doping
    athletes' personal use of, 320–322
    East Germany's use of, 310–316,
        319
    negative after-effects of, 319

Soviet bloc experimentation with,
    306–307
D'souza, Dinesh, 245
Dubois, Eugène, 84
Du Bois, W. E. B., 154, 157, 171, 334
Duke, David, 242
Dungy, Tony, 276
Dutko, Paul H., 207

Early, Gerald, 196
East African athletes
    anatomical characteristics of,
        259–261, 269
    reasons for success of, 47–50
    running accomplishments of, 29,
        30–31, 36–39, 325–326
East Germany
    development of sports programs in,
        308–310
    drug doping of athletes in, 310–316
    women athletes from, 306, 307–316
    See also Germany
Ebony magazine, 228, 275, 303, 305
Edwards, Harry, 3, 7, 18, 96, 98, 225,
    226, 228, 230, 237, 273, 334–335
Edwards, Harry F.V., 178
Edwards, Willis, 71
Egalitarianism, 212–213
Eldredge, Niles, 91
Eliot, Charles, 168
Ellis, Havelock, 168
Emerge magazine, 7
Emile (Rousseau), 75
Emotional intelligence (EQ), 243, 244
Encyclopedia Britannica, 128
Encyclopedia of Intelligence (Sternberg),
    242
Ender, Kornelia, 311
Endurance running
    black women's domination of,
        325–326
    scientific studies on, 257–259
    training and, 255–256
    See also Marathon running; Running
England, 21, 113
Enquiries into Human Faculty (Galton),
    128
Environmental factors
    athletic ability and, 274–278,
        337–338
    genetics influenced by, 289–290
    race and, 214–215, 272–274
    sports stereotypes and, 278–279

Ereng, Paul, 63
Erving, Julius, 9
Essay on the Inequality of Races (Gob-
    ineau), 125
Ethiopia, 30, 325
Ethnic groups, 108, 215, 286
Eugenics, 128, 129–130
    American eugenics movement,
        161–163, 167–169, 240–241
    intelligence testing and, 163–167
    Nazi Germany's involvement with,
        179–180, 207–208
    progressive, 168–169
    world racism and, 169–171
Eurocentrism, 103
Evans, Lee, 72, 227, 229
Eve theory of evolution, 82, 89–90, 91
Evolution, 81–95
    athletic ability and, 267
    convergence of theories of, 93–95
    Coon's theories of, 219–222
    Darwin's theories of, 117–120, 123,
        126, 130, 131
    diagram of human family tree, 85
    DNA research and, 88–90
    history of theories about, 83–88
    lineage theories of, 90–92
    map of human migration routes, 87
    mathematical study of, 122
    opposition to theories of, 119–120,
        132–133
    racial characteristics and, 116
    theoretical overview of, 81–83
Evolutionary Biology (journal), 104
Ewald, Manfred, 308
Eye color, 264

Faggs, Mae, 304
Feeblemindedness, 164
Feller, Bob, 210
Female athletes. *See* Women
Female circumcision, 50, 59
Fenn, Jim, 209
Fischer, Eugen, 179
Fisher, Ronald A., 168, 216
Fitzpatrick, Frank, 223
Flutie, Doug, 277
Football
    early black participation in, 143–144
    position discrimination in, 275–277
    racial proportion of athletes in, 19,
        284
    reintegration of, 209–210, 223

Forel, August, 133
48 Minutes (Ryan and Pluto), 20
Fossil evidence, 84, 86, 88, 91, 93,
    220–221
*Foundations of the Nineteenth Century,
    The* (Chamberlain), 133
Fowler, Bud, 146
France, 20–21
Francis, Peter, 252
Franke, Werner, 310, 315, 319, 321
Frankenburg, William, 250–251
Freeman, Ron, 229
Friedman, Max, 202
Furlong, William Barry, 305

Gaines, Bill, 227
Galápagos Islands, 117, 118
Gall, Franz Joseph, 122
Gallico, Paul, 190, 203
Galton, Sir Francis, 126–128
Gammoudi, Mohamed, 52
Gardner, Howard, 243
Garrett, Henry, 217, 241
Garrison, "Snapper," 138
Gates, Henry Louis, Jr., 335
Gates, William "Pop," 202, 211
Gault, Willie, 26
Geber, Marcelle, 250
Gebrselassie, Halle, 37, 38
Genetics
    athletic ability and, 74, 76–80, 236–237,
        264, 267–271, 288–289, 338
    disease studies related to, 287–288
    environmental influences on, 289–290
    eugenics movement and, 161–171
    geography and, 108, 109, 112
    intelligence and, 75–76, 235–236
    interbreeding and, 98–99, 115
    population clusters and, 108, 109,
        112, 259
    race and, 8, 18, 73–74, 80, 103–106,
        263–271, 338–339
    relaxation ability and, 264–266
Geography
    population groups and, 108, 109,
        112
    skin color and, 97–98
Germany
    anti-semitism in, 132, 133–134
    Berlin Olympics in, 183–187
    eugenics movement in, 130–131,
        179–180, 207–208
    nationalist fervor in, 131–132

racial hygiene movement in,
179–180, 207–208
See also East Germany
Gibson, Althea, 298
Gibson, Josh, 173
Gilliam, Jim, 234
Gladwell, Malcolm, 336
Gobineau, Joseph-Arthur, Count de, 125
Goddard, Henry, 164, 167
Goethe, Johann von, 130
Göhr, Marlies, 320
Goldman, Emma, 168
Goleman, Daniel, 243
Golf, 223
Gordon, Ed, 175
Gottlieb, Eddie, 200, 201
Gould, John, 117
Gould, Steven Jay, 82, 91, 101, 103,
238–239, 334
Gourdin, Ned, 174
Graff, Karlheinz, 321
Graham, Trevor, 324
Grant, Madison, 166–167
Gray, Johnny, 36
Green, Dennis, 277
Green, Pumpsie, 223
Greenridge, Ricardo, 27
Griffith, Darrell, 252
Griffith-Joyner, Florence, 320–321, 324
Gulcher, Jeffrey, 112
Gumbel, Bryant, 142
Gutsmuths, Johann Christoph
Friedrich, 75

Haeckel, Ernst, 131–132
Haldane, J. B. S., 168
Hannemann, Raik, 313
Hard Road to Glory, A (Ashe), 80, 194,
297
Hardy, Fred, 45, 54–56, 63, 64, 65
Harlan, John Marshall, II, 240
Harlem Globetrotters, 201–202, 203
Harpending, Henry, 92, 116
Harris, Eugene, 92
Harris, James, 275–276
Harvard Educational Review, 235
Hary, Armin, 34
Hatchell, Sylvia, 325
Hawkins, Connie, 9
Hawkins, Tommy, 231
Hayes, Rutherford B., 147
Heddy, Kathy, 311
Henderson, Edwin Bancroft, 196, 302
Henderson, Rickey, 9
Hensel, Frank, 319

Herbert, Bob, 5
Herder, Johann Gottfried von,
131
Hereditary Genius (Galton), 127
Hermann, Hans Georg, 310
Herodotus, 99
Herrnstein, Richard, 236, 238, 241
Hey, Jody, 92
Hill, Calvin, 72
Hill, Grant, 265, 337
Hill, Sonny, 198
Hilliard, Asa, 77
Himmler, Heinrich, 179
Hines, Garrett, 25–26
Hines, Jim, 229
Hingis, Martina, 298
Hinton, Charles, 140
Hirchborn, Fred, 150
*History and Geography of Human Genes,
The* (Cavalli-Sforza, Menozzi, and
Piazza), 108
Hitler, Adolf, 125, 175, 178–180,
183–187, 238
Hoberman, John, 77, 266, 335–336
Hockey, 223
Holder, Carl, 280
Holdsclaw, Chamique, 9-10, 295, 327
Hollis, Sir A. Claude, 49–50
Holman, Nat, 199, 202
Holmes, Samuel J., 170
Holocaust (World War II), 208
Holzman, William "Red," 202
Honecker, Erich, 308, 313
Hooton, Earnest A., 219
Hoover, J. Edgar, 225–226
Hoppner, Manfred, 309
Horse racing, 137–139
Horton, James, 263
Howard, Elston, 22
Hubbard, William DeHart, 174
Hudson, Marsha, 302
Human Genome Project, 108
Human Heredity (Baur, Fischer, and
Lenz), 179
Hunt, Edward E., Jr., 231
Hunt, Stanford, 152
Hunter, David, 79–80, 251
Hussein, Ibrahim, 38-39, 46, 66
Huxley, Sir Julian, 84, 168, 169
Huxley, Thomas, 119–120, 124–125
Hybridization, 93

Ice Age, 111
Iceland, 112
Identities (journal), 338

Idiot savant syndrome, 244
Ikangaa, Juma, 47
Immigrants
    basketball played by, 198–199
    restrictions placed on, 166–167
Infirmity stereotype, 152–154
Integration of sports, 223–225
    beginnings of, 141–145
    reintegration process, 209–212
    setbacks in, 147–150
Intelligence
    athletic ability and, 75–76, 139, 237,
        243, 245, 336–339
    cranial size and, 123–125, 129,
        220
    early tests of, 163–167
    genetic theory of, 162, 235–236
    measurability of, 237–242
    research on race and, 165–167,
        234–236, 238–239
    triarchic model of, 242–243
    types of, 242–245
Intelligence quotient (IQ), 165–166,
    234–236
Interbreeding, racial, 98–99, 115
International Olympic Committee
    (IOC), 182–183, 227
Ireland, 112–113
Iverson, Allen, 9, 74

Jackson, Bo, 9
Jackson, Peter, 246–247
Jackson, Reggie, 23–24
Jacob, John, 71
Jacobs, Mike, 193
Jahncke, Ernest Lee, 182
Jamaican bobsledding team, 26–27
James, Bill, 22–25
James, Larry, 229
Java Man, 84, 86
Jefferson, Thomas, 124
Jeffries, Jim, 155, 157
Jeffries, Leonard, 77
Jenkins, David, 320
Jensen, Arthur, 235, 240, 242, 244
Jews
    boycott of 1936 Berlin Olympic
        Games by, 180–183
    German racism against, 132,
        133–134, 179–183, 208
    race science and prejudice against,
        170–171
    racial classification of, 102, 109
    sports prominence of, 198–203
Jim Crow laws, 149

Jipcho, Ben, 53
Jockeys, 137–139
Johanson, Donald, 86
Johnson, Ben, 320, 321
Johnson, Brooks, 17–18, 76–77
Johnson, Cornelius, 184
Johnson, Jack, 151–152, 154–160, 189,
    196, 297
Johnson, Lyndon, 224
Johnson, Magic, 27
Johnson, Michael, 35
Jokl, Ernst, 271
Jones, Marion, 10, 295, 318, 323–325
Jones, Randy, 26
Jordan, Michael, 226, 243, 332, 334,
    337
Jumping ability, 252–253, 272
Jurgensen, Sonny, 277

Kagwe, John, 61
Kahn, Roger, 234
Kahn, Susan, 300
Kaiser Wilhelm Institute, 179, 180
Kalenjin people of Kenya, 47–50, 64,
    285–286
Kanana, Angelina, 326
Kane, Martin, 231, 236
Kapp, Joe, 277
Kaselman, Cy, 201
Keino, Kipchoge, 45, 50–56, 66, 76, 224
Kennedy, John F., 218
Kennedy, Robert, 224
Kenya, 43–67
    accomplishments of runners from,
        29, 31–32, 36–39, 50–54, 325–326
    anatomical advantages of runners
        from, 260–261
    Kalenjin people of, 47–50, 64,
        285–286
    reasons for athletic success of, 64–67,
        285–286, 289–290
    recruitment of runners from, 54–56
    resiliency of runners from, 62–64
    schooling of children in, 56–58
    training of runners in, 59–61
    women runners from, 58–59,
        325–326
Kibet, David, 45
Kidd, Kenneth, 115–116
Kind-Schneider, Petra, 319
King, Martin Luther, Jr., 218, 224, 226
King, Rodney, 8
King, William "Dolly," 211
Kinley, E. Albert, 176
Kipketer, Wilson, 38, 57, 60, 64

Kiprotich, Godfrey, 326
Kiptanui, Moses, 38, 45
Kitur, Joseph, 45
Klineberg, Otto, 170
Klobkowska, Eva, 305
Klotz, Herman "Red," 201
Knacke-Sommer, Christiane, 312
Knowles, Thelmo, 265
Koch, Marita, 320
Kolum, Limo, 54
Komen, Daniel, 36–38
Konga, Pauline, 59
Koppel, Ted, 233–234
Kosgei, Mike, 60, 61
Koskei, Kipsubai, 45
Krabbe, Katrin, 309, 322
Kratochvilova, Jarmila, 318
Krieger, Heidi, 309, 314–315
Kristiansen, Ingrid, 325, 326
Ku Klux Klan, 160, 189, 213, 241

Laettner, Christian, 272
Lamarck, Chevalier de, 118
Lancet, The (journal), 236
Landy, John, 11
Lang, Jane, 319
Lapchick, Richard, 77, 333
Latino athletes, 22, 278–279, 284
Laughlin, Harry H., 240
Lautman, Louis "Inky," 201
Law of compensation, 154
Leakey, Richard, 43, 221
Lemba people, 109
Lenz, Fritz, 179, 180, 216
Lewis, Carl, 4, 246
Lewis, Theophilus, 190–191
Lewis, William Henry, 143
Lewontin, Richard, 104, 105–106, 334
Lincoln, Abraham, 153
Linnaeus, Carolus, 100–101
Litwack, Harry, 199, 201
Lombardi, Vince, 246
London, Jack, 156
Long, Carl "Luz," 185
Lore of Running (Noakes), 257
Loroupe, Tegla, 59, 295, 325–326
Los Angeles Times, 53, 158, 230
Losson, Carl, 130
Louis, Joe, 188–197, 230, 334
Lowry, Paul, 175

Machiavellian intelligence hypothesis, 244
Mackey, Raleigh "Biz," 173

Maher, Charles, 230, 231
Mahon, Jack, 194
Mahoney, Jerimiah, 182
Mai, Volker, 310
Major League Baseball
   banning of black players from, 147–148
   reintegration of, 210
   See also Baseball
Malik, Kenan, 333
Malina, Robert, 250, 266, 270, 271, 291
Malthus, Thomas, 117, 118
Mandela, Nelson, 50
Mankind Quarterly, The, 241, 242
Manners, John, 40, 47, 49, 62, 285–286
*Man's Most Dangerous Myth: The Fallacy
   of Race* (Montagu), 215
Marathon running
   anatomical characteristics and, 258–259
   endurance studies on, 257–259
   Kenyan domination in, 38–39, 46–47, 326
   women athletes in, 325–326
   See also Endurance running; Running
Margolis, Benjamin, 278–279
Markle, Allen, 264
Marks, Jonathan, 101, 288–289, 332
Marshall, Napoleon Bonaparte, 142
Marteau, Theresa, 12
Martin, Chris, 283
Matz, Birgit Hekie, 319
Mayer, Harry H., 171
Mayer, John, 243
Mayr, Ernest, 84, 86
McFadden, Ken, 78
McGwire, Mark, 313
McNabb, Donovan, 277
McNown, Cade, 277
Mein Kampf (Hilter), 179, 238
Meissner, Renate, 311
Mendel, Gregor, 161–162
Mengele, Josef, 208
Mennea, Pietro, 34–35
"Mental age" concept, 164
Mental illness, 164
Merriman, John, 166
Metcalfe, Ralph, 175, 185
Metheny, Eleanor, 247–248
Mexican runners, 32, 284
   See also Latino athletes
Mexico City Olympics
   black power protest at, 228–230

Kenyan participation in, 52–54
threatened boycott of, 7, 225–228
Middle-distance running events, 35–38
Mikan, George, 211
Military service, 153
Miller, Johnny, 189
Miller, Kelly, 171
Mind of Primitive Man, The (Boas), 214
Mintz, Sidney, 221
Mitchell, Bobby, 223
Mitchell, Dennis, 322
Mitochondrial DNA (mtDNA), 89–90,
91, 94
Molineaux, Thomas, 140
Monogenism, 101, 131
Montagu, Ashley, 213, 214–215, 221
Montana, Joe, 277
Morceli, Noureddine, 37
Morgan, Joe, 246
Morgan, Lewis Henry, 214
Morton, Samuel George, 123–124
Moses, Edwin, 26
Moses, Yolanda, 338
Moss, Randy, 9
Motley, Marion, 210
Muindi, Alfonce, 29
Muir, Donald E., 333
Mukhopadyay, Carol, 338
Muller, Hermann J., 168, 169, 216
Multiple intelligences, 243–245
Murphy, Isaac, 137–139
Murphy, Mike, 143
Murray, Charles, 238, 241
Murray, Jim, 53
Musberger, Brent, 229
Muscle & Fitness magazine, 253
Muscle anatomy, 253–256
Muscular dystrophy, 254
Mwanzi, Henry, 47
My Awakening (Duke), 242
Myburgh, Kathy, 79, 259

Nairobi, Kenya, 44
Namath, Joe, 9
Nandi tribe, 49, 285
Narrative (Douglass), 263
National Association for the Advance-
ment of Colored People (NAACP),
171, 181
National Basketball Association
integration of, 210–211, 223
racial proportion of athletes in, 19,
20
See also Basketball

National Football League
racial proportion of athletes in, 19,
284
reintegration of, 209–210, 223
See also Football
National Hockey League, 223
Nationalism, 130–134, 169
National Science Foundation, 220
Natural selection, 118
Nature (journal), 78, 317
Nature-nurture debate, 214–215
Nazis, 132, 180, 213, 240
Ndereba, Catherine, 326
Negro National League, 188
Nei, Masatoshi, 106
Nelson, Jack, 311
Nesty, Anthony, 282
Netherlands, 20
Newcombe, Don, 233
Newman, Charlie, 200
Newsday, 6
Newsweek, 90, 304
New York Athletic Club, 227
New York Daily News, 190, 194, 203
New Yorker, The, 336
New York Times, 21, 176, 184, 221, 228,
247, 333
Ngeny, Noah, 31
Ngugi, John, 62
Nicklaus, Jack, 5–6
Nietzsche, Friedrich, 4
Nigeria, 20
Nightline (TV program), 232–234
Noakes, Timothy, 257–258, 268
Nobles, Wade, 77
Nordwig, Wolfgang, 311
Norfolk Journal and Guide, 176
Norman, Peter, 229
North, Kathryn, 255
North Africa, 31–32, 36
North American Society for the Sociol-
ogy of Sport, 339
Northern League, 241
Nuremberg Laws, 182, 183
Nyangincha, Sammy, 58

Oakland Tribune, 274
O'Connell, Colm, 57–58, 59, 63, 64, 66
Oettel, Michael, 313
Oglesby, Carole, 333
O'Leary, Daniel, 150
Olm, Kerstin, 319
Olympic Games
black power protest at, 228–230

bobsledding competition at, 25–28
threatened boycotts of, 7, 180–183,
   225–228
women's participation in, 299
Olympic Project for Human Rights, 226
Ondeiki, Lisa, 326
*On the Origin of Species by Means of
   Natural Selection* (Darwin), 119
O'Ree, Willie, 223
Organic evolution, 131
Origin of Races, The (Coon), 219
Osborn, Frederick, 169
Osborn, Henry Fairfield, 166
Osoro, Ondoro, 38, 60
Ostler, Scott, 18
Ottey, Merlene, 322
Ottley, Roi, 176
Out-of-Africa theory, 90–92, 94
Overfield, Theresa, 286
Owens, Jesse, 172–173, 175–177,
   184–187, 228, 230, 247

Paige, Leroy "Satchel," 173
Passing of a Great Race, The (Grant), 166
Passon, Harry "Chicky," 200
Patkin, Max, 202
Pearson, Karl, 130
Pearson, Roger, 241
Pegler, Westbrook, 196
Pegram, William, 150
Peking Man, 86
Péron, François, 103
Phenotypes, 18
Phillips, John, 273, 281–282, 315, 338
Phrenology, 121, 122, 129
Physical fitness, 75
Physique of the Olympic Athlete, The
   (Tanner), 248
Pickens, William, 157
Pierce, Chester, 209
Piliavin, Jane A., 278–279
Pinchot, Gifford, 168
Pintusevich, Zhanna, 323
Pioneer Fund, 240–242
Pippig, Uta, 325
Pittsburgh Courier-Journal, 182, 185
Plessy v. Ferguson case, 148
Pliny the Elder, 99–100
Ploetz, Alfred, 133–134
Pluto, Terry, 20
Poage, George, 142
Pollard, Frederick "Fritz," 144
Polygenism, 131
Population clusters, 108, 109, 112

Postmodernism, 218
Powers, Jimmy, 210
Practical intelligence, 243
Prejudice
   black stereotypes and, 153–154
   intelligence testing and, 165–167
   See also Discrimination; Racism
Press, Irene and Tamara, 305
Professional Golfer's Association, 223
Punctuated equilibrium, 91
Putnam, Carleton, 221

Quarterbacks, 275–277

Race
   academic debate on theories of,
      215–217, 220–222
   anatomical characteristics and,
      96–98, 176–178, 246–261,
      268–269, 283–284
   classification problems with, 106–113
   conceptual origins of, 99–103,
      219–220
   cranial shape/size and, 121–125,
      128–129, 220
   creationist theories of, 83
   environmental factors and, 214–215,
      272–274
   evolutionary theories of, 90–92, 116,
      219–222
   genetics and, 8, 18, 73–74, 80,
      103–106, 263–271, 338–339
   geographical factors and, 97–98, 108,
      109, 112
   intelligence and, 234–236, 238–239
   interbreeding and, 98–99, 115
   nationalism and, 130–134
   UNESCO statement on, 213–214
Race riots, 158, 224
Races and Living Races of Man (Coon
   and Hunt), 231
Race-walking, 149–150
Racial hygiene movement, 179–180
Racism
   anti-semitism as form of, 132,
      133–134
   athletic ability and, 230–231,
      236–237, 334–336
   cranial size studies and, 123–125,
      128–129, 220
   eugenics movement and, 162–163,
      169–171
   infirmity stereotype and, 152–154
   intelligence testing and, 165–167, 239

professional sports and, 145–150,
  275–279, 339–340
Social Darwinism and, 127–130
ultra-nationalism and, 130–134
See also Discrimination; Prejudice
Rainman (film), 244
Rancero, Fabian, 40
Randolph, Thomas, 331
Ratcliffe, Tom, 61
Reconstruction, 146–147
Regional continuity theory, 90–92
Reinisch, Rica, 319
Relaxation studies, 265–266
Relethford, John, 92
Retzius, Anders, 122
Reynolds, Butch, 322
Rhoden, William, 5
Rice, Grantland, 190
Rickey, Branch, 210, 233
Riddle of the Universe, The (Haeckel), 132
Riefenstahl, Leni, 186
Roba, Fatuma, 325
Roberts, Amelia, 301
Roberts, Ann, 326
Roberts, Richard, 244
Robertson, Oscar, 223
Robeson, Paul, 144–145
Robinson, Darrell, 320
Robinson, Jackie, 22, 210, 232–233
Robinson, "Mack," 185
Rodman, Dennis, 156, 273
Rogers, Frederick Rand, 299
Rono, Peter, 45, 57
Rono, Simeon, 52
Roosevelt, Franklin D., 183, 194
Rosenthal, Steven J., 238
Rotich, Paul, 62
Rousseau, Jean Jacques, 75
Rowan, Carl T., 71
Roxborough, John, 189
Roychoudhury, Arun K., 106
Rudolph, Wilma, 303–304, 305
Rugby, 76, 284
Rumbolt, Courtney Orville, 28
Runner's World, 29, 272
Running
  anatomy conducive for, 252–254,
    258–261, 269
  domination of black athletes in, 29,
    30–39, 187
  effects of drug use on, 322–326
  endurance running, 255–259, 325–326
  racial comparison of performance
    differences in, 29–34

See also Track and field events
Rupp, Adolf, 224
Rushton, J. Philippe, 74n, 239
Russell, Bill, 223, 224, 226
Ruth, Babe, 9, 247
Ruto, Paul, 45
Ryan, Bob, 20
Ryun, Jim, 52–54, 75

Sahara Desert, 113–114
Sailer, Steve, 31n
Sailes, Gary, 270
Salovey, Peter, 243
Saltin, Bengt, 259–260, 289
Samoa, 284
Sanders, Deion, 9
San Francisco Chronicle, 18
Sanger, Margaret, 168
Santee, Wes, 11
Sarich, Vincent, 81, 110, 111, 332
Scandanavians, 259–260
Schiller, Johann von, 130
Schmeling, Max, 191–192, 193, 194–195
Schmidt, Mike, 265
Schwarzchild, Henry, 221
Science journal, 217
Sedran, Barney, 202
Segregation
  Jim Crow laws and, 148–149
  legislative end of, 212
Sehorn, Jason, 331
Seikaly, Rony, 272
Seiler, Stephen, 256
Senegal, 20
Seoul Olympic Games, 320
"Separate but equal" doctrine, 148–149
Sex-education movement, 168
Sex testing of athletes, 305–306
Sharkey, Jack, 193
Shimer, Brian, 27
Shockley, William, 235
Shorter, Frank, 42
Shropshire, Kenneth, 336
Sickle cell disease, 288
Simoneau, Jean-Aimé, 254
Simpson, O. J., 8, 224, 246
Skiing, cross-country, 259–261
Skin color
  geographical distribution and, 97–98
Skin color *(cont.)*
  racial classification based on,
    101–102, 108–109
Slaney, Mary Decker, 322
Slavery

"breeding" process and, 71–73, 263
    origins of, 261–262
Slowe, Lucy, 298
Slupianek, Ilona, 313
Smedley, Audrey, 96
Smith, Akili, 277
Smith, Charles Hamilton, 123
Smith, Earl, 336, 340
Smith, Red, 228
Smith, Sybil, 7
Smith, Tommie, 225, 228–229
Snyder, Jimmy "the Greek," 71–73,
    261
Snyder, Larry, 184
Soccer, 20–21, 76
Social Darwinism, 127–130
Sosa, Sammy, 284
Sotomayor, Dennis, 322
South Africa, 227
Soviet Union, 305–307
Sowell, Thomas, 195
Spahn, Morris "Moe," 202
Spencer, Herbert, 118, 126
SPHAs (South Philadelphia Hebrew As-
    sociation), 199–203
Sporting Life, 146, 147
Sports
    banning of black players from, 147–150
    early participation by blacks in,
        139–145
    position discrimination in, 275–279,
        339–340
    reintegration of, 209–212, 223–225
    studies on black superiority in,
        230–231, 278–279, 334–336
    women's participation in, 297–300,
        317–328
    See also names of specific sports
Sports Illustrated, 7, 12, 71, 224, 230,
    231, 236–237
Sprints
    anatomy conducive for, 252–254
    black women's domination of,
        323–325
    effects of drug use on, 322–323
    superiority of black athletes in,
        34–35, 174–176, 184–187, 323–325
    See also Running; Track and field
        events
Stacking, 275, 339–340
Stanford-Binet intelligence test, 165
Stankov, Lazar, 244
Stephens, Helen, 299, 303

Stereotypes
    African American, 152–154, 266
    canine, 280–281
    sports, 278–279
Sterilization, 167, 180, 240
Sternberg, Robert, 242–243
Steroid use. *See* Drug doping
Stoddard, Lothrop, 165–166
Stoneking, Mark, 89
Straus, Lawrence, 94
Streeter, John, 153
Stringer, Chris, 94–95
Sullivan, John L., 246
Suriname, 20
Swimming, 282–283, 298
Swisher, Carl, 86

Tanner, James M., 248
Tanui, Moses, 38, 45, 61
Tarahumara Indians, 284
Tattersall, Ian, 86, 93
Taylor, John "Doc," 142
Taylor, Marshall "Major," 149, 247
Tay-Sachs disease, 288
Temple, Eddie, 303
Temu, Naftali, 52
Tennessee State University, 302, 303
Tennis, 298
Tergat, Paul, 40
Terman, Lewis, 164–165
Testosterone, 310–312, 314
Theory and Practice of Physical Culture
    (journal), 307
Thompson, Jack, 284
Thorne, Alan G., 88
Tilden, Samuel J., 147
Time magazine, 304
Tolan, Thomas "Eddie", Jr., 175
Track & Field News, 54
Track and field events
    anatomy conducive for, 252–254,
        259
    black women in, 300–302, 323–325
    effects of drug use on, 322–326
    endurance events, 38–39, 255–259,
        325–326
    middle distance events, 35–38
    racial comparison of performance
        differences in, 29–35
    sprinting events, 34–35, 174–175
    superiority of black athletes in,
        142–143, 174–176, 184–187,
        323–325

women's participation in, 298–299,
300–302, 322–326
See also Running
Training
endurance improvements through,
255–256
of Kenyan runners, 59–61
musculature and, 254–256
Transforming Anthropology (journal),
338
Treasury of American Folklore, A
(Botkin), 153
Triarchic model of intelligence, 242–243
Trinkaus, Erik, 93
Troeger, Walther, 312
Truman, Harry, 208
Turner, Miki, 274
Tuskegee Institute, 300–301
Tyson, Mike, 5
Tyus, Wyomia, 304

Ulbricht, Walter, 308
Ultra-nationalism, 130–134, 169
UNESCO Statement of Race, 213–214
Universalism, 213
USA Today, 22

Valois, Henri, 241
VanDerveer, Tara, 274
Van Horn, Keith, 331
Vecsey, Peter, 252
Velzian, John, 43, 59–60, 63, 75
Verschuer, Otmar, Baron von, 180
Virchow, Rudolf, 132–133
Vogt, Karl, 124

Walker, Herschel, 27
Walker, Moses "Fleet," 146, 148
Walking races, 149–150
Wallace, George, 172
Walsh, David, 190
Walsh, Stella, 295–296, 302, 324
Wangui, Pasqualine, 59, 326
Ward, Susan, 317
Washburn, Sherwood, 221
Washington Generals, 201, 203
Washington Post, 71
Webb, Beatrice, 168
Webb, Spud, 20, 252
Wells, H. G., 168
West African athletes
anatomical characteristics of,
248–249, 253–257, 268–269
running accomplishments of, 31, 34–36

Weston, Adele, 258
Weston, Edward, 149
Whipp, Brian, 317
White supremacy, 133, 158,
179–180
Whitfield, Malvin, 35
Whitney, Glayde, 242
Wilberforce, Samuel, 119–120
Wiley, Monica, 274
Wiley, Ralph, 7, 76, 332
Will, George, 78
Willard, Jess, 159
Williams, Doug, 71, 277
Williams, Ed, 150
Williams, Jason, 331–332
Williams, Linda, 297
Williams, Venus and Serena, 10, 295,
298
Williams-Beuren syndrome, 244
Willis, Bill, 210
Wills, Maury, 9
Wilson, Allan, 81, 88, 89
Winter, Bud, 225, 265
Winters, Jesse "Nip," 173
Witt, Katarina, 309
Wockel, Barbwel, 320
Wolpoff, Milford, 82–83, 88, 94
Women
athletic participation by, 297–300,
322–328
basketball played by, 327–328
black athletes as, 58–59, 298,
300–304, 319–321, 323–328
endurance running and, 325–326
sexually ambiguous, 296, 305–306,
314
sprinting events and, 322–325
steroid use by, 310–316, 319–321,
322–323
Women's National Basketball Associa-
tion (WNBA), 327
Wooden, John, 231
Woodring, Harry I., 240
Woods, Tiger, 98, 334
Works Progress Administration (WPA),
140
World Health Organization, 236
Worthy, Morgan, 264
Wykoff, Frank, 177

Yerkes, Robert M., 165

Zilhão, João, 93
Zollner, Fred, 211

PublicAffairs is a publishing house founded in 1997. It is a tribute to the standards, values, and flair of three persons who have served as mentors to countless reporters, writers, editors, and book people of all kinds, including me.

I.F. Stone, proprietor of *I. F. Stone's Weekly*, combined a commitment to the First Amendment with entrepreneurial zeal and reporting skill and became one of the great independent journalists in American history. At the age of eighty, Izzy published *The Trial of Socrates*, which was a national bestseller. He wrote the book after he taught himself ancient Greek.

Benjamin C. Bradlee was for nearly thirty years the charismatic editorial leader of *The Washington Post*. It was Ben who gave the *Post* the range and courage to pursue such historic issues as Watergate. He supported his reporters with a tenacity that made them fearless and it is no accident that so many became authors of influential, best-selling books.

Robert L. Bernstein, the chief executive of Random House for more than a quarter century, guided one of the nation's premier publishing houses. Bob was personally responsible for many books of political dissent and argument that challenged tyranny around the globe. He is also the founder and longtime chair of Human Rights Watch, one of the most respected human rights organizations in the world.

For fifty years, the banner of Public Affairs Press was carried by its owner Morris B. Schnapper, who published Gandhi, Nasser, Toynbee, Truman, and about 1,500 other authors. In 1983, Schnapper was described by *The Washington Post* as "a redoubtable gadfly." His legacy will endure in the books to come.

Peter Osnos, *Founder and Editor-at-Large*